LIBRARY OF HEBREW BIBLE/ OLD TESTAMENT STUDIES

461

Formerly Journal for the Study of the Old Testament Supplement Series

READING THE LAW

Studies in Honour of Gordon J. Wenham

edited by

J. G. McConville
and
Karl Möller

t&t clark

NEW YORK • LONDON

T & T Clark International, 80 Maiden Lane, New York, NY 10038

T & T Clark International, The Tower Building, 11 York Road, London SE1 7NX

T & T Clark International is a Continuum imprint.

Library of Congress Cataloging-in-Publication Data
   McConville, J. G. (J. Gordon)
   Reading the law : studies in honour of Gordon J. Wenham / J.G. McConville and Karl Möller.
     p. cm. -- (The Library of Hebrew Bible/Old Testament studies, 461)
   Includes bibliographical references and index.
   ISBN-13: 978-0-567-02642-2 (hardcover : alk. paper)
   ISBN-10: 0-567-02642-6 (hardcover : alk. paper) 1. Bible. O.T.--Criticism, interpretation, etc. I. Wenham, Gordon J. II. Möller, Karl, 1966- III. Title. IV. Series.
   BS511.3.M333 2007

   221.6--dc22

                   2007036011

Printed in Great Britain by Biddles Ltd, King's Lynn, Norfolk

CONTENTS

It is an honour and pleasure for both of us to have the opportunity to edit this collection of essays for Gordon Wenham. Together with six of the other contributors to this volume, we are among the large number who have had their introduction to Old Testament research from him. We cover a large span of his career, at Queen's University, Belfast, where McConville was his first PhD student, to the University of Gloucestershire, where Möller did his work in the 90s. Both of us became in time his colleagues, and experienced the energy, vision and commitment that went into making him so successful a leader in the promotion of good biblical scholarship. His example as a scholar has been immensely important to both of us, not only in laying the foundations of our work, but as we try to build on them. As students and colleagues we have also been privileged to know him as a friend, who unfailingly gave us loyal support and encouragement.

In joining with colleagues to honour Gordon Wenham, we are not only paying tribute to a fine scholar, but also to one for whom scholarship is a matter of Christian vocation and service. The meticulous scholarship is *soli deo gloria*, and part of a life of discipleship. In pursuit of this, he has never been afraid of controversy, yet his integrity and unselfishness have ensured his wide esteem, as the present volume attests. It may be added that a large number of others might have contributed to this volume, and some who would have liked to were prevented from doing so for reasons beyond their control.

Gordon Wenham's mature work was carried on at the University of Gloucestershire (under its several successive names), where he was the first both to accept a research student (Kiuchi), and to hold a Chair. His leadership in research made an incalculable contribution to the development of a research culture at Gloucestershire, and thus to its achievement of university status.

Since this volume was conceived, he has retired, a little earlier than your editors had quite anticipated. It is, it seems, less a retirement than a refocusing of energy, for Gordon's surprising youthfulness has always been a topic of comment. The volume nevertheless marks a significant milestone in a full and fruitful career, and we join with our fellow-contributors in wishing him and Lynne many happy and successful years to come.

Gordon McConville
Karl Möller

ABBREVIATIONS

AB	Anchor Bible
ABD	*Anchor Bible Dictionary.* Edited by D. N. Freedman. 6 vols. New York, 1992
AeUAT	Ägypten und Altes Testament
AnBib	Analecta Biblica
ANET	*Ancient Near Eastern Texts Relating to the Old Testament.* Edited by James B. Pritchard. 3d ed. Princeton, 1969
AOAT	Alter Orient und Altes Testament
ARM	Archives royals de Mari
ARWAW	Abhandlungen der Rheinish-Westfälischen Akademie der Wissenschaften
ATANT	Abhandlungen zur Theologie des Alten und Neuen Testaments
ATD	Das Alte Testament Deutsch
AV	Authorized Version
BBB	Bonner biblische Beiträge
BBET	Beiträge zur biblischen Exegese und Theologie
BHT	Beiträge zur historischen Theologie
BibInt	*Biblical Interpretation: A Journal of Contemporary Approaches*
BIS	Biblical Interpretation Series
BSac	*Bibliotheca Sacra*
BTAT	Beiträge zur Theologie des Alten Testaments
BTB	*Biblical Theology Bulletin*
BZ	*Biblische Zeitschrift*
BZAW	Beihefte zur *ZAW*
CBQ	*Catholic Biblical Quarterly*
CBQMS	*Catholic Biblical Quarterly*, Monograph Series
CBSC	Cambridge Bible for Schools and Colleges
CD	Karl Barth, *Church Dogmatics.* Edited by G. W. Bromiley and T. F. Torrance. 5 vols. in 14 parts. Edinburgh, 1936–77
ConBOT	Coniectanea biblica, Old Testament
Cyr.	J. N. Strassmeier, *Inschriften von Cyrus, König von Babylon 538–529 v. Chr.* Babylonische Texte 7. Leipzig, 1890
DBATB	Dielheimer Blätter zum Alten Testament: Beiheft
EI	*Eretz-Israel*
EncJud	*Encyclopaedia Judaica.* 16 vols. Jerusalem, 1972
ESV	English Standard Version
EvQ	*Evangelical Quarterly*
ExpTim	*Expository Times*

FAT	Forschungen zum Alten Testament
HALAT	*Hebräisches und Aramäisches Lexikon zum Alten Testament.* Edited by L. Koehler, W. Baumgartner and J. J. Stamm. 5 vols. Leiden, 1967–95
HALOT	*The Hebrew and Aramaic Lexicon of the Old Testament.* Edited by L. Koehler, W. Baumgartner and J. J. Stamm. Translated by M. E. J. Richardson et al. 4 vols. Leiden, 1994–99
HAT	Handbuch zum Alten Testament
HKAT	Handkommentar zum Alten Testament
HOS	Handbook of Oriental Studies
HS	*Hebrew Studies*
HSM	Harvard Semitic Monographs
HSS	Harvard Semitic Studies
HUCM	Monographs of the Hebrew Union College
IBC	Interpretation: A Bible Commentary for Teaching and Preaching
ICC	International Critical Commentary
IEJ	*Israel Exploration Journal*
Int	*Interpretation*
IOS	Israel Oriental Studies
ISBE	*International Standard Bible Encyclopedia.* Edited by G. W. Bromiley. 4 vols. Grand Rapids, 1979–88
ITQ	*Irish Theological Quarterly*
JAAR	*Journal of the American Academy of Religion*
JAOS	*Journal of the American Oriental Society*
JBL	*Journal of Biblical Literature*
JE	*The Jewish Encyclopedia.* Edited by C. Adler et al. 12 vols. New York, 1901–1906
JJS	*Journal of Jewish Studies*
JNES	*Journal of Near Eastern Studies*
JPSV	*Jewish Publication Society Version*
JSNT	*Journal for the Study of the New Testament*
JSOT	*Journal for the Study of the Old Testament*
JSOTSup	*Journal for the Study of the Old Testament*: Supplement Series
JSPSup	*Journal for the Study of the Pseudepigrapha*: Supplement Series
JSS	*Journal of Semitic Studies*
JTS	*Journal of Theological Studies*
KD	Karl Barth, *Die Kirchliche Dogmatik.* 5 vols. in 14 parts. Zurich, 1932–70
KHAT	Kurzer Hand-Kommentar zum Alten Testament
KUB	*Keilschrifturkunden aus Boghazköi*
KUSATU	Kleine Untersuchungen zur Sprache des Alten Testaments und seiner Umwelt
LAPO	Littératures anciennes du proche-orient
LCL	Loeb Classical Library
LHBOTS	Library of Hebrew Bible/Old Testament Studies
NAB	*New American Bible*
NAC	New American Commentary

NASB	*New American Standard Bible*
NCB	New Century Bible
NIBCOT	New International Biblical Commentary on the Old Testament
NICOT	New International Commentary on the Old Testament
NIDOTTE	*New International Dictionary of Old Testament Theology and Exegesis.* Edited by W. A. VanGemeren. 5 vols. Grand Rapids, 1997
NIV	New International Version
NJB	*New Jerusalem Bible*
NRSV	New Revised Standard Version
OBO	Orbis biblicus et orientalis
OBT	Overtures to Biblical Theology
OTE	*Old Testament Essays*
OTG	Old Testament Guides
OTL	Old Testament Library
OtSt	Oudtestamentische Studiën
OTS	Old Testament Studies
PWCJS	*Proceedings of the World Congress of Jewish Studies*
RAI	Royal Anthropological Institute
RB	*Revue Biblique*
REB	Revised English Bible
RSM	S. Dalley, *A Catalogue of the Akkadian Cuneiform Tablets in the Collections of the Royal Scottish Museum.* Edinburgh, 1979
RSV	Revised Standard Version
SAA	State Archives of Assyria
SBAB	Stuttgarter biblische Aufsatzbände
SBL	Society of Biblical Literature
SBLDS	SBL Dissertation Series
SBLSymS	SBL Symposium Series
SBLWAW	SBL Writings from the Ancient World
SBM	Stuttgarter biblische Monographien
SBS	Stuttgarter Bibelstudien
SBT	Studies in Biblical Theology
SBTS	Sources for Biblical and Theological Study
SJOT	*Scandinavian Journal of the Old Testament*
SJT	*Scottish Journal of Theology*
STAR	Studies in Theology and Religion
SubBi	*Subsidia Biblica*
TBü	Theologische Bücherei
TCL	Textes cuneiforms du Louvre
TDOT	*Theological Dictionary of the Old Testament.* Edited by G. J. Botterweck, H. Ringgren and H.-J. Fabry. Grand Rapids, 1974–
THAT	*Theologisches Handwörterbuch zum Alten Testament.* Edited by E. Jenni and C. Westermann. 2 vols. Munich, 1971–76
ThSt	Theologische Studien
ThWAT	*Theologisches Wörterbuch zum Alten Testament.* Edited by G. J. Botterweck and H. Ringgren. Stuttgart, 1970–

TLOT	*Theological Lexicon of the Old Testament*. Edited by E. J. and C. Westermann. Translated by M. E. Biddle. 3 vols. Peabody, Mass., 1997
TLZ	*Theologische Literaturzeitung*
TOTC	Tyndale Old Testament Commentaries
TP	*Theologie und Philosophie*
Trans	*Transeuphratène*
TynBul	*Tyndale Bulletin*
UBL	Ugaritisch-biblische Literatur
UF	*Ugarit-Forschungen*
VD	*Verbum domini*
VT	*Vetus Testamentum*
VTSup	*Vetus Testamentum*, Supplements
WBC	Word Biblical Commentary
WHJP	*World History of the Jewish People*
WMANT	Wissenschaftliche Monographien zum Alten und Neuen Testament
WVDOG	Wissenschaftliche Veröffentlichungen der deutschen Orient-Gesellschaft
ZAW	*Zeitschrift für die alttestamentliche Wissenschaft*
ZTK	*Zeitschrift für Theologie und Kirche*

INTRODUCTION

Gordon Wenham's remarkable range as an Old Testament scholar is evident in the voluminous list of his writings which appears elsewhere in this volume. His interests include biblical criticism, the Old Testament's context in the ancient world, Hebrew linguistics and discourse analysis, theology, ethics, hermeneutics and pedagogy.

Gordon is perhaps best known for his commentary writing, with his towering Genesis commentary in pride of place, furnishing the Word Biblical Commentary with an enviable beginning. That commentary alone exhibits the gamut of his scholarship, with its attention to the Hebrew text and other versions, its alertness to ancient Near Eastern context, its application of narrative analysis, its probing of critical approaches, and its theological and hermeneutical acumen. In *Leviticus* (NICOT), he found a new dimension in the work of Mary Douglas, and adapted it into an understanding of the sacrificial laws within the context of a penetrating theological analysis that book, in a thesis that has become highly influential. In this book, and his commentary on Numbers (TOTC), he also demonstrated his considerable interest in biblical and ancient Near Eastern law, an area in which he published a number of articles as well. As his original work was on Deuteronomy, another book that features strongly in his publishing record, he has left few Penta-teuchal stones unturned, and his recent introduction to the Pentateuch in the series Exploring the Old Testament comes from a vantage-point on the subject that few can equal. It also displays incidentally his excellence as a teacher, a passion known particularly to his immediate colleagues, as well as to generations of students who have witnessed the sacrifice of the teddy-bear.

His recent writing shows an enhanced interest in ethics and appli-cation. The ethical dimension of his scholarship is not new, as his work on marriage and divorce illustrates, as well as a string of articles. But with his *Story as Torah* it has sought new theoretical foundations, draw-ing on contemporary hermeneutical developments, and providing fresh avenues into the reading of difficult Old Testament texts with a view to ethical reflection. At the same time, it exhibits his well-established interest in reading Old Testament narrative, with Genesis and Judges providing the main examples. His anticipated work on the Psalms, trailed in the most recent volume in the Scripture and Hermeneutics Series (ed. Bartholomew), and likely to issue in at least two volumes, pursues a particular interest in a "canonical" approach to that book, but can be expected to sound literary and theological notes as well.

The foregoing sketch does little justice to the topography of Gordon's work, but may at least indicate the lie of the land. It will be apparent that with such a varied scholarly *oeuvre*, it was no light matter to decide on a topic for the present volume. The title *Reading the Law* benefits from the accommodating semantics of both "reading" and "law," where "law" stands for Torah, and thus its various connotations. The volume falls into five parts illustrating aspects of the theme.

The first part groups four essays that focus on aspects of Pentateuchal law, three of them connected by the topic of the "neighbour." David Clines explicates the "neighbours" (רעים) of the Book of the Covenant as members of a peer group. He is interested in the relationship between the laws and the social construction of manhood in Israel. In this assessment, "neighbour" transcends kinship categories, but is quite distinct from full social inclusiveness. McConville is likewise interested in the relationships among Israelites, but in contrast places Israel in Leviticus within the Pentateuchal narrative beginning with creation, and sees it as partly fulfilling the destiny of humanity. He argues that the place of the "alien" (גר) in Israel is a symptom of the true nature of Israel as inclusive and non-nationalistic. Nobuyoshi Kiuchi examines the command "love your neighbour (רעך)," not asking who the neighbour is, but rather what is involved in the concept "love." He wants to move away from an understanding of neighbour love in terms of conventions of loyalty. This love has a strong emotive aspect, but he sees the command as an impossible ideal. Jacob Milgrom builds on his massive work on the Priestly literature with an argument showing that Exodus, Leviticus and Numbers are pre-exilic in provenance, on the basis that clearly identifiable interpolations by the redactor of H must be exilic. Readers will notice resonances with Gordon Wenham's thesis concerning the relatively early date of P ("The Priority of P").

The second part consists of three essays on aspects of law in the prophetic literature. Ronald Clements and Thomas Renz examine the understanding of תורה (Torah) in Isaiah and the Book of the Twelve respectively, coming to different conclusions on these distinct corpora. Clements argues that Isaiah has been subjected to a revision which interprets תורה as references to an extant body of Mosaic law. Accordingly he argues that this should be reflected in translation, in place of translations such as "message" or "instruction." The consequence is that the prophecy is by no means deterministic in outlook, but presses the Deuteronomic call to "Choose life!" (Deut 30:19). In Renz's understanding, the existence of an extant body of law, known as תורה, is assumed by the prophets, and attributable to the fact that written Torah was a relatively early influence in Israel. תורה in the prophets refers overwhelmingly to "priestly instruction or divine law." However, the prophets were reluctant to refer directly to it, because they were chiefly concerned to expose their hearers' fundamental apostasy rather than individual breaches of the law. The relative paucity of allusions to תורה, and to instances of it, is because rebellion had made Torah unable to function. Raymond Westbrook approaches "law" from the perspective of legal procedures in the ancient Near East. He examines the trial of Jeremiah in Jer 26, and attempts to provide "a coherent account of the legal procedure" in it which would allow the text in turn to be read as coherent. He especially examines the roles of the participants, and finds that "all the people" is constituted as a mixed tribunal by virtue of its formal assembly for the purpose (v. 9), and that recognition of this clarifies the use of various terms in the account.

The third part examines aspects of law and ethics in the Writings. Examining Ps 101, Möller explores the function of the king's self-committing declarations to observe the standards of God's law both in its original context in ancient Israel and for modern readers. Utilizing concepts from speech-act theory, he investigates the performative, self-involving and commissive language of Ps 101, arguing that "in singing or praying this Psalm, *we*, its modern readers, are…committing ourselves to the behaviour the ancient psalmist thought appropriate for a king." This is argued in contrast to most modern commentators, who tend to limit the role of Ps 101 in today's context to a didactic one, thus ignoring its commissive nature. Robin Parry investigates Lam 1, aiming to show that "laments may be a richer resource for understanding ancient Israelite ethics and for funding contemporary theological ethics than is usually realized." He considers the ethical assessments in Lam 1 of Jerusalem's enemies, Jerusalem's allies, Jerusalem itself, and Yahweh. He also considers the ethical impact the chapter has on its readers, both its human readers and also Yahweh, whose "ethical reader-response to Lamentations" requires investigation, since God was "the primary intended audience" of the lament. Hugh Williamson, in a return to Ezra–Nehemiah, shows how Torah played a vital role in the self-understanding of the post-exilic community in Yehud. The community's use of Torah is placed in the context of its historical situation in such a way as to illumine both the books' view of history and the function of Torah. While Ezra and Nehemiah prove insufficient as evidence for a coherent reconstruction of the historical situation of which they purport to give an account, they show that "reading the Torah" enabled the community to find and express its identity, and its faith in the sovereignty of the God of Israel.

The fourth part returns to the "Torah" in the narrower sense of the Pentateuch, but consists of readings of parts of Genesis and Exodus with particular theological or other contemporary interests. Craig Bartholomew builds on his work on pilgrimage and offers a theology of "place," based on a reading of Gen 1–3, arguing that place "is central and foundational to human life and identity." An intriguing aspect is the portrayal of Eden as a landscaped and constructed place of human habitation. He goes on to suggest that it is essential to regain this sense of "placedness" in a disorientated postmodern world. Desmond Alexander, paying attention to the redactional structure of Gen 37–50, focuses on the theme of royalty in that narrative. He argues that the final editor of Genesis was strongly influenced by this concept when selecting and structuring the content of chs. 37–50. This "regal dimension of the תולדות יעקב" also helps integrate the Joseph narrative into the patriarchal narratives of chs. 12–36, and shows that the "generations"-formula "is more than simply a bridge between Canaan and Egypt." Walter Moberly offers a theological exposition of the story of the manna in Exod 16, reflecting on its significance in the wider Christian canon. Rejecting "rationalistic" explanations of the story, he understands the manna "as a symbolic concretization of divine grace." While Deut 8:3 indicates that the story is understood to be "about learning a fuller understanding of human life," the resonance of Exod 16 in the Lord's Prayer ("Give us this day our daily bread") encourages us to expect "whatever is needed for sustaining life in ever-renewed openness to God within the disciplines of grace. Robert Gordon provides a discussion of the week of creation in Gen 1 ("the week that made the world"), asking what the text is seeking to communicate. While Gen 1 is often perceived as using "fiat" language, he shows that God is portrayed here principally as a workman. It is as builder and craftsman— and as we might say—as inspector of buildings, that God reviews his work on each of the days of creation, pronouncing the result "good," and cumulatively "very good"… the human experience of the working week has provided the construct within which the divine acts of creation and cessation from work are presented."

The final part is united by a broad interest in history, conceived in a number of ways. Richard Hess performs a philological and religious-historical analysis, in which he finds a semantic connection between the divine name Shuwala, a West Semitic deity known from Emar and in a variety of ancient Near Eastern texts (Hurrian, Hittite), and the biblical Sheol. One result is that Sheol may be better explained in terms of the character of this underworld deity, with echoes of Ninurta, than in terms of the Hebrew word-group "ask, enquire." Alan Millard, pursuing a well-known interest in ancient writing, turns to the Ten Commandments. He argues that the Exodus narrative about the giving of the two stone tablets presupposes that the contents of the Ark were the definitive copy of the terms of the covenant in the form of two copies of the Ten Command-ments, and that these served as the treaty documents of the covenant between Yahweh and Israel. Pekka Pitkänen takes up the topic of history itself, and shows how its writing reflects the interests of those who write it. He investigates this in relation to the book of Joshua, noticing how memory plays a crucial part in that narrative. Then, in a reading of Joshua's application of the Deuteronomic law of חרם (*ḥērem*), he notes the dangers of a view of history that asserts the subject's own interests at the expense of others. Finally, John Rogerson develops a similar point as a first step in what he describes as a "communicative theology of the Old Testament." He argues that history is a function of the *present*; that is, as "cultural memory" (Assmann), the Old Testament selects and discards, always adjusting to the needs of the present. For modern readers, history is not a "thing" to be recovered by research. Rather, we engage with memories of the past, bringing our own questions, and believing we may find God's voice in it.

The subject-matter of our volume may thus be seen to correspond to many of Gordon Wenham's interests, under the broad umbrella of the notion of "reading the law." The note on which the preceding paragraph ended, with John Rogerson's indication of a belief that we may find God's voice as we read and engage with the Old Testament, is a fitting one with which to draw this Introduction to a close. For it chimes with what we earlier identified as the motivating energy of our honouree. Not only the editors, but all the contributors, are pleased to offer this volume as a tribute to an admired and respected colleague.

Part I

READING PENTATEUCHAL LAW

BEING A MAN IN THE BOOK OF THE COVENANT[*]

David J. A. Clines

No one is born a man. Male children are turned into men by learning how to be a man, behave as a man, perform the role of a man.[1] Masculinity is not a natural or inevitable state of affairs, but a socially constructed way of being, created especially through the language that surrounds males from their earliest days. Masculinity is a script, written for men by their societies, a script that men in their various cultures act out their whole lives long.

When we turn to the laws of the Book of the Covenant, it stands to reason that this text—like the rest of the Hebrew Bible—written by males, addressed to males, and read, pretty exclusively, by males, will be likely to be suffused with masculine ideals and ideology, which is to say, that it will be one instantiation of the social script for masculinity in ancient Israel. Not one, however, of the many studies of Israelite law in general or of the Book of the Covenant in particular appears to have undertaken an analysis of masculinity in the Hebrew laws—despite the existence of some excellent gender studies focusing on women[2]—and I take the opportunity offered by the invitation to contribute to this volume in honour of Gordon Wenham, a respected and energetic scholar and a long-time friend, to outline my perception of masculinity in this text.[3]

---

[*]   An earlier form of this study was read in a symposium on "Feminist Herme-neutics: Gender and Law in the Bible and the Ancient Near East" at the Annual Meeting of the Society of Biblical Literature, San Antonio, Texas, in November, 2004.

1.   On gender as performativity, see especially Judith Butler, *Bodies That Matter: On the Discursive Limits of "Sex"* (London: Routledge, 1993).

2.   See especially Cheryl B. Anderson, *Women, Ideology and Violence: Critical Theory and the Construction of Gender in the Book of the Covenant and the Deuter-onomic Law* (JSOTSup 394; London: T&T Clark International, 2004); Victor H. Matthews, Tikva Frymer-Kensky and Bernard M. Levinson, *Gender and Law in the Hebrew Bible and the Ancient Near East* (JSOTSup 251; London: T&T Clark International, 2004).

3.   I might refer to Gordon Wenham's own paper "Legal Forms in the Book of the Covenant," *TynBul* 22 (1971): 95–102.

1. *A Man's Status*

The dominant impression one gets from the Book of the Covenant about what it means to be a man in its society is that as a man one is not essentially an individual, a self-determining moral agent, but rather a member of a band of "neighbours" (רעים)—which is something like a band of brothers, but without the implication of kinship.[4]

The intended readers of the Book of the Covenant will understand that they are of the same standing as the others addressed by the text. There is hardly a whiff of social hierarchy here. There is just one reference to a man who stands outside of and above the community of "neighbours," that is, the "ruler" (Exod 22:28 [Heb. 27]), and tellingly, the one thing readers must be careful to do is not to "revile" him—which must apparently be something a band of neighbours is sorely tempted to do. As long as they do not badmouth the ruler, they are apparently free to ignore him altogether, for there is nothing else in the Book of the Covenant that draws him to their attention.

The "ruler" aside (and we do not care in the present quest who exactly this נשיא is, whether a priestly figure or a tribal head), the readers of the laws of the Book of the Covenant, who are shaped, even constituted, by it, are "neighbours," all essentially on the same footing. There are other kinds and ranks of human beings who must be envisaged, of course. There are slaves, and women, and children, and aliens. But they are not readers of this law; they are not its addressees, they are not neighbours. All of the neighbours are neighbours to one another, and that is their defining characteristic.

The neighbours of the Book of the Covenant are not equal in every respect, of course, for there are poor men among them (Exod 22:25–27 [24–26]), for example; but poor men and rich men are equally neighbours. A poor man is a neighbour (explicitly at Exod 22:26 [25]), but a rich slave or a wealthy alien is not. There are bad men among the band of neighbours too, thieves (22:2 [1]) and sheep- and ox-stealers (22:1–4 [21:37–22:3]), and kidnappers (21:16), bribe-takers and bribe-givers (23:8), but they are still neighbours. There are feckless and irresponsible men, like the man who lights a fire in a field and lets it get out of control so that it destroys the crops (22:6 [5]), or like the man who digs a pit (or is it a cistern?) and neglects to cover it so that an ox or an ass falls into it (21:33–34)—but these too are neighbours. Their wrong has been in acting in an unneighbourly fashion—but they are still neighbours.

---

4. רע is a quite imprecise term, of course; for its range of meanings, see, for example, J. Kühlewein, "רע *rʿ* companion," *TDOT* 3:1243–46.

Being a man in the Book of the Covenant means in the first place that a male is inevitably a social animal, a member of a peer group from which he derives his identity.

2. *A Man with Other Men*

As a community of neighbours, the men of the Book of the Covenant do not have a common cause, a project. They are not banded together with a goal in view. What binds them together is rather the fact that they all alike have to get along with one another, maintaining structures that will keep them neighbours, and repairing damage that happens to be done from time to time to the common weal.

One of the structures that needs maintaining is the custom of looking out for one another. In the absence of banks, as one commentator thoughtfully puts it, people are forever borrowing from one another and lending to one another. One day a man will be giving to his neighbour an ass or an ox or a sheep, or some other animal, to look after for him (22:7, 10–13 [9–12]). The next the neighbour will be borrowing an animal from him (22:14 [13]). It is not a matter of sharing common property, for the property belongs clearly either to one or the other; but this typical village habit of constantly lending and borrowing leads potentially to conflict, which must be prevented as far as possible for the sake of neighbourliness.[5] The ox someone has given to a neighbour to keep for him may die or get hurt or be driven away without anyone seeing it (22:10 [9]). Or the neighbour may be borrowing an animal that subsequently dies or is hurt while it is in his care (22:14 [13]). The band of neighbours must make sure that these accidents, which *will* happen, will not get in the way of neighbourliness.

What the neighbours of the Book of the Covenant do is to institute, in advance of the need, a fair system of reparations so that the equilibrium between neighbours can be sustained despite damage to property. Clearly, their relation as neighbours is more important than the ox or the ass, and they are very anxious to avoid dispute. If they were not, they would be happy enough to solve every case on its own merits and from first principles; their provision of legal remedies *in advance* will save them from having to argue about how they can restore the neighbour relation that is threatened by the damage that has been done.

---

5. Cf. D. A. Knight, "Village Law and the Book of the Covenant," in *"A Wise and Discerning Mind": Essays in Honor of Burke O. Long* (ed. Saul M. Olyan and Robert C. Culley; BJS 325; Providence, R.I: SBL, 2000), 163–79.

3. *The Manliness of Law*

Men do not like bickering. They want clarity. They want to know where they stand. The men of the Book of the Covenant do not care to risk the network of neighbourliness on the precarious health of their animals or on circumstances over which they have no control. And they do want to have control, not because they are control freaks, or in order to dominate other men—for neighbours regard one another as equals—but in order not to be bested by events.

This is why these neighbours like law. This is why they have a Book of the Covenant. They may well accept that the laws of the Book are spoken by Yahweh (24:7), but, regardless of its origins, this is a book of a covenant between neighbours. This is a book of recipes for keeping the peace.

Moreover, when there has been an upset, for example, with a man who keeps an ox that is prone to gore people (21:28–32), and then it does it once too often and fatally, they want their law to be able to deal with that messiness and tidy it up, without remainder. They want to be able to draw a line under it, and move on.

Remainders after an upset are the very devil. They tend to be emotional freight that has nowhere to go and gets in the way of all one's other projects. If there is recrimination and bad feeling, it can go on forever, and it is not helpful. Unlike women in a patriarchal society, men, who have to make the difficult decisions, borrow their idiom from the balance-sheet, drawing the line under the variety of eventualities that make up the rich tapestry of life and adding it all up into a single figure that can be dealt with and disposed of.

This is what is meant by that much misunderstood and much maligned phrase, an eye for an eye (21:23–25). It is a man's notion of justice, leaving out of account extenuating circumstances, special pleading, sentiment, rhetoric. This is the fairness of an honest John. It is a male justice. We today may not care for the apparent savagery of an eye for an eye, but we have to admire the principle of rigorous justice, which manifests itself equally in the laws that forbid the men of the Book of the Covenant to take a bribe (23:8) or pervert a lawsuit (23:6–7) or be partial to a disputant, even if he is one of the underprivileged (23:2–3).

4. *The Avoidance of Shame*

Mediterraneans, ancient and modern, are famously supposed to inhabit an honour–shame culture.[6] And men in many cultures are notoriously fixated on the desire to gain ever more honour, invariably at the price of the dishonour of others, since the quest for honour is a zero-sum game.

Surprisingly, however, that is not the outlook of the neighbours of the Book of the Covenant. It is noticeable that this collection of laws never speaks of shame, and never either of honour. It may be suggested that the reason is that for the neighbours of the Book of the Covenant the fine has replaced shame.

Take the example of the sex laws. The men of the Book of the Covenant are pragmatists, accepting that there will always be men seducing young women (22:16–17 [15–16]). They do not call that a matter for shame; they make the man pay the marriage present and marry the woman, or else, if her father will not have it, pay the money equivalent of the marriage present. All the neighbours are satisfied, the law is upheld. There is nothing more to say or to argue. Everyone can get on with their lives.

Even serious matters like a breach of trust (22:9 [8]), which strikes at the very foundation of neighbourliness, are not brought into the scope of shame. Even that can be dealt with by the legal system: the parties come to the judges and the guilty party pays a fine of double the amount defrauded. It is all over. There is no public humiliation, no effort to win back standing in the community. The wrong has been righted, without remainder.

There is no doubt a little too much capital punishment in the Book of the Covenant for modern tastes: it is not only for murder (21:12), but for striking one's father or mother (21:15) or cursing one's father or mother (21:17), or kidnapping in order to sell as a slave (21:16), or lying with a beast (22:19 [18]), being a female sorcerer (22:18 [17]), or sacrificing to other gods (22:20 [19]). Perhaps it is best to understand that these are crimes where no possibility of reparation exists. Is it that there is too

---

6. See, among many studies, J. D. Peristiany, ed., *Honour and Shame: The Values of Mediterranean Society* (London: Weidenfeld & Nicolson, 1965); Lyn M. Bechtel, "Shame as a Sanction of Social Control in Biblical Israel: Judicial, Political, and Social Shaming," *JSOT* 49 (1991): 47–76; Bruce J. Malina and Jerome H. Neyrey, "Honor and Shame in Luke–Acts: Pivotal Values of the Mediterranean World," in *The Social World of Luke Acts: Models for Interpretation* (ed. Jerome H. Neyrey; Peabody, Mass.: Hendrickson, 1991), 25–66; Halvor Moxnes, "Honor and Shame," *BTB* 23 (1993): 167–76.

much shame involved in cursing one's father, for example, for a money fine to cope with it, and that the fine has to be capital?

As for honour, it is not one of the key concepts of the Book of the Covenant; the reason, we may suggest, is that it is socially divisive, whereas the men of the Book are neighbours, a band of brothers, not in competition with one another for honour. The one place we are hearing of honour is in the Ten Words, "honour your father and mother" (20:12). This is an exceptional use of "honour," since normally speaking a woman cannot be honoured. A woman can be shamed, she can have a minus quantity of honour, but her normal state is to be of zero honour, which cannot be augmented. The "honour" a mother is owed is nothing more than not to be struck and not to be cursed, as our Book of the Covenant tells us (21:15, 17).

5. *Men and their God*

Men who are formed by the Book of the Covenant also learn from it that part of the male role is to have contact with the deity. It actually has God saying, "Three times a year all your males shall appear before the Lord God" (23:17). Men, in other words, are those responsible for religion, religious practice and ceremony. If it had not mentioned "males" there, one might have thought that the keeping of feasts was an activity of men and women alike, remembering perhaps Hannah going up to Shiloh with her husband Elkanah for an annual festival (1 Sam 1). But even there it is Elkanah alone who is said to have "gone up" (1 Sam 1:3), and his two wives, who obviously did accompany him, are not said in the story to have gone up—in the narrative, they just turn out to be at the shrine.

Anyway, what is reinforced by the Book of the Covenant is that religion lies within the realm of males. Women may have their own religious beliefs and practices, but the maintenance of the religion of the community is not in their hands but in the men's. They are those addressed in the Ten Words, they are responsible for rooting out illegitimate worship (22:20 [19]), for dedicating their firstborn to the deity (22:29–30 [28–29]), for bringing tithes (23:19), for offering sacrifices (23:18). Religion, a public duty, performed outside the home, is necessarily a male sphere.

6. *Men on the Farm and in the Town*

The society of the Book of the Covenant is an agrarian one, obviously, and there is nothing in the life of the farm worth mentioning that is not a man's job. If the animals are to be taken to a new pasture to graze (22:5 [4]), that is for a man to do. If there is a hole to be dug, it is a man who will do it, even if he forgets to cover it over (21:33–34). If there is any borrowing or lending, of beasts or property or money (22:7 [6]), or reparation in kind or with money, the business is between men. If there is a slave to be bought (21:2), or a daughter to be sold as a slave to make ends meet (21:7), the man must do it. If there is selling of beasts (21:35) or slaughtering (20:24), if there is a fire to be lit in the field (22:6 [5]), if there is a stray beast that needs returning to its owner (23:4), it is a man that must be on hand. If there is sowing or harvesting work, or tending of vineyards, that is men's work. From their youth up the men of the Book of the Covenant are being groomed to take on the enormous burden of patriarchy. Six days a week men must work; the commandment is not permission but injunction, as much a divine command as refraining on the Sabbath. Being a man is hard work.

Finally

The men of the Book of the Covenant do not of course spend all their days reading the Book, nor do they confine their reading to that tiny collection. They learn, consciously or unconsciously, how to be men from many other texts and practices. Their mothers teach them how important it is for boys to be *strong*, and their fathers how they must use their strength to *fight* other men. And so forth. But in this essay I have written of the influence Hebrew ways of being a man have had on the Book of the Covenant, and of the influence the Book of the Covenant has had on Hebrew ways of being a man.

"FELLOW CITIZENS":
ISRAEL AND HUMANITY IN LEVITICUS*

J. G. McConville

One of the many merits of Gordon Wenham's contribution to Old Testament scholarship is his original and penetrating work on the book of Leviticus, in which he uniquely combines insights from anthropology and Christian theology.[1] Underlying his understanding of the book is a conviction that, though it may seem arcane and esoteric, it taps into things that are profound and universal, and belongs within the biblical account of the nature and activity of God in relation to all humanity. These are concerns that I wish to take up in the present essay.

My question is how the portrayal of Israel in Leviticus may imply a view of the vocation and destiny of humanity. To put it otherwise, does its picture of Israel, in its relation to Yahweh and the responsibilities it is called to exercise in its social and political life, have relevance beyond itself? The question needs some further clarification at the outset, however. In what sense can we speak of the viewpoint of Leviticus as a thing in itself? In the biblical canon, it is part of the Pentateuch, or Torah, and thus of a narrative which runs from the creation to the point at which Israel stands on the border of its promised land. In critical analysis, it forms part of that strand of the Pentateuch known as "P," or the Priestly document. That is, loosely defined, the Pentateuchal material which has at its centre the construction of the tabernacle and the arrangements for worship in it.[2] It is impossible to speak of a theology of Leviticus, ultimately, apart from both these contexts, and the argument I offer here will take account of this.

---

* I am delighted to honour Gordon Wenham, my doctoral supervisor and now friend of long standing, with this essay. He may recall trying unsuccessfully to lure me into Leviticus for my doctoral work. The present attempt is therefore no doubt overdue.

1. G. J. Wenham, *The Book of Leviticus* (NICOT; Grand Rapids: Eerdmans, 1979).

2. I shall return to the definition of P below.

We can, however, make preliminary observations about the politics of Leviticus, as it has been understood in scholarly literature, and here Leviticus is inevitably enmeshed with "P." The question about the politics of P encounters immediate challenges because of the nature of the material. Here is a writing whose accent falls heavily on worship. Moreover, it places Israel outside land, in a wilderness, a space and time between Egypt and Canaan. Israel is led, organized and given law by Moses, a figure whose role is limited precisely to this time and space outside land. Moses will be succeeded by Joshua for the purpose of the occupation of land, but beyond that the only elaborate arrangements concerning leadership in Israel are framed for the priests. While the critical interpretation of Deuteronomy has long been closely connected with a specific event in Israel's political history, the reform of King Josiah in 621 B.C.E. (2 Kgs 22–23), and that book has been strongly identified with the politics of the reform, P has not enjoyed any such clearly enunciated political interpretation. These observations raise the question whether P is "political" at all. Is it, indeed, an instance within the Old Testament of the separation of religion and politics?

Critical scholarship has placed P broadly within the exilic and postexilic periods. This, of course, is far from precise and permits of a wide range of possible settings and therefore purposes. Martin Noth, more concerned with internal development than with specific settings, placed much of Leviticus within "the Jerusalem tradition," and found that the non-narrative parts belonged "to the period around the end of the Jewish state and the beginning of the so-called exile," though the narrative framework of P was later.[3] The nature of the material, however, made attempts to date it hazardous. Lester Grabbe considers both exilic and Second Temple views, but tends himself to the latter, on the grounds that much of Leviticus describes procedures in an actual cultic setting.[4]

The question of dating might seem, at first approach, to be the crucial one for determining the orientation of the Priestly writing, but equally important is the question about the nature and purpose of the document. Where it is treated as a book of regulations, the dating becomes almost incidental. Noth evidently saw it as a book of ritual regulation, intended variously for priest and laity depending on the text. That is, its mixed material was composed "from different points of view."[5] This is a rather loose view of purpose, with little evidence of the more recent interest in audience and rhetorical situation. Noth expresses the consequences of his approach for an attempt to read Leviticus politically when he writes:

3. M. Noth, *Leviticus* (London: SCM Press, 1965 [German 1962]), 15.
4. L. L. Grabbe, *Leviticus* (Sheffield: Sheffield Academic Press, 1993), 23.
5. Noth, *Leviticus*, 10–11.

"Cultic and ritual regulations usually remain fairly constant; they are relatively independent of the ups and downs of political and historical events."[6] If that is so, they are unlikely to carry a political message.

Yet political commitments have indeed been found here. Jacob Milgrom stands apart from the convention of exilic or post-exilic dating by tracing the origins of P to the pre-monarchic Shiloh sanctuary. The priestly laws have as their primary target a kind of demythologization of pagan demonism, but they have (perhaps unintended) political consequences. An example of this, in Milgrom's analysis, is P's ruling that the altar was contagious (in holiness terms) only to objects and not to persons.[7] A major consequence of this was that the altar could no longer be used for "sanctuary" by anyone trying to escape pursuit by the authorities. This measure, therefore, "would have won the support of the king and his bureaucracy, who would have earnestly wished to terminate the sanctuary's veto power over their jurisdiction."[8] Milgrom thinks the measure was enacted under Solomon, "who used his royal power to introduce many administrative and cultic changes." In this understanding, P's priests are not quite masters in their own house, and as a result a politically conservative temper is attributed to it.

Recent post-exilic readings, however, regard matters quite differently. In such analyses the writings in question become the instrument of a powerful political programme on behalf of the returnees from Babylon, who are armed with the Persian authorities' commission to establish a temple-based administration in the province of Yehud. The image of an "Israel" centred on a temple and defined in priestly terms by holiness distinguishes it from other populations by religion and ethnicity, and is intended to strengthen the authority of the priesthood and subject the indigenous population to their definition of Israel as a people that has arrived from elsewhere and is defined by the worship of Yahweh.[9] The traditional concept of "P," or a "Priestly writing," is somewhat overtaken here by the notion of a comprehensive literary and theological project.

---

6. Noth, *Leviticus*, 15. Grabbe (*Leviticus*, 23) also sees Leviticus as "largely a description of cultic observance."

7. Milgrom's reading depends on taking the Hebrew כל in Lev 6:11, 20; Exod 29:37; 30:26–29 to mean "whatever," not "whoever"; see J. Milgrom, *Leviticus* (Continental Commentaries; Minneapolis: Fortress, 1994), 64–65. He thinks P retains traces of the older concept of holiness contagion, in which the most holy objects did transmit holiness to persons, in Lev 10:1–5, but that its tendency was to reduce this contagious power.

8   Ibid., 65.

9. P. R. Davies, *In Search of "Ancient Israel"* (JSOTSup 148; Sheffield: Sheffield Academic Press, 1992, repr. 1995), 110–15.

However, the writings known as P are central to this conception of a temple-centred community defined by holiness.

The relation of this type of priestly vision to the Jerusalem monarchy is quite different from Milgrom's because it trades on the interpretation of history found in the Former Prophets, namely that the downfall of Israel was due to its sinfulness and to the failures of the monarchs.[10] The interests of the post-exilic "hierocracy," therefore, coincide with a deeply critical stance towards the former monarchy. This does not mean, of course, that it is revolutionary. Rather, it has simply changed masters, since it is now wholly subservient to its Persian overlords.[11]

Post-exilic readings of P are by no means limited to this assessment of its politics. For Erhard Gerstenberger, the authors of the P-laws are not the priests, or at least not the priests alone, since so much of their content reflects a broader interest than the sanctuary. He advocates a "church" model for the community addressed by Leviticus, a "temple congregation—obliged as it is to renounce any development of direct political or economic power."[12] Gerstenberger agrees that the community of Yehud has the temple and priesthood at its centre and that the community depends on Persian patronage. Yet for him, P is far from being the instrument of priestly interest. On the contrary, it gives voice precisely to those who have suffered through exile, and who continue to do so through the social stratification that crept into post-exilic society in Judah after it.[13] The focus in the texts of Leviticus, therefore, is on the community throughout Judah, its primary horizons being the family and clan. These were represented by elders in local assemblies that dealt with legal matters, while a more centralized "church assembly" will also have developed both in Palestine and in the Diaspora (Neh 8). For Gerstenberger, the loss of political power has resulted in a global and faith-based conception of identity, as well as a focus on the local community.[14] The authors of Leviticus are those versed in Torah; their interests were not different from the communities of faith throughout Judah and beyond.[15]

---

10. Davies, *"Ancient Israel,"* 112.

11. Similarly, Pleins, within a more traditional critical paradigm, thought that, while Deuteronomy had put monarchy in control of the priesthood, P cut it loose; see D. J. Pleins, *The Social Visions of the Hebrew Bible: A Theological Introduction* (Louisville, Ky.: Westminster John Knox, 2000), 110.

12. E. Gerstenberger, *Leviticus* (OTL; Louisville, Ky.: Westminster John Knox, 1996), 11.

13. Ibid., 8.

14. Ibid., 11–12.

15. Ibid., 14.

This brief review illustrates quite divergent assessments of the politics
of P. And the wide discrepancies regarding dating, the attitude to the
Davidic monarchy, and the stance of the writings in regard to issues
internal to the post-exilic community are possible because of certain loud
silences in the material. Major political figures and events are absent
from the pages of Leviticus, and consequently the book is readily subsumed into overarching theories that depend on interpretations of a wide
range of other material.

Leviticus in Literary Context

The review above postponed the crucial question of delimitation that was
mentioned at the outset. That issue, however, played a part in some of
the judgments made. For example, Gerstenberger's appraisal found
important evidence in Lev 19, a chapter that lies outside stricter definitions of P and within the so-called Holiness Code (H). While H has long
enjoyed the status of an independent law code in critical scholarship, that
status is now disputed, with some finding it to have been a false trail.
Gerstenberger calls it "a wishful phantom of scholarly literature."[16] At
stake is whether an assessment of the ethics and politics of P must include
or omit the material in Lev 17–26, with its well-known mixture of ritual
and ethical provisions, of which ch. 19 is the leading example. A number
of modern interpreters insist on maintaining the distinction. Milgrom
finds in the transition from P to H (which he dates later) a change in the
concept of holiness, broadening it from a property of the priests alone to
an ideal that is open to all members of the community.[17] H, indeed, is
revolutionary, aiming for nothing less than an egalitarian society.[18] The
ideological differences between P and H are given further expression by
Israel Knohl, who finds P stringently focussed on the holiness sphere,
while H reintroduces elements of popular religion and an attachment to
the agricultural cycles and festivals. It is with H that socio-ethical concerns are found, together with a concept of repentance as the proper
response to a sense of sin. P's concerns, in contrast, are neither moral nor
political. The priests had no desire to infringe the prerogatives of the
political leadership. Moreover, "the complete separation of morality
from the cult is at the root of PT's thought."[19] It is clear, therefore, why
an appraisal of the politics requires a decision on this point.

16. Ibid., 18.
17. Milgrom, *Leviticus*, 121 (on Lev 11:44).
18. Ibid., 175.
19. I. Knohl, *The Sanctuary of Silence: The Priestly Torah and the Holiness
School* (Minneapolis: Fortress, 1995), 155. (PT, or Priestly Torah, is effectively

In my view the boundaries between P and H are by no means so clear as Milgrom and Knohl believe.[20] The question of P and H, however (posed, incidentally, by the existence of Leviticus as a book), is only part of a larger issue, namely in what literary context the Pentateuchal regulations for priests and tabernacle should properly be read. With this question in view, the boundaries of P have to be discussed in relation to the whole Pentateuchal, or indeed Hexateuchal, narrative.

The answer to this question has usually been found within the parameters of the concept of P itself, since its regulations about worship are set within a narrative that begins with the first account of creation in Gen 1:1–2:3(4a). A recent interpretation of P within this framework, and with an expressly political angle, is that of Norbert Lohfink. Lohfink finds in "P" an account of the relationship between creation and salvation that addresses modern despair about the future of the world.[21] In his view, P tells a story in which, after the flood, the nations "fill the earth" (Gen 1:28), each one finding its appointed place, the story of Israel being told as an "example."[22] Accordingly, P portrays Israel's story as a peaceful procession out of slavery and alienation in Egypt into its designated land in Canaan. The culmination of the story is found in Josh 18:1, where the "The land lay subdued before them" (NRSV), with its clear verbal echo of the creation mandate to humanity in Gen 1:28.[23] The priestly narrative is seen, in this way, as an account of a progression from dynamic events in

equivalent to P in Knohl's terms). Cf. Davies (*"Ancient Israel,"* 112–13), who finds that the dominant voice in the Pentateuch and Former Prophets is one that prefers the concepts of sin and holiness to the justice and righteousness themes more typical of the Latter Prophets and Wisdom writers.

20. I refer to R. Rendtorff for a summary of the reasons why this is so. In brief. Lev 17 is not a new beginning; ch. 17. is closer to ch. 16, because of shared themes of sacrifice, and thus to chs. 1–7, than to ch. 18; the command "You shall be holy" is not in ch. 18, but in ch. 19—and also in ch. 11! (Milgrom and Knohl are obliged to assign Lev 11:44–45 to H). Finally, ch. 26 is better seen as a closure to the whole book of Leviticus than to the motley collection in chs. 17–25. See Rendtorff, "Is it Possible to Read Leviticus as a Separate Book?," in *Reading Leviticus: A Conversation with Mary Douglas* (ed. John F.A. Sawyer; JSOTSup 227; Sheffield: Sheffield Academic Press, 1996), 22–39 (29).

21. N. Lohfink, "God the Creator and the Stability of Heaven and Earth," in *Theology of the Pentateuch: Themes of the Priestly Narrative and Deuteronomy* (Minneapolis: Fortress; Edinburgh: T. & T. Clark, 1994), 116–35 (116–17).

22. Ibid., 124, 128.

23. Ibid., 127. The shared term in the latter texts is כבש. For this term as implying non-violent occupation, see Lohfink, "'Subdue the Earth' (Genesis 1.28)," in *Theology of the Pentateuch,* 1–17 (= "'Macht euch die Erde untertan,'" *Orientierung* 38 [1974], 137–42).

the world's early history to the "stability" of nations occupying their lands, and with the created order thus fully established, the message is that "the world can and should *remain as it is*."[24] Israel, gathered for worship at the tabernacle (also in Josh 18:1), echoes God's "rest" after creation through its worship and the creative work of its regular life, liberated and distinct from the slavery of Egypt. This view is presented as a contrast to progressive, apocalyptic theologies, which also have biblical roots, as in Deutero-Isaiah's "dynamic projection of history towards the future." P resists this with a concept of the stability of creation, and therefore has an important voice in countering the modern myth of progress which exploits the world's resources in order to try to solve its enormous problems.[25]

Lohfink's analysis depends on the proposition that P can be both clearly defined and treated as a separate work.[26] This has an important effect on the interpretation of the material assigned to it. P lacks a story of the first human sin and generally shows little interest in human sinfulness. It has no narratives of war, and no story of conquest; on the contrary, it is "pacifistic," and conceives of the occupation of the land as a peaceful settlement.[27] Such consequences generally follow from a reading of P in isolation. William Brown, for example, also finds in P a divine renunciation of violence after the flood, and a peaceable occupation of land.[28]

The governing concept in such reconstructions is the view that the P narrative culminates in the completion of the tabernacle and the portrayal of worship there, though with a measure of disagreement about whether it continued to an account of the occupation of land. There are clear

24. Lohfink, "God the Creator," 125 (emphasis original). In his view, P finds the concept of the move from dynamic pre-history to stability already in Atrahasis (see pp. 122–23).

25. Ibid., 120–21; cf. pp. 134–35.

26. Ibid., 119 and n. 10. Lohfink largely follows K. Elliger's definition of P, in "Sinn und Ursprung der priesterlichen Geschichtserzählung," *ZThK* 49 (1952): 121–43 (121). Elliger, following Noth, put the end of P in Deut 34. (According to Knohl [*Sanctuary*, 2 n. 5], the "prevailing scholarly view" is that P is considered to be composed of Exod 25–31; 35–40; Lev 1–16, and parts of Genesis, other Exodus, and Numbers.) Lohfink, however, finds it in Joshua.

27. Lohfink, "God the Creator," 126–27. Thus the story of Israel's refusal to enter the land in Num 13–14 is a "rare" narrative of sin in P, and the spies are not hostile, "but a sacred group of land inspectors."

28. William P. Brown, *The Ethos of the Cosmos: The Genesis of Moral Imagination in the Bible* (Grand Rapids: Eerdmans, 1999), 60, 64, 101. He stops short of Lohfink's "pacifism," however, which he thinks anachronistic, and points out that in priestly texts Yahweh does in fact evict the inhabitants of the land in Israel's favour (Exod 14:26–28; Lev 18:24–25; 20:22–25) (p. 101 n. 179).

analogies between the work of building the tabernacle and that of creation itself. The instructions for the tabernacle culminate in a Sabbath command (Exod 31:12–17); and the report that "Moses finished the work" (Exod 40:33c) carries a close echo of God's completion of his work on the seventh day of creation (Gen 2:2).[29] This analogy of completion has led some to think that what is portrayed is a fulfilment, a *ne plus ultra*. In Israel's life before God in worship, the divine purpose at creation is complete.

If the sharp separation of P from H robbed P of an interest in politics and ethics, its segregation from the other main strands of the Pentateuch and Joshua poses new questions about its voice in these areas, not least in the downplaying of sin, violence and the need for a redemptive mastery of these. It might be responded to Lohfink's theological analysis that it is actually difficult to disencumber P of these themes. The flood narrative is incomprehensible apart from the human violence to which it is a divine response.[30] Numbers 13–14 cannot be purged either of the sin of Israel nor of its military, and violent, character.[31] And this in turn makes an account of a peaceful subjugation of land in Joshua improbable.[32] Moreover, the completion of the tabernacle can only be a relative end, since it is necessarily also a beginning.

Piecemeal answers to such questions, however, are not quite satisfactory, since the questions are subordinate to larger ones about the

29. See B. Janowski, *Sühne als Heilsgeschehen: Studien zur Sühnetheologie der Priesterschrift und zur Wurzel KPR im Alten Orient und im Alten Testament* (WMANT 55; Neukirchen–Vluyn: Neukirchener, 1982), 309; idem, *Gottes Gegenwart* (BTAT 1; Neukirchen–Vluyn: Neukirchener, 1993), 238–39 n. 102.

30. The flood is one of the main factors that persuade F. M. Cross (*Canaanite Myth and Hebrew Epic* [Cambridge, Mass.: Harvard University Press, 1973], 306) that P deliberately assimilated JE, since in his view the P version of that narrative would make no sense without it. He also demonstrates P's method of assimilation in detail in Num 33 (p. 308). See also the comments by T. E. Fretheim, *God and World in the Old Testament: A Relational Theology of Creation* (Nashville: Abingdon, 2005), 33–34. On Gen 1–2: "...the P understanding of creation is to be found *only* in Gen 1–2 as a single whole" (p. 33).

31. Num 14:2–10 (P), for example, includes the note of Yahweh's military action against the people of the land (vv. 8–9). Even if these are attributed to J, it remains to explain why P incorporated them (unless P came first; see below). See also P. J. Budd, *Numbers* (WBC 5; Waco, Tex.; Word, 1984), 151–52.

32. Where P is found in Joshua, as in Josh 18:1, it is necessary to suppose either it is a fragmentary relic of something lost, or supplementation of the Deuteronomistic account; see Brown, *Ethos of the Cosmos*, 100 (though he does not decide which way to go). Some, however, find no elements of P in Joshua; e.g. Cross, *Canaanite Myth*, 320. This assumption is equally difficult, because on Cross's hypothesis, it means that P must have truncated the "Epic tradition" (ibid.).

composition of the Pentateuch. And here a wide range of models have been adopted, as has been documented recently by Rendtorff.[33] At stake is no longer whether P assimilated J or remained independent from it, but rather which of the two blocks has priority, and whether they even existed in the form supposed by the documentary hypothesis. Even to pose certain questions, therefore (such as whether P knew and assumed material in J), makes sense only within one fundamental construction of the Pentateuch among many others. Yet treatments of the material often make assumptions about the composition of the Pentateuch which are not always articulated, with the result that discussions of a topic such as the politics of P may simply not connect with each other. We have observed widely different perspectives on the politics of P for this very reason.

In my view, therefore, Rendtorff is right when he advocates the reading of Leviticus as a book within the flow of the Pentateuchal narrative.[34] Of course Leviticus has its own character, and even the term "P" has referential usefulness. The materials concerning sacrifice and holiness can still be distinguished from other parts of the Pentateuch.[35] However, it follows from the discussion so far that an appreciation of the theology, and the political orientation, of Leviticus should embrace all the contents of the book, and also place it in the context of the Pentateuchal narrative as such (and perhaps the Hexateuch). This means that the regulations about sacrifice will be read as part of the same theological expression as the ethical imperatives in the call to all Israel to be holy; religion will not be separate from politics. And it means too that P will not be set at odds with those parts of the Pentateuchal narrative that emphasize the sin of humanity and of Israel, and portray the conflict between Yahweh and the forces of Chaos in the progress towards promised land.

The Politics of Leviticus

I have tried to establish in the argument so far that the politics of Leviticus emerges from the book as a whole, set within the Pentateuchal narrative beginning with creation. The immediate implication of this is

---

33. R. Rendtorff, "What Happened to the 'Yahwist': Reflections After Thirty Years," available online at <http://sbl-site.org/Article.aspx?ArticleId=561> (accessed 13 September 2006). The paper was given at the International Meeting of SBL in Edinburgh, 2006.

34. Rendtorff, "Is it Possible?," 22–27. He argues especially that the book of Leviticus cannot be understood apart from the preceding book of Exodus (pp. 26–27).

35. Differences between the various corpora of law, for example, are well documented and need no special illustration here.

that Leviticus participates in a story about humanity, not just about Israel. We need to go beyond this, however, to ask what kind of relationship is intended between Israel and the rest of humanity. Does the story of humanity find its culmination in Israel? Or does the story of Israel serve the wider interest of the destiny of humanity? The recognition of the creation context does not yield answers to these questions in itself. We saw that Lohfink could not decide if Israel's story was representative. And for Davies, the creation setting led precisely to a politics of introspection and control.

Genesis begins with humanity as the "image" of God (Gen 1:26), then tells how it ramifies into the nations of the earth, yet focuses down on a branch of the line of Abraham. The language of "image" fades out, yet, as John Strong has rightly argued, the concept re-emerges at certain points, as when Moses is made "like God" to Pharaoh (Exod 7:1). He then proposes that, as in the ancient Near East, kings were seen as "testimonial steles" to the power of the god in a land, Yahweh at creation was setting up such a stele in "an erstwhile chaotic land,"[36] and that in due course Israel functions as such to Pharaoh (in reality Persia), because through it God demonstrates his glory and power (Exod 7:3–5; 14:4, 15–18).[37]

This account rightly places the portrayal of Israel in relation to the nations. Yet its role is not fully told in terms of the demonstration of Yahweh's power. Equally important is the theme of "righteousness," manifest first in Noah (אִישׁ צַדִּיק, Gen 6:9) as that which marks him out from the rest of humanity and thus as the quality needed for the renewal of humanity after the flood. Abraham too is regarded as possessing righteousness (צְדָקָה) on account of his faith (Gen 15:6). And this has further implications, because by virtue of his vocation to it, he is entrusted with a kind of responsibility for it in respect of the nations (Gen 18:17–19), which extends even to pressing Yahweh on the justice of his judgment on Sodom (vv. 20–33). Pharaoh perhaps inadvertently touches on the deep-lying significance of his contest with Yahweh when he attempts to stall the plague of thunder and hail, and pronounces Yahweh to be "in the right" (הַצַּדִּיק, Exod 9:27). In these instances the obligation of "righteousness" is assumed to lie on all nations, as it did

36. John T. Strong, "Israel as a Testimony to Yhwh's Power: The Priests' Definition of Israel," in John T. Strong and Steven S. Tuell, *Constituting the Community: Studies in Honor of S. Dean McBride* (Winona Lake, Ind.: Eisenbrauns, 2005), 89–106 (94–96). Notably, Strong explains the *priests'* view of Israel through the Pentateuchal story.

37. Ibid., 104–5.

upon the earliest human beings.[38] In Genesis, the special focus on Israel
is always in a relationship of tension with a pervasive interest in the
nations, highlighted when Abraham is told that his descendants will
bring blessing to the "families of the earth" (Gen 12:3), and indeed that
"nations and kings" will proceed from him and Sarah (Gen 17:6, 16); in
the blessing of Ishmael, and the provision of lands for the descendants of
Lot and for Esau; and in the portrayal of Egypt as a place of refuge for
the family of Jacob, and an arena within which the God of creation
blesses human beings with plenty. While the mood changes in exodus,
the underlying issue remains the rule of Yahweh in all the world. And
when Israel, the elect and covenant people of Yahweh, is portrayed as "a
kingdom of priests" (Exod 19:6), there is perhaps a thematic echo of
Abraham's role at Sodom.

When these "universalist" perspectives of Genesis and Exodus are
observed, it emerges that Israel's embodiment of the "image of God"
cannot be limited to the demonstration of Yahweh's power and glory.
The relationship between Israel and the rest of created humanity is more
complex. And this is true as we go right into the heart of the tabernacle.

It is widely recognized that the symbolism of the tabernacle represents
the created universe as a kind of microcosm.[39] We have also observed the
echoes of the first account of creation in the completion of the tabernacle
(Exod 40:33c; cf. Gen 2:2). Such echoes continue in the ordination of
Aaron and his sons, in their seven-day preparation (Lev 8:33–35) before
making the offerings which bring the sanctification of priests and tabernacle to their climax (ch. 9). The links between the tabernacle and creation narratives are not limited to the first account, however, but also, as
Gordon Wenham has shown, to the story of Eden. The expulsion of the
man and the woman from the garden to the east, and the cherubim placed
to foreclose their return (Gen 3:24), find correspondences in the location
of the door to the tabernacle on the east side of the court (Exod 27:13–
15; 38:13–15; cf. 26:27), in the symbolism of cherubim woven into the
curtains of the tabernacle (26:1) and the veil covering the most holy
place (26:31), and in the figures of gold attending the close presence of
God in the most holy place (25:18–22).[40] The approach of Israel to God

38. I have elaborated this argument in *God and Earthly Power: An Old Testament Political Theology, Genesis–Kings* (LHBOTS 454; London: T&T Clark
International, 2006), 30–73.

39. E.g. Janowski, *Gottes Gegenwart*, 216–23; cf. Clements, *God and Temple*,
6–9.

40. G. J. Wenham, "Sanctuary Symbolism in the Garden of Eden Story," in
Proceedings of the Ninth Congress of Jewish Studies (Jerusalem: World Union of
Jewish Studies, 1986), 19–25.

in the tabernacle is therefore a return, albeit restricted or provisional, to the presence that was lost at Eden.[41] In a telling moment at the climax of the Day of Atonement ritual, this restricted presence of human beings to God is vividly expressed. The High Priest alone enters the most holy place to "make atonement" for the tabernacle, the holy place and the sins of Israel; and while he is there "no man" is permitted to be in the tabernacle (כל אדם לא יהיה, Lev 16:17). It is Israelites as human beings, with an echo of the creation accounts, who are excluded from the tent; by the same token, I think, it is humanity as such, in the person of the Israelite high priest, that stands in the proximate presence of God.

This reconstruction is admittedly inferential. The relationship between Israel and humanity might be expressed otherwise than as representative. Lohfink considers that Israel's case may merely be an example of the possibility of the history of a nation with God, and that "strictly speaking, a similar history would have to be traced for every nation on earth."[42] B. Janowski, however, who also elucidates the connection between creation and the redemptive purpose expressed in the worship of Israel, is closer to a representative understanding when he carefully brackets Israel and humanity together. For him, the Sinai section, including the tabernacle rituals, shows that God's creative purpose was "to have *fellowship with humanity/Israel*."[43] Moreover, the tabernacle (*das Heiligtum*) is "the place of encounter *between God and humanity or/and between Yahweh and Israel*."[44] This fits best, in my view, with the situation of the story of Israel within one of humanity, in which the redemption portrayed in the life of Israel is an answer to the problem of the sin of humanity as such. Israel's story has its own integrity and particularity, but it discloses at the same time the destiny of the world.

I now want to bring together some threads of the argument so far. I have argued that the sections of Leviticus which deal with sacrifice and

41. Fretheim rightly cautions against the idea that the tabernacle is a restoration of Eden in any simple way, taking issue with, among others, Brown; see Fretheim, *God and World*, 47, and n. 86 on p. 313, and cf. Brown, *Ethos*, 219–28.

42. Lohfink, "God the Creator," 129. He agrees that the nature of Israel's role is not obvious, but considers it possible that "the cultic presence of God as salvation" applies somehow to the whole world. He clearly sees the theological significance of P from this perspective.

43. "*Gemeinschaft mit dem Menschen/Israel* zu haben," Janowski, *Gottes Gegenwart*, 238 (emphasis original). He also cites Genesis Rabbah 3:9, on the tabernacle as the completion of the creation, realizing God's fellowship with *humanity/Israel* (p. 245, emphasis added).

44. "[A]ls Ort der Begegnung *zwischen Gott und Mensch bzw. zwischen JHWH und Israel*," *Gottes Gegenwart*, 246 (emphasis added); cf. Janowski, *Sühne*, 311–12.

atonement are inseparable from the parts of the book traditionally ascribed to H, and also that the book as a whole participates in a story that is humanity's as well as Israel's. It follows, I think, that the representative character of Israel is manifest not only in its presence to God in worship, but also in its vocation to exhibit "righteousness" in its life. We have already seen that the ethical imperatives are regularly subsumed under the idea of holiness in Leviticus, the language of "righteousness" itself being rather rare.[45]

Israel's Holiness, the Land and the Alien

In the remainder of the essay, I want to look more closely at the ethics of Leviticus, especially regarding the nature of Israel and the claim I have made to its implied universality.

The thinking of Leviticus on the nature of Israel is remarkable for its attitude to the "alien" (גר, *gēr*). Compassion for the alien is grounded in Israel's own experience as an alien in Egypt, and its deliverance from slavery there by the compassion of Yahweh (Exod 20:21 [EVV 22]; 23:9; Lev 19:33–34; cf. Exod 18:3). The ethical, economic and political consequences of this memory are profound. In relation to property tenure, the notion of Israel as "aliens" persists even into the time of land possession, and underlies the idea that ownership is neither absolute nor perpetual (Lev 25:23). And the obligation to care for the alien is more than a call to charity; it amounts to a readiness to extend to him or her in effect full membership in Israel. This concept of the openness of Israel is one of the most radical ethical implications of the narrative of Leviticus.

One important expression of the status of the "alien" is the recurrent theme which puts him on a par with "Israelites" (בני ישראל), including the formula which brackets him with the "native" Israelite (אזרח, *ᵓezrah*). The formula is found first in Exod 12:19, 48–49, in relation to regulations for the Passover, then a number of times in Leviticus and Numbers.[46] In this first occurrence of the formula, the "alien" is permitted to participate in the Passover (v. 48), while other groups are excluded. In the immediate context of this permission is the information that Israel

---

45. צדקה does not appear at all, nor does צדיק; צדק occurs once in the sense of "justice" at Lev 19:15.

46. Lev 16:29; (17:8–10, "house of Israel";) 17:13, 15; 18:26; 19:33–34; (20:2; 22:18 *gēr* and "sons/house of Israel;) 24:22; Num 9:14; 15:13–16, 22–26, (here the גר is included with the עדת בני ישראל, "the congregation of the children of Israel," and all together form the עם, "people,"] 29–30; (19:10; 35:15 [בני ישראל]). Cf. also Josh 8:33; Ezek 47:22.

went out of Egypt accompanied by a "mixed multitude" (ערב רב, Exod 12:38), an important indication that Israel's true character will not be measured by ethnicity. This first impression is confirmed when the texts that expressly unite Israelite and alien are considered more closely. Broadly speaking, they relate to the keeping of the Torah and penalties for breaking it, and the need to keep the rituals of the covenant and worship. They cover a range of the life of Israel, including the Passover (again at Num 9:14), the Day of Atonement (Lev 16:29), the command to sacrifice only at the door of the Tent of Meeting (Lev 17:8–10, 13, 15), other laws concerning sacrifice and atonement (Lev 22:18; Num 15:13–16, 29–30; 19:1–10), the prohibition of idolatry and the basic command to keep the covenantal laws (Lev 18:26; 20:2), the cities of refuge (Num 35:15). In Joshua, native and alien are united in covenant renewal (Josh 8:33); and in Ezekiel, the alien joins the native in the right to inheritance in the land (Ezek 47:22).

The assumption behind this range of privileges and obligations is that the alien can become Israelite to all intents and purposes. In effect, he can be part of the "assembly" or "congregation" of Israel. This formal membership of the people is indicated in a number of texts. In the Day of Atonement ceremony, the alien is included in the command to "afflict yourselves" and the prohibition of work, and thus in the "you"-address to Israel and the purpose of atonement (Lev 16:29–30).[47] When the atoning actions of the priest are then described for the five categories of sanctuary, tent, altar, priests and "all the people of the assembly" (כל עם הקהל, Lev 16:33), the alien is presumably included in the last named. In the prohibition of sacrificing away from the "door of the Tent of Meeting," both the alien and the "man of the house of Israel" (איש איש מבית ישראל) are subject to the penalty "he shall be cut off from his people" (ונכרת האיש ההוא מעמיו; cf. Lev 20:3).[48] In the congregational offering for unwitting sin (Num 15:22–26), the alien is effectively included in "all the congregation of the children of Israel" (כל עדת בני ישראל), equated in turn with "all the people" (כל העם) (vv. 25–26). Finally, Num 15:15

---

47. Milgrom (*Leviticus 1–16* [AB 3; New York: Doubleday, 1991], 1055) thinks the alien is subject only to the prohibition of work and not to the command to afflict oneself in penitence, and argues the alien "is bound by prohibitive commands and not by performative ones." I see no justification in the text for excluding the alien from the command to self-affliction. See also R. Rendtorff, "The GĒR in the Priestly Laws of the Pentateuch," in *Ethnicity in the Bible* (ed. Mark G. Brett; Leiden: Brill, 2002), 77–87 (83–84), who includes the "alien" in the practice of self-denial, and also points to the "you"-address in v. 30 as probably including him also.

48. מעמיו is literally plural, but the meaning is indistinguishable from the singular מעמו; cf. Lev 20:3.

prefaces the equality-formula with the word הקהל ("the assembly"), with
the probable meaning: "As for the assembly, there shall be one statute for
you and for the alien," again implying the latter's inclusion in it.

I have already suggested that the attitude to the alien is deeply symbolic for the nature of Israel, because it is a consequence of Israel's
former status as aliens in a foreign land, a status which continues in a
certain sense. The equality-formula, "native and alien," seems also to
express something of the real character of Israel, rather than being
merely an adventitious provision for a certain kind of social problem.
The term אזרח, while it is not referentially different from "Israelite,"[49]
occurs almost exclusively in the equality-formula, and is therefore virtually unnecessary apart from it.[50] It hardly denotes Israel as an ethnicity,
since we have already observed that Israel's lineage was evidently porous
(because of the "mixed multitude," Exod 12:38; and the mixed marriages
of key figures such as Abraham, Joseph and Moses). Rather, its meaning
apparently consists simply in making a distinction with the alien. To put
it differently, the concept אזרח exists in the interests of elucidating the
nature of Israel, precisely by pointing to the alien's integration. How may
this distinction be imagined?

The laws of Leviticus, in themselves and in their literary context,
envisage a society that was subject to change, like most others. The alien
is, by definition, a person in transition. His transitional situation emerges
clearly from the Passover commands, which permit but do not compel
participation. His integration, therefore, presupposes a wish and commitment to integrate. This voluntary process no doubt distinguishes
the alien from the other groups that are regarded differently, namely the
"foreigner" (בן נכר, Exod 12:43), the "hired worker" (שכיר) and
"stranger" (תושב, Exod 12:45). With these different groups, we glimpse
something of the plurality and changing composition of Israel as a
society, which no doubt gave rise to the question as to who properly
belonged to the people called Israel. The answer given in Leviticus is
unequivocally in terms of allegiance to Yahweh. As the "alien" may be
distinguished from the "stranger" by virtue of declared and enacted
allegiance, so the bought slave is distinguished from the hired man, by
circumcision and right of participation in Passover (Exod 12:44).[51]

49. So rightly Christiana van Houten, *The Alien in Israelite Law* (JSOTSup 107;
Sheffield: Sheffield Academic Press, 1991), 120.

50. Cf. Rendtorff, "*GĒR*," 81. Lev 23:42, on Tabernacles, is the only exception,
where the אזרח is to keep the feast and there is no reference to the גר (contrast Deut
16:14). (Ps 37:35 has the only other reference to the אזרח in MT, but in a disputed
text; cf. LXX and *BHS*.)

51. Cf. J. I. Durham, *Exodus* (WBC 3; Waco, Tex.; Word, 1987), 173.

In one case, the expression "native and alien" apparently serves to include all members of society under certain laws and principles that operate in Israel. In the story of the son of an Israelite woman and an Egyptian father (Lev 24:10–23), the man's blasphemy against "the Name" leads to Moses consulting God then pronouncing a death sentence (v. 14; cf. Exod 22:27 [EVV 28]). There follow a number of generalizing commands, beginning with blasphemy itself, where the point is made that all are subject to it, "the alien and the native" (v. 16). The equality-formula recurs in v. 22, still in the context of the same case. The striking curiosity of the story lies in the identity of the offender. His mixed parentage seems to be at the heart of the incident. He is never named; rather, the focus is all on his parents. His Israelite mother is mentioned four times in two verses (vv. 10–11); we learn that her name was Shelomith, and that she belonged to the tribe of Dan. Forms of the word "Israel" occur frequently; the offender goes out among "the people of Israel," and fights with "a man of Israel." The Egyptian father is mentioned only once, but it is the man's paternity that calls forth the insistent contrast with "Israelites." Yet the connection with what follows is not straightforward, partly because the man would not seem to fit the category of "alien," and partly because the need to seek a special word from God on the matter can be explained simply as a first case of the offence itself, by analogy with the case of Sabbath-breaking in Num 15:32–36.[52]

Rather than suppose, therefore, that the offender must be classed as an alien, on the grounds of the connection between the case and the equality-formula, it is preferable to take the divine pronouncement to mean that blasphemy is punishable by death, and that this applies invariably, whoever the offender is (vv. 15–16). The equality-formula, in this context (v. 16b), lies close to the "whoever"-clause in v. 15b (איש כי יקלל אלהיו). It is striking that the response to Moses' enquiry, and the

---

52. Noth (*Leviticus*, 179–80) thought the man must be regarded as a foreigner by virtue of his paternity. Gerstenberger (*Leviticus*, 361), in contrast, points out the analogy with the case of Sabbath-breaking in Num 15:32–36. It might be argued that the man must have the legal status of an alien since the law would not make sense otherwise; so van Houten, *Alien*, 144–45. But against this is both the man's maternal line and the fact that, according to Deut 23:8–9 (EVV 23:7–8), Egyptians might become members of the assembly. The latter point is not decisive for the present case, admittedly, since the passage in Leviticus does not give enough information to match this individual to the terms of that command (namely the third-generation proviso—curiously matched here by the three generations on his mother's side). However, there is not enough evidence either to show that the man falls simply into the category of "alien." Cf. again Gerstenberger, *Leviticus*, 361: "This mixed parental pair can hardly serve as an illustration of the stipulation following in v. 22…since the perpetrator is at least a potential Israelite by way of his mother."

extension of it in further commands through to v. 23, is couched in quite universal terms.[53] The verdict on the blasphemer is followed immediately by the basic principle that anyone guilty of murder (that is, killing a נפש אדם) should likewise be put to death. The echo of the post-flood command to Noah about murder as a capital offence is unmistakeable (Gen 9:5–6). The compensation for murder by the life of the murderer leads into further prescriptions about compensation, in which instances of the *lex talionis* are bracketed by requirements to make good the culpable killing of valuable livestock. Here too principles are articulated about fundamental issues in human relations, illustrated by the twice-repeated אדם (vv. 20–21, echoing the one in v. 17). The uniting theme in vv. 17–22 is the demand for absolute respect of the fellow human being.[54] With this established, the equality-formula is repeated, and the account of the incident ends with the execution of the blasphemer. In this instance, the equality-formula has served, not to legislate specifically about the alien, but by a sort of extension to embrace all members of the society under basic principles of law and religion.

The inclusion of the alien is often explained as a consequence of the holiness of the land.[55] It is true that the language of defilement (טמא) is applied to the land in Lev 18:24–28, where Yahweh is said to have "punished its iniquity" (ואפקד עונה אליה, v. 25), and the land itself to have "vomited out its inhabitants" (cf. 18:28; Num 35:34; Deut 21:23). However, the notion of the land's defilement need not mean that this land is intrinsically more "holy" than other lands.[56] The concept of the land as holy is surprisingly muted, at best inferred from the presence of the tabernacle in it.[57] Aaron makes no atonement for it, though he does so for sanctuary, tent, altar, priests and people (Lev 16:33). In the Jubilee laws, it is the Jubilee itself that is said to be holy (25:10–12), not the land,

53. Gerstenberger (ibid., 364) finds the law in v. 17 so "indeterminate" that he suspects "a religiously pluralistic society as the background."

54. The biblical *lex talionis* differs from ancient Near Eastern laws such as the Code of Hammurabi in not making distinctions of social class in the application of law; cf. e.g. CH 196–223, and Gerstenberger, *Leviticus*, 368; see also Wenham, *Leviticus*, 281–86.

55. For example, Milgrom thinks the inclusion of the alien in the prohibition of work on the Day of Atonement (Lev 16:29) can only be explained on the grounds that breaking this command would pollute the land. As this notion is a special concern of H, Lev 16:29–34 must be an appendix from that source; see Milgrom, *Leviticus 1–16*, 1065.

56. *Pace* van Houten, *Alien*, 140.

57. *Pace* Milgrom (*Leviticus*, 324), who claims that both land and Sabbath are "sanctums."

though the land is in the centre of attention there. Furthermore, the application of holiness-related terms to the land is not systematically pursued. When it is said that the land will "enjoy its sabbaths," in consequence of Israel's expulsion from it (26:34–35, 43), this concept does not prevent it from being occupied by Israel's "enemies" in their absence (26:32). It seems, therefore, that the personification of the land in terms drawn from the holiness sphere is a trope intended to show the devastating effect of the people's sin. (This appears, I think, from 18:25, which resists being forced into a systematic statement: Yahweh punishes the land for its iniquity, yet the land vomits out its inhabitants. The connection is not a logical one.) This trope serves the essential point, namely the importance of covenant faithfulness on the part of Yahweh's people. It is by virtue of the covenant that they are bound in obedience to Yahweh, as is clear from the continuation of this fundamental relationship even in exile and apart from land (Lev 26:40–42, 44–45).

The close connection between land and people is best understood in relation to Israel's role as representative and witness to the nations, and correspondingly the land as microcosm of the earth. Milgrom rightly points out a parallel between land in Lev 26 and the earth in the flood narrative (P), where the earth is said to have become corrupt and is therefore engulfed (Gen 6:11–12).[58] There is indeed a harmony, in principle, among the elements in the created order, and this is reflected both in the devastation of the earth and its people in the flood narrative, and in the devastation of Israel and its land in the events that led to exile. But this falls short of ascribing holiness in a special way to Israel's territory. Rather, the land is an arena within which Yahweh demonstrates his holiness. The aspect of witness to the nations is evident in the astonishment of the "enemies" who occupy the land after Israel (Lev 26:32), just as the exodus from Egypt had happened "in the sight of the nations" (Lev 26:45).

For the same reasons, it strains the evidence to claim that "aliens" in Israel are subject to its laws and religious standards on the grounds of the holiness of the land. The idea of a necessary link between the land and the alien's obligations is further belied by the voluntary nature of Passover participation, and by the non-eligibility of other groups resident in the land. Rather, as we have seen above, "aliens" are counted alongside Israel because they are eligible, by choice, to become members of the covenant people, the "assembly" (קהל, or עדה) of Israel.

---

58. Milgrom, *Leviticus*, 324 (the text is cited wrongly as Gen 16:11–12). He goes on to speak of a cleansing of the land, as if Israel had to "atone to the land" (p. 323).

The relationships between land, people and the alien are further illustrated by the Jubilee laws, which thus provide an extended instance of the concept of Israel in Leviticus. At their heart is the concept that both the land and Israel belong to Yahweh (Lev 25:23, 55). How does this concept bear on our discussion so far?

We have observed that the language about land in Leviticus sometimes suggests that it is seen as an agent in its own right. The tendency is also manifest in the Jubilee context, where it "yields [gives] its fruit" (25:19). Its existence as an entity over against Israel is summed up in Yahweh's declaration that "the land is mine" (v. 23), with the immediate corollary that it may not be sold in perpetuity. This land is not under Israel's absolute control, but rather is put at Israel's disposal by the grace and favour of one beyond themselves. There is an analogy here with humanity's relationship to the earth, since in the creation narratives the earth has an existence prior to the advent of humanity (in both creation accounts), and human beings are placed in it "to work and keep it" (לעבדה ולשמרה, Gen 2:15). Ellen Davis has pointed out the honour bestowed upon the land in this phraseology.[59] The close relationship between אדם and אדמה can be disrupted, as Cain found when he was sentenced to wander in the earth because of his crime of murder (Gen 4:11–16). For him, the land would no longer "give" its "strength" (כחה); as he is driven from the earth (אדמה), so he is hidden from the presence of God, and by the same token vulnerable to any human predator (Gen 4:14). Israel does not "possess" the land any more than humanity "possesses" the earth. The land, by its nature, makes demands, requires to be treated in a certain way, will refuse to give "life" if it is not. The "triangular" relationship of God, land and people[60] is much in evidence here. To the mutuality of God and Israel, in which Israel keeps God's commands, corresponds a mutuality of Israel and land, in which the land "gives" its fruit and Israel eats its fill (Lev 25:18–19). The land, though an independent entity, is not a free agent, for it is subject to God's "command" of blessing upon his people (v. 21). And throughout the chapter runs an interface between the "fear" of God (vv. 17, 36, 43), radical respect for the neighbour, and the ethics of land-use.

59. Ellen F. Davis, *Getting Involved With God: Rediscovering the Old Testament* (Cambridge, Mass.: Cowley, 2001), 192–94. She has developed the theme in her recent Hulsean Lectures, Cambridge, 2006.
60. This triangular relationship, in which the triad of God, the earth and humanity is paralleled by Yahweh, the land of Israel and the people of Israel, has been well described by C. J. H. Wright, *God's People in God's Land: Family, Land and Property in the Old Testament* (Grand Rapids: Eerdmans; Exeter: Paternoster, 1990).

The concept of the land as God's is at the heart of the logic of Lev 25. The formulation in v. 23 is the culmination of a passage on the sale of land calculated according to time elapsed since the Jubilee, in which the land itself is not sold, but only its capacity to produce crops over a specified period. Equally, it grounds all that follows: the fundamental right and obligation to "redeem" land (vv. 25–28),[61] with qualifications and exclusions (vv. 29–34); the obligation to support those who have had to "sell" land, motivated by the "brotherhood" of Israelites and the gift of the land of Canaan after deliverance from Egypt (vv. 35–38); the extreme case of the poor falling into debt-service, with qualifications and exclusions (vv. 39–46); the possibility of debt-service to a גר or תושב ("sojourner") (vv. 47–55).[62] The rationale of God's ownership of land is maintained throughout. While Israelites may "sell" themselves to other Israelites as a remedy for poverty (v. 39), this "selling" is analogous to the "selling" of land, as it does not imply the permanent subjugation of the person who serves in this way, nor indeed the status of "slave" (עבד), since Israel is in an עבד-relationship only to God (vv. 42, 55). The service given to the fellow Israelite is comparable to the exchange of money, since both illustrate the close relationship between land, labour, produce and value. The "selling" of the person is in reality the selling of his capacity to enable the land to produce.

While Israel does not own the land absolutely, there is nevertheless a close bond between it and the land, expressed by the term "holding" (אחזה), which applies both to Israel in relation to "the land of Canaan" (14:34; cf. 25:24) and to families and their particular "holdings" (e.g. 25:13, 25, 27). These "holdings" have a force compelling the return of individuals and families each to their villages or clans (משפחתו, v. 10) in the Jubilee. The Jubilee concept is thus somewhat paradoxical, since it both resists the notion of absolute ownership and also establishes an inalienable bond between people and land, and between families and lands in particular.

The Jubilee laws are important, therefore, to Leviticus' understanding of social ethics. But how do they contribute to the theme of the inclusion of the גר? The laws scarcely give a complete or coherent picture. The basic image of the "alien" is that of a dependant, since together with the "sojourner," he is a paradigm for the poor "brother" who falls into debt and therefore needs to be maintained (v. 35). Yet in another case, it is the גר (or תושב) who has become rich, and to whom the Israelite "brother"

61. Note the redemption "to/for the land" (לארץ); here too the land itself seems to have an interest in the provision made.
62. Cf. Milgrom, *Leviticus*, 298–99.

sells himself to discharge debt (v. 47). His status in relation to the
"brother" is both like and unlike. He is distinguished (at least by silence)
from the תושב in the sense that he may not be sold as a "slave," that is, as
property that may be passed from generation to generation (vv. 45–46a).
This provision ranges the תושב along with the "nations," while the
omission of the גר leaves him on the side of the Israelite. But he is unlike
the Israelite in the sense that one who has entered debt-service with him
may be redeemed before the Jubilee (vv. 48–55), while this possibility is
not held out to the debt-slave of the full Israelite.

The laws of the Jubilee probably afford only a very imperfect portrayal of conditions that obtained at any particular time in Israel regarding the place of the "alien" in society. The individual prescriptions are
focussed on quite specific points, and may leave things unsaid which
would affect the total picture. But they are consistent with the notion of a
tendency towards the full inclusion of the "alien" in Israelite society, a
tendency that finds further fulfilment in the law of Ezek 47:21–23, in
which the alien is expressly included in the possession of property as
"inheritance." Leviticus 25 is therefore a point on the way in the Old
Testament's movement towards liberation, its limitations evidenced by
its incomplete disavowal of chattel-slavery, and its preferential treatment
of the Israelite (and "alien") compared with other nations.

Conclusion

My concern has been to understand the portrayal of Israel in Leviticus in
relation to the divine purpose for humanity declared in its larger literary
context. Should the story of Israel in P be comprehended exclusively in
terms of Israel's own destiny, or was it in some way representative of the
destiny of humanity? Was there a universal significance in the particular
experience? The enquiry fell into two related parts. First, it was argued
that Israel's presence to God in the tabernacle worship was at the same
time a partial recovery of the presence of humanity to God. The completion of the tabernacle, therefore, was not an end in itself, but a symbolic
realization of the destiny of humanity.

The second part was based on the premise that Leviticus embraced not
only the worship events and practices that were the principal subject of
chs. 1–16, but also the ethical and political thinking in chs. 17–26
(traditionally H). Here the topic of universality was pursued chiefly by
means of a study of the גר ("alien") in relation to the "Israelite." The
material in Leviticus (and elsewhere in P) went further than other law
codes towards the full integration of the alien. While the process of

integration did not seem to be complete, it was principled rather than accidental. That is, it was based on the alien's free decision to become a member of the קהל, or "assembly," of Israel, rather than his settlement in the "holy" land.

These two strands of the argument point towards the universal significance of the story of Israel in P. This literature therefore participates in the development of a concept of nationhood in the Pentateuch. That concept is more advanced in Deuteronomy, where the interrelated understandings of land, people, law and institutions are worked out somewhat systematically.[63] But while Deuteronomy also has a universalizable concept of people or nation, it is the Priestly literature that insists most emphatically on the inclusion of the outsider. Such inclusion is even essential to a true understanding of Israel in P. Israel is to include aliens because they themselves were aliens, and in an important sense remain so (Lev 25:23b). The included alien, therefore, is a necessary mark of Israel, having a kind of sacramental significance, comparable in a way to the Levite in Deuteronomy.[64] This concept of Israel—both inclusive and constituted by unity in worship—is evidently distinct from a genetic or "primordial" concept; indeed, the narrative seems deliberately to preclude such an impression (Exod 12:38). The story of Israel, therefore, is carefully conceived to be at the same time the story of humanity.

How far, then, are the ethical and political commands in Leviticus prescriptive generally? In them, the historicality and particularity of Israel are evident. The historical and cultural differences between ancient Israel and modern societies need no elaboration here. We have seen too that the centrally important idea of the inclusion of the alien is still in the process of development. Yet it is clear that a close connection exists between the nature and vocation of Israel (to be a people of God, standing before him in worship) and its ethical and political commitments. There is no disjunction here between "religious" and "political"; all comes under the rubric of "holy." Israel as humanity recovering the lost presence of God is the same Israel that resists the permanent concentration of property in the hands of a few, and is radically open to the inclusion of those who were previously not "Israel." Such inclusion is

---

63. The most exhaustive treatment of this is J.-M. Carrière, *La théorie du politique dans le Deutéronome* (ÖBS 18; Frankfurt: Peter Lang, 1997). See also Steven Grosby, *Biblical Ideas of Nationality Ancient and Modern* (Winona Lake, Ind.: Eisenbrauns, 2002); and McConville, *God and Earthly Power*, 74–98.

64. By "sacramental" I mean signifying something beyond itself, yet where the signifier is by its nature part of what is signified. In Deuteronomy, the Levite signifies by his landlessness the fact that Israel possesses land only as gift.

also exclusive in an important sense, namely its predication on acceptance of Yahweh as God. As a political concept, this might be read as
fundamentally at odds with modern notions of inclusion. But two preliminary responses might be made to this: first, that the portrayal of God
in the Bible is itself universal, and second, that all societies have ultimate
values. These may or may not be overtly expressed, but do increasingly
play a part in modern discourse about inclusion, and even fall broadly
under the category of "worship."

COMMANDING AN IMPOSSIBILITY?
REFLECTIONS ON THE GOLDEN RULE
IN LEVITICUS 19:18B*

Nobuyoshi Kiuchi

The attitude of exegetes to biblical law is often affected by their conviction about the nature of the biblical text in question. The underlying premises of the biblical laws have been debated over the last few decades.[1] Yet, it appears that one aspect of the laws, namely, their practicability, has not so far received much attention. Does God assume that the Israelites can observe his commandments? Is it appropriate for an exegete to approach the text on the assumption that the addressee, or audience, is deemed to be capable of doing so? Or does God simply lay out the ideal, setting aside the question of practicability? One may well consider that these questions should come after uncovering the exact meaning of the laws. Yet, the present writer's work on a commentary on Leviticus[2] has convinced him that an exegete's attitude toward the above questions often determines the course of his or her interpretation, as well as the definition of the meanings of the words and phrases.

In Leviticus the Lord addresses himself to people and priests through Moses. However, it is remarkable that nowhere in the book is it mentioned explicitly that the people can observe the Lord's commandments, nor indeed that they cannot, except for ch. 26 in which the future of the Israelites is heavily clouded by their disobedience to them.

---

* It is a privilege to dedicate this short essay to the honouree who has inspired the present author in many ways and for a number of years in exploring the Lord's true intention in and behind the Law.

1. For instances, see B. Lindars, ed., *Law and Religion: Essays on the Place of the Law in Israel and Early Christianity* (Cambridge: James Clarke, 1988); E. B. Firmage, B. C. Weiss, and J. W. Welch, eds., *Religion and Law: Biblical-Judaic and Islamic Perspectives* (Winona Lake, Ind.: Eisenbrauns, 1990).

2. N. Kiuchi, *Leviticus* (Apollos Old Testament Commentary 3; Nottingham/ Downers Grove, Ill.: InterVarsity, 2007).

In order to exemplify this and to provide a fresh way of looking at the laws, I shall offer a certain interpretation of one of the most famous passages in Leviticus, namely, the so-called Golden Rule in 19:18b. As we survey various exegetical questions, it will be clear that one's interpretation of the law is affected by one's general stance towards the Law. In what follows, I begin, therefore, by observing the literary features of Lev 19, then discussing its meaning, and finally considering the implication of the result for the purpose of the law.

1. *Interpretative Problems with Leviticus 19:18b*

Leviticus 19:18b reads as follows:

ואהבת לרעך כמוך אני יהוה

A common understanding of the commandment is that one ought to love one's neighbour as much as possible, even as one loves oneself, and that the endeavor toward this is called holiness. This position is nuanced differently by different scholars. For example, G. Wallis,[3] followed by J. Hartley,[4] states:

> ...even if the Old Testament does not explicitly demand self-denial and altruism, it advocates the kind of behavior which equates concern for the well-being of one's neighbour with the assertion of one's own will. In no case should one allow one's own selfish interests to prevail when this would be harmful to his neighbour.

While this comment should be accepted from a humanitarian point of view, is this really what Lev 19:18b states? In particular, the view expressed seems optimistic in failing to take account of situations in which one's interest conflicts with the neighbour's. Also debatable is whether or not the commandment talks about the "will" of the addressee, and how אהב is related to this.

As to the last question J. W. Kleinig comments,

> The love that the Lord commands is not basically an emotional attitude, a matter of sentiment, but an act of benevolence, a matter of will, for feelings cannot be commanded. The Lord commands his people to act in a loving way toward their neighbours and care for them as they care for themselves.[5]

---

3. G. Wallis, "אהב ʾāhabh," *TDOT* 1:99–118 (111).
4. J. Hartley, *Leviticus* (WBC 3; Dallas: Word, 1992), 318.
5. J. W. Kleinig, *Leviticus* (Concordia Commentary; St. Louis: Concordia, 2003), 412.

It is this kind of comment that led the present writer to examine the commandment in question anew. For, is it not reasonable to ask whether the Hebrew term אהב means to "love" in the sense of a human emotion?

There are other hurdles to overcome in obtaining the clear message of the commandment. First, there is an ongoing debate over the syntax of v. 18b, specifically as to whether כמוך ("like yourself") qualifies ואהבת ("You shall love") or רעך ("your neighbour"). Second, though usually neglected by exegetes, the exact meaning of כ deserves re-examination. Third, it is necessary to define the meaning of אהב ("to love"), as there is a question whether it includes such elements as outward conduct, or will that is separated from emotions. We first examine the syntax of v. 18b.

a. *The Wider Context, Verses 2–18*
Despite the apparent variety of topics, Lev 19 is generally viewed as consisting of two parts, vv. 2–18 and vv. 19–34. Indeed, the first part, after the command to become holy (v. 2), begins with the prohibition of idolatry, and ends with the apparently most comprehensive and positive commandment of neighbourly love in v. 18b.

Moreover, the first part could be further viewed as consisting of two parts, the first stressing the divine–human relationship (vv. 2–5) and the second the inter-human relationship (vv. 6–18). One can note a gradual flow of the author's concern from divine–human to inter-human (vv. 3–4 [prohibition of idolatry], vv. 5–8 [ban on illegal way of eating the fellowship offering], vv. 9–10 [concern for the needy], vv. 11–18), yet even in these last, the negative and positive commandments are to be viewed under the aspect of the Lord's presence, as the repetitive "I am the Lord" indicates.

Regarding vv. 11–18, there is a notable repetitive literary feature that our honouree is to be credited for uncovering, in which different words for "neighbour" are used, and each of the four subsections is closed by the formula "I am the Lord."[6] As the section progresses, the terms relating to the neighbour appear more frequently. Thus,

vv. 11–12	עמיה	I am the Lord
vv. 13–14	רעך	I am the Lord
vv. 15–16	עם,עמיה	I am the Lord
vv. 17–18	רעך,עם,עמיה,אח	I am the Lord

In addition to Wenham's comment, it can be observed that there is also a progressive focus in vv. 11–18 on the inner attitude of the addressee.

---

6. G. J. Wenham, *The Book of Leviticus* (NICOT; Grand Rapids; Eerdmans, 1979), 267.

Such a literary feature is unlikely to be accidental; it would represent the author's intention that aims to emphasize the grand principle in v. 18b.

In content, then, what is the relationship between the prohibition of idolatry and the command of neighbour-love? It is generally assumed that the first part of this chapter contains many references to the Ten Commandments, such as the Sabbath observance, prohibition of stealing, and fear of one's parents. Prohibition of idolatry is the second commandment. However, while love of God is mentioned in the second commandment (Exod 20:6), it is not in this chapter. Instead, the term "love" (אהב) is used for inter-human relationships in v. 18, and it is noteworthy that it is not simply said that one ought to love one's neighbour, but to love one's neighbour *as oneself*, if we adopt a traditional understanding of the commandment (see below). In view of the second commandment, one must assume that herein lies an implication that simply loving another can be a kind of idolatry.

b. *The Immediate Context, Verses 17–18*
Some observation of the context may contribute to the interpretation of neighbour-love in v. 18b. From v. 17b onwards, the laws explicitly mention human inner states such as hating, grudging and loving. The injunctions flow from hating (v. 17) to grudging (v. 18a) and then to loving (v. 18b). For our purpose, it should be asked whether loving in v. 18b is emotional or not. At least, it appears that as "hating" is contrasted with "loving," the latter includes one's inner emotion or attitude. Regarding שׂנא ("hate"), B. J. Schwartz comments that hatred in the Bible is not always emotional but can be either emotional or behavioral, and that is why in v. 17 it is specified by "in your heart," in order to address the emotion alone.[7] While this comment is right as regards Lev 19:17, it may be questionable if שׂנא is said to be behavioral. Schwartz cites such passages as Jer 12:8, Amos 6:8, Mal 1:3, and Ps 5:6 as pointing to that meaning.[8] However, it may equally well be that, just like the meaning of אהב in v. 18b, this verb also refers to an overall attitude to the object, and that is why its meaning looks as though it includes outward conduct.

The two verbs in v. 18a, namely, "revenge" and "bear a grudge," stand in contrast with אהב in v. 18b. While the former ("revenge") is behavioral, the latter ("bear a grudge") refers to one's inner emotion. This fact by itself may not appear to provide a key to understanding whether אהב in v. 18b is emotional or behavioral term. However, it is obvious that

7. B. J. Schwartz, *The Holiness Legislation* (Jerusalem: Magnes, 1999 [Hebrew]), 319.
8. Ibid., 319 n. 75.

"revenge" comes from one's inner hatred, and the whole section aims to prohibit hatred already in one's heart. Thus, from this consideration it is probable that אהב refers to emotions, rather than to outward conduct.

More importantly, Schwartz proposes a novel interpretation of vv. 17–18. He proposes two ways of looking at the passage.[9] The first reading follows the order of the commands, namely, negative commands are followed by positive ones ("Don't do this" [v. 17a and v. 18a], but "Do this" [v. 17b and v. 18b]), and each of the verses closes with a summary statement ("and you will not bear guilt because of him" [v. 17b], "I am the Lord" [v. 18b]). The second reading works from hindsight, that is, by seeing the beginning and end of the passage as general statements and the middle (v. 17b and v. 18a) as their details. However, while the first reading is intelligible, the second one appears to be slightly artificial, particularly when Schwartz uses the terms "general" and "details." At any rate, from such a reading he draws the conclusion that the only positive command in this passage is "Rebuke him" in v. 17b (הוכח תוכיח), and that v. 18b is the *result* of "not hating in the heart," "rebuking," and "not taking revenge and bearing a grudge," so that it is not a command in itself.[10] One may wonder if God's command only becomes such when it is specific. It is preferable, in my view, to suppose that what is commanded in v. 17 is repeated in a heightened form in v. 18, and therefore that v. 18b is also a command.

c. *The Syntax of Verse 18b*
Two interpretations of the syntax of the passage have appeared, one traditional, and the other favored mainly by Jewish scholars. The focus of the interpretation revolves around the question what the phrase כמוך qualifies. The traditional interpretation takes it to qualify "and love," whereas some Jewish scholars take it qualify "your neighbour." According to the former position, the command dictates the mode of "loving," while the latter says in effect "your neighbour who is like you."

I begin with a re-examination of the latter position as it may sharpen the problem of interpreting this commandment. A Jewish exegete, A. Ehrlich, argues on the basis of the practicability of the command that כמוך qualifies רעך ("your neighbour"), and means איש אשר כמוך ("a man who is like you").[11] In a similar vein, Muraoka argues for the

---

9. Ibid., 317–18.
10. Ibid., 320–21.
11. A. B. Ehrlich, *Randglossen zur hebräischen Bibel* (Hildesheim: Georg Olms. 1968 [repr. of 1st ed., Leipzig: Hinrichs, 1908]), 2:65. This position is also adopted by NEB when it renders "You shall love your neighbour as a man like yourself."

substantivization of בּ.[12] However, he provides no example of such a use of בּ except for this passage, and it is difficult to apply it to the בּ in 19:34, since there is no noun corresponding to "your neighbour" in v. 18b, and therefore כמוך in this case more probably means "as yourself." Most recently, A. Schüle has discussed the David–Jonathan narrative, in which the phrase אהב כנפשו in 1 Sam 18:1, 3 and 20:17 is used to describe Jonathan's love for David, and means "as he loved himself." He argues, however, that this case refers to a "substitutional self-dedication to the others," and thus differs contextually from Lev 19:18b, which addresses itself to the care of the needy and socially oppressed.[13] However, Schüle's argument is problematical in some respects. First, he does not provide a linguistic discussion of the use of בּ in Lev 19:34. Second, his characterization of the context of Lev 19 is one-sided. Particularly vv. 17–19 should not be viewed merely socially, or from the viewpoint of the third party. The commandment is given directly to the addressee. And in this regard, the David–Jonathan relationship represents, though a rarity in the Old Testament, a fulfillment of the command in Lev 19:18b. Moreover, it may be argued that if one resolves to observe the commandment in Lev 19:18b, one cannot do so without putting oneself in a relationship such as that between David and Jonathan.

Therefore, I conclude that in Lev 19:18b כמוך qualifies ואהבת ("you shall love"), not רעך ("your neighbour"). As rightly pointed out by H.-P. Mathys, the above position, mostly adopted by Jewish scholars, strongly anchors in the assumption that the law is practicable.[14]

With regard to the meaning of בּ in כמוך, to my knowledge, no exegete has paid attention to its exact nuance. It is agreed that the preposition בּ conveys either resemblance or exact similitude.[15] However, while the preposition is properly translated "like," it often means exact similitude, rather than approximation. Let us take some examples from Leviticus to demonstrate this point:

12. T. Muraoka, "A Syntactic Problem in Lev xix 18b," *JSS* 23 (1978): 291–97.

13. A. Schüle, "»Denn er ist wie Du«: Zu Übersetzung und Verständnis des alttestamentlichen Liebesgobots Lev 19, 18," *ZAW* 113 (2001): 515–34.

14. H.-P. Mathys, *"Liebe Deine Nächsten wie Dich Selbst": Untersuchungen zum alttestamentlichen Gebot der Nächstenliebe (Lev 19, 18)* (OBO 71; Göttingen: Vandenhoeck & Ruprecht, 1986), e.g. 19–20.

15. P. Joüon and T. Muraoka, *A Grammar of Biblical Hebrew* (Subsidia Biblica 14/I-II; Rome: Editrice Pontificio Istituto Biblico, 1991), §133g: "*k* expresses a relation of either perfect (equality) or imperfect (resemblance) similitude; the meaning may therefore be exactly like, or more or less like, but in many cases without any precise nuance."

וּתִקְרֶאנָה אֹתִי כָּאֵלֶּה

...and things like these have happened to me. (10:19)

Aaron refers to the death of his two sons, Nadab and Abihu and its consequences, recounted in vv. 1–9. The preposition כ here functions to make the reference imprecise. So כ here has the role of expressing resemblance.

כִּימֵי נִדָּתָהּ תִּהְיֶה טְמֵאָה הִוא

As in the days of her menstruation, she shall be unclean. (15:25)

The phrase כִּימֵי נִדָּתָהּ refers to the degree of defilement, and not to the length of period, hence the proposed translation. It is not approximation or resemblance, but exact similitude regarding the degree of defilement that is expressed by כ.

כַּחַטָּאת כָּאָשָׁם תּוֹרָה אַחַת לָהֶם הַכֹּהֵן אֲשֶׁר יְכַפֶּר־בּוֹ לוֹ יִהְיֶה

The reparation offering is like the sin offering, there is the same instruction for them; the priest who makes propitiation with it shall have it. (7:7)

The idiomatic כ...כ expresses exact similitude, which is, in this case, confirmed by "the same instruction." Needless to say, the exact similitude lies in the handling of the remaining flesh alone.

These examples show that it is important to pay attention to the semantic function of כ (i.e. what is compared with what) as well as its nuance in a given passage. Thus, in view of the different nuances that כ might express, it is worth considering in what nuance the כ in Lev 19:18b is used.

First of all, those exegetes who advocate Ehrlich's position and translate כָּמוֹךָ as "[your neighbour] as yourself" find it difficult to be exact about in what sense the addressee resembles his/her neighbour. However, the text is not explicit about the point of resemblance. At any rate, even in this position it is clear that כ is understood as expressing resemblance only.

What happens when we take the traditional understanding of the command? At this juncture we recall the literary feature of vv. 11–18 observed by Wenham (see above). It is striking that the last sub-unit, vv. 17–18, begins with the prohibition of hating one's אָח ("brother"). However, what is the purpose of this literary feature, in terms of כָּמוֹךָ and רֵעֲךָ in v. 18b? Self-evidently, the addressee is not identical with his/her neighbour. Thus, in line with my interpretation of the syntax of the command and the increasingly frequent use of the neighbour-related terms in vv. 17–18, it is more likely that כָּמוֹךָ expresses exact similitude, rather than just resemblance, and that v. 18b virtually says that the neighbour ought to be treated as more than "a brother."[16]

At the same time, the repetitive use of the neighbour-related terms in vv. 17–18 aims to inculcate in the mind of the addressee(s) the need to overcome hatred and vengeance on their own part. If so, to understand כ in כמוך as expressing resemblance ("more or less similar") would make ambiguous the contrast made between hatred and vengeance on the one hand, and love on the other. This understanding would leave room for degrees of resemblance, and thus in practice for degrees of endeavor, while the goal of the command would not appear in the text. Therefore, I propose that כמוך should be understood "exactly like yourself."

Thus, this interpretation would increase the impracticability of the command even more than when the preposition is simply understood as expressing resemblance.

However, what does loving one's neighbour as oneself mean? For this question it is necessary to clarify the meaning of אהב.

2. *The Meaning of* אהב *in the Legal Material*

The verb אהב occurs only twice in Leviticus, in Lev 19:18 and 34, whereas it occurs 220 times in the Old Testament. (Notably, before Deuteronomy it appears just four times in the legal part of the Penta-teuch, at Exod 20:6 and 21:5 besides the two occurrences in Lev 19:18, 34.) While the term has commonly been classified according to whether it expresses divine–human, or inter-human relationships, it is clear that the term in Lev 19:18b and 19:34 refers to inter-human love.[17]

If the term אהב here is an emotive or attitudinal term, as argued above, it may be asked how God can command it, since any human emotion or attitude exists before it is commanded. The same holds true regarding its antonym שׂנא, meaning to "hate." In fact, in Lev 19:17 the Lord forbids the Israelites to *hate* his/her neighbour *in their hearts*. Thus, in the context of vv. 17–19, it can safely be inferred that אהב in v. 18b is mentioned, at least, as an opposite of inner-human emotion or attitude of hatred. Furthermore, the context stresses that the love commanded in v. 18b is to be shown not just to human beings in general but also to (a) person(s) by whom the addressee is supposedly offended. It is common-place that when one is offended, one tends to bear a grudge and to hate.

---

16. That את and רע constitute a fixed word pair may be confirmed by Exod 32:27; Deut 13:7; 15:2; Jer 9:3; Ps 35:14; Job 30:29, etc.

17. A basic analysis of the term is provided by P. J. J. S. Els, "אהב ʾhb," *NIDOTTE* 1:277–99.

Therefore, the reader is here commanded to *love* such a person whom he/she *tends to hate*, but once hatred is entertained, the law in v. 17 is violated, which is then far from the observance of the commandment in v. 18b!

It appears that the majority of exegetes take the meaning of אהב as emotive, but, as it appears impossible that God commands human emotions, they stress that the love must be translated into outward benevolent conduct. Apart from the question whether God is actually commanding the addressee to control his/her emotions, in this case, love, it is questionable if אהב itself denotes outward conduct. On the one hand, it is observed above that the context of vv. 17–18, particularly, the explicit mention of "hating in the heart" in v. 17, implies that the אהב in v. 18b is a purely emotive or attitudinal term. On the other hand, in an attempt to demonstrate that אהב has outward conduct in view, Milgrom, for instance, adduces a number of Deuteronomic passages, such as Deut 7:8; 10:18–19; 11:1, and says, "the very context of this strophe (vv. 17–18) implies that love must be translated into deeds."[18] Milgrom does not deny that אהב is an emotive term. However, does his inference about translation into deeds not derive from his assumption that the commandment is practicable? Further, a problem with his philology lies in neglecting the point that if one term is explicated by another, or another phrase, the sense of the former cannot be equated with that of the latter. Thus, the question how God can command emotions still remains. In my view, the exegetical thrust of our passage is that, although love should be naturally translated into outward conduct, אהב in Lev 19:18b is an emotive term and/or one that expresses one's total attitude to his/her neighbour.

With these considerations in mind, I examine below Exod 20:6 and 21:5 and their related passages as they bear upon אהב in our passage. Exodus 20:6 describes God's character as follows:

> ...but showing steadfast love to thousands of those who love me (לאהבי)
> and keep my commandments (ולשמרי מצותי). (RSV)

It appears that love of God is equated here with observance of his commandments. However, this is so on the level of its content, not on the semantic level. As it stands, the second commandment indicates that the content of אהב is also closely related to "worship" (השתחוה) and "serve" (עבד), and one cannot argue that אהב is co-terminous with either of

---

18. J. Milgrom, in discussing the same commandment in Lev 19:33–34, comments that the verb actually means "doing good, treating kindly" (*Leviticus 17–22* [AB 3A; New York: Doubleday, 2000], 1653).

these.[19] On the other hand, since these latter express the total attitude of a person to his/her God, the term אהב also belongs to this level of meaning; it is not just a temporary emotion, but a total favorable attitude. The comprehensiveness of the meaning of אהב matches that of the meaning of the term מצות which covers other related terms such as חקים and משפטים (Lev 26:34).

Exodus 21:5 deals with the release of a Hebrew slave:

> But if the slave plainly says, "I love (אהבתי) my master, my wife, and my children; I will not go out free." (RSV)

In considering the reason why the slave wishes to remain with his master, scholars have suggested specific circumstances, such as that a slave may face a worse situation if he goes free,[20] but Chirichigno is no doubt right when he comments, "he [the slave] chooses to remain because he has formed a close relationship to his lord, not because he has no other choice."[21] The "close relationship" is precisely what אהב expresses. אהב is the basic motive here regardless of other conceivable circumstances.

This use of אהב is an inter-human one, but could this love of the master be classified as a violation of the second commandment, according to which the slave ought to love only the God of Israel? It may be so. However, the context of Exod 21:5 indicates clearly that this love is a self-sacrificial love, by which the slave resolves to remain with his master at the sacrifice of legitimate freedom. In this instance, freedom does not lie in the choice between freedom and bondage, but in choosing bondage, which may be higher than the ordinary sense of freedom.[22] It seems that just as fear of the parents (Lev 19:3) does not constitute idolatry, neither does this case.

In Exod 23:4–5 there is the following command:

> If you meet your enemy's ox or his donkey going astray, you shall bring it back to him. If you see the donkey of one who hates you lying down under its burden, you shall refrain from leaving him with it; you shall rescue it with him. (ESV)

One might say that this command aims to promote and encourage neighbourly love. Yet neither the term אהב nor any of its related terms

---

19. אהב occurs in parallel with עבד in the following passages: Gen 29:18, 30, Deut 10:12; 11:13; 22:5; Jer 8:2.

20. Cf. G. C. Chirichigno, *Debt-Slavery in Israel and the Ancient Near East* (JSOTSup 141; Sheffield: JSOT Press, 1993), 230.

21. Ibid., 231.

22. Cf. 1 Cor 9.

appears to describe the addressee's attitude. Moreover, is this command not given precisely because the natural thing may well be not to assist the enemy who needs help? As we have seen, it has often been held that the love commanded in Lev 19:18b must be expressed outwardly, that is, by doing benevolent things to the person who offends or persecutes the addressee. Yet one wonders if such a view does not distinguish between a law like Exod 23:4–5 and Lev 19:18b in terms of the occurrence of אהב.

The difficulty of implementing "neighbourly love" is also implied in the following wisdom saying:

> If your enemy is hungry, give him bread to eat,
>   and if he is thirsty, give him water to drink,
> for you will heap burning coals on his head,
>   and the LORD will reward you. (Prov 25:21–22, ESV)

Again, although such a commended action may approximate to אהב, the term is not used.[23] It could be that the actions commended aim to orient the readers towards the goal in Lev 19:18b. Yet, if the term has an emotive element, then the latter should be distinguished from any endeavor towards it.

In view of the above, we are faced with a question whether אהב in Lev 19:18b includes various kinds of outward conduct that are mentioned in the context up to v. 18b. Commentators have generally assumed that, as the commandment in v. 18b appears most positive, it must be comprehensive and include all these. However, while it is indeed comprehensive, it is so in the sense that אהב refers to the underlying disposition of a person, not referring necessarily to some specific action that is motivated by אהב.

This invites a further question whether אהב includes conduct, or whether the verb expresses any performance of benevolent acts toward one's neighbour in the rest of the Old Testament.

a. *The Meaning of* אהב

If one approaches various rules in Exodus–Leviticus on the assumption that they are "laws" which are similar in nature to modern laws, one would scarcely conclude that God commands human emotions. Inevitably, exegetes would tend to make the laws practicable in interpreting them. In the case of our passage, this tendency has appeared in the understanding of the syntax of v. 18b, and the failure to neglect the delicate nuance of כ in כמוך.

---

23. Cf. Rom 12:19–20.

Now, there is another issue that may concern the correct understanding of the commandment, that is, the meaning of אהב. It has been pointed out above that the verb itself may not refer to any specific benevolent action towards the neighbour. This can also be argued by reference to a number of other Old Testament passages that some scholars have adduced to demonstrate that love consists in doing something.

b. *Inter-human Love*
As אהב in Lev 19:18b is a term used for inter-human relationship, I focus my examination on that context. The occurrences of אהב in interpersonal contexts can be classified by the viewpoint of who loves whom, such as Abraham loving Isaac (Gen 22:2), but more important for our concern is to explore the meaning of the term אהב by raising the question whether it occurs independently or not, and if it is followed by a mention of some reason for its use, or what relation outward conduct has to it. The result of the examination is as follows:

    (1) Human love such as filial love etc. is assumed by God as a given, but something more than that is demanded as in the case of Abraham offering his only son Isaac (Gen 22:2).

    (2) Love has degrees; one loves a certain person more than the others (Gen 29:18, 30; 37:3, 4).

    (3) There are cases in which the mention of love is followed by some reason (Gen 37:3; 1 Sam 18:16).

    (4) The mention of love stands alone, or love is mentioned as the underlying motive for other actions (Gen 29:18, 30; 34:3; 1 Sam 18:20; 20:17; 2 Sam 13:1, 4, 15; 1 Kgs 5:15; 11:1).

As the instances of אהב show, human love is not free from selfishness or egocentricity (a notable exception is the case of David and Jonathan). Yet, even within this limitation, "love" often becomes the underlying motive for some action(s), and it cannot be replaced by its consequential outward act(s). When love is said to be motivated by a specific reason (such as Jacob's love for Joseph because he was the child of his old age), the fact that the reason is not an act implies that אהב refers to one's overall attitude towards the other person. On the other hand, the cases in which אהב is followed by some kind of act may be taken as though the act and the human will operating in it are the content of אהב, yet in such cases it can equally be supposed that the person's action is motivated by אהב.

Thus, it is concluded that אהב in the inter-human context describes the condition of human relations such as ones between father and son, friends, man and woman, and it represents an overall favorable emotional attitude towards the person loved.

It is thus erroneous to assume that אהב includes the human will to love, or any action. These latter may represent a person's effort to love others, but the verb אהב itself is an underlying emotive attitude towards another person. Certainly, if אהב has no accompanying actions, then the "love" may lack credibility, yet it is also possible that any particular benevolent action may not arise from אהב.

In sum, אהב is a comprehensive emotive and/or attitudinal term. It is used in this sense in Lev 19:18b in contrast with שנא in v. 17a, and by itself does not refer to outward actions.

c. אהב *Also Means "to Like"*

The second issue regarding the meaning of אהב is whether there are degrees of intensity in "love." This question has not featured prominently in the history of the command's interpretation, yet it arises in relation to the command in v. 17 that prohibits hating in one's heart. Is the commandment in v. 17 concerned with the extreme degree of hatred, and that in v. 18 with the same polar opposite degree of love? If one reads these commandments this way, the laws' scope of application would be rather minimized. At the same time, the addressee would excuse himself from being accused of violating the commandments, if there are degrees of "hating" and "loving."

Not only are there some contexts in which אהב can be interpreted as "to like" (e.g. Gen 27:4, 9, 14; 29:30; Isa 56:10), the context of Lev 19, particularly vv. 15–16, shows that being partial leads to violation of the prohibitions, which means that the mere presence of a bias in one's mind or heart toward one's neighbour may lead one to violate the injunctions. In the light of these injunctions, it may well be possible that by שנא the legislator meant "to dislike" as well as "to hate." And the same goes for אהב: it can mean "to like" as well as "to love."

In sum, following vv. 13–16, vv. 17, 18b assume that the slightest inner discrimination against one's neighbour is judged as violation of the commandments.

3. *Self-love and the Love of Neighbour*

According to the traditional understanding of the syntax in v. 18b that I advocate, the commandment assumes self-love. Since human love has an egocentric nature, it is unlikely that self-love is commanded here; it is rather assumed (see below). And consequently, the command to love the neighbour is based on this self-love. In other words, the command does not just require the addressee to love his/her neighbour, but to love the neighbour just as one loves himself/herself. The very syntax of the passage indicates that it is illegitimate to see either self-love or neighbourly love separately. The two must be viewed in their relationship. But how is this possible?

The analogy between self-love and love of the neighbour raises the question whether the commandment is one that can be observed by human beings, given any element of egocentricity in the self-love. While there may be exceptions (such as Jonathan's love for David, 1 Sam 18:1), it appears that, though using the common term "love," this command aims to point to a kind of love that is beyond, and different from, ordinary human love. Paradoxically, then, it would seem that only by negating the egocentric self-love can one truly have love toward his/her neighbour; the command in Lev 19:18b therefore, with its stipulation "as yourself," appears to demand an impossibility. Thus, from every angle the conclusion is inevitable that the love commandment is impossible to observe, and this conclusion prompts us to consider the purpose of giving such a command.

4. Conclusion: The Purpose of the Commandment

The purpose of observing the love of neighbour is stated in Lev 19:2, namely, to become holy. However, while one may tend to regard this command as fulfilled by any human effort towards the goal, arguably such fulfilment can at best be partial. Is the holiness command, then, merely an ideal?

Nowhere in Leviticus is it stated explicitly that the addressee(s) cannot observe the Lord's commandments, and so one should be cautious before coming to conclusions about impracticability. Indeed, human efforts towards the love of neighbour love are contemplated elsewhere in the Pentateuch, and in approaching the Lord's presence one cannot but take practical steps that appear in line with the Lord's will. However, in the Golden Rule it is simply commanded that one ought to love his/her neighbour as one loves himself/herself.

Yet, as I have argued above, the meaning and formulation of the love commandment denies in effect the possibility that a person can observe the commandment. Not only my interpretation of the preposition כ (to mean as one loves oneself), but also the very command to love as an underlying emotion or attitude, puts it beyond normal human efforts. Does God not know that the addressee cannot observe the commandment? If he does, what is its purpose? Or is it permissible to see the command simply as an ideal for human beings?

While a full discussion of Lev 19 is impossible here, some further observations on it may support this view. Certain positive and negative commandments that concern outward conduct in the chapter appear to make the reader aware of the addressee's egocentric nature. For instance, in v. 3a the Lord commands to fear one's mother and father, but this command is presumably violated unless "fear" is the underlying motive for all other kinds of human conduct. Further, though the commandments in vv. 13–14 concern one's outward conduct, they rest on the "fear" of God, and it follows that any violation of them starts from the human heart, such as by looking down on one's neighbour or being partial toward the physically handicapped. Observance of these laws certainly has a beneficial effect on the community, yet can they be fully observed? In the light of the increasing emphasis on the human inner condition in vv. 13–18, it seems that in vv. 17–18 as well the laws aim to make the addressee aware of his/her egocentric nature.

In view of the discussion so far about the underlying attitudes expressed by "fear" or "love," it is clear that these refer to the condition of the human heart, and the intention that any egocentric nature be destroyed. This leads me to an inference that the giving of the love-command in its formulation in Lev 19:18b aims to make one aware of, and destroy, the egocentric in human nature. This is achieved by inculcating the realization that one cannot observe this commandment. In other words, it is simplistic to assume that observance of the law leads one to holiness. There lies an abyss between the human efforts to observe this law and holiness itself, namely, the egocentric nature. Only if one's egocentric nature is destroyed can one be said to be holy. In this regard, not just this commandment, but all the commandments aim at this realization. Indeed, it is the absence of an egocentric nature that constitutes the core idea of holiness, and fulfillment of the Law.

THE CASE FOR THE PRE-EXILIC AND EXILIC PROVENANCE OF THE BOOKS OF EXODUS, LEVITICUS AND NUMBERS

Jacob Milgrom

Elsewhere I have cited evidence demonstrating the pre-exilic provenance of H.[1] In addition, the fact that H is subsequent to and redactor of P has allowed me to claim that the entire priestly source (P and H), especially the book of Leviticus, is pre-exilic. My claim, however, is not a proof. All I have shown is that each law or pericope in which H occurs is pre-exilic, but not the entire priestly source. For example, the absence of an intermarriage ban from the list of certain illicit sexual unions (Lev 18:6–23; 20:9–21) only demonstrates that the latter is pre-exilic,[2] but not all of Leviticus. Moreover, that Ezekiel unquestionably had all of Lev 26 before him is shown by Ezekiel's extensive citations of Lev 26.[3] This conclusion is further buttressed by the evidence within ch. 26 itself. Its concept of repentance is pre-prophetic,[4] and its presumption of multiple sanctuaries (v. 30) is pre-Josianic. All well and good. Again, all that can be decided is that Lev 26 is pre-exilic, but not all of Leviticus.

In this study I shall attempt to bring conclusive evidence that, indeed, the entire book of Leviticus is pre-exilic and raise the possibility that both of its flanking books, Exodus and Numbers, must also be designated as pre-exilic. My claim is anchored on the one-verse pericope of the sabbath, Lev 23:3, that heads the festival calendar. This verse (along with v. 2 αβb) is indisputably an interpolation of the redactor H$_R$.[5] Moreover, it is possible to provide the exact date when this passage was inserted. The unique designation of the sabbath as a "feast" (מועד) that is "proclaimed" (תקראו), and the omission of the required public sacrifices

1. J. Milgrom, *Leviticus 17–22* (AB 3A; New York: Doubleday, 2000), 1362–64.
2. Ibid., 1584–86.
3. J. Milgrom, *Leviticus 23–27* (AB 3B; New York: Doubleday, 2001), 2348–52.
4. J. Milgrom, *Leviticus 1–16* (AB 3; New York: Doubleday, 1991), 373–78.
5. Milgrom, *Leviticus 17–22*, 1954–55.

for the sabbath (Num 28:9–10), pinpoint the exilic period as the only possible time for the composition and insertion of the sabbath pericope at the head of the festival calendar.[6]

This means that wherever the sabbath is an editorial interpolation (H_R) it must be attributed to the exilic period. For example, the sabbath passages (Exod 31:12–17; 35:1–3) contain distinctive H vocabulary (שבתותי, מקדשכם יהוה אני etc.). Furthermore, they are located in the interstices between the instructions and building of the sanctuary, tell-tale signs that their author is H_R. Moreover, it can be claimed that for these two sabbath passages and wherever an insertion is indisputably H_R (exilic), the literary context is *ipso facto* a pre-exilic composition.

To indicate the wide distribution of H_R, I shall cite five examples of H_R in Leviticus, five examples of H_R in Exodus, and five examples of H_R in Numbers.

H_R in Leviticus

1. *Leviticus 23:39–43*. This passage is an H_R appendix to the festival calendar. The term סכות (vv. 42–43), in particular, betrays this passage as exilic. Only in exile were the סכות-booths transferred from voluntary lodgings for pilgrims to mandatory seven-day lodgings for all Israel. These concluding verses of ch. 23 match the opening sabbath verses of the same chapter (vv. 2aβ–3) as H_R additions. H_R's reasons for those additions are obvious. In the exile, the entire festival calendar became defunct. Only the שבת and the סכות were observable, and they became the signatories of Jewish life after the destruction of the temple up to our own day.

2. *Leviticus 26:1–2*. These two verses were inserted in the interstice between two major blocks, the Jubilee (Lev 25) and the blessings and comminations (Lev 26). The first verse carries forth a condensation and application of the Decalogue.[7] It should not be overlooked, however, that the second verse also mentions the שבת, which being inside an insertion means automatically that the insertion was authored by H_R. H_R's purpose is clear: it emphasizes that the sabbath day as well as the sabbatical year (26:34–35, 43) determine Israel's national destiny. That is, H_R condemns Israel not only for neglecting the sabbatical year but also for neglecting the sabbath.

6. For the evidence, see ibid., 1956–59.
7. Milgrom, *Leviticus 23–27*, 2275–78.

3. *Leviticus 24:4*. This verse is an H$_R$ supplement to vv. 2–3.[8] It claims that the lampstand comprises more than a single lamp. It also resolves the debate between Myers[9] and Hachlili.[10] The former has shown that Israel originally had a lampstand with a single lamp, whereas the latter has demonstrated that the archaeological evidence of the (late) Second Temple period proves that the lampstand had multiple lamps. Leviticus 24:4 shows that both scholars are correct. This verse gives the precise period when the change took place—the exile. H$_R$ prescribes that in the future reconstructed Temple the lampstand will bear multiple lamps.

It should not be forgotten that in Leviticus H is subsequent to P.[11] This means that H$_R$, the redactor of H, is automatically the redactor of P.[12] The following two examples stem from P.

4. *Leviticus 11:43–45*. This passage is replete with H expressions: אני
יהוה אלהיכם (v. 44a; 18:2; 19:2, 4, 10, 25, 34, 36), והתקדשתם והייתם
קדשים (v. 44a; 20:7); כי קדוש אני (v. 44a; 19:2; 20:26); והייתם קדשים
כי קדוש אני (v. 44b; 19:2; 20:26). Like H, it contains a rationale (v. 44a). Again, like H, it uses P idioms imprecisely. For example, שקץ and טמא are used synonymously (v. 43; contrast 11:10–38).[13] That this passage is postpositional in ch. 11 indicates that H$_R$ is responsible for its placement. Its purpose is to stress that observance of the diet laws leads to holiness. Moreover, since the diet laws are independent of the sacrificial system, they would rise in importance during the exile when the absence of the temple would leave few observable rituals. To this day the Sabbath and the diet laws are the two most important factors responsible for Jewish distinctiveness. This is repeated in 20:25–26 (H), which adds that holiness is also contingent upon Israel's separation from the nations.

5. *Leviticus 16:29–34a*. This pericope bears many signs of H:
1. The second-person direct address to Israel.
2. The terminology frequently differs from the rest of this P chapter:
   a. מקדש הקדש instead of הקדש (Lev 16:2, 3, 16, 17, 20)

8. Ibid., 2090–91.
9. R. Hachlili and R. Merhov, "The Menorah in the First and Second Temple Times in the Light of the Sources and Archeology," *EI* 18 (Festschrift N. Avigad) (1985): 255–67 (Hebrew).
10. C. Meyers, *The Tabernacle Menorah* (Missoula, Mont.: Scholars Press, 1976).
11. I. Knohl, *The Sanctuary of Silence* (Minneapolis: Fortress, 1995), 1–164.
12. Ibid., 124–64, and Milgrom, *Leviticus 17–22*, 1349–52.
13. J. Milgrom, "Two Priestly Terms שקץ and טמא," *Maʿarav* 8, no. 2 (1992): 7–16.

      b.   עם הקהל instead of עם or הקהל (Lev 16:17, 24)

      c.   The description of the high priest is that of H (Lev 21:10) and not of P (Lev 4:3)

      d.   The purgation rite (כפר) purifies (טהר) the people, whereas in P it only purifies the sanctuary

3.   The mention of the גר is an unmistakable sign of H (see 17:8, 10, 12, 13, 15; 18:26 etc.).

4.   The Day of Purgation (Lev 16) is the only festival whose date is specified postpositionally, at the end of its prescription (16:29, 34a), whereas the dates of all other festival prescriptions begin pre-positionally.

Thus we are dealing with an appendix inserted by H_R. It abolishes the privileges heretofore vested in the high priest to purge the sanctuary "when he chooses" (v. 2). Instead, it establishes the entire sanctuary's purgation only "once a year" (v. 34), on the tenth of Tishri (v. 29). It imposes a national day of self-denial and abstinence from work (v. 29), and it vests control of the entire ritual with the people (v. 34; cf. Lev 21:24).[14] Though v. 33 makes it certain that this pericope dates from pre-exilic times, the emphasis on the individual, sanctuary-independent observance of the day of purgation makes it extremely apt for the Babylonian (and every) diaspora.

    Since H_R is the redactor of both P and H, it follows that he is the redactor of the entire book of Leviticus.

H_R in Exodus

H_R is clearly detectable in Exodus. The following are five examples:

1. *Exodus 6:2–9.* A host of scholars[15] have identified this passage ending with אני יהוה as H. This is part of the larger priestly passage, Exod 6:2–7:6, which may stem from the pen of H_R, but it also may be a P composition to which H_R attached 6:2–9. The latter's dependency on Lev 26:13,[16] in addition to its incorporation of the JE term סבלת מצרים,[17] makes it likely that it is the handiwork of H_R.

    14.   For other examples of H_R's intrusion into P, see Lev 3:16b–17; 6:12–18aα; 7:22–27; 10:10–11.

    15.   Cited by Knohl, *Sanctuary*, 17 n. 24.

    16.   Demonstrated by N. F. Lohfink, "Abänderung der Theologie des priesterlichen Geschichtswerks im Segen des Heiligkeitsgesetzes: Zu Lev 26, 9:11–13," in *Wort und Geschichte* (Festschrift K. Elliger; ed. H. Gese and H. P. Rüger; Neukirchen–Vluyn: Neukirchener, 1993), 129–36. Amended by Milgrom, *Leviticus 23–27*, 2298.

2. *Exodus 24:15b–18a.* As noted by earlier scholars,[18] the priestly
redactor is intent on supplementing Exod 24:12–15a, 18b (JE).[19] That this
priestly addition is the work of the redactor H_R is shown by its repetition
of the same ending "and he (Moses) ascended on the mountain" (v. 18aβ;
cf. v. 15a), which makes no sense sequentially but only as a correction:
Moses does not ascend directly to the summit of the mountain but must
first tarry six days on the mountain's side. Thereafter YHWH, who is
concealed within the כבוד (the cloud-encased fire), summons Moses to
his presence on the mountain top. Thus, Moses received the tablets not in
full view of the deity but within the darkness of the cloud encasing his
earthly presence, the כבוד fire. H_R was obliged to conclude his supplement with the same ending as JE—Sinai's ascension—in order to accord
with the priestly view that YHWH's instruction concerning the Tabernacle
(Exod 25:1–31:17) were revealed to Moses on Sinai's mount. It should
also be noted that the mountain top in the priestly view corresponds with
the adytum of the Tabernacle. The high priest may enter the adytum only
after he covers it with a cloud raised by an incense source that covers the
כפרת, symbolic of YHWH's earthly presence in his sanctuary (Lev 16:13).

3. *Exodus 27:20–21 and Numbers 8:1–4.* These two passages on the
menorah were inserted by H_R in Exodus between the P prescriptions on
the Tabernacle (Exod 25:1–27. 19) and the consecrations of the priests
(Exod 28), and in Numbers between the gifts of the chieftains (Num 7)
and the ordinations of the Levites (Num 8:5–22). Perhaps it was the
presence of Lev 24:1–4 (H) that compelled H_R to infix a duplicate of
these verses in Exod 27:20–21, at a point immediately after the prescription to build the sanctuary and its sanctums (Exod 25:1–27:19).[20]
As shown by Knohl,[21] it was the lack of the menorah's function in its
description (Exod 25:31–40) that compelled H_R to add it after all the
other sanctions were described.

17. Knohl, *Sanctuary*, 17 n. 24.
18. J. Wellhausen, *Die Composition des Hexateuchs und die historischen Bücher
des Alten Testaments* (4th ed.; Berlin: de Gruyter, 1963; originally published 1885),
96–97; S. R. Driver, *The Book of Exodus* (Cambridge: Cambridge University Press,
1929; originally published 1911), 25b; A. T. Chapman, *The Introduction to the
Pentateuch* (Cambridge: Cambridge University Press, 1911), 201.
19. But see A. Toeg, *Lawgiving at Mount Sinai* (Jerusalem: Magnes, 1977),
79–80 on v. 12 (Hebrew).
20. Concerning the placement of Num 8:1–4, see J. Milgrom, *Numbers* (Philadelphia: The Jewish Publication Society of America, 1990), 60, and Y. Ts. Mosh-
qovitz, *The Book of Numbers* (Jerusalem: Mosad Harav Kook, 1988), 87 (Hebrew).
21. Knohl, *Sanctuary*, 47–48.

4. *Exodus 29:38–46*. H$_R$ appends a prescription on the תמיד (vv. 38–42) and a rationale for the Tabernacle (vv. 43–46) to a passage on the altar (vv. 36–37). Exodus 29:38–46 ends with אני יהוה אלהיכם, a tell-tale signature of H. The placement here of this pericope on the תמיד was probably motivated by the statement in Num 28:6 that the תמיד ritual was performed in the wilderness beginning with its ordination at Sinai.[22] That the תמיד pericope is dependent on Numbers and that without it the text reads smoothly make it highly probable that this is the work of a priestly editor, namely H$_R$.

The תמיד is copied and condensed mainly from Num 28:3–8 (P). In the condensation H$_R$ excised the golden libation vessels (v. 7) and explicitly prohibited their use because of their implication that YHWH imbibed drink in his chambers.[23]

5. *Exodus 31:12–17; 35:1–3*. As I have demonstrated elsewhere,[24] these two passages contain H's terminology, the plural construct שבתת (31:13; cf. Lev 18:3, 30; 23:38); the superlative שבת שבתון (31:13; 35:2; cf. Lev 16:31; 23:3, 32; 25:4); and YHWH's sanctifying of Israel מקדש ישראל (31:13; cf. Lev 20:8; 21:8, 15, 23; 22:16, 32), all of which make it certain that these inserts into the P text are the work of H$_R$.[25]

The common denominator of all five examples is that they interrupt the flow of the text, but once they are removed the text reads smoothly. This is a clear sign that they are the work of a redactor. Moreover, the redactor can be identified. All the examples are priestly additions, indeed that of H (note H's signature nos. 1, 4, 5). This makes it likely that the redactor is H$_R$. Finally, the fact that two of the examples either contain a JE term (no. 1) or are attached to JE passages (nos. 1 and 2) raises the possibility that H$_R$ had the text of both JE and P before him. In other words, H$_R$ was the redactor of the book of Exodus.

H$_R$ in Numbers

The following are five examples from Numbers:

1. *Numbers 3:11–13*. This is an H$_R$ interpolation, as shown by YHWH's first-person address with the subject אני (3:12, 13) and the object לי (3:12, 13), the characteristic H formula אני יהוה (3:13), and the use of

---

22. See Milgrom, *Numbers*, 239–40.
23. See Milgrom, *Leviticus 17–22*, 1338, 2093.
24. Ibid., 1338–39; *Leviticus 23–27*, 2003a.
25. For further evidence and details, see Milgrom, *Leviticus 17–22*, 1338–39.

rationales (3:12, 13). The passage 3:11–13 is an insertion explaining 3:5–10 (P), namely, the right of the Levites to assume a cultic office.[26] Thus, H informs us that the Levites replaced the firstborn, who hitherto had officiated at the family hearth to worship the departed ancestors.[27] Since this passage is an insertion—without it the text reads smoothly—it most likely stems from H_R.

2. *Numbers 8:14–19*. That the Levites replaced the firstborn (Num 3:11–13) is repeated here (vv. 16–17). Furthermore, v. 19 provides a rationale—a *bona fide* H characteristic—explaining the purpose of the Levite appointment, to ransom the Israelites.[28] Remove vv. 14–19 and the text reads smoothly: vv. 20–22 report Israel's compliance with the prescriptions of vv. 5–13. Thus vv. 14–19 have been inserted by H_R.[29]

3. *Numbers 9:9–14*. This law cites two criteria for postponing the פסח offering: distance and impurity. The narrative (vv. 1–8), however, speaks only of impurity. Thus, the formulation of the law must be subsequent to the text of the narrative. Since the narrative (vv. 1–8) is clearly a product of H,[30] the law (vv. 9–14) can be attributed to H_R. A post-Deuteronomic date, in the time of H_R, must be postulated when distance from one legitimate (Jerusalem) sanctuary became a major deterrent for pilgrimages from afar.

4. *Numbers 13:1–17a; 14:26–35*. These two priestly passages have been artfully affixed before and after JE's version of the story of the scouts by a priestly redactor.[31] Knohl has shown that the redactor must be identified as H_R.[32] YHWH addresses Israel directly by the subject אני, a distinctive H word (13:2; 14:35). Moreover, P and JE expressions have been fused into the priestly account.[33] Thus the priestly account and its fusion with the JE story is the work of H_R.

---

26. S. E. Loewenstamm, "Law, Biblical," in *The World History of the Jewish People* (ed. B. Mazar; Tel Aviv: Massada), 3:231–67.
27. Cf. Milgrom, *Numbers*, 17–18.
28. Cf. Milgrom, *Numbers*, 369–71.
29. See further Milgrom, *Leviticus 17–22*, 1340–41.
30. See the evidence compiled by Knohl, *Sanctuary*, 121.
31. See Milgrom, *Numbers*, 387–90.
32. Knohl, *Sanctuary*, 90.
33. The fact that Ezekiel borrows many of these passages does not absolutely prove that they originate with H. Ezekiel may have found them in P!

5. *Numbers 15*. That the entire chapter stems from H was first observed by Kuenen.[34] This can be substantiated by examining each of the chapter's five pericopes (vv. 1–16, 17–21, 22–31, 32–36, 37–41),[35] in particular the final one, vv. 37–41, as follows.

H's major earmarks are concentrated in the final pericope (vv. 40–41): והייתם קדשים לאלהיכם, "so you shall be holy to your God" (v. 40b; cf. Lev 19:2; 20:26; 11:45 [H]) and H's signature אני יהוה אלהיכם, literally "I am YHWH your God" (v. 41), which, however, should be rendered "I YHWH your God (have spoken)."[36] Furthermore, H breaks with the priests' exclusive right of שעטנז (garments of wool and linen) by commanding the lay person to wear it on the outer garment.[37] Thus, all of Israel can become "a kingdom of priests and a holy people" (Exod 19:6).

This pericope concludes not only ch. 15 but also the larger unit, chs. 13–15, the failure of the scouts to report objectively their reconnaissance of Canaan. It also points forward to the adjoining Korahite rebellions (ch. 16). H_R anticipates Korah's challenge by unfurling its quintessential postulate: everyone in Israel can achieve holiness if he or she fulfils the divine commandments. Thus, Num 15:37–41 serves as a transition between two large blocks, Num 13–15 and Num 16–18.[38]

In the introduction to my commentary on Numbers,[39] I observed that this book consists of an alteration of law (L) and narrative (N), totalling 12 units: 1:1–10:10 (L); 10:11–14:43 (N); 15 (L); 16–17 (N); 18–19 (L); 20–25 (N); 26:1–27:11 (L); 27:12–27:28 (N); 28–30 (L); 31:1–33:49 (N); 33:50–36:13 (L). Mary Douglas[40] refined my observation in an extensive treatment.[41] The implication of this construction of the book of Numbers is of signal importance. Chapter 15 is a link in this structure. Remove it and the entire structure collapses. Thus, if as shown, H_R has placed ch. 15 in its present position, he is also responsible for structuring the rest of the book. The conclusion is ineluctable: H_R is the redactor of the book of Numbers.

34. A. Kuenen, *An Historical-Critical Inquiry into the Origin and the Composition of the Hexateuch* (trans. B. H. Wickstied; London: Macmillan, 1886), 96.

35. Kuenen, *Composition*, 1341–44.

36. See Milgrom, *Leviticus 17–22*, on Lev 18:2b.

37. For the complete discussion, see Milgrom, *Numbers*, 410–14.

38. Knohl, *Sanctuary*, 90.

39. Milgrom, *Numbers*, xv–xvi.

40. M. Douglas, *In the Wilderness* (Sheffield: Sheffield Academic Press, 1993), 102–22.

41. For the placement of ch. 15 in its present position, see the remarks of the mediaeval commentators Ibn Ezra, Ramban and Hezzequni at the beginning of the chapter. See also my explanation in *Leviticus 17–22*, 1343.

The above passages indicate that H_R is the editor of H in Leviticus, and of P and JE in Exodus and Numbers. Note that all these examples are editorial insertions, as shown by the fact that they interrupt the flow of the text, but once they are removed the text reads smoothly. This can only mean that the context of the H_R insertions must be pre-exilic. Also, since these example show a wide distribution of H_R in Exodus and Numbers, as well as in Leviticus, the inescapable conclusion is that H_R is the editor of all three books. H_R, the exilic redactor, must have had all the materials represented in Exodus, Leviticus and Numbers before him, before rearranging them in the order represented in the present Masoretic text.

There is insufficient evidence of H_R in Genesis and Deuteronomy for us to conclude that H_R was actually editor of the entire Torah, and that the entire Torah was composed in the exilic period. But recently I have come to the conclusion that all of the first story of creation (Gen 1:1–2:4a) is the work of H_R.[42] If this is correct, then H_R indeed played the deciding role in editing the book of Genesis. He would have attached his story of creation to J's creation story as a needed polemic against Babylonian theology.[43]

---

42.   J. Milgrom, "H_R in Leviticus and Elsewhere in the Torah," in *The Book of Leviticus* (ed. R. Rendtorff and R. A. Kugler; Leiden: Brill, 2003), 33–37.

43.   See J. Milgrom, "The Alleged 'Hidden Light,'" in *The Idea of Biblical Interpretation* (Festschrift James H. Kugel; ed. H. Najman and J. H. Newman; Leiden: Brill, 2004), 41–44.

Part II

Reading the Law in the Prophets

THE MEANING OF תורה IN ISAIAH 1–39

Ronald E. Clements

1. תורה *in Isaiah*

The question of the meaning of the Hebrew word תורה (*torah*) in the book of Isaiah has occupied the attention of scholars for some considerable time and it may appear that there is little that is new to be said in regard to it. In 1973 J. Jensen published a monograph devoted to this particular topic[1] and the detailed entry devoted to the usage of the noun תורה by F. Garcia López and H.-J. Fabry in *ThWAT*[2] further explores the potential for understanding both the term and its usage. Nevertheless, in spite of several studies, the relevance of the precise connotation of the noun to the current state of Isaiah studies is considerable. Marvin Sweeney has placed the issue in the forefront of recent discussion[3] and it is noteworthy that the most recent commentary by Brevard S. Childs reflects afresh on the question.[4] It is not at all difficult to see that the sharply focused occurrences of the noun in Isa 1:10; 2:3 and 42:4 take on a distinctly wider significance if they are considered as references to a recognized body of legal and instructional tradition existing in a written documentary form. Yet in all three instances the preferred conclusion of several recent translations of these passages is to translate the noun simply as "teaching" or "instruction" and to assume that it refers to an undefined range of prophetic instruction which cannot be identified precisely with the preserved Pentateuchal תורה.

---

1. J. Jensen, *The Use of* "tôrâ" *by Isaiah: His Debates with the Wisdom Tradition* (CBQMS 3; Washington: Catholic Biblical Association, 1973).
2. F. García López and H.-J Fabry, "תורה tôrâ," *ThWAT* 8:597–637; cf. also G. Liedke and C. Petersen, "תורה tôrâ Weisung," *THAT* 2:1032–43 (trans. Martin Biddle, *TLOT* 3:1415–22).
3. M. A. Sweeney, "The Book of Isaiah as Prophetic Torah," in *New Visions of Isaiah* (ed. Roy F. Melugin and M. A. Sweeney; JSOTSup 214; Sheffield: Sheffield Academic Press, 1996), 50–67.
4. B. S. Childs, *Isaiah: A Commentary* (OTL; Louisville, Ky.: Westminster John Knox, 2001), 30.

Altogether there are seven recorded instances in Isa 1–39 where the noun is used. Of these, four (2:3; 5:24; 8:20; 24:5) are regarded by *ThWAT* as secondary to the eighth-century prophet, Isaiah of Jerusalem. Accordingly, the authors conclude that only three occurrences (in Isa 1:10; 8:16; 30:9) are authentic to the original prophet. These presumed original occurrences are then understood, not to refer to תורה in the later (post-Deuteronomic) sense of a tradition of sacred written instruction, but as references to a prophetic message.

A primary goal of this re-examination of the meaning attached to such a key theological term is to press the claim for a coherent and consistent interpretation of it in Isa 1–39 and to relate this interpretation firmly to the preserved תורה of the Five Books of Moses, or, at least, to a Deuteronomic nucleus of this. Once this interpretation is established as a fundamental exegetical guideline, then further important conclusions fall into place, not only regarding the literary and theological structure of Isa 1–39, but also regarding the nature of the relationship between "The Law and the Prophets" as the foundation of *Tanakh*—the Hebrew biblical canon.

The central role of a written and authoritative תורה for the post-587 B.C.E. Jewish community is sufficient to explain why the introduction of such a key concept in Isa 1 and 2 was particularly important. However, the wider issue of the structure of the Hebrew canon becomes a matter of far-reaching theological concern once it is recognized that a significant editorial revision has affirmed that the message of the book of Isaiah, like that of the prophet Jeremiah, should also be interpreted in the light of the Mosaic תורה. Where recent scholarship has focused particular attention on the comprehensive תורה-revision in respect of Jeremiah,[5] the introduction of a similar revision in the book of Isaiah has tended to be overlooked. Moreover, in the case of the Isaiah book, the editorial reasoning which undertook such a revision can more readily be explained. In the instances of its occurrence in Isa 1–39, the impact of this תורה-revision is all too easily discounted by the translation of the Hebrew תורה to mean simply "message, instruction."

2. *The Several Meanings of the Noun* תורה

We can begin by noting that, although there are a total of 220 occurrences of the noun תורה in the Hebrew Bible, a significant and distinctive enlargement of meaning can be directly linked to the introduction of a

5.   T. Römer, "How Did Jeremiah Become a Convert to Deuteronomistic Ideology?," in *Those Elusive Deuteronomists: The Phenomenon of Pan-Deuteronomism* (ed. L. S. Schearing and S. L. McKenzie; JSOTSup 268; Sheffield: Sheffield Academic Press, 1999), 189–99.

book of תורה in Deut 4:44.[6] Not only did this development mark a most distinctive shift in the understanding of the term, but it marked the beginning of a change of focus in Israel's religion from cultic religious observance to a comprehensive written book of polity and conduct. It was the beginning of "the religion of a book."

Quite clearly, prior to this development, the noun conveyed a much less specific range of meaning. Whether its primary roots should be traced to parental or priestly instruction has been a matter for debate. Assuming the correctness of the derivation from a verb ירה ("to aim, direct, point"), a relatively broad connotation for the original usage to describe "instruction, direction, teaching" of many kinds can convincingly be claimed. The term could be used for instructions and regulations given by priests (cf. Lev 6:2, 7 etc.), for the spoken utterances of prophets (cf. Hag 2:11 etc.) and for the pronouncements of parents and teachers of wisdom (cf. Prov 4:11; 31:26 etc.). In this context, it appears that all kinds of instruction, some given orally and some in writing, could be included under such a heading. It also appears that such instructions were not necessarily of a religious or ethical nature, but could relate to relatively mundane secular activities.

In Deut 4:44 תורה is used as a comprehensive description for the legislative rulings given by Moses to Israel as the charter of its national existence. It is defined as comprising "decrees" (עדות), "statutes" (חקים) and "ordinances" (משפטים, Deut 4:45). Moreover, such instruction was written down and carefully preserved (Deut 31:24). From the time of this comprehensive Deuteronomic definition onwards it is evident that a distinctive frame of reference became attached to the noun which applied it to a body of authoritative written pronouncements. These included historical traditions, cultic and legal rulings, ethical advice generally, and admonitions. All these now became directly associated with the figure of Moses and with the tradition of Israel's national origins from a group of landless slaves who had escaped from Egypt. In the wake of this development, the written תורה became progressively more and more central to Israel's national life and the noun became increasingly associated with this highly specific reference to a unique body of national legislative and ethical tradition. It aimed at regulating Israel's life and conduct at every

6. Cf. Barnabas Lindars, "Torah in Deuteronomy," in *Words and Meanings: Essays Presented to David Winton Thomas* (ed. P. R. Ackroyd and Barnabas Lindars; Cambridge: Cambridge University Press, 1968), 117–36. G. Braulik, "Die Ausdrücke für 'Gesetz' im Buch Deuteronomium," *Bib* 51 (1970): 39–66; repr. in *Studien zur Theologie des Deuteronomiums, SBA: Altes Testament* (Stuttgart: Katholisches Bibelkwerk 1988), 11–38.

level, but was believed from a relatively early stage to possess an authority which was more than national in its range.

It is no cause for surprise that the date of this Deuteronomic reformulation of the concept of תורה and its application to a specific body of written laws and regulations has been much discussed and contested. The conclusion adopted here carries a wide level of support and is that it originated sometime between the late seventh and mid-sixth centuries B.C.E. Its introduction is presented as a re-introduction rather than a new departure (2 Kgs 22:3–23:25) and was linked to the reform of King Josiah. Therefore the earliest date that can be claimed for this Deuteronomic redefinition of תורה is 623–22 B.C.E., but some time up to a century later is more probable.

In reconstructing the nature and consequences of this development in the historical course of Israelite–Jewish religion, it is evident that the change in the understanding of תורה represented a definable turning-point. From being a temple-based cult, the worship of YHWH moved in progressive stages into becoming "the religion of a book." The existence of this written תורה made conscientious and effective religious observance practicable for people living in exile and outside the normal orbit of the most prestigious religious sanctuary in Jerusalem. The foundation concept of תורה, and the necessity of obedience to its demands, was thereby elevated into becoming the central focus of religious life. Obedience to the revealed תורה came ultimately to define what was acceptable or unacceptable in membership of the community of Israel. No longer was it understood as a reference to any broad and occasional instruction, but instead it became identified with a specific body of tradition, preserved in a written document and eventually extending to include all five books of the Pentateuch. With this Deuteronomic re-interpretation of תורה, the essential foundation of a canonical Hebrew Bible was laid.

3. *The Meaning of* תורה *in Isaiah 1–39*

The issue, so far as Isa 1–39 is concerned, is whether any or all of the seven occurrences of the noun which occur in this part of the book are to be interpreted as referring to תורה, understood in the Deuteronomic/ post-Deuteronomic sense of a written code of ethical and religious teaching, or whether they refer, less specifically, to instruction given by the prophet on a particular occasion, or even to some undefined tradition of instruction.

We can begin by noting the seven instances where the noun occurs:

(1)

"Hear the word of YHWH,
    You rulers of Sodom!
Listen to the תורה of our God,
    You people of Gomorrah! (Isa 1:10)

(2)

For out of Zion shall go forth תורה
    And the word of YHWH from Jerusalem. (Isa 2:3)

(3)

For they have rejected the תורה of YHWH of hosts,
    And have despised the word of the Holy One of Israel. (Isa 5:24)

(4)

Bind up the testimony, seal the תורה among my disciples. (Isa 8:16)

(5)

Concerning תורה and testimony.
    Surely those who speak like this
    will have no future (literally "dawn"). (Isa 8:20)

(6)

The earth lies polluted under its inhabitants;
    for they have transgressed תורות
violated statutes,
    broken the everlasting covenant. (Isa 24:5)

(7)

For they are a rebellious people, faithless children
    children who will not listen to the תורה of YHWH. (Isa 30:9)

Of these seven passages, I have already noted that F. Garcia-López
and H.-J. Fabry in *ThWAT* regard only four (viz. 1:10; 2:3; 8:16; 30:9) as
authentic to the eighth-century prophet Isaiah of Jerusalem. Not surprisingly there are scholars who would contest this conclusion and who
regard all the passages as authentic to Isaiah, interpreting it as meaning
simply "message, instruction," which is undoubtedly feasible, but which
appears unlikely.[7] However, such a comprehensive conclusion is based
on over-riding assumptions regarding the authorship and date of the
sections where it appears and does not concern itself directly with wider,
and more controversial, issues concerning the more likely dates of the
relevant passages.

There are several significant points which require to be made. First is
the fact that there are grounds for questioning whether the occurrences of

7. Cf. the translation and commentary of J. N. Oswalt, *The Book of Isaiah:
Chapters 1–39* (NICOT; Grand Rapids: Eerdmans, 1986), 94, 112, 230 etc.

the noun in 1:10 and 2:3 can be ascribed to a prophet of the eighth century B.C.E., since a number of scholars regard the passages in which they occur as late additions to the original book, concluding that this at one time began with ch. 5 and remained in this form well into the post-exilic (Persian) era. A similar conclusion is applicable in the case of Isa 24:5, which occurs in the late post-exilic section of Isa 24–27. The entire context of this section is late, as noted by Garcia-López and Fabry.

Chapter 1, with its clear purpose of making an appeal for repentance and a return to YHWH, is now also widely regarded as one of the later parts to have been added to the book, although suggestions have been proposed that it may have drawn elements from elsewhere in the book where original, eighth-century B.C.E. material is to be found. The chapter has clearly been designed to serve as an introduction to the whole composition. Its appeal is directly to the reader, urging a penitent and committed response to obey the תורה. This introduction is followed by "The Little Book of Zion," comprising 2:1–4:6. This short unit largely consists of an indictment of the citizens of Jerusalem for failure to conform to the demands of תורה. It shows every sign of having been composed from more than one unit of prophetic invective, but the emphasis on conformity to the rules of תורה is paramount. As a consequence, both the present ch. 1 and the following unit in Isa 2:1–4:6 stand apart from the main core of the book in Isa 5:1–35:36 by this primary focus on calls for obedience to the demands of the Mosaic legislation. They focus on issues relating to divisions within the city of Jerusalem which reflect indifference to the prescriptions of תורה. Both sections place the authority of תורה as central to the wellbeing of the city and extend this to a vision of world peace which can only be realized through obedience to this divine instruction on the part of all nations (so Isa 2:3).

All the signs are that neither of the instances of the use of the noun in chs. 1 and 2 of the Isaiah book should be traced back to the eighth century B.C.E. Rather, they show every sign of having been introduced with the express purpose of linking the message of the main core of the book, which focuses on national and international political issues, with the central authority of תורה.

Accordingly, the occurrences of the noun תורה in 1:10 and 2:3 can be added to 24:5 as expressive of the interests of post-exilic sections of the Isaiah book. In this case, the number of passages where the noun is used which can be claimed to have originated with the eighth-century Isaiah is reduced significantly further from the four listed by Garcia López and Fabry.

With such a conclusion, the case for translating the noun simply as "teaching, instruction," with no direct reference to a written Mosaic book, is almost totally removed. The remaining instances of the noun's possible use in the less specific sense are reduced to a maximum of two special cases. However, the primary argument here is to question whether this approach of making a distinction between authentic and inauthentic parts of the text, and translating particular words accordingly, can any longer have any justification. The book of Isaiah was clearly intended to be read as a unity and its vocabulary understood in conformity with this.[8] In this case, the argument for understanding all of the references to תורה as referring to the Mosaic law book is overwhelmingly strong, irrespective of conclusions regarding the date of particular passages.

In pursuing the issue further we can note that the interpretation of תורה as a comprehensive body of rulings revealed through Moses is already evident in the case of the re-interpretation in 8:20 of the reference to תורה in Isa 8:16. Isaiah 8:1–4 relates an episode in a sequence of events concerning children of the prophet which form a central part of the book. This can still be defended as constituting Isaiah's "memoir."[9] It is evident that the reference in Isa 8:16 was originally to the instruction given to the two witnesses, the priest Uriah and Zechariah the son of Jeberechiah, mentioned in Isa 8:2. This account recorded the name Maher-Shalal-Hash-Baz on a tablet (גליון) which was then sealed until its public display was called for. The unusual name was subsequently given to a male child born to a woman, described as "the prophetess" (v. 3). The point is made that this woman had not conceived when the mysterious name was first written on the tablet. The two witnesses who attested the inscribing of the name evidently recorded the date when this was done. The inference appears to be that the tablet was sealed so that the name remained hidden until the next step in the prophetic action had been completed.[10]

8. This point is especially made by Sweeney, "The Book of Isaiah as Prophetic Torah," especially his comments on pp. 62–65.

9. My treatment of this important section of Isa 1–39 and a defense of the recognition of it as authentic to the eighth-century prophet is set out in "The Prophet as an Author: The Case of the Isaiah Memoir," in *Writings and Speech in Israelite and Ancient Near Eastern Prophecy* (ed. Ehud Ben Zvi and Michael H. Floyd; SBLSS 10; Atlanta: SBL, 2000), 89–102.

10. This section of the "Isaiah Memoir" and the giving of significant names to three children is discussed in my essay, "The Immanuel Prophecy of Isaiah 7:10–17 and Its Messianic Interpretation," in my *Old Testament Prophecy: From Oracles to Canon* (Louisville, Ky.: Westminster John Knox, 1996), 65–77. A fuller treatment is now available in T. Wagner, *Gottes Herrschafft. Eine Analyse der Denkschrift (Jes 6,1–9,6)* (VTSup 108; Leiden: Brill, 2006).

The impregnation of the prophetess was followed by the normal period of pregnancy and the subsequent birth acquired significance by revealing the child's name as that inscribed on the tablet. This sequence of actions is interpreted as a message relating to the threat currently facing King Ahaz of Jerusalem. It affirms that, by the time the child could speak his first words, "Mummy" and "Daddy," the capital cities of the two nations which posed this threat, Syria and Israel (Ephraim), would be devastated and plundered by the forces of Assyria. This interpretation of the name is spelled out with complete clarity in Isa 8:4:

> For before the child knows how to call "My father" or "My mother" the
> wealth of Damascus and the spoil of Samaria will be carried away by the
> king of Assyria.

So, the significance of the name on the tablet, its being specially witnessed by respected figures of the community, and the pregnancy and birth of a child to the prophet, were ways of spelling out in dramatic fashion a message regarding the sovereignty of God over human affairs and schemes. Within a period of two or three years, the threat to Jerusalem and its king which was causing such alarm would have come to nothing.

The verses that follow in Isa 8:5–8 elaborate the message further by foretelling the disastrous consequences of the forthcoming military intervention from Mesopotamia. Verses 9–10 elaborate this message still further in an even more wide-ranging sense and form part of a comprehensive apocalyptic re-interpretation of Isaiah's prophecies affirming that many nations will come to fight against Jerusalem, but will encounter disaster there.

The central feature is focused on the introduction of the child's name, Maher-Shalal-Hash-Baz, which is interpreted as a warning to Ahaz, the king of Jerusalem, affirming the over-riding sovereignty of God. No matter what action the human participants took, the will of YHWH, God of Israel would prevail.

This is also clearly the message conveyed by the prophet in two earlier confrontations with King Ahaz, focused similarly on names given to children. The explanations attached to them (Isa 7:7–9, 16–17) make this plain. These mysterious names form a sequence of three prophecies, all of which convey essentially the same point. They serve as affirmations that YHWH, God of Israel, has sovereign control over all events. Opinions have been divided over whether this broad, but cryptically expressed, message regarding the sovereignty of YHWH, God of Israel, was intended to be understood as an assurance to King Ahaz or a threat. In many respects it is deliberately ambiguous on this front, and although it appears to be re-assuring by asserting that the enemies who were threatening King Ahaz were merely human (cf. Isa 7:4–9) and could not thwart the purposes of God, it has a double-edge to it.

In any case, the king's failure to respond to this message, and to those of the previous messages implicit in the other children's names, drew forth the prophet's anger and hostility, as Isa 8:5–6 shows. However, the separation of the summary of the prophet's instructions in v. 16 from their reference to the events described in vv. 1–4 tends to hide the connection. By the introduction of the intervening vv. 5–15, the message implicit in the name inscribed on the tablet is interpreted in a larger political framework. The prophet's original instruction is referred to in 8:16 as "a תורה and a 'testimony' (עדות)." However, in the present edited presentation, a more comprehensive interpretation of the significance of the name is introduced. This is clearly brought out in 8:20 by interpreting these instructions as a reference to the Mosaic תורה. The reference at the beginning of v. 20 is designed to provide a marginal notation for the reader—"concerning the תורה and the testimony." By making this fresh interpretation, this brief note gave rise to a far-reaching and influential tradition concerning the "two witnesses" who would unlock the secrets of the "Last Days."[11]

The exultant assurance that is introduced in vv. 9–10 about the power-lessness of nations that threaten Jerusalem no longer relates the message of the child's name to the eighth-century problems confronting King Ahaz, but instead applies the prophet's emphasis on divine sovereignty to a still future eschatological day of judgment upon all nations. It forms part of the overall revision of the interpretation which has now re-shaped and given a new context to the "Vision of Isaiah" in Isa 5–35. This has made it into a book concerning Jerusalem and a great battle which will determine the city's destiny among the nations. The additional appended note in v. 20—"Surely, those who speak like this will have no future (dawn)!"—provides a warning of judgment affirming the central role of תורה for the community. The complicated literary history and unfamiliar lines of reasoning which hold this section of the Isaiah book together have occasioned great difficulty for translators throughout the ages. Nevertheless, there is a connecting thread that holds all the parts together.

---

11. For the development and elaboration of this theme in Deutero-Zechariah, cf. the treatment in Marvin A. Sweeney, "Zechariah's Debate with Isaiah," in *The Changing Face of Form-Criticism for the Twenty-first Century* (ed. M. A. Sweeney and Ehud Ben Zvi; Grand Rapids: Eerdmans, 2003), 335–50; also idem, commentary on Zech 9–14 in *The Twelve Prophets* (Berit Olam; Collegeville, Minn.: Liturgical Press/Michael Glazier, 2000), 2:656–706.

This is that ultimately YHWH, God of Israel, is sovereign over all nations. Isaiah's cryptic message to King Ahaz, contained in the strange name given to the child, just as the Immanuel name had previously been similarly used, was a message concerning the ultimate power and authority of God over all human plans and schemes.

It may appear that this complex exposition of the description of Isaiah's recording of the name of a child who was still to be conceived has little to do with the wider use of the noun תורה in Isa 1–39. Yet this is not the case, since it is not simply the prophetic action in recording the name, but the message of the name itself which is regarded as uniquely significant. This is borne out by the way in which it is linked to the Mosaic תורה in v. 20.

Bearing this example in mind, it is open to suggest that a comparable process of inner-biblical exegesis has encouraged the reference to תורה in Isa 30:8–9. Here the command to the prophet to write down the accusation against Israel for disobedience (Isa 30:8) has attracted an allusion back to the inscribing of the tablet with the mysterious sign-name of 8:1–4. This has prompted the link in 30:9 to the broad accusation that the people are rebellious children (cf. Isa 1:2). We can then suggest that the duplication of the description of the written indictment of Israel in v. 8 ("tablet," לוח and "writing," ספר), which is often regarded as the result of a scribal gloss, arose from the desire to highlight the connection with the tablet of Isa 8:1.

The belief that a final climactic *dénouement* involving many nations would occur outside Jerusalem has further encouraged similar reinterpretations of the first of the sign-names given to the prophet's children, that of Shear-Jashub (Isa 7:3). These are now preserved in Isa 10:20–23 and, gloomily, offer no hope for Israel's national future. The message of the name is applied directly to Israel, instead of to Israel's enemies, as in the initial action in Isa 7:3–9.

The overall character of this later, post-exilic, reworking of Isaiah's prophecies focuses primarily on constructing a vision of "the end" in which Israel's destiny among the nations would finally be resolved. Its link to the original message of the children's names rests on the fact that it elaborates on the theme of the sovereignty of YHWH, God of Israel, over all nations. Such reinterpretations of names and themes, originally spelt out in Isaiah's "Memoir" of his prophecies to King Ahaz, present the future fate of the entire region as already determined by a plan of God, which is awaiting fulfilment. This is expressed most sharply in Isa 10:23:

> For YHWH God of host will make a full end, as decreed, in all the earth.

The "full end" that has been "decreed" refers back to the threat which closes the original prophet's commissioning vision (Isa 6:10–13). The fixed and immutable character of this plan as divinely ordained is spelt out explicitly by describing it "as decreed" (i.e. in the word of prophecy). The same affirmation is then further taken up in Isa 28:22 and yet again in Dan 9:27. In this way, the belief that recorded prophecy foretold a predetermined catastrophe which would engulf the earth became explicit. We can compare this short note in Isa 10:23 with the repeated emphasis that is set out in Isa 14:24–27, asserting that God's victory over "the Assyrian" (probably intended as a cover name for enemies from the east generally) will take place "as God has planned"!

This emphasis on the sovereignty of Israel's God over all nations became one of the central themes of later Jewish apocalyptic literature. Isaiah's message thereby provided the seed-bed of apocalyptic themes concerning world judgment which became widely popular in later Jewish thinking, sometimes with unrealistic expectations and disastrous consequences. In this respect, the emphasis upon divine sovereignty over human history, expressed in Isaiah's use of children's names conveying cryptic messages, clearly had a dangerous dimension when it became too focused on hidden meanings and coded messages located in written prophecies. The contrast between divine power and human frailty was a salutary warning when applied to the ambitions of ancient imperial rulers (as in Isa 10:15–19; 37:23–29), but it became a dangerous illusion when pressed into a principle of historical determinism.

It is welcome, therefore, to see how, by introducing an emphasis on divine justice and compassion expressed in תורה, this presentation of a deterministic interpretation of Isaiah's message concerning the sovereignty of God was qualified. Warnings of coming judgment on the world of nations occasioned the need for setting them in a larger context concerning the nature and purpose of God. This is achieved by introducing in chs. 1–4 the message that all prophecy must be read against a background of תורה. Israel had not been judged already and sentenced to an inevitable doom, since the message of תורה offered the possibility of life through obedience and loyalty.

The concern to show that law, not fatalism, controlled Israel's future is further brought out in Isa 1–39 in the linking of the account of Jerusalem's deliverance in 701 B.C.E. (36:1–37:38) with the story of King Hezekiah's sickness and repentance in 38:1–22. More than any other experience of the enigmatic events of biblical history, the contrast between the triumph of Jerusalem's escape from disaster in 701 B.C.E. and its humiliation and confusion after the catastrophe of 587 B.C.E.

called for reflection. Great damage was done to the interpretation of
biblical prophecy when the two major parts of the Isaiah book (Isa 1–39
and 40–66) were split asunder in the interests of a "modern" criticism. By
doing this, the biblical concern that required that both events be understood in relation to each other was overturned. Certainly the dramatic
tensions and contrasts between such historical events yield to no easy
explanations. Nevertheless, by reading the Isaiah book as a single whole,
the modern reader is enabled to see that the ancient scribes did not hide
their faces from the problem. Many of the same tensions and concerns
reveal themselves in the conclusions drawn from the different consequences following the closely similar prophecies of Micah and Jeremiah
in Jer 26:16–24. Even the seemingly contradictory outcomes of events,
when Israel's rulers had been forewarned of danger, must be understood
in the light of God's justice and mercy as explained by Moses.

The source to which ancient scribes looked to understand these
contrasting events was that of תורה and, overall, we are led to conclude
that all the references to תורה that are now to be found in Isa 1–39 are
understood to be references to the law-book of Moses. When this interpretation was established, this was probably not as extensive as the
present Pentateuch. Nevertheless the basic understanding that a book of
תורה formed the authoritative guidebook for the community of Israel was
fully recognized. It showed that divine anger against idolatry and wrongdoing was not an unpredictable and arbitrary threat to human existence.
Against such arbitrariness the rule of law enshrined in the Mosaic תורה
provided a means of grace to guide the wayward, first of Israel, but
ultimately of all nations (cf. Isa 2:3). In this way, God's revealed word of
תורה upheld the message of divine sovereignty over human history,
while at the same time firmly rejecting any notion of fatalistic determinism. No nation was judged already!

Isaiah's threat's and warnings, extolling the sovereignty of God, are
shown to be subordinate to the message of hope and assurance that
God's creation of the world and calling Israel out of Egypt had brought
into being. This point is made fully explicit in the opening chapter of the
book which declares unequivocally that the future was open for Israel to
choose, overturning the legacy of past disasters through repentance and
obedience. This is now most firmly spelt out in Isa 1:2–31 and is central
to what has often been described as a "Deuteronomistic" world-view (cf.
especially Deut 28:1–68).

Even the reference in Isa 8:16 to Isaiah's instructions as constituting a
תורה is no longer an exception to this understanding, since it too has
been reinterpreted in the fuller and more specific sense in 8:20. In sum, I

conclude that the prophecies of Isa 1–39, which major recent studies have shown to be the product of a complex process of editorial reworking of earlier texts, has been subjected to a thoroughgoing תורה-redaction. This shows most clearly where the term is used in Isa 1:10 and 2:3, but the overall need for this emphasis was to counter the deterministic view of history which the late apocalyptic reworking of Isaiah's prophecies had encouraged.

I conclude therefore that, so far as the present shape of the Isaiah book is concerned, all the occurrences of the noun תורה in Isa 1–39 are to be understood in the later sense of a reference to a written body of instruction, rules and regulations mediated by Moses. This set the pattern for understanding the relationship between "The Law and the Prophets" as a central feature of the structure of the Old Testament canon.[12] Altogether, it is not surprising that a variety of opinions has arisen over exactly how the noun should be translated and understood in the Isaiah book. Nevertheless, I reiterate the point that the attempts to make a sharp distinction between an eighth-century "prophetic" understanding of the noun which Isaiah authentically employed, and a later, post-Deuteronomic, sense when the term was understood to refer to the law-book of Moses is neither probable, nor valid. Throughout the present book, the existence of a written book of תורה, ascribed to Moses, is presumed and provides the key to understanding its warnings and threats.

4. *Determinism and the Moral Imperative*

The question of the meaning of תורה in Isa 1–39 is inseparably linked to the wider theological issue of the relationship between prophecy and a deterministic view of history.[13] It is popularly accepted by many that, if prophecy can foresee with remarkable accuracy into the distant future, then surely all history is already complete and everything has already happened! Such at least appears to be the conclusion of a thoroughgoing historical determinism, which builds on schemes of prophetic foretelling of specific future events. The fulfilment of prophecies after intervals

12. Cf. Stephen Chapman, *The Law and the Prophets* (FAT 27; Tübingen: Mohr Siebeck, 2000), especially pp. 241–82; also idem, "'The Law and the Words' as a Canonical Formula within the Old Testament," in *The Interpretation of Scripture in Early Judaism and Christianity: Studies in Language and Tradition* (ed. Craig A. Evans; JSPSup 33; Sheffield: Sheffield Academic Press, 2000), 26–74.

13. Cf. Jacques Berlinerblau, "Free Will and Determinism in First Isaiah: Secular Hermeneutics, the Poetics of Contingency, and Émile Durkheim's *Homo Duplex*," *Journal of the American Academy of Religion* 71 (2003): 767–91. I am particularly indebted to Dr. W. S. F. Pickering for drawing my attention to this important article.

spanning several centuries presumes their inevitability and predetermined character and builds on the theological affirmation that, in the last resort, the will of God cannot be thwarted.

It is undoubtedly a relevant feature that, within the prophetic corpus of the Hebrew Bible, the book of Isaiah is the one that appears most explicitly to present such a deterministic view of world history. On this account it has become a foundation text for an apocalyptic world-view. Yet this is far from being the only, or even the most memorable, reason why it has remained a widely cited text of biblical prophecy. As a book, it provides many of the most familiar themes and images which have continually appeared, and continue to appear, in popular interpretations of the end of world history. Many of its key themes re-emerge in the Old Testament, in the visions of Zech 9–14, and beyond the immediate biblical canon in 1 Enoch and the sectarian writings from Qumran. It is no occasion for surprise therefore that it is extensively cited in the New Testament.[14] When we move beyond the biblical period into the sphere of Christian liturgy and political theory, we encounter afresh key images and concepts which first appeared with this eight-century figure whose words were written down in a crisis that confronted ancient Jerusalem.

Yet, when read in its completed form, the book of Isaiah is not a work extolling historical determinism. It recognizes that its readers, both ancient and modern, are faced with a choice:

> If you are willing and obedient,
>   You shall eat the good of the land;
> But if you refuse and rebel,
>   You shall be consumed by the sword,
> For the mouth of YHWH has spoken. (Isa 1:18–20)

In this way the book of Isaiah's prophecies do not present threats and warnings which leave no hope. Threats are not God's last word either to Israel or to all humankind. Moses had already spoken long before and the word he has given is unequivocal; "Choose life so that you and your descendants may live!" (Deut 30:19).

---

14. Steve Moyise and M. J. J. Menken, eds., *Isaiah in the New Testament* (London: T&T Clark International, 2005).

TORAH IN THE MINOR PROPHETS

Thomas Renz

The relationship between Torah and prophecy has been a matter of controversy for some time. The traditional Jewish view of the prophets as expositors of Torah is probably based on Deuteronomy.[1] It found its antithesis in the view of "the prophet as a specially gifted person of marked individuality who stands apart from public expressions of religion and its institutions," with the law being disparaged as the ossified Jewish form of a once lively Israelite faith, a view usually connected with one of its most eloquent exponents, Julius Wellhausen.[2] In a recent overview of scholarly study of prophecy and the prophetic books, Joseph Blenkinsopp observed:

> One of the most contentious issues in the study of prophetic texts from Wellhausen to von Rad, Noth, and Zimmerli was the relation between prophecy and law. Though the issue has lost none of its edge, it is now at least agreed that it cannot be posed in a straightforward way in terms of relative priority. Even if we were sure of the date of the legal compilations, especially the so-called Book of the Covenant (Exod 20:23–23:19),

1. Deuteronomy's exposition of the nature of (true) prophecy is summarized by J. Blenkinsopp thus: "The chief function of the prophet is...to promulgate the law, preach its observance after the manner of Moses, and transmit it to posterity. A secondary function is the prediction of the future, which, when successful, can serve to validate the prophet's mission (Deut. 18:18–20)" (*Sage, Priest, Prophet: Religious and Intellectual Leadership in Ancient Israel* [Louisville, Ky.: Westminster John Knox, 1995], 120). H. Barstad, "The Understanding of the Prophets in Deuteronomy," *SJT* 8 (1994): 236–51, suggests that Deuteronomy holds a negative view of prophecy; K. Jeppesen offers a rejoinder in "Is Deuteronomy Hostile Towards Prophets?," *SJT* 8 (1994): 252–56.

2. The quotation is from W. McKane, "Prophecy and the Prophetic Literature," in *Tradition and Interpretation: Essays by Members of the Society for Old Testament Study* (ed. G. W. Anderson; Oxford: Clarendon, 1979), 163–88 (164), who thus characterized "the older view," contrasting it with later scholarship which gave greater recognition to cultic dimensions of prophecy.

we would still have to allow for a much older legal tradition to which
individual prophets could have appealed.[3]

There is little agreement among biblical scholars about the extent of
earlier traditions to which the prophets could have appealed, or indeed
the extent to which the prophetic books allow us to reconstruct the
message of the prophets after which they are named. This is due to a
number of factors, such as the general lack of confidence in establishing
a close relationship between literary forms and socio-historical realities,[4]
ongoing disagreements about the significance of covenant notions for the
prophetic indebtedness to tradition,[5] controversies about the age of
various cultic institutions, and different understandings of the interrelationship between prophet and society.[6]

At present, any specific reconstruction of the complex history of the
different corpora of literature, accounting for influence going both ways,[7]
will meet only limited agreement. It is thus difficult to enter the discussion at any point without making assumptions which will not be widely
shared. The following essay seeks to honour Gordon Wenham by taking

---

3. J. Blenkinsopp, "Prophecy and the Prophetic Books," in *Text in Context:
Essays by Members of the Society for Old Testament Study* (ed. A. D. H. Mayes;
Oxford: Oxford University Press, 2000), 323–47 (338).

4. This is evident, for example, in the "Setting" sections of many volumes in the
Forms of the Old Testament Literature series.

5. Thus the prominence given to covenant ideas in commentaries varies significantly. I am not aware of recent systematic discussions of the issue along the lines
of R. E. Clements, *Prophecy and Covenant* (SBT 43; London: SCM Press, 1965),
and *Prophecy and Tradition* (Growing Points in Theology; Oxford: Blackwell,
1975); R. V. Bergren, *The Prophets and the Law* (HUCM 4; Cincinnati: Hebrew
Union College Press, 1974), 80–150. Also relevant is the prophetic lawsuit genre
whose existence is controversial; see K. Nielsen, *Yahweh as Prosecutor and Judge:
An Investigation of the Prophetic Lawsuit* (JSOTSup 9; Sheffield: JSOT Press,
1978), who argues that the prophetic lawsuit presumes a covenantal relationship
between Yahweh and Israel.

6. See, e.g., R. R. Wilson, *Prophecy and Society in Ancient Israel* (Philadelphia:
Fortress, 1980); D. L. Petersen, *The Roles of Israel's Prophets* (JSOTSup 17;
Sheffield: JSOT Press, 1981); R. P. Carroll, "Prophecy and Society," in *The World
of Ancient Israel: Sociological, Anthropological and Political Perspectives* (ed.
R. E. Clements; Cambridge: Cambridge University Press, 1989), 203–25. Cf. Blen-
kinsopp's comparison of prophets with (dissident) intellectuals in *Sage, Priest,
Prophet*, especially 144–54, 164–65.

7. See, e.g., B. Peckham, "The Function of the Law in the Development of
Israel's Prophetic Traditions," in *Law and Ideology in Monarchic Israel* (ed. B.
Halpern and D. W. Hobson; JSOTSup 124; Sheffield: Sheffield Academic Press,
1991), 108–46.

seriously his reconsideration of the temporal and theological priority of Torah traditions,[8] and by imitating his careful reading of the biblical texts, which he demonstrated so masterfully in his commentaries on books of the Pentateuch.

Once we recognize that the prophets had access to a substantial body of traditions which stand in continuity to what we now call the Torah (or Pentateuch) and spoke judgment in the light of these traditions, we face the challenge that "there seems to be no instance of a prophetic indictment based explicitly on a law."[9] In the following I want to explore whether there are hints in the prophetic literature which may help explain this absence of explicit references. A few general observations on Torah and prophetic literature will be followed by an overview of the use of the term תורה in Hosea–Malachi. A conceptual study of Torah would need to examine also the use of legal terms and any references to Sinai, covenant, Moses, divine standards, etc., but the semantic study of תורה will form an important contribution to the fuller conceptual study which cannot be offered here. The scroll of the Minor Prophets offers material written over a period of more than three hundred years, yet the individual books appear stitched together in such a way as to encourage reading them as a collection.[10] An investigation of the Minor Prophets is obviously limited in scope, but the body seems substantial enough to warrant the exercise in the hope that it will offer insights into the relationship between prophets and the Torah, maybe even helping us to understand why the prophets did not appeal to legal traditions with which they were familiar and which would have served their purpose.

---

8. As is well know, Gordon Wenham particularly sought to demonstrate the antiquity of P, following arguments developed by Jewish scholars such as Jacob Milgrom. See, e.g., "The Priority of P," *VT* 49 (1999): 240–58. Doing research on Ezekiel as his doctoral student, one of my tasks, whose fruit entered the thesis (published as *The Rhetorical Function of the Book of Ezekiel* [VTSup 76; Leiden: Brill, 1999]) only tangentially, was to explore the relationship between P and Ezekiel. I, too, concluded that (much of) the P material is earlier than Ezekiel. See now also R. Levitt Kohn, *A New Heart and a New Soul: Ezekiel, the Exile and the Torah* (JSOTSup 358; Sheffield: Sheffield Academic Press, 2002).

9. Blenkinsopp, "Prophecy," 338–39.

10. The question whether we are dealing with one coherent book or not is of course widely discussed at present. See, e.g., J. D. Nogalski and M. A. Sweeney, eds., *Reading and Hearing the Book of the Twelve* (SBL Symposium Series 15; Atlanta: SBL, 2000). I am impressed by the stitching devices often observed but less persuaded by the various attempts to show a more thoroughgoing redaction across the whole corpus.

1. *Characteristics of Torah*

It would be wrong to equate the *characteristics* of Torah and of prophetic literature with what is *distinctive* about them, but observing how
Israel's canonical traditions differ from those of their neighbours may
provide clues for understanding the relationship between its various
parts. Israel's legal material is distinct from that of its ancient Near
Eastern neighbours in two ways, first in its claim to be divine revelation,
establishing a legal sphere independent of the ruler which integrated
"religious" (cultic) and "secular" (non-cultic) areas of life, and secondly
in its attribution to a figure of the distant past, Moses.[11] The former in
particular fits with the observation that most often תורה is used with
reference to a divine standard, whether this standard finds expression in
cultic regulations, legal stipulations, judicial decisions, or more general
teaching.[12] This is, of course, not to say that there was no instruction or
law-giving in ancient Israel or Judah which failed to make implicit or
explicit reference to the God of Israel.[13] But at least for one group among
the Israelites all legitimate תורה had its ultimate origin in the God of
Israel, and it is this perspective which has been canonized.[14] This is true

11. See, e.g., S. Greengus, "Law," *ABD* 4:242–52 (244–45); F. Crüsemann, *The
Torah: Theology and Social History of Old Testament Law* (trans. A. W. Mahnke;
Minneapolis: Fortress, 1996), 1–16. Cf. G. J. Wenham, "Law and the Legal System
in the Old Testament," in *Law, Morality and the Bible* (ed. B. N. Kaye and G. J.
Wenham; Leicester: InterVarsity, 1978), 24–52 (26–27).

12. The main exception is the use of תורה in Prov 1–9 for parental instructions,
but given the close interrelationship between divine and parental wisdom in chs. 1–9,
the use of תורה may well serve to associate the parental teaching offered in Proverbs
with divine teaching. The תורה references in Prov 28–29 appear to be to divine
"law" and the teaching of the capable wife in 31:26 is obviously related back to the
teaching of Lady Wisdom in chs. 1–9. For the תורה of the wise being a fountain of
life (13:14), cf. 14:27 (10:11; 16:22), confirming the close relationship between
wisdom and "the fear of Yahweh."

13. Thus the חקות עמרי (Mic 6:16) may well have made no reference to the
covenant God of Israel, whether these were written statutes or unwritten customs,
but we do not know. The chapter on the king as imparter of תורה in G. Östborn,
TŌRĀ *in the Old Testament: A Semantic Study* (Lund: Håkan Ohlssons Boktryckeri,
1945), 54–88, focuses on Second Isaiah's Servant, Moses and Joshua, and demonstrates that there is no canonized concept of royal תורה independent of Yahweh.

14. For this reason there is more to be said about the canonical role of תורה in
Proverbs than M. V. Fox, *Proverbs 1–9* (AB 18A; New York: Doubleday, 2000), 79,
allows for in his critique of the close association between wisdom and law made by
G. Baumann, *Die Weisheitsgestalt in Proverbien 1–9* (FAT 16; Tübingen: Mohr–
Siebeck, 1996). תורה was conceivably an innocuous term for any sort of teaching in
ancient Israel but within the canon it is undoubtedly a loaded term.

even of Deuteronomy, which has sometimes been thought to reflect a secularizing tendency.[15] While providing for a secular judiciary in the cities (16:18–20; cf. 1:15–18), Deuteronomy involves Levitical priests at the central sanctuary along with "the judge" to decide on disputed matters (17:8–13; cf. 19:17).[16] The judicial system is an expression of divine government.[17]

Even with biblical authors envisaging a judicial system which implements divine תורה, we should not think of תורה as statute law in the Anglo-Saxon legal tradition. We need to bear in mind the differences between forms of judicial arbitration in primarily oral cultures and the "rule of law" in many modern Western societies.[18] The biblical language of God's "laws" may be more akin to the use of the term "law" in phrases such as "the laws of nature" or "the law of diminishing returns."[19] This

15. Classically M. Weinfeld, *Deuteronomy and the Deuteronomy School* (Winona Lake, Ind.: Eisenbrauns, 1992 [reprint of the 1972 Oxford University Press edition]). It is now generally acknowledged that "secularization" may be a misleading term. For discussion, see J. Milgrom, "The Alleged 'Demythologization' and 'Secularization' in Deuteronomy," *IEJ* 23 (1973): 151–56; N. Lohfink, "Opferzentralisation, Säkularisierungsthese und mimetische Theorie," in *Studien zum Deuteronomium und zur deuteronomistischen Literatur* (SBAB 20; Stuttgart: Katholisches Bibelwerk, 1995), 3:219–60; I. Wilson, *Out of the Midst of the Fire: Divine Presence in Deuteronomy* (SBLDS 151; Atlanta: Scholars Press, 1995).

16. Cf. the account of Jehoshaphat's judicial reforms in 2 Chr 19:4–11, which has no parallel in the book of Kings. Verse 11 implies separate legal procedures for disputes involving the sacred and those involving the secular realm.

17. Cf. J. G. McConville, *Deuteronomy* (Apollos Old Testament Commentary 5; Leicester: Apollos, 2002), 291–93. The disputes referred to here are matters of criminal and civil law and the priests were probably not expected to resort to divination, so also J. H. Tigay, *Deuteronomy* (Philadelphia: The Jewish Publication Society of America, 1996), 164–65; D. L. Christensen, *Deuteronomy 1:1–21:9* (rev. ed.; WBC 6A; Nashville, Tenn.: Thomas Nelson, 2001), 374–77. A similar principle is reflected in Exod 18:13–27 where the covenant mediator Moses has the last word.

18. Cf. D. Patrick, *Old Testament Law* (London: SCM Press, 1986), 189–222; B. S. Jackson, "Ideas of Law and Legal Administration: A Semiotic Approach," in Clements, ed., *The World of Ancient Israel*, 185–202. See also W. M. Schniedewind, *How the Bible Became a Book: The Textualization of Ancient Israel* (Cambridge: Cambridge University Press, 2004).

19. The main difference is that phrases like "the laws of nature" refer to our normal experience (conforming to them does not require special effort) and it is usually not a bad thing, and sometimes even a good thing, if the law can be "broken." In biblical perspective, divine law is frequently broken without much effort but with harmful consequences. A more precise but lesser known parallel may be with the classical "law" of India, see already B. S. Jackson, "From *Dharma* to Law," *The American Journal of Comparative Law* 23 (1975): 490–512.

may indeed be one reason why, anachronistically put, "quoting chapter and verse" was of no concern to the prophets.[20] In this respect the situation in Israel and Judah was probably quite similar to that in other parts of the ancient world. M. T. Roth notes: "In numerous studies of a range of legal situations, little correspondence has been found between the provisions in the law collections and contemporary practice. Furthermore, no court document or contract makes a direct reference to any of the formal law collections."[21] A number of scholars are attracted to the idea that ancient codes were largely academic exercises.[22] This conclusion presumes too much. Roth rightly cautions against arguing simply from the lack of citation "that the law collections had little or no impact on the daily operation of legal affairs."[23] It is evident, however, that ancient legal practice does not conform to the model of modern, Anglo-Saxon legislation in which quotation and exegesis of legal statutes are paramount.

Nevertheless, 2 Kgs 17:13 declares that the prophets were Yahweh's instruments to warn Israel and Judah to turn from evil ways and to keep his commandments (מצות) and statutes (חקות), in accordance with the תורה which he had commanded their ancestors and which he had sent them (שלח) by his servants the prophets. Here at least we have a conception of Torah being sent through the prophets.[24] The earlier part of this verse, asserting that Torah had been commanded to their ancestors, as well as v. 37, which speaks of "the statutes (חקים) and the ordinances (משפטים) and the law (תורה) and the commandment (מצוה) that he wrote for you," strongly imply that the Torah sent through the prophets is

---

20.   The limited availability of written texts and the logistical problems involved in consulting scrolls should also be borne in mind in this context; see S. Niditch, *Oral World and Written Word: Orality and Literacy in Ancient Israel* (London: SPCK, 1997), 60–77.

21.   M. T. Roth, *Law Collections from Mesopotamia and Asia Minor* (SBLWAW 6; 2nd ed.; Atlanta: Scholars Press, 1997), 5. J. A. Dearman, *Property Rights in the Eighth-Century Prophets* (SBLDS 106; Atlanta: Scholars Press, 1988), 106, notes that the Yabneh Yam letter about a seized garment and even a text as late as Neh 5 similarly do not appeal to relevant Pentateuchal texts.

22.   E.g. A. Fitzpatrick-McKinley, *The Transformation of Torah from Scribal Advice to Law* (JSOTSup 287; Sheffield: Sheffield Academic Press, 1999), especially Chapter 3, following the later work of B. S. Jackson and R. Westbrook.

23.   Roth, *Law Collections*, 5. Fitzpatrick-McKinley is right to point out how much scholars such as J. Halbe, E. Otto, F. Crüsemann and L. Schwienhorst-Schönberger presume about the relationship between written law and society.

24.   This is the only verse in the Hebrew Bible that has תורה as the object of sending (שלח). A similar idea is found in Zech 7:12, on which see below.

pictured as an already extant (written) body of laws (cf. 21:8 etc. and the reference to Moses earlier in 1 Kgs 2:3).[25]

2. *Characteristics of Prophetic Literature*

There are two ways in which Israel's prophetic traditions are distinct from other prophetic material unearthed in the region. First, it took the shape of literature. It was not unusual for prophecies to be carefully written down and filed. There is indeed a large quantity of prophetic texts known to us, but from all we know they were not written for posterity or put together in larger literary complexes anywhere else in the ancient Near East. Secondly, the literature reflects the proclamation of certain judgment.[26] Both characteristics arguably point to an awareness on the part of the editors, and maybe the prophets themselves, of a larger over-arching perspective within which both the end of the nation and a more long-term divine purpose could be conceived. From the point of view of their editors, the prophets did not speak for the moment only but contributed to a body of literature which has the Torah with its definition of the relationship between Yahweh and Israel and Israel's place in the world as its logical foundation.[27] While this may go beyond the per-spective of the prophets themselves, the fact that most prophets in Israel and Judah were not writing prophets with a "canon consciousness" does not seem to me sufficient reason to think that none were. It is true that the prophets of whom we read in biblical *narratives* behave and speak in ways similar to prophetic figures elsewhere in the ancient Near East, which is different from the portrayal of "classical" prophets in the prophetic literature. But this is not a sufficient reason to suppose that Hosea and Amos, Micah and Isaiah could not have been any different

25. Cf. Dan 9:10–11 which uses the plural תּוֹרוֹת for the teachings set forth (נָתַן לְפָנֵי) by the prophets and associates the singular תּוֹרָה with Moses (also v. 14).

26. See, e.g., R. G. Kratz, "Das Neue in der Prophetie des Alten Testaments," in *Prophetie in Israel* (ed. I. Fischer, K. Schmid and H. G. M. Williamson; Altes Testament und Moderne 11; Münster: LIT, 2003), 1–11 (10). Kratz rightly points out that the former has long been observed (e.g. by von Rad) and points to J. Jeremias, "Das Proprium der alttestamentlichen Prophetie," *TLZ* 119 (1994): 483–94, for the latter. In distinction to Kratz and Jeremias, I would want to distinguish more care-fully between the *proclamation* of "certain" judgment and the *expectation* of certain judgment. Cf. my "Proclaiming the Future: History and Theology in Prophecies against Tyre," *TynBul* 51 (2000): 17–58.

27. In this context it may also be observed that the largest part of prophetic denunciations and announcements concern whole communities or the leadership of a community; cf. Bergren, *The Prophets and the Law*, 151–78.

from the prophets who feature in the narrative literature. The books associated with these prophets suggest an understanding of prophecy which differs from classical ancient Near Eastern types of prophecy. The question which cannot be addressed here, and which may in any case have to be answered differently for different prophets, is whether this shift is entirely the product of later writers or whether prophets such as Amos consciously departed from traditional understandings, in which case we might speak of an emerging "canon consciousness" on the side of such prophets.

While prophetic teaching can be called תורה,[28] particularly in the book of Isaiah (e.g. 8:16), the overwhelming majority of references to תורה in the prophets is to priestly instruction or divine law, and it is possible that the prophets, where they are said to impart Torah, are portrayed as imitating the priests.[29] The differentiation made in Jer 18:18 between prophetic דבר, priestly תורה and the עצה of the wise appears to apply to much prophetic literature.[30] Maybe acknowledging that divine law was anchored in the past (Moses) and leaving cultic תורה to be given by the priests, the prophets rarely promulgate תורה as a substitute for previously given (priestly) תורה.[31]

Deuteronomy 18:15–22 distinguishes between true and false prophets, with the latter speaking what God had not commanded (צוה). As Yahweh's ambassadors, the prophets were expected to work within the framework of his תורה just as much as the other office holders reviewed in this section of Deuteronomy (judges, priests, king), but the passage does not state that the prophets were primarily preachers or enforcers of the תורה. Christensen summarizes the prophetic responsibility as "exer-

---

28. Cf. the lengthy treatment in Östborn, TŌRĀ *in the Old Testament*, 127–68.

29. So Östborn, TŌRĀ *in the Old Testament*, 128 (following Proksch); cf. p. 143. Östborn suggests that this may be particularly appropriate for temple prophets (pp. 129–30). The "torah of the temple" (תורת הבית in Ezek 43:12; cf. 43:11; 44:5 and maybe 44:24) is an obvious example.

30. דבר is very common for the prophetic word. Ezek 7:26 differentiates in a similar way but uses חזון for the prophetic communication. It is possible that Ezekiel thought more specifically of prophets closely associated with the court and that חזון is a technical term used in connection with court or temple prophets, but this is by no means certain.

31. The main exception is Ezek 40–48, which was written in the wake of the destruction of the temple and the nation. Isa 56:3–7 implicitly revises existing regulations, but see R. D. Wells, Jr., "'Isaiah' as an Exponent of Torah: Isaiah 56:1–8," in *New Visions of Isaiah* (ed. R. F. Melugin and M. A. Sweeney; JSOTSup 214; Sheffield: JSOT Press, 1996), 140–55. Prophecies, of course, could be revised in some circumstances; see Isa 16:13–14; Ezek 29:17–21; cf. 1 Sam 2:27–36.

cised in three general areas, as reflected in the types of oracles associated with the classical prophets: in matters of war (war oracles), in matters relating to the king (royal oracles), and in matters relating to the people in general (as monitors of the covenant agreement between God and his chosen people)."[32] This is a helpful reminder of the diversity of tasks undertaken by prophets. The last may appear the most prominent in the canonical literature but covenant monitoring is not what defined a prophet in Israel and Judah. Indeed, it does not account very well for the prevalence of oracles about other nations.[33]

a. *Hosea*

The only two prophetic books among the Twelve in which תורה is used more than once are the first and the last of the Twelve. Hosea opens with allusions to Torah traditions in the naming of his children, but our concern here is the actual uses of the term תורה of which the first is in ch. 4. The chapter opens with a general condemnation in v. 1 (no faithfulness, no loyalty, no knowledge of God), which is followed by an itemization of wrong practices in v. 2 which may allude to the ten commandments. The wrongness of the practices condemned in v. 2 is considered obvious and does not require citation of any documents. Verse 3 specifies the "natural" consequence of this destruction of the fabric of society. From v. 4 onwards, the priests are addressed and made ultimately responsible for the catastrophe because of their neglect of the תורה of their God (v. 6).[34] Israel's lack of understanding is the result of the priests' failure to uphold תורה (cf. Jer 2:8). Hosea assumes that the priests have to

---

32. Christensen, *Deuteronomy 1:1–21:9*, 409–10. The summary given by Tigay, *Deuteronomy*, may imply a permanent role ("The prophets served, in sum, as the monitors of Israel's fulfilment of its covenant obligations to God and as primary bearers of Israel's religious and moral ideology," p. 176), but McConville rightly points out that in contrast to priest and king mentioned earlier the prophet has no ceremony of institution, suggesting that "the prophet will be appointed by Yahweh as need arises" (*Deuteronomy*, 302), although he too speaks later of a distribution of political functions (p. 205), which to me suggests a more regularized involvement of prophets in the political processes. The historical narratives know of royal prophets and there may have been court prophets in Israel and Judah, but it seems to be doubtful that Deuteronomy speaks specifically of court prophets.

33. Cf. H. M. Barstad, "No Prophets? Recent Developments in Biblical Prophetic Research and Ancient Near Eastern Prophecy," *JSOT* 57 (1993): 39–60 (53–56). There are attempts to interpret oracles concerning other nations as directly related to the covenant traditions, but these seem to me forced.

34. A. A. Macintosh, *Hosea* (ICC; Edinburgh: T. & T. Clark, 1997), 136, rightly observes the logical progression here (*pace* Weiser and Wolff).

conform to a given divine תורה and do not have the authority to create it. It would not have been possible to charge them for failing to uphold תורה, if תורה denoted priestly instruction here.[35] The prophet does not claim new insights into the תורה and sees no need to substantiate the accusation with examples. The assumption is that the basic contents of this תורה are known among the addressees of the prophetic book.[36] Indeed, far from explaining Torah to help the people live in obedience to it, the prophets are a means of judgment in 6:5 (cf. 9:7–8).

In Hos 8, rebellion against Yahweh's תורה parallels transgression of the covenant which constitutes Israel as Yahweh's people (v. 1).[37] This is elaborated upon in terms of king-making without reference to the covenant God and unfaithfulness expressed both in the "cultic" (idols) as well as the "political" (Assyria) realm. Certainly the latter, and probably the former as well, would be considered breaches of the covenant in any suzerain–vassal relationship. Verse 12 implies that this divine תורה includes written instruction.[38] But the "principal requirements" of God's תורה "are considered as those of an alien god" and disregarded.[39] Here it is not specified who is responsible for upholding תורה, but the co-text refers to altars and sacrifices, thus reinforcing the impression gained in

---

35. Cf. H. W. Wolff, *Hosea* (Philadelphia: Fortress, 1974), 79, who notes that "Hosea's portrayal of the priest is similar to the Chronicler's description of the teaching Levites" and appeals to Deut 33:10 and 31:9ff as further evidence for the exercise of such a role among priests. The reference to prophets in 4:5 establishes that Hosea's indictment of the northern priests for failing to uphold תורה is relevant for false prophecy as well and may have been prompted by a close association of false prophets with the temple establishment. Cf. Macintosh, *Hosea*, 139.

36. The existence of such a "common ground" is also stressed by Bergren, *The Prophets and the Law*, with regard to passages other than the one discussed here; see, e.g., pp. 205–7.

37. For the phrase "transgressing [God's] covenant," cf. 6:7. See also Josh 7:11, 15; 23:16; Judg 2:20; 2 Kgs 18:14; Jer 34:18. The only instance in biblical law where breaking a law equates to transgression (עבר) of the covenant is apostasy in Deut 17:2. The language of covenant breaking (פ־ר) is used for falling away from Yahweh in Lev 26 and Deut 31.

38. So also, e.g., Wolff, *Hosea*, 144; Macintosh, *Hosea*, 326; and Crüsemann, *Torah*, 17–20. The proposal put forward by F. I. Andersen and D. N. Freedman, *Hosea* (AB 24; New York: Doubleday, 1980), 509, that the verb should be attached to the preceding, suggesting the writing down of Ephraim's sin, produces a rather awkward sentence and is therefore implausible.

39. This reading follows Macintosh, *Hosea*, 325–26, who in my view rightly considers the wordplay on רבבה/רבב as a means of contrasting the *multitude* of altars with the *weightiness* of God's law and identifies the use of זר as elliptical—"(those of) an alien" (god is added *ad sensum*).

ch. 4 that the priests have the particular responsibility of upholding the divine תורה.⁴⁰

b. *Joel*

Joel does not use תורה, although priests feature prominently as authority figures.⁴¹ While many phrases in the book of Joel can be correlated with the language of covenant curses and blessings,⁴² there is no analysis of any violations to explain the suffering of covenant curses. The absence of the term תורה is therefore not surprising. The lack of detail combined with the focus on the catastrophes suffered by Judah suggests that the fact that Yahweh's standards had been violated was not considered to require any proof.

c. *Amos*

The book of Amos refers to God's תורה in the judgment oracle against Judah, which, in using the root פשע (2:4; cf. 1:3, 6, 9, 11, 13; 2:1), implicitly equates rejection (מאס) of Yahweh's תורה with the extreme instances of wrongdoing listed in the preceding strophes against other nations. The rejection of Yahweh's תורה is parallel to and presumably expressed in the failure to keep Yahweh's precepts (חקים), a failure which in turn made room for deception by false prophets.⁴³ The formulaic language suggests that the reference is to Yahweh's commands

---

40.   The priests are also condemned in Hos 6:9. Apart from the gloss in 4:5, prophets are only referred to positively (6:5; 9:7–8). They are never called to responsibility for failing to uphold תורה. The court officials are condemned in 7:5 for their self-indulgence and consequent inability to advise appropriately. There is no explicit reference to divine standards of justice, although there is a suggestion that their tolerance of "wickedness" (vv. 1–3) has clouded their judgment. They can therefore not be absolved as easily from the responsibility for upholding תורה. Nevertheless, 7:5 refers to specific events ("on the day of our king," presumably the first anniversary of Pekahiah's accession or coronation; see Macintosh, *Hosea*, 261), while the indictment of the priests is more general.

41.   Cf. J. R. Linville, "The Day of Yahweh and the Mourning of the Priests in Joel," in *The Priests in the Prophets: The Portrayal of Priests, Prophets and Other Religious Specialists in the Latter Prophets* (ed. L. L. Grabbe and A. Ogden Bellis; JSOTSup 408; London: T&T Clark International, 2004), 98–114, who explores "how the book of Joel affirms the legitimacy and centrality of Judah's Persian-era priesthood" (p. 98).

42.   D. Stuart, *Hosea–Jonah* (WBC 31; Waco, Tex.: Word, 1987), 228, is particularly impressed with parallels to Deut 32.

43.   For this interpretation of the last part of the verse, see K. Möller, *A Prophet in Debate: The Rhetoric of Persuasion in the Book of Amos* (JSOTSup 372; London: Sheffield Academic Press, 2003), 192. The only other references to rejection (מאס) of Yahweh's תורה are in Isa 5:24 and Jer 6:19 (cf. 8:8–9).

generally rather than to any specific exhortations,[44] whether or not this body of commands was available in written form. Given the obviousness of the criminal nature of the wrongdoing condemned among the nations, the oracle suggests that the fact of the rejection of Yahweh's תורה should have been equally obvious to those with eyes to see and ears to hear.[45] There is certainly no hint of Amos introducing a new set of ethical standards. Of course, the real climax of the indictments put forward here comes with the oracle against the northern kingdom. In condemning Israel, Amos offers detailed accusations of wrongdoing rather than a general, albeit equally damning, complaint about rejection of the divine תורה. It is true that the people of Israel needed to be persuaded that they fell far short of divine standards, but there appears to be no serious disagreement as to what these standards were and hence the call to repentance can be expressed in the most general terms as seeking Yahweh (5:6), seeking good and not evil, hating evil and loving good (5:14–15).

d. *Micah*

תורה does not occur in any of the books which focus on the fate of a foreign nation: Obadiah, Jonah and Nahum. The only other reference to be discussed prior to Habakkuk and Zephaniah is therefore the future-oriented prophecy in Mic 4, which is also found in Isa 2.[46] In its Micah context, the prophecy contrasts the teaching and judging of Yahweh,

44. E. Bons believes that תורה may refer to prophetic instruction here ("Das Denotat von כזביהם 'ihre Lügen' im Judaspruch Am 2,4–5," *ZAW* 108 (1996): 201–13) but he allows that it might refer to a pre-Deuteronomic written law of Yahweh. He points out that the language here is not akin to Deuteronomy or DtrH, *pace* H. W. Wolff, *Joel and Amos* (Philadelphia: Fortress, 1977), 163, and others. Cf. F. I. Andersen and D. N. Freedman, *Amos* (AB 24A; New York: Doubleday, 1989), 296–300. The idea that חקים are cultic ordinances in distinction to civil laws is questionable even in phrases combined with משפטים and certainly implausible here. Other attempts to narrow the meaning of חק are equally unpersuasive, at least outside P and H; see H. Ringgren, "חקק," *TDOT* 5:139–47.

45. It is perfectly possible, even likely, that those in control of Israelite society were oblivious to the injustice perpetrated by them; cf. A. Phillips, "Prophecy and Law," in *Israel's Prophetic Tradition: Essays in Honour of Peter R. Ackroyd* (ed. R. Coggins et al.; Cambridge: Cambridge University Press, 1982), 217–32 (220–21). Those suffering from the injustice were likely aware of the fact that the divine "law and order" was not being upheld.

46. W. Gisin, *Hosea: Ein literarisches Netzwerk beweist seine Authentizität* (BBB 139; Berlin: Philo, 2002), 28–35, usefully compares how the prophecy is embedded in the books of Isaiah and Micah. I find Gisin's overall method (for which this comparison is meant to serve as a test case) questionable, but his case for the priority of Micah is well argued.

which allows nations to resolve differences without resorting to war (4:2–3), with the perversion of justice by Israel's leaders and the violence associated with it (3:9–10).[47] The salvation prophecy stresses the certainty of judgment by claiming that "the judgment upon the priests, prophets and heads of Israel will result in Yahweh himself removing these officials and carrying out their tasks."[48] The beginning and end of the condemnation in ch. 3 focuses on leaders who held a degree of military and judicial authority,[49] but a middle section condemns prophets for giving unreliable oracles (3:5–7). Micah contrasts himself with them as one who is "filled with power by Yahweh's spirit and with justice and might to declare to Jacob his transgression and to Israel his sin" (3:8).[50] Verse 11, which stands out as spoken to a third party, lists three groups: (1) rulers whose job is שׁפט, the judicial or executive action that restores the peace to a community after it has been disturbed;[51] (2) priests who teach (ירה); and (3) prophets who tell the future (קסם).[52]

47. Cf. Gisin, *Hosea*, 32; and C. S. Shaw, *The Speeches of Micah: A Rhetorical-Historical Analysis* (JSOTSup 145; Sheffield: Sheffield Academic Press, 1993), 97–127.

48. Shaw, *Speeches*, 102.

49. They were probably not military commanders and judges in the narrow sense of the word. For discussion, see Shaw, *Speeches*, 110–11; and W. McKane, *Micah: Introduction and Commentary* (Edinburgh: T. & T. Clark, 1998), 99–102. McKane believes that Micah uses traditional terms in vv. 1 and 9 to address and condemn new style "officials of the king's secretariat" (p. 102). This is quite possible, although McKane's discussion suggests too neat a separation of judiciary and executive roles.

50. Reading את as a preposition (cf. LXX ἐν πνεύματι κυρίου; other versions imply "strength of Yahweh's spirit"; see McKane, *Micah*, 109). For the phrase את רוח יהוה, which is often considered a gloss, see the discussion in J. E. Robson, *Word and Spirit in Ezekiel* (LHBOTS 447; London: T&T Clark International, 2006). The contrast to 2:11 is particularly noteworthy.

51. Cf. the pertinent entries in *THAT* 2:999–1009 (G. Liedke) and *NIDOTTE* 4:213–20 (R. Schultz).

52. The root is often used for (inductive) divination but it is not clear that it is restricted to it (see, e.g., J. K. Kuemmerlin-McLean, "Magic [OT]," *ABD* 4:468–71 [468]; *HALOT*, 3:1115–16; contrast L. Ruppert, "קסם," *TDOT* 13:72–78). Hence "divine" (RSV, NAB, NASB, NJB, JPSV) and "practice divination" (ESV) may be too narrow, although they preserve the link to v. 7 where it is hard to avoid translating the noun as "diviners." The rendering "give oracles" (NRSV) slightly obscures the future orientation that seems inherent in קסם and "tell fortunes" (NIV) brings with it unhelpful fairground connotations, obscuring the fact that the activity is not condemned as such. For a discussion of the relationship between prophecy and divination, see T. W. Overholt, *Channels of Prophecy: The Social Dynamics of Prophetic Activity* (Minneapolis: Fortress, 1989), 117–47 (esp. 140–47).

The use of יָרָה Hiphil in connection with priests is not surprising.[53] In Lev 10:11, Aaron, representing the priesthood, is instructed to teach (יָרָה) Israel God's statutes (חֻקִּים) as mediated through Moses. Similarly, in Deuteronomy, the Levites are said to be responsible for teaching Israel the מִשְׁפָּטִים and תּוֹרָה of Yahweh (33:10).[54] In 2 Kings, Jehoash is reported to have been well instructed by the priest Jehoiada (12:3) and the Assyrian king is said to have send for one of the exiled priests to return to Samaria to teach its new inhabitants "the מִשְׁפָּט of the god of the land" (17:27–28). In Ezekiel's vision, the Levitical priests are to teach "the difference between the holy and the common" and "between the unclean and the clean" (Ezek 44:23).[55] Finally, the Chronicler equates the absence of a "teaching priest" (כֹּהֵן מוֹרֶה) with the absence of תּוֹרָה (2 Chr 15:3).[56] Thus there is broad support for the claim that priestly responsibilities included giving authoritative direction on Yahweh's תּוֹרָה.[57] The lack of reference to Torah mediators in Micah's prophecy does not necessarily imply a change in this regard, but is a feature of the judgment on the present incumbents. A similar line of argument with regard to leaders more generally, and the king in particular, is found in Ezek 34 where many scholars see a conflict between the emphasis in the first part on Yahweh taking "shepherd" responsibilities away from present incumbents and upon himself and the existence in the second part of a new David as "shepherd" of Israel. But the rhetorical emphasis on God taking charge again, whether as king or teacher of Torah, need not rule out the use of human mediators. While it must be acknowledged that

53. Cf. S. Wagner, "יָרָה III," *TDOT* 6:339–47 (343–44); G. Liedke and C. Petersen, "תּוֹרָה," *THAT* 2:1032–43 (1035–38) = *TLOT* 3:1415–22 (1418–19); and Östborn, TŌRĀ *in the Old Testament*, 89–111.

54. Cf. the application to the specific case of skin disease in Lev 14:57 and Deut 24:8.

55. In so far as teaching this differentiation to the Israelites goes beyond merely making the differentiation (Lev 10:10; distinguished from the teaching ministry in Lev 10:11), this could be said to involve a broadening of responsibilities. But this may read too much into a subtle difference of phrasing.

56. This is an allusion to Hos 3:4; cf. H. G. M. Williamson, *1 and 2 Chronicles* (NCB; London: Marshall, Morgan & Scott, 1982), 267. See also 2 Chr 17:7–9 for officials and Levites (including priests) teaching (לִמֵּד) Torah. Note also n. 35 above.

57. As pointed out by G. J. Wenham, *The Book of Leviticus* (NICOT 3; Grand Rapids: Eerdmans, 1979), 159; cf. L. L. Grabbe, "A Priest Is Without Honour in His Own Prophet: Priests and Other Religious Specialists in the Latter Prophets," in Grabbe and Bellis, eds., *The Priests in the Prophets*, 79–97 (92). Contrast this with the claim made by Z. Zevit in an essay in the same volume ("The Prophet Versus Priest Antagonism Hypothesis: Its History and Origin," 189–217) that the priests "*were essentially technicians, mechanics*" (p. 208, emphasis original).

Micah does not speak of a renewed priesthood in the way Ezekiel speaks of a new David, neither does the text hint at the abolishment of priesthood. It is therefore extremely unlikely that a priest-less religion is envisaged.

e. *Habakkuk*

Apart from clauses with אבד in Jer 18:18 ("surely, Torah from the priest will not become lost") and Ezek 7:26 ("Torah will be lost from the priest") and היה in Mal 2:4 (see below), Hab 1:4 is the only place in the Hebrew Bible that has תורה as the subject of a verb.[58] The verb is translated rather loosely as "is ignored" in NASB but more literally as "is paralyzed" in NAB and ESV.[59] The verb suggests growing frozen or numbed, that is, becoming weak and ineffectual.[60] This is the result of strife and contention (ריב מדון, v. 3).[61] With Torah unable to function properly, justice (משפט) never comes forth (יצא), that is, never prevails. The "wicked/guilty" (רשע) hem in or crowd out "the righteous/innocent" (הצדיק) and so justice comes forth bent.[62] A few scholars insist that justice either does or does not come forth and seek to resolve the "contradiction" in this verse by assuming that different authors were responsible for different parts of the verse.[63] But this seems to me an over-literal and rather unimaginative reading: justice does not come forth where it comes

58.   In the book of Psalms תורה is occasionally the subject of a verbless clause (19:6; 37:31; 40:9; 119:72, 77, 92, 142). Cf. Prov 6:23; Jer 8:8, as well as Prov 13:14 (תורת חכם) and 31:26 (the תורת חסד of the capable wife).

59.   The verb פוג is found in the MT only here and in Gen 45:26, Pss 38:9; 77:3. An emendation to the last word in Ps 88:16 would add another reference. Cf. the nouns פוגה (Lam 2:18) and הפגות (Lam 3:49).

60.   Cf. J. G. Janzen, "Eschatological Symbol and Existence in Habakkuk," *CBQ* 44 (1982): 394–414; and M. D. Johnson, "The Paralysis of Torah in Habakkuk I 4," *VT* 35 (1985): 257–66 (259–60). Johnson's restriction of the meaning of תורה in Hab 1:4 to (Deuteronomic) promises (which failed to materialize) is unwarranted.

61.   The (internal Judean) strife and contention may well be the result of (Babylonian) destruction and violence, at least from Habakkuk's perspective, but this depends on how ch. 1 as a whole is read. For a critique of the traditional view that the oracle in 1:5–11 is a response to the complaint in 1:2–4, see, e.g., Johnson, "Paralysis," pp. 261–63; G. T. M. Prinsloo, "Reading Habakkuk as a Literary Unit: Exploring the Possibilities," *OTE* 12 (1999): 515–35; and D. Cleaver-Bartholomew, "An Alternative Approach to Hab 1,2–2,20," *SJOT* 17 (2003): 206–25.

62.   This is the only occurrence of the verb but two adjectives of the same root are known and help to clarify the meaning (Judg 5:6; Ps 125:5; Isa 27:1).

63.   E.g. L. Perlitt, *Die Propheten Nahum, Habakuk, Zephanja* (ATD 25/1; Göttingen: Vandenhoeck & Ruprecht, 2004), 50–51.

forth perverted. Justice is not done in Judah even if "justice" is still spoken.

תורה and משפט (singular or plural) are referred to in the same breath quite frequently.[64] The most interesting parallels for our purposes are in the book of Isaiah. The Servant is said twice to bring forth (יצא) justice to the nations (42:1, 3). Because he establishes (שׂים) justice in the earth, the coastlands wait for his teaching (תורה, v. 4). In Isa 51:4 it is Yahweh himself who calls his people to listen to him and take note that תורה will come forth (יצא) from him and that he will set (רגע Hiphil) justice as a light to the peoples.[65] The prophecy discussed above in which the going forth (יצא) of תורה leads to Yahweh judging (שׁפט) between many peoples (Mic 4:2–3; cf. Isa 2:3–4) is of course closely related to these texts and may well have been their source.

Habakkuk's choice of metaphor is intriguing and implies that תורה does not refer to the (perverted) instruction given in Judah. While there is a wordplay with משפט, which in the sense of a sentence being spoken is present and in the sense of true justice being spoken is absent, תורה is used only to refer to what is in effect absent. It is not clear whether Torah was absent, rendered unable to function according to its purpose, because Torah teachers distorted its contents (cf. Jer 8:8) or whether Torah teaching was appropriately given but ignored. While the latter cannot be excluded, the former seems to account better for the imagery of Torah itself being hampered and fits with the portrayal of the judicial system as corrupt.

f. *Zephaniah*

In Zephaniah, four types of leaders are accused of wrongdoing, as Jerusalem has failed to accept correction and draw near to God (3:2). Officials and judges brutally seek their own interest (3:3), prophets act as treacherous insurrectionists[66] and priests profane what is holy,[67] doing violence (חמס) to תורה (3:4). This failure of leadership contrasts with the righteous judgment of Yahweh (3:5), similar to the logic of Mic 4 and Isa 2

---

64.   Lev 26:46; Num 15:16; Deut 4:8; 17:11; 33:10; 1 Kgs 2:3; 2 Kgs 17:34, 37; 2 Chr 19:10; 30:16; 33:8; Ezra 7:10; Neh 8:18; 9:13, 29; 10:30; Ps 89:31; Isa 42:4; 51:4; Ezek 44:24; Mal 3:22.

65.   For Torah as light, cf. Prov 6:23.

66.   See A. Lange, "Die Wurzel *PHZ* und ihre Konnotationen," *VT* 51 (2001): 497–510.

67.   Ps 134:2 and Dan. 8:13–14 indicate that the direct article is not strictly required for קדשׁ to refer specifically to the sanctuary (maybe also in Obad 17 where *HALOT* glosses as "holy area"), hence "defile the temple" is also possible (cf. NASB, NIV).

(see above). It is noteworthy how prophets and priests are here more closely associated with each other than priests and judges.

The denunciation of Jerusalem's leaders in Ezek 22 is dependent on Zeph 3.[68] Ezekiel's omission of the judges is well explained by Sweeney:

> Ezekiel portrays the crimes of officials as those of corrupt judges. Furthermore, the book of Ezekiel never refers to judges. In that the Mosaic tradition in Exod 18:21–23 makes very clear that judges are to be chosen from among the officials of the people, it would appear that Ezek 22 presupposes both Zeph 3:3–4 and Exod 18:21–23.[69]

The way Ezekiel expands on the charge that the priests have done violence to Torah is relevant in the context of our discussion. Ezekiel pluralizes קֹדֶשׁ to refer to "my holy things" and states that the priests "have made no distinction between the holy and the common, neither have they taught to distinguish between the unclean and the clean, and they have disregarded my Sabbaths, and I am profaned among them" (22:26). If the profanation of what is holy may be linked to the violence done to תּוֹרָה, which seems plausible, this violence consists not only of ignoring the distinctions made in the Torah but also of failing to teach these distinctions to the people. In any case, it is obvious that not only the priest Ezekiel but already Zephaniah took disregard of the "cultic" law as seriously as cases of injustice. The condemnation of priests is not a condemnation of priesthood, but belongs to the wider denunciation of Jerusalem's upper class in the book.

g. *Haggai and Zechariah*
In Hag 2:11–12, the prophet Haggai is asked to go to the priests to request a תּוֹרָה concerning the question whether consecrated meat makes holy the things with which it gets in contact.[70] It is not necessary to assume that the question is meant to elicit previously unknown information, although

---

68. Cf. M. Fishbane, *Biblical Interpretation in Ancient Israel* (Oxford: Clarendon, 1985), 461–63.

69. M. A. Sweeney, *Zephaniah: A Commentary* (Hermeneia; Minneapolis: Fortress, 2003), 163. If my analysis of the Masoretic division of the text (*Colometry and Accentuation in Hebrew Prophetic Poetry* [KUSATU 4; Waltrop: Spenner, 2003]) is correct, the Masoretes may have considered the denunciation of the "officials" (scanned as a monocolon) as a summary statement, embracing the three groups which each get a bicolon (judges, prophets, priests).

70. P. J. Budd, "Priestly Instruction in Pre-Exilic Israel," *VT* 23 (1973): 1–14, usefully distinguishes such priestly direction from the "priestly technical oracle," often given in response to a military enquiry, "priestly proclamation" at cultic assemblies and "priestly verdict" in judicial pronouncements.

this is possible.[71] In any case, the priestly ruling is destined to become a vehicle for a prophetic message. A similar, but here clearly genuine, request for a priestly ruling is found in Zech 7:2–3, but the term תורה is not used and the prophets are included among those from whom a decision is sought.[72]

Zechariah 7:12 looks back to pre-exilic failure "to hear the Torah and the words that Yahweh of hosts had sent by his spirit through the former prophets," which resulted in divine outpouring of wrath. "In tandem," התורה and הדברים "apparently represent two categories of authoritative revelation" and may even refer to two canonical corpora.[73] Thus the words of the prophets (cf. 7:7) are distinguished from התורה, even if in agreement with it. Interestingly, Zech 1:6 speaks of the prophets having been commanded Yahweh's words and "statutes" (חקים), thus attributing Torah-like qualities to the prophetic word. This may reflect post-exilic developments. Prior to the destruction of Jerusalem it may not have been obvious that the prophets were adding to a written divine standard; in post-exilic perspective this is what they had been doing.[74]

h. *Malachi*
Malachi's first disputation was directed to the whole community. His second disputation is directed specifically to the priests (1:6–2:9). The first part is focused on persuading the audience of the need to give true honour to Yahweh (1:6–14),[75] the second rebukes the priest for failing to

71. Cf. the question in v. 13 whose answer was probably not in doubt. The situation assumed is a שלמים offering, which made it possible for lay people to take consecrated meat back home. The concept of contagious holiness is implied in Lev 6:20 (Eng. 27) and Ezek 42:13–14. For a brief discussion, see J. Kessler, *The Book of Haggai: Prophecy and Society in Early Persian Yehud* (VTSup 91; Leiden: Brill, 2002), 204.

72. Indeed, the answer comes through the prophet Zechariah (see 8:19).

73. C. L. Meyers and E. M. Meyers, *Haggai, Zechariah 1–8* (AB 25B; New York: Doubleday, 1987), 402, cf. p. 406. Cf. the use of דברים for post-exilic prophecies in 8:9. *Pace* Östborn, *TŌRĀ in the Old Testament*, 142–43, who argues that תורה here designates the prophetic message because its content (cf. 7:9–10) agrees with the prophetic utterances.

74. This is of course not to say that prophecies had not been written down prior to the destruction of Jerusalem. I believe the initial impetus for the writing down of prophecies was the (impending) end of the northern kingdom.

75. Both Codex Leningradensis and Aleppo Codex take 1:14 with the next subunit. For the common demarcation of the text also adopted here, see, e.g., A. E. Hill, *Malachi* (AB 25D; New York: Doubleday, 1998), 172; and K. W. Weyde, *Prophecy and Teaching: Prophetic Authority, Form Problems, and the Use of Traditions in the Book of Malachi* (BZAW 288; Berlin: de Gruyter, 2000).

give proper instruction to the people (2:1–9). Levi had given "true instruction" (תורת אמת), turning many away from iniquity (v. 6). Indeed, the people are right to seek תורה from the mouth of the priest, because the priest is Yahweh's messenger (v. 7). Yet the contemporary priests "have caused many to stumble over Torah" (v. 8), not acting graciously in their administration of Torah (v. 9).[76] Commentators disagree over the meaning of the phrase המצוה הזאת in vv. 1 and 4. There are two main options. The phrase either refers to the responsibilities entailed in Yahweh's covenant with Levi or to the prophetic verdict.[77] If the latter, the passage "may reflect a confluence of priestly (and levitical) and prophetic functions" in the post-exilic community.[78]

The final reference to תורה in the Twelve is in the concluding paragraph: "Remember the Torah of my servant Moses (תורת משה עבדי), that I commanded him at Horeb for all Israel, the statutes (חקים) and ordinances (משפטים)" (3:22 [Eng. 4:4]). There is no explicit acknowledgment of the need for Levites to "set forth the sense" of Torah (cf. Neh 8:8) here, but there is of course no assumption of individual families owning and consulting their own copies of the Torah. Thus the need for (priestly) mediators to help the community follow this injunction is surely taken for granted. The final word, however, belongs to a future "prophet Elijah" (presumably a prophet of the stature of Elijah) who will succeed where his predecessors failed in leading the people to such a change of heart as will keep them safe from divine wrath (3:23–24 [4:5–6]). We must assume that this prophet will help the community in the most effective way to "remember the Torah."

i. *Summary*

In Hag 2:11 and Mal 2:6–9 תורה refers to a priestly ruling. All other occurrences of תורה in the Minor Prophets scroll are best understood as a reference to a publicly known, probably written, divine standard. This may be the case either because such a publicly known, written divine standard was already recognized from an early time onwards, as Macintosh argues for Hosea, or as a result of a fifth-century (or later) redaction

76. For this interpretation of the final clause of v. 9, see Hill, *Malachi*, 217–18.
77. For the former, see, e.g., P. A. Verhoef, *The Books of Haggai and Malachi* (NICOT; Grand Rapids: Eerdmans, 1987), 237–38; and Hill, *Malachi*, 196–97. For the latter, B. Glazier-McDonald, *Malachi: The Divine Messenger* (SBLDS 98; Atlanta: Scholars Press, 1987), 64–65; and Weyde, *Prophecy*, 170–72.
78. Weyde, *Prophecy*, 171. Cf. Zech 1:6 above and the use of צוה in Nah 1:14. Weyde lists additional parallels which I find less convincing. He also thinks that the portrayal of Levi suggests a prophetic function (pp. 194–95, 199–201).

of a Book of the Twelve. The answer to this question obviously depends, on the one hand, on evidence outside the Minor Prophets scroll for the early existence of such a publicly known, written standard, and, on the other hand, on further evidence for the redactional unity of the Book of the Twelve or lack thereof. The fact that the latest תורה references are the ones referring to priestly directives is a complicating factor for the view that uniformity was created at a late redactional stage.[79]

The prophets are not uniformly portrayed as exegetes and teachers of the Torah. In fact, the best examples for the view of prophecy as exposition of Torah are two prophetic books often considered rather uncharacteristic of classical prophecy, namely, Jonah and Nahum. Both books can be seen as lengthy expositions of Exod 34:6–7. Those primarily responsible for the teaching of תורה are the priests. The prophetic denunciation of priests is not a rejection of the cult or priesthood—quite the opposite. The prophets arraign the priests for failing to be proper priests.[80] Similarly, Jeremiah does not object to the exercise of rule (רדה) by priests but to the fact that in his time such exercise of rule had come under the spell of false prophets (Jer 5:31; 27:16; cf. Isa 28:7 for false visions of prophets going together with wrong decisions by priests).[81] It is unwarranted to claim that "the absence of positive statements about the priesthood by the classical prophets suggests that they had a low regard for the whole institution, or at least viewed the priests as subordinate figures dependent on the prophets for their instruction."[82] The fact that prophetic statements

79. These references stand alongside references to Torah as divine standard in Zech 7:12; Mal 3:22 (Torah of Moses). There is thus no linear development of the meaning of the term תורה.

80. Cf. Östborn, *TŌRĀ in the Old Testament*, 108–10, 145, 148; and R. R. Hutton, *Charisma and Authority in Israelite Society* (Minneapolis: Fortress, 1994), 160–63.

81. Bergren observed that for Amos the cultic practice of his time fostered and benefited from injustice and was therefore condemned as rebellion (*The Prophets and the Law*, 111–12). More generally, for a number of prophets "what would normally had been praiseworthy had become indictable—*in the context of disobedience* (p. 132, emphasis original; see pp. 129–46 for a discussion of the rejection of sacrifice in Isa 1:2–3, 10–20; Jer 2:4–13; Mic 6:1–8). Later he argues that "there was a tradition for which the ritual requirements of the law were not part of the covenant" (p. 223; see pp. 214–20 for his general discussion of the prophets' attitude to ethical and cultic demands) but one need not follow him in this to affirm the former statements.

82. J. E. Tollington, *Tradition and Innovation in Haggai and Zechariah 1–8* (JSOTSup 150; Sheffield: JSOT Press, 1993), 83. Cf. T. L. Fenton, "Israelite Prophecy: Characteristics of the First Protest Movement," in *The Elusive Prophet: The Prophet as a Historical Person, Literary Character and Anonymous Artist* (ed.

about priests are largely negative is no more surprising than the fact that the prophets did not speak positively about other prophets.[83] For the "orthodox" prophets the cultic and the ethical were interconnected.[84] It is obvious that the prophets were not satisfied with proper cultic procedures apart from social justice and righteous living. Given frequently expressed concern about idolatry, however, I see no reason to think that these prophets would have been entirely unconcerned about proper cultic procedures as long as justice prevailed.[85] Indeed, I am not convinced that they would have shared the assumption commonly made today that justice can be practised in a society whose cultic practices are corrupt.[86]

3. *Conclusion*

Habakkuk's metaphor of a numbed Torah is striking and unique, but it represents a more widespread attitude towards Torah among the prophets as reflected in the prophetic literature. The prophets who announce "inevitable" judgment on Israel or Judah do not accuse their addressees of the occasional infringement of divine standards but of downright rebellion against Yahweh. Such rebellion finds expression in a widespread rather than just occasional neglect of Yahweh's commandments. This in turn leaves Torah effectively unable to function, particularly as society's leadership is fully implicated in the apostasy.[87] Where the apostasy is detailed with reference to the breaking of divine standards, most prophets choose the most easily visible, that is, blatant, violations of divine Torah. This did not require the quotation of written command-

J. C. de Moor; OtSt 45; Leiden: Brill, 2001), 129–41, who thinks that "the disdain for the entire cultic apparatus is total" (p. 135).

83. A. G. Auld drew the conclusion from this that the prophets did not consider themselves prophets; see Auld's "Prophets and Prophecy in Jeremiah and Kings," *ZAW* 96 (1984): 66–82, and "Prophets Through the Looking Glass: Between Writings and Moses," *JSOT* 27 (1983): 3–23.

84. I find Fenton's arguments to the contrary ("Israelite Prophecy," pp. 134–35) unpersuasive.

85. The assumption that the prophets were antagonistic to the priesthood is critiqued by most contributors to Grabbe and Bellis, eds., *The Priests in the Prophets*.

86. See Zeph 3:4, discussed above, and maybe Hos 4 (note the condemnation of improper cultic practices in vv. 12–14) for an early and Mal 1:6–2:9 for a late example. See Kessler, *The Book of Haggai*, 210–18, for a thorough discussion of the nature of the offence in the last case.

87. This is the element of truth in Fenton's characterization of the prophets as a protest movement ("Israelite Prophecy").

ments. Because the fundamental problem, as these prophets perceived it, was disloyalty to Yahweh, it is possible to say that "the prophet was the appointed interpreter of the law" in pointing to "the true essence of the law."[88] This need not imply prioritizing the ethical over the cultic aspects of Torah, however, but is a matter of directing the people to loyalty to Yahweh as the wellspring of all true conformity to Torah.[89] It should be borne in mind, however, that the prophets are not simply portrayed as preachers of loyalty to Yahweh but as people who announced that Yahweh himself will intervene in punishing rebellion and restoring justice so that one day "the earth shall be filled with the knowledge of the glory of Yahweh" (Hab 2:14; cf. Isa 11:9).[90]

88.   F. Delitzsch, *Isaiah* (Commentary on the Old Testament 7; Peabody, Mass.: Hendrickson, 1989 [originally published in 1861]), 1:90. Cf. p. 54 of the final (fourth) edition of the German original (1889).

89.   This is, of course, not a demand for spirituality apart from obedience but for an orientation of one's entire life to Yahweh. Cf. Deut 6:5; 10:12–13; 13:4–5 (13:3–4); 30:6; Josh 22:5; Mark 12:28–34.

90.   The prophets portrayed in the Minor Prophets scroll were largely concerned with announcing God's purpose for the future. The prophetic announcement regularly concerns the future of entire communities which probably distinguishes it from priestly divination of the future.

THE TRIAL OF JEREMIAH*

Raymond Westbrook

Chapter 26 of the book of Jeremiah belongs to an exceedingly rare category of trial report in the ancient Near East, in that it focuses on issues of law and not of fact. It is concerned not with the evidence but with the legal arguments that were presented to the court prior to its decision.[1] This small contribution in honour of Professor Wenham will review in brief scholarship on the forensic aspects of the report and attempt to provide a coherent account of the legal procedure involved in the prophet's trial.

The difficulties of the account in Jer 26 have led to a long tradition among exegetes of excision, emendation, and source criticism.[2] Not a few have despaired altogether of making sense of the narrative. Thus one commentator remarks: "Too many discrete strands make up the story for a coherent account to be derived from it."[3]

The biblical narrative should not, however, be dismissed as unrealistic or confused simply because it does not fit modern concepts of forensic jurisprudence or reporting. When seen in the context of ancient Near Eastern litigation, many of the seeming discrepancies fall away. The events described may be divided into a number of stages.

* A draft of this study was presented as a lecture to the Department of Bible of the Tel Aviv University on January 2, 2006. I am grateful to the members of the department for their comments and criticisms. Responsibility for the opinions expressed remains entirely my own.

1. There are many litigation records in cuneiform, but they report only the evidence and the bare verdict. The sole comparable report to Jer 26 is the Nippur Murder Trial, discussed below.

2. For a typical division into diachronic layers and a summary of the scholarship, see H. J. Stipp, *Jeremia im Parteienstreit* (BBB 82; Frankfurt am Main: Anton Hain, 1992), 17–72.

3. R. P. Carroll, *Jeremiah: A Commentary* (OTL; Philadelphia: Westminster, 1986), 520. Likewise F. L. Hossfeld and I. Meyer, who take the view "dass wir einem Text mit erheblichen Unebenheiten gegenüberstehen" ("Der Prophet vor dem Tribunal," *ZAW* 86 [1974]: 30–50 [32]).

1. *The Offence (vv. 1–6)*

The facts in this case are not in dispute. Jeremiah has made in public the statements for which he is put on trial and he does not deny them. The trial is about whether they constitute an offence under the law. The only relevant law in the Bible is Deut 18:20–22, which decrees the death penalty for a prophet who falsely purports to prophesy in the name of YHWH when he has no such mandate. To distinguish between a false and a real prophet, the law proposes a "wait and see" test: if the prophecy is fulfilled, it came from YHWH. We have no way of knowing whether the Deuteronomic law was in force or even in the minds of the participants in Jeremiah's trial.[4] What we are entitled to assume is that the Deuteronomic rules were not created *ex nihilo* and for the most part reflected traditional law. That said, the death penalty is a far more credible aspect of the law than its "wait and see" test.

2. *Seizure and Accusation (vv. 7–9)*

The seizure of Jeremiah by so many people at once may be dismissed as hyperbolic, but in a forensic context seizure can be a formality, a symbolic act to initiate pre-trial proceedings, especially when accompanied by formal words of accusation, as here in vv. 8–9.[5] In Deut 21:19, a father and mother are expected to "seize" their rebellious son and bring him before the elders—a daunting task for aged parents against a strapping young man, if conceived in purely physical terms. In Jeremiah's case, the question of how he is brought before the court is moot, because the court comes to him.

The verbal accusation is: "You shall surely die! Why did you prophesy…?" (v. 9). As H. J. Boecker points out, it is common in the biblical idiom for the accusation to be formulated as a question to the accused.[6]

---

4. The lack of citation is of no weight because the system of citation of statutes characteristic of Rabbinic law had not yet developed. It is attested with certainty only in post-exilic sources: R. Westbrook, "The Character of Ancient Near Eastern Law," in *A History of Ancient Near Eastern Law* (ed. R. Westbrook; 2 vols.; Handbook of Oriental Studies 72; Leiden: Brill, 2003), 1:1–90 (19–21).

5. Cf. E. Dombradi (*Die Darstellung des Rechtsaustrags in den altbabylonischen Prozessurkunden* [2 vols.; Freiburger altorientalische Studien 20; Stuttgart: Franz Steiner, 1996], 1:295–302), for the Old Babylonian period, although she distinguishes between criminal and civil trials. In the former, the person may be physically detained until brought before the court.

6. H. J. Boecker, *Redeformen des Rechtslebens im Alten Testament* (WMANT 14; Neukirchen–Vluyn: Neukirchner, 1964), 25–31, 67; see also P. Bovati,

The accuser may at the same time propose the punishment, which is the accuser's estimation of the seriousness of the offence.[7] Although presented as if it were a sentence, it is merely a proposal, conditional upon trial and conviction.[8]

Boecker notes that atypically the proposed punishment in this verse precedes the accusation, which he attributes to the heated emotions of the accusers.[9] It is noteworthy, however, that the accusation in question does not state what crime has been committed; it simply repeats the accused's words without any expression of wrongdoing. This is equally atypical for the interrogative form of accusation, where the offence is made explicit either before or after the question. Thus in 1 Sam 26:15–16, in a quasi-forensic context, David accuses Abner and his guard: "Why did you not guard your lord the king, for someone came to slaughter the king your lord. It is not good what you have done: by the life of YHWH, you are all deserving of death, because you did not guard your lord..."

In Jer 26, I suggest, the appropriate punishment precedes the accusation for two reasons. First, it serves to define the crime: Jeremiah can only face the death penalty if his prophecy in the name of YHWH is false. Second, the trial and the role of the accusers are atypical in that the facts are not at issue. There is no need to prove that the offence was committed.

3. *The Court (vv. 9–10)*

The three components of the accusers are the priests, the prophets, and "all the people" (כל העם). At the close of the accusation it is said that all the people gathered (v. 9, ויקהל) around Jeremiah in the Temple of YHWH. Some commentators translate the verb "thronged about," which raises difficulties in the sequence of events, since they must already have gathered around Jeremiah at the moment of seizure.[10] Far better is the view of those commentators who see in the use of the verb here the constitution of a court.[11] As Bovati puts it, "this phrase does not describe

---

Re-Establishing Justice (trans. M. J. Smith; JSOTSup 105; Sheffield: JSOT Press, 1994), 75.

7. Boecker, *Redeformen*, 72.
8. Bovati, *Re-Establishing Justice*, 85–88.
9. Boecker, *Redeformen*, 59.
10. W. L. Holladay, *Jeremiah 2* (Hermeneia; Minneapolis: Fortress, 1989), 106; J. R. Lundbom, *Jeremiah 21–36* (AB 21B; New York: Doubleday, 2004), 289–90. Cf. G. Brin, *The Prophet in his Struggles* (Tel Aviv: Miphʿalim Universitayyim, 1983), 53, who regards the actions of the accusers as those of a lynch mob.
11. E.g. C. Rietzschel, *Das Problem der Urrolle* (Gütersloh: Gerd Mohn, 1966), 97 n. 10; K. M. O'Connor, "Do Not Trim a Word: The Contributions of Chapter 26 to the Book of Jeremiah," *CBQ* 51 (1989): 617–30 (621).

the threatening press of the crowd around Jeremiah so much as the formation of a juridically competent assembly which has a decisive role within the trial."[12] At this point, however, the nobles intervene. Furthermore, in v. 17 yet another group, the elders of the land, are mentioned as being present. The question is then: Which of these various groups formed the court and what role did they play?

Bovati hesitates to ascribe the role of a court to "all the people." That function belongs to the nobles, who will pass sentence. The public assembly acts "almost like the jury in a modern assizes" to endorse their decision.[13] Boecker likewise insists that the trial is conducted by the nobles, but with participation by the people, which may be a special feature of Jerusalem courts. He also invokes the idea of a jury, drawing on a parallel from German legal history.[14] H. C. Brichto refers to the king's officials and the עם as judge and jury respectively.[15]

A different approach is that of H. Schulz, who considers the only true court to be כל קהל העם in v. 17. In his view, this is a special "cultic court" (*Kultgericht*) comprised of every other group mentioned—the priests, the prophets, the accused, the nobles, the elders and the people— and at the same time separate from them. The scenario imagined by Schulz is that the various parties or groups address various other groups during the course of the proceedings, but only the elders address the whole court. Their opinion must therefore have been the one adopted by the court, although not actually recorded in the text.[16]

For V. H. Matthews and D. C. Benjamin, "all the people" is a technical legal term for a quorum, which means that enough people are present for the trial to be official. Wherever the term appears, it means "officially" rather than referring to a group of jurors or spectators. When "all the people" gather round Jeremiah, the state court was officially called into session.[17]

Whatever their individual merits, the difficulty with all these reconstructions is the models that they use. Bovati, Boecker, and Brichto rely on anachronistic parallels drawn from their own legal systems. Judges and juries in modern courts, whether in the Civil or Common Law

---

12. Bovati, *Re-Establishing Justice*, 229.

13. Ibid.

14. Boecker, *Redeformen*, 59 n. 1: *"Rechtssasse."*

15. H. C. Brichto, *Toward a Grammar of Biblical Poetics* (New York: Oxford University Press, 1992), 228.

16. H. Schulz, *Das Todesrecht im Alten Testament* (BZAW 114; Berlin: Töpelmann, 1969), 120–22.

17. V. H. Matthews, and D. C. Benjamin, *Social World of Ancient Israel 1250– 587 BCE* (Peabody, Mass.: Hendrickson, 1993), 236.

systems, have different functions; such differentiation cannot be projected back into an ancient tribunal. Schulz and Matthews and Benjamin invent novel institutions that are otherwise unknown. Even if we accept the possibility of Schulz's special "cultic court," not elsewhere attested in the Bible, the idea of a forum in which some factions address other factions but not the plenum has no parallel in any recorded legal system. Nor is it surprising, since such a cacophonic arrangement between groups within earshot of each other would be unworkable.

Similarly, Matthews and Benjamin's idea of the totality being a quorum, if taken strictly, would mean that the court could never sit, since full attendance of every possible participant is unattainable in practice. If all the people means less than everyone, on the other hand, then the phrase begs the question of what is the minimum needed for a trial to be official. It also begs the question of what makes a group action official. The one biblical text that Matthews and Benjamin cite in support illustrates the problem. In Gen 19:4, all the people of Sodom gather outside the house in which Lot is a guest and demand his production. It is difficult to see their demand as the authoritative act of a duly constituted assembly—as opposed to a threatening mob—given that the action that they are said to contemplate is hardly of a juridical nature. Nonetheless, both Schulz' and Matthews and Benjamin's analyses are helpful, as we shall see below, in their emphasis on the inclusive nature of the tribunal.

A better approach in my view is to examine the copious data from Israel's neighbors, from around the time of Jeremiah and previously. It is true that there is no evidence from the ancient Near East as to the actual formalities whereby a court was constituted. There is a great deal of evidence, on the other hand, about the composition of courts of law, indicating cultural patterns that were long-standing and widespread. Three types of forum can be discerned:

(a) A single official sitting as judge or a college referred to simply as "the judges."

(b) A large assembly of lay persons (Sumerian: *ukkin*; Akkadian: *puḫrum*; Hittite: *pankuš, tuliya*). There is never any mention of a quorum, but the members are referred to as "citizens" (*mār banî*), "the men of GN," "the sons of GN," and the like (see below under c). The qualification for membership would thus seem to be the status of an adult male citizen.

(c) A mixed tribunal of officials and citizens. This form of court was quite common. In the Neo-Babylonian and Persian periods, for example, an assembly (*puḫrum*) of free citizens (*mār banî*) or local elders (*šībūt āli*) in Babylonian cities is frequently found sitting as a court for both civil and criminal matters, sometimes

alone and sometimes in conjunction with officials, both royal and
temple.[18] In a case from the reign of Cambyses, employees of the
Eanna Temple at Uruk who stole ducks from the temple are
examined by an assembly consisting of temple administrators
and free citizens (*mār banî*) and after they confess are sentenced
by a plenary tribunal consisting of the chief administrator and the
royal treasurer of the Eanna Temple, and the assembly of the
men of Babylon and the men of Uruk.[19] In another case from the
reign of Cyrus, the city scribe of Sippar, an official of the Shamash Temple, and the elders sit in a mixed tribunal to decide
whether a slave is private or temple property (Cyr., 332), while
in a property dispute from the reign of Neriglissar, the court is
composed of the governor of Babylon, the judges, and the elders
of the city (RSM, 69).[20]

The Hittite terms *tuliya* and *pankuš*, the subject of a philological study by
G. Beckman, are particularly helpful in revealing the ancient conceptu-
alization of large, mixed tribunals. *tuliya* is the equivalent of Akkadian
puḥrum and is used to describe an assembly, inter alia, acting as a court.
pankuš as an adjective means "every." Beckman concludes that where
the noun *pankuš* stands alone, it has the meaning "totality (of those present on a given occasion)"—it is inclusive, rather than exclusive. For
example in a ritual text (*KUB*, XII, 8:3:1–4): "Then the men of GN enter.
Three men wail and the congregation (*pankuš*) sings thus…" When
employed in the political and juridical sphere, it is synonymous with
tuliya, or more precisely, the *pankuš* is assembled in a *tuliya*.[21]

   In the light of this evidence, "all the people" (כל העם) should not be
taken as an authoritative body in itself; it merely designates all those
present in the Temple. It is through the action described by the verb קהל
that they constitute themselves as a court. Although mentioned separately, the priests and prophets are also a component of the court, since
"all the people," like the *pankuš*, is an inclusive term. Thus it is that in
v. 8 Jeremiah can be said to have addressed "all the people" without
mention of the priests and the prophets, even though the previous verse

   18.   M. A. Dandamaev, "The Neo-Babylonian Citizens," *Klio* 63 (1981): 45–49;
J. Oelsner, B. Wells, and C. Wunsch, "Neo-Babylonian Period," in Westbrook, ed.,
A History of Ancient Near Eastern Law, 911–74 (919).
   19.   H. H. Figulla, "Lawsuit Concerning a Sacrilegious Theft at Erech," *Iraq* 13
(1951): 95–102.
   20.   Edited by F. Joannès, *Rendre la justice en Mésopotamie* (Saint-Denis:
Presses Universitaires de Vincennes, 2000), 234–37.
   21.   G. Beckman, "The Hittite Assembly," *JAOS* 102 (1982): 435–42 (438).

had informed us that the priests and the prophets heard it too. The court thus constituted is then joined by the nobles to form a mixed tribunal.

The whole process is referred to summarily in v. 17, where the elders address "all the קהל of the people," that is, those present constituted as a court. What formality was needed to give the court authority is not stated, but in this final form it included all those mentioned separately: the people, the priests and prophets, and the nobles. My conclusion thus supports the inclusive approach of Schulz and of Matthews and Benjamin, but is based on real ancient models, not putative ones.

If there is a technical aspect to the phrase "all the people," it is that it cannot refer to every living soul even among those present. To qualify as a court, it must exclude persons who are not eligible, such as foreigners, women, and slaves, if any were present (cf. the merism in Gen 19:4: "young men and old, all the people"). On the other hand, it would have included not only Jerusalemites but the inhabitants of the towns of Judah, whom Jeremiah had been commissioned to address in the Temple. Some of them, the "elders of the land," publicly voice their opinion during the proceedings. The examples given above from Babylonian trials are sufficient to negate Matthews and Benjamin's judgment that "from a sociological point of view these elders from a village assembly are out of place in a state court."[22]

To summarize: by the action described in v. 9 (ויקהל), the priests and prophets and the remaining male citizenry constitute themselves as a court in order to pursue Jeremiah in a formal trial. Their previous role as accusers, however, does not bode well for the fairness of the trial, for there was no rule in ancient law that precluded a man from being judge in his own cause.[23] The priests and prophets who are singled out as the motivating force behind the accusation have an obvious interest in protecting their monopoly over authorized prophecy. Fortunately, the nobles of Judah, evidently palace officials, intervene. In our understanding, they join the court that is about to sit in order to form a mixed tribunal of officials and citizens.

4. *The Trial (vv. 11ff.)*

Because the trial turns upon the law, not the facts, the proceedings have nothing of the character of a conventional hearing in which the prosecution and defence present conflicting narratives and adduce evidence in support, and the judges decide on the true version of events.

22. Matthews and Benjamin, *Social World of Ancient Israel*, 236.
23. Examples from the Bible are to be found in B. Wells, *The Law of Testimony in the Pentateuchal Codes* (Wiesbaden: Harrassowitz, 2004), 50–51.

To place the biblical report in context, I would invoke the parallel of the only other known trial report of a purely legal issue from the ancient Near East. In a murder trial conducted before the Assembly of Nippur, as reported in a literary account copied in Old Babylonian scribal schools, the established facts were that three men had conspired to kill a priest. After the murder, the conspirators had informed the victim's wife of what they had done, but she kept silent.[24] The central issue of the hearing being reported is the culpability of the victim's wife. The report presents it in the form of a debate among different factions within the Assembly. As in Jeremiah's trial, the guilt or innocence of all the accused is formulated in terms of their liability to the death penalty.

Nine men of various professions, such as bird-catcher and potter, who are clearly ordinary citizens, address the Assembly, speaking in favor of the death penalty for the conspirators and the wife. Two men, an army officer and an orchard-keeper, then argue in the woman's defence. The Assembly then deliberates (l. 43: en₃-tar-re-eš-am₃) and sides with the majority, adding its own arguments. It concludes: "her guilt exceeds (the guilt of) those who kill a man."

Here also we see the term assembly (*puḫrum*) is used in a non-exclusive manner. The report then states that the Assembly, having resolved the case, delivered all four for execution.

On the basis of this parallel, I would argue that the report of Jeremiah's trial is in fact a series of orations by factions within the court. The only difference—and it is a significant difference for the structure of the narrative—is that the defendant gets to speak on his own behalf.

5. *Oration of the Priests and Prophets (v. 11)*

The priests and prophets reiterate the charges previously made against Jeremiah. They now refer to the defendant in the third person, addressing their remarks to the nobles and all the people. Boecker takes this change to indicate that a prosecutor is addressing a court officially in session.[25] The priests and prophets do not repeat the facts, but take them as known

24. Editions by T. Jacobsen, "An Ancient Mesopotamian Trial for Homicide," in *Toward the Image of Tammuz and Other Essays on Mesopotamian History and Culture* (ed. W. L. Moran; HSS 21; Cambridge, Mass.: Harvard University Press, 1970), 193–214; and M. T. Roth, "Gender and Law: A Case Study from Ancient Mesopotamia," in *Gender and Law in the Hebrew Bible and the Ancient Near East* (ed. V. H. Matthews, B. M. Levinson, and T. Frymer-Kensky; JSOTSup 262; Sheffield: Sheffield Academic Press, 1998), 173–84.

25. Boecker, *Redeformen*, 71, 150 n. 4.

("as you have heard with your own ears"), even though a part of the court, namely the nobles, had not in fact been eyewitnesses to Jeremiah's prophesying. The latter are deemed to be cognizant of the facts. The issue is thus one of pure law. When the priests and prophets put the case for the prosecution, they are not presenting to the court a version of events (nor, obviously, evidence to support it), but a legal argument. They function as a faction within the tribunal rather than as an external entity.

As we have seen, the offence is not made explicit in the accusation. It only emerges from Jeremiah's defence that he is accused of falsely purporting to prophesy in the name of YHWH. The argument of the priests and prophets appears to be that Jeremiah's lack of a mandate is self-evident from the content of his prophecy. They thereby infer that a "wait and see" test, such as prescribed in Deut 18:21–22 (if the prophecy is fulfilled, it came from YHWH), would not be applicable.

6. *Jeremiah's Oration (vv. 12–15)*

Jeremiah's speech to the court in his defence:
(a)   agrees upon the facts (v. 12, "all the words that you have heard");
(b)   asserts his divine mandate from YHWH;
(c)   points out that the prophecy is conditional, and may be averted by appropriate measures. This argument may also be an oblique reference to a "wait and see" test, effectively neutralizing its danger for Jeremiah. It places responsibility for his prophecy not being fulfilled with the government and people (cf. Jonah 3:4–10);
(d)   warns the court of the consequences of a guilty verdict. Bovati adduces this verse in support of his view that there is no such thing as a "neutral" defence; defence is to accuse the accuser.[26] His analysis, however, does not fit the account of the trial. Jeremiah addresses not those who have accused him ("the priests and prophets" or even "the priests and prophets and all the people") but emphatically the whole court ("all the nobles and all the people"). It is not a charge of false accusation that he is bringing, but a warning of perversion of justice through a wrongful verdict. If the trial had turned on an issue of fact, then the court, even if it had wrongly convicted the accused, could claim its innocence because it had been misled by the false evidence of the accusers. There is no such escape for the court here, where

26.   Bovati, *Re-Establishing Justice*, 331–32, especially n. 161.

the issue is purely one of law: Do Jeremiah's words amount to
false prophecy (without allowing for "wait and see")? A guilty
verdict would therefore be a conscious wrongdoing (according to
Jeremiah), and execution of the death sentence would amount to
murder. Furthermore, murder pollutes the immediate area where
it has been committed and the persons implicated. An official
verdict of the Jerusalem court would pollute the members of the
court, the city, and its inhabitants. Thus the wheel will come full
circle: pollution in turn will bring down divine wrath, with similar
consequences to the curse pronounced in the original prophecy.

7. *Oration of the Nobles and All the People (v. 16)*

The remainder of the court rejects the argument of the priests and
prophets, addressing them as an isolated minority. Although the inference
is that the overwhelming majority unreservedly embraces Jeremiah's
argument, curiously, no reasoning is presented, only a conclusion of
Jeremiah's innocence. It should logically mark the end of the report, even
if not followed by an explicit notice of Jeremiah's acquittal. Instead, the
narrative continues with notices of the fate of two other prophets.

It is these extra verses that have done most to persuade scholars that
the chapter is a composite account that has lost any pristine coherence it
might have had through editing.[27] It is true that they appear to disrupt the
chronological (and logical) sequence followed hitherto and seem otiose
after the climax of the court's pronouncement in v. 16. Brichto, however,
has rightly discerned that a deliberate narrative technique is employed
here: "...this chapter exploits the narrative technique of dividing the
story into episodes, a synoptic episode relating the entire story in brief,
followed by a resumptive episode in which additional details are
provided."[28]

Brichto does not explain the advantage of this technique, which seems
to result in a resounding anti-climax. That, in my view, is exactly the
point. The narrative is not a dry court report but a propagandistic account
of the trial. The purpose of the narrator (or editor) is to paint Jeremiah in
the best light. The progress of the trial is sketched in the bold lines of a
good courtroom drama: Jeremiah is accused, Jeremiah makes a magnifi-
cent speech in his own defence, the court acquits him. The impression is

---

27. Typical is the judgment of O'Connor: "The inconsistencies and contradic-
tions of these verses...indicate that vv 17–24 do not form part of the original
narrative" ("Do Not Trim a Word," 623).

28. Brichto, *Toward a Grammar of Biblical Poetics*, 227.

thereby given that it was Jeremiah's speech that won the day. There are, however, two inconvenient facts that would temper this impression and for that reason they are relegated to postscripts. Paradoxically, the structure of the narrative, in seeking to play down uncomfortable facts, vouches for the basic credibility of the report.

8. *Oration of Members of the Elders of the Land (vv. 17–19)*

Those elders who address the court (apparently not all of them) are once again a faction within the forensic assembly. They are among the inhabitants of the cities of Judah who had come to Jerusalem to worship at the Temple, and would thus have been among Jeremiah's audience who were subsequently constituted as a court, albeit (the text emphasizes) a small minority.

The elders present arguments that directly correspond to Jeremiah's (in a way that the statement of the court in v. 16 does not): a previous prophet had made a conditional prophecy of disaster; King Hezekiah's government had heeded him and taken the appropriate apotropaic measures; the disaster was thereby averted; to act otherwise in this case would be a wrongful act with dire consequences for the perpetrators. This argument from precedent may well have been decisive, as Schulz claims, or at least may have had more weight in the court's decision than Jeremiah's oration. Certainly, it was sufficiently important that it could not be omitted from a report of the trial. The narrative, however, relegates it to a postscript after the acclamation that Jeremiah's words receive, so as to give the impression that the latter's rhetoric brought about his acquittal.

9. *The Case of Uriah (vv. 20–24)*

A second example is given of a prophet who gave much the same message as Jeremiah, but who was pursued, extradited, and executed by King Jehoakim. The case is distinguished from the present one by the protection given Jeremiah by a royal official. Bovati argues that this and the previous notice are both part of the speech by the elders, who present two contradictory precedents. The latter is to be followed, since it was a decision of the reigning king. Accordingly, Jeremiah had by no means been acquitted by the nobles in v. 16, but the trial continues and would have ended in Jeremiah's execution were it not for the intervention of the official in an unstated manner.[29]

---

29. Bovati, *Re-Establishing Justice*, 331–33 n. 161. Brichto attributes the second precedent to another set of elders, but no mention is made of them in the text (*Toward a Grammar of Biblical Poetics*, 228–29).

It is anachronistic to turn the elders into some form of legal experts who summarize the relevant precedents (like the official in some trials in modern Civil Law systems). From the pattern of the Nippur Homicide Trial, it is more likely that the elders argued for one point of view only. As elders, they would be the obvious repository of memories of a case that had occurred more than a hundred years earlier. Their expertise counter-balances any expertise that the priests and prophets could claim in the assessment of prophecy.

In my view, the second notice is not part of the forensic debate. A vague reference to the content of the prophecy cited as being "just like the words of Jeremiah" begs the very questions (the content of the prophecy and its conditionality) that are at issue. It uses the language of the outside narrator (the reliable narrator, as Brichto calls him), not the language of the participants in the debate, who refer to Jeremiah as "this man" (vv. 11 and 16).[30] On Bovati's hypothesis, it is difficult to explain how the intervention of the royal official Ahikam son of Shaphan could have taken place. Ahikam neither presents arguments nor is he assigned any forensic role.

Above all other verses of the chapter, v. 24 is regarded by scholars as the ultimate misfit. Attributing the outcome of Jeremiah's trial to the intervention of a named official, in unexplained circumstances, seems to contradict the verdict, if not the whole of the proceedings just previously narrated. "Not only is Jeremiah's rescue mysterious in v 24; the reason he requires rescue is also obscure."[31] Nonetheless, it is my opinion that v. 24 is an integral part of the second postscript and vital to understanding the course of the trial and its result.

The second postscript, by the narrator, is a further acknowledgment that in reality it was not just Jeremiah's inspired rhetoric that won his trial. The last-minute participation by the nobles ensured that the court was sufficiently stacked in Jeremiah's favor—enough to overcome the unfavorable reaction that his preaching had previously aroused in its

---

30. Stipp suggests that the phrase "concerning this city and this land" in v. 20 indicates direct forensic speech (*Jeremia im Parteienstreit*, 20–21). On the contrary, it is simply a quotation from the prophecy, to show its parallel with Jeremiah's prophecy "concerning this house" and "this city" (v. 6). The meaning of the verse is: there was another man who made an "about this house and city" prophecy just like Jeremiah. Cf. C. Hardmeier, "Die Propheten Micha und Jesaja im Spiegel von Jeremia xxvi und 2 Regum xviii-xx: Zur Prophetie-Rezeption in der nach-joschijanischen Zeit," in *Congress Volume: Leuven, 1989* (ed. J. A. Emerton; VTSup 43; Leiden: Brill, 1991), 172–89 (177).

31. O'Connor, "Do Not Trim a Word," 624.

audience. The nobles' intervention seems unmotivated until we realize that it was the work of Ahikam, who had persuaded his fellow courtiers to act.[32]

Thus it was the influence of Jeremiah's friends at court already at the outset of the trial, with help from a few local dignitaries who managed to dredge up an old precedent, that was really responsible for Jeremiah's acquittal.

32. For Ahikam's position, see Lundbom, *Jeremiah 21–36*, 298–99. On the role of the Shaphanides, see B. Seidel, "Freunde und Feinde Jeremias unter den Beamten Judas der spätvorexilischen Zeit," *BZ* 41 (1997): 28–53. The narrative implies in v. 10 that it was entirely an initiative of the nobles, without the king's knowledge. This time Jeremiah is being saved from the people, not from the king, but it would not be wise to let the king hear of it. In Jer 36:10–19, where the prophet's message has been committed to writing, courtiers sympathetic to him (including Ahikam's brother) feel themselves unable to hide it from the king, so they hide Jeremiah instead.

Part III

READING THE LAW IN THE WRITINGS

READING, SINGING AND PRAYING THE LAW: AN EXPLORATION OF THE PERFORMATIVE, SELF-INVOLVING, COMMISSIVE LANGUAGE OF PSALM 101*

Karl Möller

1. *Introduction*

The title of the present collection of essays, *Reading the Law*, reflects Gordon Wenham's long-standing interest in the Pentateuch or Torah,[1] in biblical ethics[2] and in biblical criticism and hermeneutics, that is, in how

---

* I wish to thank Dr Thomas Renz, who kindly read and very helpfully commented upon an earlier draft of this essay.

1. This is exemplified by his 1970 doctoral dissertation, "The Structure and Date of Deuteronomy: A Consideration of Aspects of the History of Deuteronomy Criticism and a Re-Examination of the Question of Structure and Date in the Light of That History and of the Near Eastern Treaties" (King's College, University of London), his commentaries on Genesis (*Genesis 1–15* [WBC 1; Dallas: Word Books, 1987]; and *Genesis 16–50* [WBC 2; Dallas: Word Books, 1994]), Leviticus (*The Book of Leviticus* [NICOT; Grand Rapids: Eerdmans, 1979]) and Numbers (*Numbers: An Introduction and Commentary* [TOTC; Leicester: InterVarsity, 1981]; see also *Numbers* [OTG; Sheffield: Sheffield Academic Press, 1997]), his recent textbook on the Pentateuch (*The Pentateuch* [Exploring the Old Testament 1; London: SPCK, 2003]) and many articles on the Pentateuch and its interpretation, including "Pondering the Pentateuch," in *The Face of Old Testament Studies: A Survey of Contemporary Approaches* (ed. David W. Baker and Bill T. Arnold; Grand Rapids: Baker Book House, 1999), 116–44.

2. See "The Restoration of Marriage Reconsidered," *JJS* 30 (1979): 36–40; "Matthew and Divorce: An Old Crux Revisited," *JSNT* 22 (1984): 95–107; "Attitudes to Homosexuality in the OT," *ExpTim* 102 (1991): 359–63; "The Gap Between Law and Ethics in the Bible," *JJS* 48 (1997): 17–29; *Story as Torah: Reading Old Testament Narrative Ethically* (OTS; Edinburgh: T. & T. Clark, 2000); "The Ethics of the Psalms," in *Interpreting the Psalms: Issues and Approaches* (ed. Philip S. Johnston and David G. Firth; Leicester: Apollos, 2005), 175–94; Gordon J. Wenham and William E. Heth, *Jesus and Divorce* (2d ed.; Carlisle: Paternoster, 1997); and Gordon J. Wenham, William A. Heth and Craig S. Keener, *Remarriage*

we *read* the biblical texts.[3] More recently, Wenham has turned his attention to "the ethics inculcated by the Psalms, an area that seems to have been largely overlooked by recent biblical scholarship."[4]

In the present study I intend to make a small contribution to the long overdue exploration of this area by considering the function of the statements in Ps 101 that talk about the king's determination to observe the standards of God's law. A number of commentators have noted that the king's self-committing declarations, together with the reference to Yahweh's loyalty and justice (חסד and משפט) in v. 1, suggest that our psalm needs to be understood against the background of the covenant.[5] This justifies an approach that considers Ps 101 as a reading of, or a reflection upon, the Torah,[6] which after all contains an elucidation of the ethical standards of the covenant.

In his exploration of the ethics of the Psalms, Wenham has identified some key themes, such as references to the principles of the Decalogue and an approach to ethics "through the description of the righteous and the wicked,"[7] which leads to the principle that "the righteous are supposed

---

after Divorce in Today's Church: 3 Views (ed. Mark L. Strauss; Grand Rapids: Zondervan, 2006).

3.   Gordon Wenham's interest in biblical criticism and hermeneutics is most apparent in his works on Pentateuchal criticism and interpretation (e.g. "Method in Pentateuchal Source Criticism," *VT* 41 [1991]: 84–109; and "The Priority of P," *VT* 49 [1999]: 240–58), his adoption of the insights associated with literary critics such as Edwin Good, Jacob Licht, Robert Alter, Meir Sternberg and others in his two-volume Genesis commentary, his engagement with the work of cultural anthropologist Mary Douglas in the commentary on Leviticus and his more recent deployment of rhetorical criticism in *Story as Torah*.

4.   Wenham, "The Ethics of the Psalms," 194.

5.   The covenant is mentioned in connection with Ps 101 by Sigmund Mowinckel, *The Psalms in Israel's Worship* (trans. D. R. Ap-Thomas; 2 vols.; repr. of the first English edition [Oxford: Basil Blackwell, 1962], Grand Rapids: Eerdmans, 2004), 1:66, 68; Hans-Joachim Kraus, *Die Königsherrschaft Gottes im Alten Testament: Untersuchungen zu den Liedern von Jahwes Thronbesteigung* (BHT 13; Tübingen: J. C. B. Mohr [Paul Siebeck], 1951), 75; Otto Kaiser, "Erwägungen zu Psalm 101," *ZAW* 74 (1962): 195–205 (202); Helen Ann Kenik, "Code of Conduct for a King: Psalm 101," *JBL* 95 (1976): 391–403 (esp. 403); Leslie C. Allen, *Psalms 101–150* (WBC 21; Waco, Tex.: Word, 1983), 3; Konrad Schaefer, *Psalms* (Berit Olam: Studies in Hebrew Narrative & Poetry; Collegeville, Minn.: Liturgical Press, 2001), 249; and Adrian Curtis, *Psalms* (Epworth Commentaries; Peterborough: Epworth, 2004), 201.

6.   Again, the Torah is referred to in connection with Ps 101 by Hans-Joachim Kraus, *Psalms 60–150: A Continental Commentary* (trans. Hilton C. Oswald; Minneapolis: Fortress, 1993), 278.

7.   Wenham, "The Ethics of the Psalms," 187.

to imitate God."[8] Wenham considers Ps 101 as an example of the latter, but most importantly he notes that "this identification with the divine standpoint extends to everyone who prays the Psalms."[9] It is this notion of us identifying with the divine standpoint that I wish to investigate. In reading, singing or praying Ps 101 we, as readers in the twenty-first century, are reading, singing or praying Israel's ancient law. More importantly, in rehearsing the king's self-involving language we too are committing ourselves to the ethical values promoted in this psalm.

Utilizing some concepts associated with speech act theory, I intend to examine this notion of self-involvement and the light it might shed on our reading of a text like Ps 101. However, before I invoke the concepts of speech act theory, it is important to have a close look at the psalm's genre, setting and function.

2. *The Genre, Setting and Function of Psalm 101*

A good number of psalms concerned with ethical conduct are couched in third-person language: "Happy are *those who do not follow* the advice of the wicked" (Ps 1:1);[10] "O LORD, who may abide in your tent? Who may dwell on your holy hill? *Those who walk blamelessly*, and do what is right…" (Ps 15:1–2); "Who shall ascend the hill of the LORD? And who shall stand in his holy place? *Those who have clean hands and pure hearts*…" (Ps 24:3–4); "Give the king your justice, O God, and your righteousness to a king's son. *May he judge* your people with righteousness, and your poor with justice" (Ps 72:1–2); "Happy are *those who fear* the LORD, who greatly delight in his commandments" (Ps 112:1).[11]

---

8. Ibid., 192.

9. Ibid., 193.

10. Unfortunately, the translation of the NRSV obscures the fact that in the Hebrew (which has אֲשֶׁר יִהָאִישׁ) it is the individual who is pitched against the crowd. The scenario envisaged by our text is that of "the one against the many," the "moral individual" against the "immoral society," as Sarna rightly notes (see Nahum M. Sarna, *On the Book of Psalms: Exploring the Prayers of Ancient Israel* [New York: Schocken, 1995]; originally publ. in 1993 as *Songs of the Heart: An Introduction to the Book of Psalms* [New York: Schocken], 25, 31; see also Norbert Lohfink, "Die Einsamkeit des Gerechten: Zu Psalm 1," in his *Im Schatten deiner Flügel: Große Bibeltexte neu erschlossen* [Freiburg: Herder, 1999], 163–71).

11. Again, in Pss 15:2 and 24:4 the Hebrew text uses masculine singular participles, which are rendered in the singular by RSV, ESV and NIV. The opening of Ps 112 parallels Ps 1 in its use of אֲשֶׁר־אִישׁ. NRSV'S striving for political correctness in the use of non-gendered language, which is laudable to be sure, once again unfortunately obscures the wording of the Hebrew.

Psalm 101, by contrast, employs first-person verbs ("*I will walk* with integrity of heart," v. 2) and thus, with the obvious exception of Ps 119, is perhaps one of the best examples of "the self-involving language of worship"[12] being used with a clear ethical thrust. An initial reading in English translation suggests that Ps 101 contains an individual's vow concerning their future conduct. However, a survey of twentieth-century Psalms scholarship reveals that this is not the only possible interpretation, which is perhaps not surprising, given that the tenses employed by the psalmist can be construed as future or past. How they are understood depends largely on our perception of the psalm's genre, setting and function as well as the question in v. 2.

As regards the genre of Ps 101, Allen is not alone in noting that our passage "is difficult to analyze in form-critical terms."[13] McCann even claims that it "has always been something of an enigma to commentators."[14] According to Kenik, it "consists of no clearly defined *Gattung*";[15] and Broyles maintains that "the genre and function of this psalm are difficult to determine because it is unique."[16] Earlier on, Mowinckel had suggested that "elements from hymn and psalm of lament and prayer are here combined to make a new unity."[17]

However, this uncertainty about the psalm's form-critical classification has not prevented scholars from reaching conclusions concerning its function. For instance, Allen notes that most commentators regard Ps 101 as a vow of loyalty "whereby the king commits himself to the ideals of the Davidic covenant."[18] Mowinckel speaks of a new king's "charter," characterizing Ps 101 as a psalm of promise[19] and a vow "to rule Yahweh's people wisely."[20] Croft regards it as "a solemn

---

12. Wenham, "The Ethics of the Psalms," 194.

13. Allen, *Psalms 101–150*, 3.

14. J. Clinton McCann, Jr., "The Book of Psalms: Introduction, Commentary, and Reflections," in *The New Interpreter's Bible*. Vol. 4, *The First Book of Maccabees, The Second Book of Maccabees, Introduction to Hebrew Poetry, The Book of Job, The Book of Psalms* (ed. Leander E. Keck et al.; Nashville: Abingdon, 1996), 639–1280 (1081).

15. Kenik, "Code of Conduct for a King," 391.

16. Craig C. Broyles, *Psalms* (NIBCOT 11; Peabody, Mass.: Hendrickson, 1999), 388.

17. Mowinckel, *The Psalms in Israel's Worship*, 1:66.

18. Allen, *Psalms 101–150*, 3.

19. Mowinckel, *The Psalms in Israel's Worship*, 1:65, 67.

20. Ibid., 1:56; similarly Hermann Gunkel, "Die Psalmen," in *Zur neueren Psalmenforschung* (ed. Peter H. A. Neumann; Darmstadt: Wissenschaftliche Buchgesellschaft, 1976), 19–54 (51).

confession" of the king's "intent to administer justice in his realm,"[21] a "promise to Yahweh for the coming year" and an "oath of allegiance."[22] Weiser speaks of "the lofty ideal principles whereby the conduct of a ruler shall be guided,"[23] Crim of the "king's statement of loyalty to the ethical demands of his office,"[24] Kidner of a "king's resolve,"[25] Mays of a "declaration of commitment to the righteous conduct that belonged to the ideal of a king"[26] and a "vow to develop a character and to practice a life that is coherent with a theological morality."[27] Terrien calls our psalm a "royal program,"[28] Davidson a "royal manifesto,"[29] Curtis a "declaration of intent,"[30] Broyles a vow.[31] Kraus, having similarly identified vv. 2–8 as a "declaration of loyalty," is adamant that the speaker of the psalm does not look back to the past but offers some kind of vow,[32] committing himself to pure and loyal conduct in the future. In this respect, Ps 101 differs from Ps 18:22–24 [Eng. 21–23] with its backward-looking purification oath.

Turning to the setting of our psalm, we begin by noting that what Kaiser calls the earlier, historicizing approach to the Psalms[33] had concluded that it is a prayer by David as he renews his procession with

21. Steven J. L. Croft, *The Identity of the Individual in the Psalms* (JSOTSup 44; Sheffield: JSOT Press, 1987), 29. Croft's choice of the term "confession" seems somewhat odd, given that what he has in mind is a declaration of intent.

22. Ibid., 100.

23. Artur Weiser, *The Psalms: A Commentary* (trans. Herbert Hartwell; OTL; London: SCM Press, 1962), 649.

24. Keith R. Crim, *The Royal Psalms* (Richmond, Va.: John Knox, 1962), 111–12.

25. Derek Kidner, *Psalms 73–150: A Commentary on Books III–V of the Psalms* (TOTC 14b; Leicester: InterVarsity, 1973), 357.

26. James L. Mays, *Psalms* (IBC; Louisville, Ky.: John Knox, 1994), 321.

27. Ibid., 322.

28. Samuel Terrien, *The Psalms: Strophic Structure and Theological Commentary* (The Eerdmans Critical Commentary; Grand Rapids: Eerdmans, 2003), 692.

29. Robert Davidson, *The Vitality of Worship: A Commentary on the Book of Psalms* (Grand Rapids: Eerdmans, 1998), 328–29.

30. Curtis, *Psalms*, 201. Martin Leuenberger, *Konzeptionen des Königtums Gottes im Psalter: Untersuchungen zu Komposition und Redaktion der theokratischen Bücher IV–V im Psalter* (ATANT 83; Zurich: Theologischer Verlag, 2004), 172, similarly speaks of a *"königliche Deklaration."*

31. Broyles, *Psalms*, 388.

32. Kraus, *Psalms 60–150*, 277; for a similar view see Terrien, *Psalms*, 691–94; and William L. Holladay, *The Psalms Through Three Thousand Years: Prayerbook of a Cloud of Witnesses* (Minneapolis: Fortress, 1993), 38.

33. Kaiser, "Erwägungen zu Psalm 101," 197.

the ark to Jerusalem,[34] that it "belongs to the time during which the Ark was in the house of Obed-Edom, where David had left it behind through terror at the misfortune of Uzzah,"[35] or that it is a song celebrating the accession to power of the Maccabean ruler Jonathan.[36] Explanations such as these have now been largely abandoned, however.[37]

Eaton captures the general drift of recent scholarship well in speaking of "a formal, ceremonial setting." However, he is far less in tune with current Psalms interpretation in envisaging a connection of Ps 101 with the rites of enthronement or their renewal associated with the autumn festival.[38] In this Eaton follows the lead of scholars such as Mowinckel, Hooke and the Uppsala school, represented by Engnell and Widengren, who have sought to understand (many of) the royal psalms against the background of the Babylonian New Year or *akitu* festival.[39]

34. Thus A. F. Kirkpatrick, *The Book of Psalms* (Cambridge: Cambridge University Press, 1902), 589–90; and Wilhelm Martin Leberecht de Wette, *Commentar über die Psalmen* (ed. Gustav Baur; 5th ed.; Heidelberg: J. C. B. Mohr, 1856), 495.

35. Franz Delitzsch, *Psalms* (Commentary on the Old Testament 5; repr. of the first English edition [Edinburgh: T. & T. Clark, 1871], Peabody, Mass.: Hendrickson, 1996), 637–38.

36. Ferdinand Hitzig, *Die Psalmen übersetzt und ausgelegt* (2 vols.; Leipzig: C. F. Winter, 1863–65), 2:269; and Bernhard Duhm, *Die Psalmen* (KHAT 14; 2d ed.; Freiburg: J. C. B. Mohr [Paul Siebeck], 1922), 364.

37. For instance, Th. Booij, "Psalm CI 2—'When Wilt Thou Come to Me?,'" *VT* 38 (1988): 458–62 (458), notes that "it does not seem plausible that Jerusalem was called the city of YHWH [as in Ps 101:8] before the ark was taken there." Based on his analysis of the composition and redaction of the book of Psalms, Leuenberger (*Konzeptionen des Königtums Gottes im Psalter*, 173–74), has recently argued that in Books 4 and 5 the phrase לדוד does not imply any historical reference to David or the time of David. This precludes any historicizing explanation that attempts to relate the psalms contained in these books to specific situations in the life of David. Back in the nineteenth century, historicizing interpretations had already been challenged by Hermann Hupfeld, *Die Psalmen übersetzt und ausgelegt* (4 vols.; Gotha: F. A. Perthes, 1855–62), 3:68.

38. John Eaton, *The Psalms: A Historical and Spiritual Commentary with an Introduction and New Translation* (London: T&T Clark International, 2003), 351.

39. See Peter H. A. Neumann, "Einleitung," in Neumann, ed., *Zur neueren Psalmenforschung*, 1–18 (13–14). For Mowinckel's views on this issue, see *The Psalms in Israel's Worship*, 1:56, 66–67; cf. also S. H. Hooke, "Myth and Ritual: Past and Present," in *Myth, Ritual and Kingship: Essays on the Theory and Practice of Kingship on the Ancient Near East and in Israel* (ed. S. H. Hooke; Oxford: Clarendon, 1958), 1–21; and Geo Widengren, "Early Hebrew Myths and Their Interpretation," in Hooke, ed., *Myth, Ritual and Kingship*, 149–203. Other scholars who have assumed an enthronement setting include Kurt Galling, "Der Beichtspiegel: Eine gattungsgeschichtliche Studie," *ZAW* 6 (1929): 125–30 (128); Nic. H. Ridderbos, "Psalmen und Kult" (trans. Heinz Wolters), in Neumann, ed., *Zur neueren Psalmen-*

Many who advocate this view argue that the focus of the king's words in Ps 101 is on his past rather than his future conduct.[40] The king, that is to say, is pleading his just rule hitherto in a setting that has been compared by Johnson to the symbolic rite of humiliation found in the *akitu* festival.[41]

Interestingly, however, ascertaining the setting of Ps 101 in and of itself does not lead to a conclusive answer as to whether its focus is on the king's past or future actions. This is best illustrated by comparing the views of Johnson and Mowinckel who agree in relating our passage to a setting that is comparable to the *akitu* festival. They part company, however, when it comes to determining the tenses of the verbs, for whereas Johnson thought that the past was in view in our text, Mowinckel opted for a future interpretation.

This takes us back to the question of the psalm's genre, because having referred to the views of those who regard our passage as a vow of loyalty, a king's charter or an oath of allegiance, we now need to take account of the fact that scholars preferring to take vv. 2b–8 as relating to the king's past conduct have come to different conclusions. Pointing to the *qinah* metre found in these verses, a number of interpreters have argued that we are dealing with a lament, an individual complaint or a supplication from distress, with vv. 2b–8 being said to be comparable to the Babylonian king's protestation of innocence made on the occasion of the *akitu* festival.[42] That is to say, having asked God when he will come to his rescue (v. 2a), the Israelite king in vv. 2b–8 goes on to talk about his past conduct, which was blameless, thus meriting Yahweh's salvific intervention on the king's behalf.

forschung, 234–79 (275); and James L. Crenshaw, *The Psalms: An Introduction* (Grand Rapids: Eerdmans, 2001), 78.

40. See, e.g., Aubrey R. Johnson, *Sacral Kingship in Ancient Israel* (2d ed.; Cardiff: University of Wales Press, 1967), 113–14; Mitchell Dahood, *Psalms III: 101–150: Introduction, Translation, and Notes with an Appendix: The Grammar of the Psalter* (AB 17A; New York: Doubleday, 1970), 2; and Allen, *Psalms 101–150, ad loc.*

Booij, "Psalm CI 2," 459, noting that the *Lutherbibel* renders the imperfects in vv. 2b–8 in the present tense, has argued that they "point to an existing situation." Thus, rather than talking about the past or the future, the king claims *always* to live by the standards laid out in these verses.

41. On the *akitu* festival, see now Julye Bidmead, *The* Akitu *Festival: Religious Continuity and Royal Legitimation in Mesopotamia* (Gorgias Dissertations: Near Eastern Studies 2; Piscataway, N.J.: Gorgias, 2002).

42. Thus, e.g., Johnson, *Sacral Kingship in Ancient Israel*; Dahood, *Psalms III*, 2; Allen, *Psalms 101–150*, 4; John S. Kselman, "Psalm 101: Royal Confession and Divine Oracle," *JSOT* 33 (1985): 45–62; and Eaton, *Psalms*, 351.

While this is not the place to offer a detailed critique of the views of those who interpret Ps 101 in the light of the *akitu* festival,[43] some comments are pertinent at this point. First of all, it is important to note that, in contrast to the strong focus on ancient Near Eastern cultic-mystical schemes that characterized Swedish Psalms scholarship in particular,[44] there has been a tendency in German interpretation of the royal psalms to relate them to Israelite traditions, such as the Nathan oracle in 2 Sam 7, instead.[45]

Secondly, it is worth pointing out that Croft has proposed an alternative reconstruction of the royal humiliation ritual to the one suggested by Johnson and Eaton,[46] arguing that Ps 101 is part of this royal ritual.

43. See, however, Davidson's assessment, in *The Vitality of Worship*, 328, that "the details...of such a festival are far from clear...and [that] it is questionable whether it is needed to account for the language of this psalm."

44. See the views of Mowinckel, Engnell and Widengren mentioned earlier.

45. This was of course the view of Gerhard von Rad, "Erwägungen zu den Königspsalmen," *ZAW* 58 (1940–41): 216–22. Kraus, *Die Königsherrschaft Gottes im Alten Testament*, 74–75, does not detect any specific allusions to the Nathan oracle in Ps 101, but he does relate it to an Israelite institution in speaking of the royal Zion festival (*"dem königlichen Zionfest"*).

The existence of an Israelite enthronement festival celebrating Yahweh's enthronement in analogy to that of an ancient Near Eastern king has been denied by Diethelm Michel, "Studien zu den sogenannten Thronbesteigungspsalmen," *VT* 6 (1956): 40–68; and Werner H. Schmidt, *Königtum Gottes in Ugarit und Israel: Zur Herkunft der Gottesprädikation Jahwes* (BZAW 80; 2d ed.; Berlin: Alfred Töpelmann, 1966), esp. 74–79. For a different view, see Odil Hannes Steck, *Friedensvorstellungen im alten Jerusalem: Psalmen, Jesaja, Deuterojesaja* (ThSt 111; Zurich: Theologischer Verlag, 1972), 10, 15 (esp. nn. 7, 8, 16), who does not, however, include Ps 101 among the psalms identified as part of the cultic ceremony celebrating Yahweh's enthronement.

For further discussion of the issues mentioned in this paragraph, see Martin Noth, "Gott, König, Volk im Alten Testament: Eine methodologische Auseinandersetzung mit einer gegenwärtigen Forschungsrichtung," *ZTK* 47 (1950): 157–91; Karl-Heinz Bernhardt, *Das Problem der altorientalischen Königsideologie im Alten Testament, unter besonderer Berücksichtigung der Geschichte der Psalmenexegese dargestellt und kritisch gewürdigt* (VTSup 8; Leiden: E. J. Brill, 1961); Hans-Joachim Kraus, *Geschichte der historisch-kritischen Erforschung des Alten Testaments* (4th ed.; Neukirchen–Vluyn: Neukirchener, 1988), §97; and John Day, *Psalms* (OTG; Sheffield: Sheffield Academic Press, 1992), Chapter 5.

46. John Eaton, *Kingship and the Psalms* (London: SCM Press, 1976; 2d ed.: The Biblical Seminar 3; Sheffield: JSOT Press, 1986), built upon Johnson's work on Pss 18, 89 and 118 in relation to the Babylonian humiliation rites, arguing that all the royal psalms identified by Gunkel ought to be understood in this context. Later on, in *Festal Drama in Deutero-Isaiah* (London: SPCK, 1979), Eaton modified his position, allowing for the possibility that some royal psalms might be best interpreted in

Again, this is not the place to offer a full discussion of Croft's proposal, but it should be noted that he is able to make sense both of the *qinah* metre and the question in v. 2a (to which we shall turn in a moment) while still taking the statements in vv. 2b–8 as referring to the future, which even Eaton concedes is "the more obvious [solution] grammatically."[47] Croft maintains:

> The lament metre of the psalm and the otherwise difficult phrase מתי תבוא אלי ("When wilt thou come to me?") are both adequately explained by the fact that the king, having made his confession [this Croft finds in Pss 5; 7; 17; 26; 139], probably in the ritual dress of sackcloth and ashes and with fasting, is now waiting for his vindication in the festal epiphany of Yahweh. The oath or promise for the future in vv. 2b–8 forms the counterpart to the earlier confession: having given account of his stewardship over the previous year he promises to continue to show righteousness in all his dealings in the year to come.[48]

At this point, some further comments on the metre of Ps 101 are in order. Some, like Dahood, are adamant that the entire psalm "is a lament composed in a uniform 3+2 or *Qinah* meter."[49] Others, however, have found it more difficult to be quite so categorical. For instance, according to Kraus, there are exceptions to the 3+2 *qinah* metre in v. 5aγ/b, which has a 4+2 metre.[50] Booij similarly notes that sometimes the metre is 4+2 (or 2+2+2), that is, in v. 3 line 1, v. 4 and v. 5 line 2; in v. 8a Booij finds

---

relation to other ceremonies. For Eaton's comments on Ps 101 in relation to these questions, see his *Psalms*, 351.

Johnson's earliest work on these issues was "The Role of the King in the Jerusalem Cultus," in *The Labyrinth: Further Studies in the Relation between Myth and Ritual in the Ancient World* (ed. S. H. Hooke; London: SPCK, 1935), 73–111; but see also his *Sacral Kingship in Ancient Israel*. Eaton was not the only scholar to build on Johnson's work; another example is Ivan Engnell, *Studies in Divine Kingship in the Ancient Near East* (Uppsala: Almquist & Wiksells, 1943; 2d ed.: Oxford: Basil Blackwell, 1967). For criticisms of the notion of an Israelite royal humiliation rite, see Mowinckel, *The Psalms in Israel's Worship*, 2:253–55; Tryggve N. D. Mettinger, *King and Messiah: The Civil and Sacral Legitimation of the Israelite Kings* (ConBOT 8; Lund: C. W. K. Gleerup, 1976), 307; Croft, *The Identity of the Individual in the Psalms*, 85–88; and Day, *Psalms*, 105–6, among others.

47. Eaton, *Psalms*, 515.

48. Croft, *The Identity of the Individual in the Psalms*, 100.

49. Dahood, *Psalms III*, 2; see also Oswald Loretz, *Die Königspsalmen: Die altorientalisch-kanaanäische Königstradition in jüdischer Sicht. Teil 1: Ps 20, 21, 72, 101 und 144* (UBL 6; Münster: Ugarit-Verlag, 1988), 162.

50. Kraus, *Psalms 60–150*, 277; see also Kaiser, "Erwägungen zu Psalm 101," 198.

a 2+2 metre.[51] Interestingly, therefore, according to Booij, there are significant parts where the metre is not the 3+2 *qinah* metre characteristic
for laments. In addition, it has been shown that the *qinah* metre can be
used also in other texts and therefore does not automatically render the
passage in question a lament.[52]

This then takes us to the question in v. 2, מתי תבוא אלי, which has
led to much discussion among commentators. The wording itself is
straightforward enough and has been translated along the lines of "when
will you come to me?" by RSV, ESV and NIV.[53] However, some commentators, arguing that a question is rather unexpected and out of place in the
context of Ps 101, have treated v. 2aβ as a gloss[54] or have emended מתי
to אמת ("truth"), reading "truth will come" or "may truth come."[55] Yet

51. Booij, "Psalm CI 2," 461 n. 7.

52. See, e.g., Nivard Johann Schlögl, *Psalmen, aus dem kritisch hergestellten
hebräischen Urtext ins Deutsche metrisch übersetzt und erläutert* (Die heiligen
Schriften des alten Bundes 3; Vienna, 1915), xv; and J. P. M. van der Ploeg,
Psalmen: uit de grondtekst vertaald en uitgelegd (De boeken van het Oude Testa-
ment 7; Roermond: Romen, 1974), 2:168. See also in this context Raymond de
Hoop, "Lamentations: The Qinah-Metre Questioned," in *Delimitation Criticism: A
New Tool in Biblical Scholarship* (ed. Marjo C. A. Korpel and Josef M. Oesch;
Pericope 1; Assen: Van Gorcum, 2000), 80–104.

53. The NRSV translates "when shall I attain it?," which is essentially a different
way of saying "when will *it* come to me?" The translators of the NRSV therefore
identify the subject of the phrase not as God, but as the attaining of the "blameless
way."

54. Thus, e.g., Justus Olshausen, *Die Psalmen* (Kurzgefasstes exegetisches
Handbuch zum Alten Testament; Leipzig: S. Hirzel, 1853), 391; Charles Augustus
Briggs and Emilie Grace Briggs, *The Book of Psalms* (ICC; 2 vols.; Edinburgh:
T. & T. Clark, 1909), 2:313; and Klaus Seybold, *Die Psalmen* (HAT I.15; Tübingen:
J. C. B. Mohr [Paul Siebeck], 1996), 393.

55. For this view, which apparently originated with Halévy, see Hermann
Gunkel, *Die Psalmen* (HKAT 2.2; 4th ed.; Göttingen: Vandenhoeck & Ruprecht,
1926), 432, 434; Weiser, *Psalms*, 648; and Kraus, *Psalms 60–150*, 277. Eaton's
treatment of the question in v. 2a is inconsistent, for he translates it as "O when will
you come to me?," only to go on to claim that the psalmist sings of חסד and אמת,
"the basic covenantal values of committed goodwill and faithfulness" (*Psalms*, 350–
52), thus clearly presupposing an emendation of מתי to אמת.

Michael L. Barré, "The Shifting Focus of Psalm 101," in *The Book of Psalms:
Composition and Reception* (ed. Peter W. Flint and Patrick D. Miller, Jr.; VTSup 99;
Leiden: Brill, 2005), 206–23 (208), assuming an original defective orthography (i.e.
מתי תבא אלי instead of מתי תבוא אלי), has argued that the text ought to be vocalized
as מְתֵי תָּבֵא אֵלָי ("the men you bring to/before me"), which would tie in with his
view that the original focus was on the king's instruction of his courtiers, that is, the
men God has brought before him. Summaries of other suggested emendations can be

these text-critical operations have been rightly rejected by Booij on the grounds that the Hebrew clause makes perfect grammatical sense and is supported by the ancient versions.[56]

According to others, the question in v. 2, far from being out of place, is of paramount importance. For instance, Terrien has argued that "the short but unexpected prayer, "When wilt thou come to me?," may well have been the key to [the psalm's] preservation, not only in the official Judaism of the Persian period but also among the members of the Qumran community."[57] As regards the Persian period, Terrien notes that "the plaintive petition for God's intimate manifestation covers a profound anxiety over the absence of the Lord. A great void lies behind the begging for presence."[58]

Importantly for our purposes, the question in v. 2 is one of the key reasons for regarding Ps 101 as a lament psalm.[59] Kaiser seeks to back this up by arguing that the use of מתי within the Psalms is restricted to lament psalms.[60] Interestingly, however, one of the passages Kaiser lists in this connection is Ps 119:82, 84. To be sure, the immediate context of the two uses of מתי in Ps 119, that is, the *kaph* section (vv. 81–88), is one of lament. Yet that should not detract us from the fact that the psalm as a whole is hardly a typical lament but is better characterized as a wisdom psalm. This is worth mentioning because many of the psalmist's statements in Ps 119 are quite similar to the kinds of statements made by the king in Ps 101, which explains why a number of interpreters have detected wisdom influences in our passage too.[61]

found in Iohannes Bapt. Bauer, "'Incedam in via immaculata, quando venias ad me?' (Ps. 100 [101]:2)," *VD* 30 (1952): 219–24; and Kaiser, "Erwägungen zu Psalm 101," 198–99. To mention one further example, Hitzig (*Die Psalmen übersetzt und ausgelegt*, 2:271), translated "ich will achten auf des Redlichen Weg, wenn er an mich gelangt," thus rendering מתי as a conjunction (for this view, see also Hupfeld, *Die Psalmen übersetzt und ausgelegt*, 69).

56. Booij, "Psalm CI 2," 458.

57. Terrien, *Psalms*, 694.

58. Ibid., 694.

59. Kselman, "Psalm 101," finds the answer to that question in vv. 6–7 (Eng. 8) understood as a divine oracle (see esp. p. 57).

60. Kaiser, "Erwägungen zu Psalm 101," 199–200.

61. Thus, e.g., Othmar Keel, *Feinde und Gottesleugner: Studien zum Image der Widersacher in den Individualpsalmen* (SBM 7; Stuttgart: Katholisches Bibelwerk, 1969), 118; Kenik, "Code of Conduct for a King"; Walter Brueggemann, "A Neglected Sapiential Word Pair," *ZAW* 89 (1977): 234–58 (esp. 244–45); Louis Jacquet, *Les Psaumes et le Cœur de l'Homme: Etude Textuelle, Littéraire et Doctrinale.* Vol. 3, *Psaumes 101–150* (Gembloux: Duculot, 1979), 2–3; J. Emmette

Just as the occurrence in Ps 119 of a section dominated by lament does not turn the entire psalm into a lament psalm, so the question in Ps 101:2 should not lead us to regard that psalm as a lament either. Indeed, Kaiser appears to be clutching at straws when he says: "*Den breiten Raum des Liedes nimmt dann eine in der Tat programmatisch wirkende Unschuld- serklärung des Königs ein, deren Breite nicht dazu verführen darf, von ihr aus die Gattung des ganzen zu bestimmen.*"[62]

Why though should the fact that most of the psalm is devoted to the king's declaration of loyalty or intent[63] not lead us to take this as deter- minative of its genre? In response to this question, Kaiser would point to the question in v. 2, yet we have already seen that Croft is able to make perfect sense of that question without turning the entire psalm into a lament. The same is true for Terrien who, while detecting "a begging for presence," does not feel compelled to read the remainder of the psalm as a summary of the king's past loyalty.[64]

Even more important than Kaiser's observation that large parts of the psalm are constituted by statements that in his view should not be taken as determinative of its genre (because they would undermine his char- acterization of the psalm as a lament) is the concomitant observation that "constitutive elements of the lament, namely the petition to God for help or deliverance and the recitation of various sufferings about which the psalmist is complaining" are absent. Thus rightly Barré, who goes on to say that "with the absence of [these] elements one cannot classify a Biblical Hebrew poem as a lament."[65]

Loretz makes a similar point in relation to the suggestion that the king's statements in vv. 2b–8 be understood as a protestation of his innocence. We saw above that these assertions have sometimes been compared to the Babylonian king's protestation of innocence made on the occasion of the *akitu* festival. However, as Loretz rightly notes, a comparison of the

Weir, "The Perfect Way, a Study of Wisdom Motifs in Psalm 101," *EvQ* 53 (1981): 54–59; Kselman, "Psalm 101"; and Barré, "The Shifting Focus of Psalm 101."

62. Kaiser, "Erwägungen zu Psalm 101," 201.

63. Kaiser's characterization of vv. 2–8 as a declaration of innocence (rather than of loyalty or intent) is, of course, based on his rendering of the verbs as past tense.

64. In the interpretation suggested by Kaiser (see esp. ibid., 205), who is fol- lowed in this by Allen, *Psalms 101–150*, 4, the declaration of innocence serves as the motivation for God's desired appearance: "I have done justly" (vv. 2c–8), therefore "when will you come to me?" (v. 2b). For this interpretation, see also Kselman, "Psalm 101."

65. Barré, "The Shifting Focus of Psalm 101," 208. Leuenberger, *Konzeptionen des Königtums Gottes im Psalter*, 176 n. 179, too, maintains that Ps 101 is not a lament psalm.

words spoken by the Babylonian king with Ps 101:2b–8 clearly shows that the latter passage is much better understood as a programmatic declaration or an annunciation of the ideals of the royal regime rather than a profession of the king's innocence.[66]

That the king's words in vv. 2b–8 can be understood as a vow or promise without regarding the question in v. 2a as inappropriate has been shown by Davidson who notes that "the plea for help is…being strengthened by a *promise of commitment* to the values which are close to the heart of God."[67] Curtis similarly speaks of "a declaration of good intent occasioned by a time of distress."[68] I therefore agree with Kaiser's conclusion that the plea in v. 2a asks Yahweh to acknowledge and live up to the covenant relationship,[69] without, however, following him in characterizing Ps 101 as a psalm of lament or in construing the verbs in vv. 2b–8 as past tense.

Earlier on, I noted that the determination of the psalm's setting in and of itself does not lead to conclusive results concerning the translation of the verbs in vv. 2b–8 as either future or past tense. The same can be said for the determination of the genre of Ps 101, as for instance McCann's exegesis illustrates. While noting that there is much in the text that would lead one to think of it in terms of a royal pledge or oath, McCann ultimately follows Allen in regarding the psalm as a royal complaint because of the question in v. 2. However, this does not lead him to interpret our passage as looking back to the king's past behaviour.[70]

Since the arguments advanced in favour of understanding Ps 101 as a lament have turned out to be unconvincing, I am finding myself in agreement with those who describe our text as a royal vow or pledge. Moreover, if Ps 101 is indeed a vow, then the verbs in vv. 2b–8 are best rendered as future, which is the most obvious solution grammatically anyway.[71] In these verses, in what is highly self-involving language, the

66. Loretz, *Königspsalmen*, 162–65.

67. Davidson, *The Vitality of Worship*, 329 (my italics). Alternatively, Davidson notes, "the thought may be that only if his plea is answered will the king be able to fulfill the promises expected of him."

68. Curtis, *Psalms*, 201.

69. See Kaiser, "Erwägungen zu Psalm 101," 202.

70. See McCann, "The Book of Psalms," 1081–83.

71. The fact that all the verbs in vv. 2b–8 are translated as past tense in the LXX (i.e. as either aorist or imperfect) does not invalidate this conclusion. In fact, the translation of the LXX appears to be a deliberate move designed to enhance the portrayal of the king as a wisdom figure who has not committed any sins. This is consistent with other developments in the textual tradition of Ps 101, as Barré ("The Shifting Focus of Psalm 101," 221–22) has shown. For instance, Targum Psalms seeks to make the connection with David more consistent by introducing v. 2b with

king promises that his future reign will be characterized by an adherence to the standards of the law.

It is this self-involving language, the idiom of vow and promise, that deserves a closer look as we move on to consider the ways in which this type of language might affect our own reading of Ps 101. However, first it should be noted briefly that, although modern Psalms scholarship has almost unanimously followed Gunkel in regarding Ps 101 as a royal psalm,[72] there are still some who prefer the common pre-Gunkel

---

אמר דוד ("David said") while also paraphrasing בקרב ביתי ("within my house") in the same verse with בגו בית אולפני ("within my house of instruction").

72. See, e.g., Hermann Gunkel, *Introduction to Psalms: The Genres of the Religious Lyric of Israel* (trans. James D. Nogalski; Mercer Library of Biblical Studies; Macon, Ga.: Mercer University Press, 1998), 99; see also Allen, *Psalms 101–150*, 3; Hans-Joachim Kraus, *Theology of the Psalms* (trans. Keith Crim; Minneapolis: Fortress, 1992), 107; and Dahood, *Psalms III*, 2, who describes Ps 101 as "distinctly royal, the work of a king or for a king."

A modification of the royal interpretation is Seybold's suggestion to regard Ps 101 as a palimpsest. According to this view, an old royal text in which the ruler explains the principles of his politics (i.e. vv. 2aα, 3–5, 7) has been turned into a prayer outlining a priestly dignitary's religious aims by means of several additions to the original wording (Seybold, *Psalmen*, 393; idem, *Die Psalmen: Eine Einführung* [Stuttgart: Kohlhammer, 1986], 89; followed by Leuenberger, *Konzeptionen des Königtums Gottes im Psalter*, 175–76; see also Loretz, *Königspsalmen*, 165–69; and Markus Saur, *Die Königspsalmen: Studien zur Entstehung und Theologie* [BZAW 340; Berlin: de Gruyter, 2004], *ad loc.*). It seems doubtful, however, that such a neat distinction between the king's political agenda and the religious ambitions of the alleged priest can be maintained. Mowinckel's description of Ps 101 as a king's "religious charter" does seem to do more justice to the political and religious context of ancient Israel (*The Psalms in Israel's Worship*, 67).

Another literary-critical theory is that of Briggs and Briggs (*Book of Psalms*, 2:314), who argued that the original psalm "was probably composed for the community of the Restoration before Nehemiah," whereas the glosses in vv. 5 and 8 "are Maccabean in tone." Verses 1–2a in turn were "designed to make the Ps. more appropriate for public worship." Based on extensive text-critical manoeuvres, Moses Buttenwieser (*The Psalms, Chronologically Treated with a New Translation* [Chicago: University of Chicago Press, 1938], 811–12) found in Ps 101 a personal prayer followed by a divine speech. Loretz (*Königspsalmen*, 144), rightly notes that Kselman's views resemble Buttenwieser's to a large degree, even though Kselman was evidently unaware of this: "the thesis that the 'I' of vv. 6–7 (and perhaps v. 8) is no longer the voice of the king, but of Yahweh, in the form of a divine oracle to the king, has not to my knowledge been previously recognized" (Kselman, "Psalm 101," 45). Earlier on, Karl Budde ("Psalm 101," *ExpTim* 8 [1896–97]: 202–204; idem, "Zum Text der Psalmen," *ZAW* 35 [1915]: 175–95 [191–92]) had argued that the original version of Ps 101 featured a verse after v. 1 that introduced the speaker of vv. 2–8 as Yahweh.

understanding. According to the advocates of this view, the psalm is best read collectively, taking the people as a whole as the intended speakers.[73]

It should also be noted that recent scholarship has shown a strong interest in the relation of Ps 101 to its context in the book of Psalms.[74] This is reflected also in Gordon Wenham's own brief comments on our passage. It has been argued in recent years that Pss 90–106, Book 4 of the Psalter, reflect the situation of the exile, a time when there was no king in Israel/Judah, and that Book 4 in its entirety is designed to answer the question posed in Ps 89:49: "Lord, where is your steadfast love of old, which by your faithfulness you swore to David?" Taking his cue from these considerations, Wenham has argued that the inclusion of Ps 101 should be seen as a "reaffirmation of faith": "Despite Israel's present predicament, God is going to restore a Davidic king and bring the Messiah, but he will require loyal and faithful servants, just as the original David did. In the meantime the LORD is king and he too seeks integrity, loyalty and humility in his servants."[75]

McCann similarly understands our passage as a response to the break-down of the monarchy, noting that "the voice of an imagined future king says, in effect, 'I shall do everything right.'"[76] Interestingly, this kind of interpretation is not as new as one might think, given that the interest in the Psalms as a carefully arranged book is a recent one. Yet already Kirkpatrick thought that Ps 101 may have been placed after Pss 93 and 95–100 in order to show how God's kingship could work itself out through a second David.[77]

---

73. Scholars who reject a royal understanding of Ps 101 include Buttenwieser, *Psalms*, 811–12; and Joachim Becker, "Die kollektive Deutung der Königspsalmen," *TP* 52 (1977): 561–78 (577); idem, *Messiaserwartung im Alten Testament* (SBS 83; Stuttgart: Katholisches Bibelwerk, 1977), 73.

74. There has been a veritable flood of studies of the composition and redaction of the book of Psalms in recent years, which cannot be listed here. For a recent investigation containing an extensive bibliography, see Leuenberger, *Konzeptionen des Königtums Gottes im Psalter*. See also Wenham's recent article, "Towards a Canonical Reading of the Psalms," in *Canon and Biblical Interpretation* (ed. Craig G. Bartholomew et al.; Scripture & Hermeneutics Series 7; Milton Keynes: Paternoster, 2006), 333–51.

75. Gordon J. Wenham, "Rejoice the Lord is King: Psalms 90–106 (Book 4)," in *Praying by the Book: Reading the Psalms* (ed. Craig Bartholomew and Andrew West; Carlisle: Paternoster, 2001), 89–120 (98).

76. McCann, "The Book of Psalms," 1081.

77. Kirkpatrick, *The Book of Psalms, ad loc.*

3. *The Performative, Self-Involving, Commissive Language of Psalm 101*

One of the encouraging developments in Old (and New) Testament studies in recent years has been the renewed interest in theological interpretation and in questions such as how academic biblical interpretation can make a fruitful contribution to Christian belief and living in today's world. This interest has already led to the publication of many important and refreshing works, including Moberly's *The Bible, Theology, and Faith*[78] and the *Dictionary for Theological Interpretation of the Bible*,[79] to name but two examples. Additional fruits of this focus on theological interpretation of the Bible are the recent establishment of the SBL Theological Hermeneutics of Christian Scripture group and the *Journal of Theological Interpretation*, the inaugural issue of which appeared in spring 2007.

The question of how academic biblical interpretation can make a fruitful contribution to Christian belief and living in today's world has always been at the heart of Gordon Wenham's work, as is evident not least in his interest in reading the Old Testament ethically.[80] It is therefore fitting in this tribute to his work to consider the ways in which academic interpretation of Ps 101 can make a contribution to contemporary Christian belief and living.

One way of conceiving this task might be to investigate and comment on the messianic interpretation of Ps 101. We saw earlier that the very inclusion of our psalm in the book of Psalms is often attributed to the fact that it had come to be understood messianically.[81] No king had ever been able to maintain as high a standard as is pledged in Ps 101, hence the expectation of a messianic figure developed, a figure who would live up to the ideals proclaimed in our passage.

Taking his cue from this line of interpretation, Davidson compares our psalm to "the kind of promises we expect to hear from politicians in a party manifesto leading up to an election," which "are rightly greeted with a fair measure of cynicism, because they are seldom delivered." He

---

78. R. W. L. Moberly, *The Bible, Theology, and Faith: A Study of Abraham and Jesus* (Cambridge: Cambridge University Press, 2000).

79. *Dictionary for Theological Interpretation of the Bible* (ed. Kevin J. Vanhoozer et al.; London: SPCK, 2005).

80. See especially *Story as Torah* and "The Ethics of the Psalms."

81. See my earlier references to the works by Kirkpatrick, McCann and Wenham, which are representative of a widespread tendency to offer messianic interpretations of the royal psalms.

goes on to say that "it is hardly surprising, therefore, that such a royal psalm was given a future messianic interpretation, with the promises understood as a future hope to be fully realized only in an ideal kingdom yet to come."[82] In other words, we are still in some respects in the same boat as the ancient Israelites, because we still await the full realization of this ideal kingdom. In a similar vein, Terrien comments that our psalm "may urge Christians to pray for an existential messianism."[83] Kidner also favours a messianic interpretation of Ps 101, noting that "for its perfect fulfilment we are forced to look beyond our approximations, to the Messiah Himself."[84]

While I believe that Christians can legitimately interpret the royal psalms (including Ps 101) messianically, I am uneasy with conclusions such as Terrien's that what our text essentially does is to urge us to pray for what he calls an "existential messianism." Such a reading does not even begin to do justice to the theological potential of Ps 101, as I shall endeavour to demonstrate in what follows.

Another avenue to pursue might be to take our lead from what has been called the democratization of our passage. Schaefer, for instance, speaks of "the ruler's acknowledgment of the responsibility as judge to promote justice in society" becoming "a basis for the worshipper's examination of his or her own adherence to such a standard."[85] Mays similarly notes that "early Christian interpreters read this psalm as a charge from [Jesus] to *all* who would belong to the faithful,"[86] a point taken up also by McCann.[87] Democratization of the royal psalms is also assumed by Holladay, who argues that

> the process of democratization must have been a steady, though com-
> plicated one: if the context of pre-exilic worship was strongly centered in
> the royal court, now there was no court, and the experience of the people
> in exile would have strengthened their perception that the psalms were a
> vehicle for the worship of a people bereft of royal leadership.[88]

82. Davidson, *The Vitality of Worship*, 329.
83. Terrien, *Psalms*, 694.
84. Kidner, *Psalms 73–150*, 358.
85. Schaefer, *Psalms*, 250.
86. Mays, *Psalms*, 322 (my italics).
87. McCann, "The Book of Psalms," 1083.
88. Holladay, *The Psalms Through Three Thousand Years*, 64; see also Alfons Deissler, *Die Psalmen* (3 vols.; 4th ed.; Düsseldorf: Patmos, 1971), 3:46. Some-times, it is suggested that the democratization process that is observable in Ps 101 is the result of a variety of redactional operations. For this view, see, e.g., Leuenberger, *Konzeptionen des Königtums Gottes im Psalter*, 173–76; and see the discussion in Loretz, *Königspsalmen*, 166–67.

Of course, passages like Mic 6:8 and Matt 23:23[89] indicate that values such as חסד and משפט, of which the king sings in v. 1, are required of everyone.

Thus, when we reflect on the contribution Ps 101 might make to contemporary Christian belief and living, we need to pay attention to the notion of democratization while at the same time not losing sight of the fact that our passage is particularly suited to those in power. A helpful example of holding these two dimensions together can be found in Eaton's recent commentary, *Psalms for Life*. Eaton maintains that Ps 101

> speaks to societies today, as they struggle with the deceptions and greed that cling to political office—the slanders, treacheries, ambition and corruption that penetrate and cling to *the centres of power*. The psalm declares to modern rulers that only through dedication to God's standards can this blessing be retained.[90]

Eaton appropriately describes our psalm as a "solemn message for rulers" only to go on to say, however, that it also applies to "each of us in the little kingdoms where we have responsibility."[91]

But it is important not to stop here. Having commented, albeit only briefly, upon possible applications of the psalm, we need to move on and reflect on its actual function. Taking our lead from Clines, we might ask, "Why is there a Ps 101, and what does it do to us when we read, sing or pray it?"[92] Or, better still, "What are *we* in fact doing when we read, sing or pray Ps 101?"

These kinds of questions are not often asked. Instead, it is usually assumed that our text has something to teach. An example of this tendency is Broyles's suggestion that "Psalm 101 presents Yahweh's pilgrims with 'instruction' about what the God who inhabits the temple desires of his worshipers."[93] McCann somewhat similarly notes that the

89. In Matt 23:23 Jesus criticises the scribes and Pharisees for neglect of the most important matters of the law, which are understood to be justice, mercy and faithfulness. In talking about κρίσις ("justice") and ἔλεος ("mercy"), Jesus uses the terms employed by the LXX in its translation of חסד and משפט in Ps 101:1.

90. John Eaton, *Psalms for Life: Hearing and Praying the Book of Psalms* (London: SPCK, 2006), 263 (my italics).

91. Ibid.

92. The wording of this question is a play on the titles of Clines's articles, "Why Is There a Song of Songs, and What Does it Do to You if You Read it?" and "Why Is There a Book of Job, and What Does it Do to You if You Read it?," both published in *Interested Parties: The Ideology of Writers and Readers of the Hebrew Bible* (ed. David J. A. Clines; JSOTSup 205; Sheffield: Sheffield Academic Press, 1995), 94–121 and 122–44, respectively.

93. Broyles, *Psalms*, 389. At least, here the use of inverted commas shows that Broyles is aware that this is not quite an accurate description of what is in Ps 101.

text came to be understood "as an articulation of the values that God wills to be concretely embodied among humans—love, justice, integrity."[94] Mays specifically talks about teaching: "The psalm *teaches* that it is not good enough for those who lead to live by the legalities and govern by codes," and again, "The psalm also *teaches* that conduct depends on character."[95]

I am not suggesting that Ps 101, or the psalms generally, do not teach us anything. Of course, they do. However, their function is not properly determined by limiting it to a didactic one. Indeed, it seems somewhat ironic that commentators, who have done much to help us understand the setting and function of Ps 101 in ancient Israel (including the sometimes quite elaborately reconstructed cultic drama in which our passage is supposed to have played its part), almost by default revert to the notion of teaching when it comes to determining the psalm's function in today's context.

A more promising, because more holistic, approach to the psalms sees them not only as texts to be read and studied, but also as prayers to be prayed and as songs to be sung. An example of this is Wenham's comment that "it is in prayer that people give utterance to their deepest and most fundamental convictions. Thus the words hymn-writers and liturgists put on our lips in worship affect us profoundly: they teach us what to think and feel."[96] To be sure, there is another reference here to teaching, but in talking about prayer, hymns, liturgies, worship and feeling, Wenham expresses the possible range of functions in much wider terms.[97] Eaton helpfully applies such a perspective to Ps 101, commenting that

> Integrity in government is a heavy subject, but it is striking that here it is expressed in a song, a poem to be sung and played to the Lord. Justice indeed must rise above rules and codes of practice and deeply breathe the air of the arts; only so does it engage the imagination, the heart, the very soul, and find the way of wholeness.[98]

Eaton's reference to the imagination is important and of course highly appropriate in a commentary on what is after all a poetic text. Much has been said about metaphors, poetry and the imagination in recent years,

94. McCann, "The Book of Psalms," 1083.
95. Mays, *Psalms*, 322 (my italics).
96. Wenham, "The Ethics of the Psalms," 177.
97. I should perhaps point out that I am not suggesting that the commentators mentioned earlier show no awareness of these dimensions. All I am saying is that in modern applications of Ps 101 to our contemporary context there tends to be a heavy emphasis on its didactic role to the detriment of other possible functions.
98. Eaton, *Psalms*, 353.

and it would seem to be highly instructive to reflect on Ps 101 in the light of statements such as, "'The proper and immediate object of poetry" is not to convey knowledge; it is rather "the communication of immediate pleasure,'" or "In communicating its message through beauty of form and expression [a poem] has fulfilled its *raison d'être*."[99]

What does it mean for the king to express his determination to walk with integrity and surround himself with like-minded servants "through beauty of form and expression"?[100] If poetry is "the communication of immediate pleasure," what does it mean for the king to employ poetry in his declaration of commitment to righteous conduct? And what does it mean for us to use these words today? It seems to me that there is much scope for creative work here, and it is certainly apparent that to limit the role of Ps 101 to that of teaching is to be unduly restrictive.

However, as I said at the outset, the self-involving language of Ps 101 makes it appropriate for us to consider the contribution speech act theory might make to the interpretation and application of our passage.[101] As I

99. These are Paul Avis's statements, made in *God and the Creative Imagination: Metaphor, Symbol and Myth in Religion and Theology* (London: Routledge, 1999), 86–87, summarizing notions expressed by Samuel Taylor Coleridge, *Biographia Literaria, or, Biographical Sketches of My Literary Life and Opinions* (ed. George Watson; Everyman's Library 11; London: Dent, 1965).

100. Commentators have observed that Ps 101 is very carefully structured, using several instances of repetition. These include the phrases בדרך תמים (vv. 2, 6), בקרב ביתי (vv. 2, 7), לנגד עיני (vv. 3, 7) and אצמית (vv. 5, 8), as well as the references to Yahweh in vv. 1, 8. Kenik ("Code of Conduct for a King," 394), therefore describes our psalm as "a poetic composition designed with precision and care."

101. Studies that have applied speech act theory to the investigation of the Psalms include Donald K. Berry, *The Psalms and Their Readers: Interpretive Strategies for Psalm 18* (JSOTSup 153; Sheffield: JSOT Press, 1993), esp. Chapter 5; Stephen Breck Reid, "Psalm 50: Prophetic Speech and God's Performative Utterances," in *Prophets and Paradigms: Essays in Honor of Gene M. Tucker* (ed. Stephen Breck Reid; JSOTSup 229; Sheffield: Sheffield Academic Press, 1996), 217–30 (who argues that in Ps 50 divine performative speech is used in a context of moral exhortation); Andreas Wagner, "Der Lobaufruf im israelitischen Hymnus als indirekter Sprechakt," in *Studien zur hebräischen Grammatik* (ed. Andreas Wagner; OBO 156; Göttingen: Vandenhoeck & Ruprecht, 1997), 143–54; idem, "Die Bedeutung der Sprechakttheorie für Bibelübersetzungen, aufgezeigt an Gen 1,29, Ps 2,7 und Dtn 26,17–19," in *The Interpretation of the Bible: The International Symposium in Slovenia* (ed. Jože Krašovec; JSOTSup 289; Sheffield: Sheffield Academic Press, 1998), 1575–88 (esp. 1577–78); and Stephen Breck Reid, "Power and Practice: Performative Speech and Piety in Psalm 132," in *Psalms and Practice: Worship, Virtue, and Authority* (ed. Stephen Breck Reid; Collegeville, Minn.: Liturgical Press, 2001), 40–51. According to Reid ("Psalm 50," 224), the first to

have noted elsewhere,[102] speech act theory, as conceived by Austin, Grice, Searle and others,[103] "was developed to supersede the old logical-positivist view of language which assumed that the only meaningful statements are those which describe a state of affairs in the world."[104] Briggs similarly argues that "to understand a text as a communicative action...appears to be...a useful corrective to overly dominant models of texts as representational or, to borrow Janet Martin Soskice's term, 'reality-depicting.'"[105]

Seeking to correct what he thought of as the "descriptive fallacy," Austin attempted, albeit not entirely successfully perhaps, to distinguish between "constatives" (descriptive statements) and "performatives" (statements that "get something done").[106] However, all the flaws in Austin's

apply Austin's work on performative language to the language of the Psalms was Mettinger in *King and Messiah*.

102.   See my "Words of (In-)evitable Certitude? Reflections on the Interpretation of Prophetic Oracles of Judgement," in *After Pentecost: Language and Biblical Interpretation* (ed. Craig Bartholomew, Colin Greene and Karl Möller; Scripture & Hermeneutics Series 2; Carlisle: Paternoster, 2001), 352–86, where I have applied speech act theory to the interpretation of prophetic oracles of judgment.

103.   See, e.g., J. L. Austin, *How to Do Things with Words* (2d ed.; Oxford: Clarendon, 1975); John R. Searle, *Speech Acts: An Essay in the Philosophy of Language* (Cambridge: Cambridge University Press, 1969); idem, *Expression and Meaning: Studies in the Theory of Speech Acts* (Cambridge: Cambridge University Press, 1979); H. P. Grice, "Logic and Conversation," in *Syntax and Semantics*. Vol. 3, *Speech Acts* (ed. Peter Cole and Jerry L. Morgan; New York: Academic Press, 1975), 41–58; and idem, "Utterer's Meaning, Sentence Meaning, and Word Meaning," *Foundations of Language* 4 (1968): 225–42. Note, however, that Richard S. Briggs, *Words in Action—Speech Act Theory and Biblical Interpretation: Toward a Hermeneutic of Self-Involvement* (Edinburgh: T. & T. Clark, 2001), 5, rightly cautions against assimilating the concerns of these three philosophers under the one rubric of what he calls "speech act criticism." For a detailed account especially of Searle's work in contrast to that of Austin, see Chapter 2 of Briggs's study.

104.   Thus Raman Selden and Peter Widdowson, *A Reader's Guide to Contemporary Literary Theory* (3d ed.; New York: Harvester Wheatsheaf, 1993), 148.

105.   Briggs, *Words in Action*, 31; the reference is to Janet Martin Soskice, *Metaphor and Religious Language* (Oxford: Clarendon, 1985), 97. See also Berry, *The Psalms and Their Readers*, 109, who notes that speech act theory does not approach speaking as conveyance of information but as performance.

106.   The general distinction is made in the first lecture (Austin, *How to Do Things with Words*, 1–11). Lectures 2–4 deal with what Austin called "infelicities," reflecting his basic distinction between constatives, which can be true or false, and performatives, which are either "happy" or "unhappy" (see pp. 12–52). In lectures 5–7, Austin then discusses criteria for distinguishing performatives from constatives (pp. 53–93).

argument notwithstanding,[107] he clearly did succeed in demonstrating the performative force of language. And it is precisely this attention to the performative nature of language, that is, the question of how specific utterances are operative and have effects, that will assist us in coming to a better understanding of the "first-person performative speech" in Ps 101.[108] After all, as Vanhoozer notes, "the propositional content [the statements made, in this case, by the speaker of the psalm] is intended to function or count *as* something in the communicative act."[109] It is this "counting as" that is of interest to us here.[110]

Exploring the nature of performatives, Austin went on to differentiate between three types of performative statements, namely "locutionary," "illocutionary" and "perlocutionary" acts.[111] The first of these is defined as "the performance of an act *of* saying something," an illocution, on the other hand, is "the performance of an act *in* saying something" and a perlocution, finally, is "the performance of an act *by* saying something." Thus, we can "distinguish the locutionary act "he *said* that..." from the illocutionary act "he *argued* that..." and the perlocutionary act "he *convinced* me that..."[112]

Subsequent writers such as Black, Cohen and Searle have found it difficult to distinguish between the locutionary act and the illocutionary one, because in practice they are never separate.[113] Yet, as Briggs points out, Searle not only left Austin's category of illocutionary force in place

107.   See the discussion in Briggs, *Words in Action*, Chapter 2 §2.
108.   Reid, "Power and Practice," 47, has similarly drawn attention to the "first-person performative speech" of Ps 132.
109.   Kevin J. Vanhoozer, "The Semantics of Biblical Literature: Truth and Scripture's Diverse Literary Forms," in *Hermeneutics, Authority and Canon* (ed. D. A. Carson and John D. Woodbridge; Leicester: InterVarsity, 1986), 53–104 (92).
110.   See also in this context Vanhoozer's comment that Scripture is "composed of divine–human speech acts which, through what they say, accomplish several authoritative cognitive, spiritual and social functions" (Kevin J. Vanhoozer, "God's Mighty Speech-Acts: The Doctrine of Scripture Today," in *A Pathway into the Holy Scripture* [ed. Philip E. Satterthwaite and David F. Wright; Grand Rapids: Eerdmans, 1994], 143–81 [148]).
111.   For the basic distinction, see lecture 8 (Austin, *How to Do Things with Words*, 94–107). Lectures 9–10 (pp. 108–31) follow this up by providing criteria for distinguishing "illocutions" from "perlocutions."
112.   Ibid., 102 (my italics).
113.   See Max Black, "Austin on Performatives," *Philosophy* 38 (1963): 217–26; L. Jonathan Cohen, "Do Illocutionary Forces Exist?," *Philosophical Quarterly* 14 (1964): 118–37; and John R. Searle, "Austin on Locutionary and Illocutionary Acts," in *Essays on J. L. Austin* (ed. Isaiah Berlin et al.; Oxford: Clarendon, 1973), 141–59. For fuller discussion, see Briggs, *Words in Action*, 44–47.

but spent much effort on classifying illocutionary acts based on different "directions of fit between word and world."[114] Thus, for instance, in the case of an assertive, the direction of fit is word to world in that the speaker commits him-/herself to something being the case, whereas in a commissive the direction of fit is world to word in that the commissive commits the speaker to some future course of action: "what is spoken shapes what will be."[115] For our purposes, it is the latter category of the commissive that is of particular interest, but it is important to underline that speech acts cannot always be neatly categorized.

As we saw above, the first-person statements in Ps 101 are best understood in a commissive sense,[116] with the king committing himself, in language that is appropriately described as strongly self-involving,[117] to a certain type of future behaviour. The notion of self-involvement was first applied to the area of biblical interpretation by Donald Evans in his *The Logic of Self-Involvement*.[118] Yet, according to Briggs, whose aim it is to develop a "hermeneutic of self-involvement,"[119] this notion is still very much "an under-explored aspect of biblical language,"[120] even though it "remains the most fruitful for utilising speech act theory in a hermeneutical role in biblical interpretation."[121]

114.   See the discussion in Briggs, *Words in Action*, Chapter 2 §3, as well as his claim that "with the work of Searle, Austin's performative–constative distinction recedes further into the background, and all utterances are viewed as illocutionary acts" (p. 63).

115.   Thus Anthony C. Thiselton, *New Horizons in Hermeneutics: The Theory and Practice of Transforming Biblical Reading* (Grand Rapids: Zondervan, 1992), 296.

116.   Andreas Wagner, "Die Sprechaktklassifikation nach Searle in historischer Sprechaktanalyse," in *Aspekte der Sprachbeschreibung: Akten des 29. Linguistischen Kolloquiums, Aarhus 1994* (ed. Per Bærentzen; Linguistische Arbeiten 342; Tübingen: Niemeyer, 1995), 269–72 (271), has pointed out that the Hebrew prefix conjugation can be used to express commissives.

117.   See Briggs, *Words in Action*, 7, 150, who rightly notes that there are degrees of self-involvement.

118.   Donald D. Evans, *The Logic of Self-Involvement: A Philosophical Study of Everyday Language with Special Reference to the Christian Use of Language about God as Creator* (London: SCM Press, 1963).

119.   Briggs, *Words in Action*, 147.

120.   Briggs, *Words in Action*, 148. Thiselton, *New Horizons in Hermeneutics*. 274, similarly comments that Evans's book has been "seriously undervalued."

121.   Briggs, *Words in Action*, 5. As an example of applying speech act theory in this way, Briggs refers to Anthony C. Thiselton, "The Supposed Power of Words in the Biblical Writings," *JTS* 25 (1974): 283–99. In *A Prophet in Debate: The Rhetoric of Persuasion in the Book of Amos* (JSOTSup 372; London: Sheffield

In my discussion of the genre of Ps 101 I noted that it has been variously described as a vow, a charter, a psalm of promise, an oath, a declaration of commitment or intent, a royal programme or manifesto, or a pledge. What all these descriptions have in common is a clear tendency to think of Ps 101 not only in self-involving but also in specifically commissive terms, even if that term is not used by the commentators. The language used in Ps 101 thus indicates that "the speaker 'stands behind' the words giving *a pledge and personal backing* that he or she is prepared to undertake commitments and responsibilities that are entailed in extra-linguistic terms by the proposition which is asserted."[122]

Prichard, whose work preceded that of Austin, similarly noted that "in promising, agreeing, or undertaking to do some action we seem to be creating or bringing into existence the obligation to do it."[123] And in his study of the "language of self" in the book of Jeremiah, Polk too has argued that in pledging or lamenting we "do not describe a condition so much as enact one."[124] All these statements highlight the performative, self-involving, commissive nature of a passage such as Ps 101, which has been duly noted by commentators who have described it as a pledge or vow or with any of the similar expressions mentioned above.

However, although scholars have observed the self-involving, commissive nature of the king's words, this unfortunately has had little impact on their conclusions concerning the psalm's function in and for today's communities of faith. As we saw above, that function is regularly described in didactic terms:[125] Ps 101 teaches modern believers how to conduct themselves.

Academic Press, 2003), I have additionally drawn attention to Terry Eagleton, "J. L. Austin and the Book of Jonah," in *The Book and the Text: The Bible and Literary Theory* (ed. Regina M. Schwartz; Oxford: Blackwell, 1990), 231–36; and Walter Houston, "What Did the Prophets Think They Were Doing? Speech Acts and Prophetic Discourse in the Old Testament," in *"The Place Is Too Small for Us": The Israelite Prophets in Recent Scholarship* (ed. Robert P. Gordon; Sources for Biblical and Theological Study 5; Winona Lake, Ind.: Eisenbrauns, 1995), 133–53.

122. Thus Thiselton, *New Horizons in Hermeneutics*, 617, in a discussion of early Christian confessions (the italics are Thiselton's).

123. Harold Arthur Prichard, "The Obligation to Keep a Promise," in *Moral Obligation: Essays and Lectures* (Oxford: Clarendon, 1949), 169–79 (169).

124. Timothy Polk, *The Prophetic Persona: Jeremiah and the Language of Self* (JSOTSup 32; Sheffield: JSOT Press, 1984), 46.

125. See also, in this context, my comments on descriptive, didactic biblical theologies in "The Nature and Genre of Biblical Theology: Some Reflections in the Light of Charles H. H. Scobie's 'Prolegomena to a Biblical Theology,'" in *Out of Egypt: Biblical Theology and Biblical Interpretation* (ed. Craig Bartholomew, Mary

Let us briefly consider one further example of this tendency. In his recent commentary on the Psalms, McCann rightly notes that "the psalmist makes a *commitment* to pursue love and justice, even in the apparent absence of God."[126] However, while being quite clearly aware of the commissive nature of the psalmist's statements, he then speaks of the "*invitation* of Psalm 101…that we speak and embody the truth in love as a witness to God's claim upon our lives and our world."[127]

Of course, Ps 101 does invite us to do these things; of course, it teaches us something. But these notions do not come anywhere near to doing justice to the effect and function of its self-involving language. Is it not ironic that Old Testament experts who have spent much time and effort on identifying the genre of a passage such as Ps 101 quite regularly do not even begin to consider the implications of their conclusions for their suggestions concerning that passage's function in and for today's communities of faith?

It is at this point that speech act theory can help us become more aware of the performative force and the self-involving, commissive nature of our passage. Yes, the king does commit himself to a certain kind of future behaviour. But so does anyone who sings or prays Ps 101 today—yet this is routinely missed by modern interpreters.

Briggs's "hermeneutic of self-involvement" can assist us here by emphasizing that in passages such as Ps 101 the self-involvement occurs "as part of the communication between author and reader," because it "is raised in the discussion which takes place between the author and the real-world reader."[128] A good example of how readers are drawn into the text is Polk's work on the "language of self" in Jeremiah, because, as Briggs perceptively comments, "Polk seeks to demonstrate how the self which is constructed by Jeremiah's first-person language serves hermeneutically to mediate between the text and the reader, as a personal enactment of a corporate relationship between God and his people."[129]

Coming back to Ps 101, we can therefore conclude that in singing or praying this psalm, *we*, its modern readers, are ourselves making a pledge; we are committing ourselves to the behaviour the ancient

Healy, Karl Möller and Robin Parry; Scripture & Hermeneutics Series 5; Carlisle: Paternoster, 2004), 41–64.
126.   McCann, "The Book of Psalms," 1083 (my italics).
127.   Ibid., 1084.
128.   Briggs, *Words in Action*, 20. Alternatively, as Briggs points out, in some cases the self-involving language occurs within the narrative world, that is, on the part of the characters in that world, rather than in the communication between author and reader.
129.   Briggs, *Words in Action*, 168; the reference is to Polk, *Prophetic Persona*.

psalmist thought appropriate for a king.[130] As Reid notes in a study of "performative speech and piety in Psalm 132," "the performative speech is action. This also means that it conveys a sense of agency. At the same time…it also incites action, and the concomitant agency related to it."[131] To be sure, there are some modern commentators who understood this when they reflected on the function of Ps 101 for today. For instance, Curtis, who notes that "in stressing the characteristics of the good king, the psalm points to the characteristics required of those who wish to participate in God's kingdom,"[132] goes on to say that "the psalm has continued to provide a vehicle for *the expression of a determination* to live in accordance with God's will."[133] Eaton in a similar vein notes that "in our own domains of rule and care, we are to *pledge* ourselves again and again, morning by morning, to faithful love and justice, to honesty and kindness, that the Lord may come to us and abide with us—that he may work through us with all his fruitfulness."[134]

Unfortunately, these are the exceptions that only serve to prove the rule. Indeed, some commentators find the self-involving language of Ps 101 hard to take. In his exposition of the psalm in "The People's Bible Commentary," Coggan is positively irritated by the fact that vv. 1–6 all begin with "I." He rather disparagingly speaks of the psalm's ego-centricity and its "note of superiority, of boasting"; and he cannot but wonder whether the writer isn't "a bit over-pious."[135]

Surely, however, in the relationship between the worshipping king and his God there ought to be room for the kind of self-involving language found in Ps 101, especially if that relationship is expressed in covenantal terms, as is so clearly the case in our passage.[136] Nor, we might add, is

---

130.   See Berry, *The Psalms and Their Readers*, 128, who similarly notes that "in the act of reading, 'I praise' becomes the reader's statement… When the 'I' of Psalm 18 is read with a view toward its contemporary context…the poem takes on a heightened personal nature."

131.   Reid, "Power and Practice," 49.

132.   Curtis, *Psalms*, 202.

133.   Ibid., my italics.

134.   Eaton, *Psalms for Life*, 263 (my italics).

135.   Donald Coggan, *Psalms 73–150* (The People's Bible Commentary; Oxford: The Bible Reading Fellowship, 1999), 80. To be sure, Coggan does concede "that the writer puts his finger with a sure touch on areas of life where a godly person needs to keep watchful."

136.   See, in this context, Thiselton, *New Horizons in Hermeneutics*, 305, who notes that "the language of divine promise belongs to the context of covenant." Conversely, as Thiselton also maintains, drawing on David J. A. Clines, *The Theme of the Pentateuch* (JSOTSup 10; Sheffield: JSOT Press, 1978), 50–53, there is a

this type of self-involving language any less appropriate in the relationship of modern worshippers and their God.

We conclude therefore that in singing or praying Ps 101 we, today, follow the lead of Israel's ancient kings and psalmists in pledging ourselves, again and again, as Eaton rightly notes,[137] to the kind of ethical behaviour that is the subject of Ps 101. In reading, singing or praying this psalm, we are reading, singing or praying the law, as it were, and in doing so we commit ourselves to its values and to concomitant action. And it should come as no surprise that the singing or praying of a text like Ps 101 should have ethical and political implications. Smart, addressing "the centrally performative role of language in worship," saw quite clearly that, because of the strong ethical dimension of religious views, self-involvement in worship often runs deep in ethical and political areas.[138]

human response to the divine promise, which in Leviticus takes "the form of acts of worship, which are seen as institutional 'statutes and ordinances.'" In our psalm, the human response takes the form of a pledge or vow to adhere to the standards of the law.

137.   See the quote from Eaton, *Psalms for Life*, 263, above.

138.   Ninian Smart, *The Concept of Worship* (New Studies in the Philosophy of Religion; London: Macmillan, 1972), 31.

THE ETHICS OF LAMENT:
LAMENTATIONS 1 AS A CASE STUDY

Robin Parry

In discussions of Old Testament ethics it is laws, wisdom literature and prophetic oracles that have always had pride of place. In more recent days narrative texts have begun to play a more prominent role, in part thanks to Professor Gordon Wenham's fine study.[1] Professor Wenham's current work on the ethics of the Psalms is also sure to contribute to an even more rounded approach to Old Testament ethics. In the midst of this exciting retrieval of sidelined parts of the Old Testament for ethical reflection, I would like to draw attention to the literature of lament. I have chosen Lam 1 as a case study. In some ways this is an odd choice as it does not conform to a "pure" lament form but blends elements of the dirge and the communal lament.[2] However, Lam 1 is interesting for several reasons. First, it presents two different voices and hence two slightly different perspectives on Jerusalem's plight. Second, the poem provides ethical assessments on at least four different sets of characters. Third, the way that readers are drawn into the ethical assessment of the situation is especially interesting and full of potential for contemporary reading. Finally, the wider canon opens up new avenues of exploration on Yahweh-as-ethical-reader of Lamentations. I shall only be able to comment on the latter two points briefly.

1. The Ethical Assessments in Lamentations 1

a. Ethical Assessment of Jerusalem's Enemies
The narrator's focus is on Zion's distress and for the most part Zion's enemies are simply the means by which this distress has come. The

---

1. G. J. Wenham, *Story as Torah: Reading the Old Testament Ethically* (Edinburgh: T. & T. Clark, 2000).
2. C. Westermann, *Lamentations: Issues and Interpretation* (trans. C. Muenchow; Edinburgh: T. & T. Clark, 1994), 114–19.

results of their actions are clear: Zion has moved from being "great amongst the nations" to being like a widow and a forced labourer; from being full of people to being alone (1:1). Her daughter, Judah, has gone into exile (1:3, 5); the temple is destroyed and the cult has ceased functioning (1:4); her leaders have been captured (1:6); her citizens are starving to death because of the siege and its aftermath (1:11). Ethical evaluation of the enemies is not uppermost in the narrator's concerns in these descriptions although he clearly pities Jerusalem in all her suffering and thus *implicitly* condemns those who inflicted it.

There are a couple of moments when the narrator's distaste at the enemies comes closer to the surface. The first is in 1:7. Having just drawn out his readers' compassion for Jerusalem whose "people fell into the hands of an adversary and there was no one to help her" (1:7c), he immediately adds that the adversaries "mock over her destruction." Mockery is clearly the exact opposite to the kind of response the narrator is seeking to elicit from his readers and this makes its cruelty jar all the more. To mock someone suffering so greatly is clearly presented as despicable.

The second more evaluative moment is in v. 10 when the narrator speaks of how Jerusalem was forced to watch "nations enter her sanctuary." The desecration of Israel's most sacred site by the adversary is a deeply shocking thing to the narrator. He makes this shock clear by picturing it as the rape of Jerusalem by Gentile nations. He recalls the command of Yahweh that such nations not enter the assembly (Deut 23:3–6) to drive home just how inappropriate this action is. It is obvious that the reader is intended to disapprove of the behaviour of the adversary.

Jerusalem's very first words aim to draw Yahweh's attention to the enemy. She cries out that she is in distress "because an enemy has magnified [himself]" (1:9c). The gloating self-exaltation of the enemy over her is presented as a motive for Yahweh to pay attention. Presumably Jerusalem is appealing to God's own loss of honour that accompanies the loss of honour of his people.

When Jerusalem first speaks of the details of what the enemies did it is interesting that she speaks of their actions not as the deeds of a human foe but *as the actions of Yahweh* (1:13–15). In 1:16–20 she then portrays the suffering she has experienced at the hands of the enemy but the focus is on the pain and not the ethics of their deeds. However, the climax of the poem (1:21–22) sees a shift towards a clear ethical critique of the enemy. Speaking to Yahweh, Jerusalem prays:

> They heard that I was groaning.
>> There is no one to comfort me.
> All my enemies heard of the evil that had befallen me.
>> They rejoiced that you had done it.
> You brought the day that you proclaimed.
>> May they become like me.
>
> Let all their evil doing come before you,
>> and deal harshly with it,
>> as you dealt harshly with me,
>> on account of all my transgressions.
> For many are my groans,
>> And my heart is faint.[3]

Here Jerusalem draws attention to the same mocking at her downfall that the narrator had critiqued in 1:7d. In a very similar way to the narrator, she juxtaposes a comment on her pain intended to solicit compassion (1:21a; cf. 1:7c) with the cruel anti-compassionate response of the enemy (1:21b; cf. 1:7d). This serves to highlight just how wicked their response was. The shock of the reader at this response is accentuated by the fact that in 1:21a the subject is not revealed—all we know is that some people ("they") have heard her groaning and have appreciated that there is no one to comfort her. Jerusalem has been calling out for someone to see and hear her pain (1:9c, 11c, 12a, 17, 18b, 19, 20), so in 1:21a the reader is led to hope that *at last* Jerusalem has found a comforter. That hope is dashed with the revelation in 1:21b that the hearers respond not by offering comfort but by *rejoicing* at the evil she has suffered! Jerusalem prays that the evil done by the enemy (רעתם), which is the cause of the evil suffered by her (רעתי), would be dealt with harshly by Yahweh. Clearly, even though she sees the work of the enemy as the work of Yahweh, she judges it to be wrong and precisely the kind of behaviour that Yahweh ought to punish.

b. *Ethical Assessment of Jerusalem's Allies*
Jerusalem's political allies are not favourably portrayed by the narrator. In 1:2 he writes:

> Bitterly she weeps in the night,
>> and her tears are upon her cheeks,
> For there is no comforter
>> from amongst all those who love her.
> All her companions have betrayed her,
>> they have become to her as enemies.

---

3. All translations are my own.

Jerusalem is pictured as a desolate woman sitting alone and weeping uncontrollably. Her sorrow is compounded by the fact that there is no one to comfort her from amongst all those who supposedly love her. It was customary for friends and relatives of those in mourning or sorrow to stand in solidarity with them and offer comfort (e.g. Gen 37:35; 50:21; Ruth 2:13; 2 Sam 10:23; Eccl 4:1). The expressions "those who love her" (1:2d) and "her companions" (1:2e) refer to the cities or states surrounding Judah that she had been on good terms with in the past. As Berlin points out, "A nation was obligated to mourn the loss of an ally, and to provide comfort to his survivors."[4] Jerusalem's political allies provide no such support and disgracefully abandon her to her fate. Clearly this negative portrayal of Zion's political "allies" *assumes* ethical beliefs about the duty of keeping treaty obligations, and the importance of standing in solidarity with one's friends (political or otherwise) in the midst of loss.[5]

Jerusalem's main focus is not on her former allies. Indeed, it is not until 1:19a that she mentions them as part of a summary statement of her predicament. She explains: "I called to my lovers. *Even they* deceived me." Interestingly, this single line performs a dual function. In part, by describing them as illicit "lovers,"[6] it serves as an implicit confession on Jerusalem's part that her relationships with these allies were inappropriate. The alliances often involved religious duties that would have compromised her sole devotion to Yahweh. But whilst Jerusalem is, in part, making a confession, she is primarily making a protest against her so-called "allies": *"Even they* deceived me!" These alliances would have been motivated, in part, by the desire for increased security. In this case such security was not forthcoming. Jerusalem's ethical objection to the behaviour of her allies is very close to that of the narrator. What is interesting is that her reference to them as illicit "lovers" serves to cast the narrator's more neutral phrase "those who loved her" in a new and darker light. Thus, whilst the narrator's focus is firmly on the crimes of the "friends" against Jerusalem, we see now that he does not portray the city as blameless in the events that unravelled.

c. *Ethical Assessment of Jerusalem*
The narrator is clear that Jerusalem's suffering is a consequence of her sins. We have just seen how this is implicit in his reference to "those

---

4. A. Berlin, *Lamentations* (OTL; Louisville, Ky.: Westminster John Knox, 2002), 50.

5. The narrator also describes the stand-offish attitude of Zion's allies in 1:8b, 17b–c.

6. מאהביׄ designates *illicit* lovers; see, e.g., Jer 22:20–22; 30:14; Ezek. 16:33, 36; 23:5, 9, 22; Hos. 2:5–13.

who love her" in 1:2—a very subtle allusion, seen only in retrospect, to
her adultery. There are also some early and subtle hints that Jerusalem is
being punished for her sins. These come in the form of allusions to the
covenant curses of Deut 28. First, in 1:3 we read of the exile of Judah
and how "she has not found a resting place." This seems to draw on Deut
28:64–65: "Then the LORD will scatter you amongst all nations …
Among those nations you will find…*no resting place for the sole of your
foot.*" The readers would recognize the signs of the divine curse in
Judah's homelessness.[7] The next allusion to the covenant curses comes in
1:5a: "Her adversaries have become [the] head, her enemies prosper."
Readers will recall Moses' warning to Israel that if they break the covenant then the alien in their midst "will become the head [i.e. the master],
and you will become the tail [i.e. the servant]" (Deut 28:44). So in these
three subtle ways the narrator, whilst focusing on Zion's pain, *hints* at
her culpability. All subtlety is abandoned in 1:5b where he says plainly,
"For Yahweh has brought affliction, *on account of her many transgressions.*" The word פשעיה ("transgressions") suggests the breach of
covenant stipulations and that fits the context well with its allusions to
the covenant curses of Deuteronomy. Again, in 1:8–9b, the narrator
writes,

> Jerusalem sinned grievously,
>> therefore she became a mockery.
> All those who honoured her despise her,
>> for they saw her nakedness.
> Indeed, she herself groans,
>> and turns away.
>
> Her impurity was in her skirts,
>> she gave no thought to her future,
> and she has declined amazingly!
>> There is no one to comfort her.

In 1:8a we find the root חטא ("to sin") which, according to Renkema,
"points more towards a breach of community relationships."[8] This sin, he
says, is a breach of Jerusalem's relationship with God by virtue of the
fact that the community relationships that have been violated by
Jerusalem were established by Yahweh. The result of Jerusalem's sin is
that she became a נידה (*nidah*). What is a נידה? The word only appears
in this verse, but I tentatively follow those who see the Hebrew root as

7. Against Renkema's resistance to seeing any allusions in Lam 1:3 to "rest"
theology or Deut 28; J. Renkema, *Lamentations* (Historical Commentary on the Old
Testament; Leuven: Peeters, 1998), 109–10.
8. Ibid., 132.

נוּד.9 Now נוּד can mean one of two quite distinct things: (a) "wanderer," the idea being that Jerusalem is exiled for her sin (the problem is that in Lam 1 *Zion* is not exiled—*her children* are); and (b) "to shake the head" in mockery, scorn, or horror (Jer 18:16; 48:27; Ps 44:15). Hence Jerusalem is the object of head-nodding. I think this option makes the most sense of the word in the context of 1:7–9.

Those foreigners who used to hold Jerusalem in high esteem (i.e. the former allies; cf. 1:2) now despise her as something worthless (cf. 1:17) because she has been publicly humiliated by having her naked body exposed for all to stare at. In the ancient world, to have one's naked body exposed, especially the genitals, was utterly shaming. Her nakedness points both towards the city "stripped" of its walls, its palaces and riches by the foe,[10] and towards the exposure of her sins. Two cultural backgrounds may combine in this text: first, the practise of invading armies stripping their captives naked to humble them (Isa 20:3–4); and second, the practise of punishing a woman guilty of sexual impropriety by exposing her genitalia in public (Hos 2:3; Ezek 16:35–39; 23:29). Perhaps the two images are both at work here: Yahweh strips Jerusalem as punishment for her infidelity and to do that he uses the adversary who attack and strip her as a defeated foe.

Lamentations 1:9 opens with the comment that "her impurity is in her skirts," that is to say, in the lower part of her garments.[11] I follow Berlin in seeing this as a reference to her sexual immodesty.[12] Jerusalem did not

9. Others see the root as נדד. The nominal form can refer to the ritually unclean state of a menstrual woman (Lev 15:19–33; 25:19). Whilst a menstruating woman was not considered morally "unclean," the concept of ritual impurity could be *metaphorically extended* to cover moral uncleanness (Ezek 36:7).

10. Other Old Testament texts see the metaphorical stripping of a city as divine judgment; see, e.g., Nah 3:5–6; Jer 13:26; Isa 47:2–3; Lam 4:21.

11. Those who take the נידה in 1:8 as a "menstruant" usually maintain that this is a reference to menstrual blood staining her robes; e.g. D. R. Hillers, *Lamentations* (AB 7A; New York: Doubleday, 1992), 86; and I. Provan, *Lamentations* (NCB; Grand Rapids: Eerdmans, 1991), 45. If we follow this line, it may suggest that "Jerusalem's moral impurity was as obvious for all to see as a bloodstain on the skirt of a menstruating woman. O'Connor's claim that the blood is proof of sexual intercourse is implausible; K. M. O'Connor, *Lamentations and the Tears of the World* (New York: Orbis, 2003), 22. One may expect a woman to bleed after her first act of sexual intercourse but such is hardly Jerusalem's situation! Also unlikely is Dobbs-Allsopp's suggestion that the blood on her skirts might be there following an attack; F. W. Dobbs-Allsopp, *Lamentations* (Interpretation; Louisville, Ky.: Westminster John Knox, 2002), 64. The text does not mention "blood," *but "uncleanness"* in her skirts *may* be menstrual blood.

12. Berlin, *Lamentations*, 54–55. The skirts of a robe were sometimes associated with one's modesty.

consider the consequences her behaviour would have for her future. She
went ahead with reckless abandon never expecting her actions to catch
up with her—but they did, and when they did her reversal of fortunes was
breathtaking.

However, in spite of the fact that the narrator sees Jerusalem as morally culpable, his attitude towards this sinful woman is most instructive.
Whilst he is clear that she has rebelled, he is seeking to elicit sympathy
from his audience for her plight. He does this in two ways. On the one
hand, he does not dwell on the exact nature of her sins. She broke the
covenant (implicit in 1:3b, 5a), she committed "many transgressions"
(1:5), she "sinned grievously" (1:8). What *exactly* did she do? We are not
told explicitly, although reading into the images we can say that the narrator hints that she committed adultery against Yahweh through foreign
alliances. This serves not to undercut the severity of the sin but to de-
emphasize it. On the other hand, the narrator does tell us about her pain
at great length and in particular detail. This dual strategy serves to elicit
sympathy for the sinner.

The first observation to make about Jerusalem's self-assessment is that
she does not claim to be an innocent victim, but owns her responsibility
for the fate that has befallen her. The first reference to her sin is found in
1:14a-b:

> He fashioned a yoke of my transgressions,
>   in his hand they were entwined,
> they ascended upon my neck,
>   he caused my strength to fail.

From being caught in Yahweh's net (1:13), Jerusalem is now, like a
prisoner of war, constrained in a yoke.[13] This yoke, however, has been
constructed by Yahweh not from wood but out of her rebellions. The
image suggests an organic relationship between Jerusalem's sins and her
current suffering. It is not simply that her sins motivate Yahweh to
punish her in response, although that idea is clearly present. The image
goes further, suggesting that as punishment for her rebellions *Yahweh
has taken those very sins and woven them into a weapon against her*—
a yoke that binds her and weighs down heavily on her neck. Possibly
this indicates the way in which Jerusalem's illicit affairs with foreign

---

13. O'Connor sees in this sequence "a scene of domestic violence in which a
powerful, angry man beats his wife, hurls her about, and leaves her for dead"
(*Lamentations*, 26). But this is to misread the metaphors, which all depict Yahweh as
a military opponent and not as an angry husband (husbands did not catch their wives
in nets and put them in yokes).

nations have recoiled against her and those nations now become her yoke.[14]

The next self-reference to Zion's sin comes at the beginning of her second main speech: "Yahweh is indeed righteous, for against his mouth I have rebelled." There may be an allusion to rebellions of the exodus generation by the choice of the word מרה ("rebellion"). The rebellion in the wilderness is often referred to in this way (Num 20:10, 24; 27:14; Deut 1:26, 43; 9:7, 23–24), indeed several of those references use the very expression found here—"to rebel against the mouth" (Num 20:24; 27:14; Deut 1:26, 43; 9:23). The likelihood of an exodus allusion is increased by the presence of other such exodus allusions in Lamentations.[15] If such an allusion is intended, we may see that God's people are as rebellious now as they were in the exodus generation. Which of Yahweh's words has she rebelled against? Is this just a general reference to the covenant stipulations that he had given at Sinai? Perhaps, although Renkema argues that the expression to "rebel against (the) mouth" "is always used for resistance to a particular command given in a particular situation, but never with respect to commandments which have eternal validity."[16] Thus he suggests that it may be the words of the prophets such as Jeremiah that Jerusalem rebelled against. Either way, Jerusalem again admits that she has sinned (cf. 1:14) and, as such, she concurs with the narrator's assessment in 1:5 and 1:8.

The third admission of guilt is found in the use of the word מאהבי ("lovers") to describe her former allies (1:19a). We have already considered this. In her closing prayer (1:20–22) she makes two final references to her moral culpability. First, in 1:20b she says to Yahweh, "I have indeed rebelled" (cf. 1:18), and in 1:22b she says, "you [Yahweh] dealt harshly with me, on account of all my transgressions."

The second observation to make is that, like the narrator, she places more emphasis on her suffering than on her sin. The bulk of her words (1:9c, 11c, 12–16, 18–22) are designed to elicit pity and compassion for herself and her children. Whilst she does not deny her sin, her aim is salvation. In her first main speech (1:12–16) there is only *one* passing reference to her transgressions (1:14). The tone changes in the second

---

14. But we must also note that the image is not one of some kind of "natural justice" built into the fabric of the world. Throughout the verse it is emphatically Yahweh who is behind the pain—"*He* fashioned a yoke…," "*he* caused my strength to fail," "*my Lord* gave me into the hands…"

15. On such, see Dobbs-Allsopp, *Lamentations*, 75–77.

16. Renkema, *Lamentations*, 181. He cites Num 20:24; 27:14; Deut 1:26, 43; 9:23; Josh 1:18; 1 Kgs 13:21, 26.

main speech (1:18–22), which opens with a confession of Yahweh's righteousness in punishing her "for against his mouth have I rebelled" (1:18a). Immediately, however, the focus shifts back again to her sorrow (1:18b). The implicit owning of responsibility in the reference to her former allies as illicit "lovers" is placed in a context that focuses attention on *their* wronging her and on the suffering of her citizens. Similarly, the admission "I have indeed rebelled" (1:20b) is found in the midst of a call for Yahweh to observe her distress. Finally, the recognition that Yahweh has dealt with her harshly "on account of all my transgressions" (1:22b) is part of a plea that Yahweh apply the same standards to her foes, presumably so that she can have some relief from the distress they are causing her.

The third observation to make is to note how the narrator and Jerusalem converge and diverge in their assessment of Zion's situation. They clearly agree that Jerusalem has sinned. Both speak of her "transgressions" (פשעים, the narrator in 1:5b and Zion in 1:14a, 22b). Their vocabulary parts ways a little as the narrator speaks of her "sins" (חטא, 1:8a) and she talks of her "rebellions" (מרה, 1:18a, 20b), but whilst the nuances may differ there is no reason to suppose that they would disagree on the substance of her crimes. The narrator intensifies Zion's sin by speaking of her "*many* transgressions" (1:5b) and how she "sinned *grievously*" (1:8a) whilst she merely speaks of her "transgressions" and her "rebellions." However, we ought not to leap too quickly to the conclusion that the narrator emphasizes her sin more. He only refers to her "transgressions" once (1:5b) whilst she refers to them twice (1:14a, 22b); he only refers to her "sin" once (1:8a) whilst she refers to her "rebellion" twice (1:18a, 20b). He speaks neutrally of her allies as "those who loved her" (1:2b) whilst she refers to them as illicit lovers (1:19a). Thus it is Zion and not the narrator who leads the readers to assess her relationship with the foreign allies negatively. On the other hand, it is the narrator alone who speaks of Zion as disgraced by being stripped naked and raped (1:8b, 10). Perhaps it is his male perspective that allows him enough distance to speak of such things. Zion herself is so humiliated that she just groans and averts her gaze from the onlookers (1:8c). She cannot bring herself to speak of her humiliation in such terms. But it is not clear that by speaking of her humiliation this way he *accentuates* her sins so much as nuances them differently. It seems to me that Zion and the narrator do not differ much in their ethical assessment of her behaviour.

d. *Ethical Assessment of Yahweh*
In Lam 1, the narrator, for the most part, evaluates Yahweh's role as an ethically blameless one. When he first makes it clear that Yahweh is the

cause of Jerusalem's troubles, he immediately explains that this was "on account of her many transgressions" (1:5). It is interesting, however, that the narrator does not place much emphasis on Yahweh's role. The only explicit links between Yahweh and her decimation come in 1:5b and 1:17b. The rest of the time the narrator either ignores Yahweh's role in order to focus on her plight or merely implies it.

At only one point (1:10) does the narrator express some ethical reservation at what Yahweh has done. He says:

> An adversary has stretched out his hand
>   over all her precious things.
> Indeed, she saw nations
>   enter her sanctuary
> concerning whom you had commanded,
>   "They shall not enter your assembly."

He speaks of her metaphorical rape as the pagan nations desecrate the temple and then he is appalled at the shocking horror of the image.[17] He turns to Yahweh with an implicit accusation: "*You yourself* commanded that these nations should not enter your assembly! How could you allow them to force their way in?" It is just a crack in the theology that the narrator holds together so well throughout the rest of this poem. In Lam 2 this theological crack will widen.

Jerusalem places a far greater emphasis on Yahweh's role than does the narrator. Her first main speech (1:12–16) is basically an "accusation against Yahweh" drawn from the communal lament tradition.[18] She described in 1:13–15 the affliction that Yahweh has brought upon her "on the day of the burning of his anger" (1:12c). All the initial descriptions are of the work of the Babylonians seen in terms of their ultimate cause (Yahweh). He sent fire into her bones (1:13a)—possibly a metaphorical allusions to the fires set within the heart of the city itself by the enemy. He spread a net to trap her (1:13b) and made a yoke to take her prisoner (1:14a-b). However, Jerusalem's valiant men were no match for "the Lord in my midst" who treated them with disdain (1:15a). "The Lord *in my midst*" is an expression which in times past would have indicated Yahweh's dwelling with his people to bless and protect them. But Yahweh's holy presence in Jerusalem now becomes a devastating

---

17. Some feminist readers have taken exception to the "pornographic" display of the broken body of the raped mother. By doing this the text itself "rapes" her again. My feeling is that whilst such imagery is indeed deeply disturbing, it serves not the purposes of the voyeur but of the city herself by portraying the *deep horror* of her situation in order to elicit *compassion*.

18. So Westermann, *Lamentations*, 91–93, 132–36.

curse. In the normal order of things Adonai-in-her-midst called holy assemblies (מוֹעֵד) of worship and sacrifice. Now, in a painful twist of the temple traditions, Adonai-in-her-midst calls an assembly (מוֹעֵד) *against* her. Not an assembly of joyous pilgrims (such assemblies are no more, 1:4), but an assembly of enemy troops who shatter her young men. This is a dreadful exchange of the joyful Zion festivals for a "festival" in which the "pilgrims" are an enemy army. The picture of the festival is possibly expanded on in the image of wine (1:15c). But the wine for this feast is the blood of Daughter Judah crushed under the feet of the Lord in his winepress! Whilst she does not *explicitly* say that Yahweh's treatment of her is wrong, the "accusation" contains an implicit protest.

Jerusalem's second speech (1:18–22) is much less of a protest. Indeed, she opens with the confession, "*Yahweh is indeed righteous*, for against his mouth have I rebelled" (1:18a). The point is that Yahweh's punishment of her is justified because of her sin. Similarly, the call for Yahweh to notice the evil of her enemies and to "…deal harshly with it, as you dealt harshly with me, on account of all my transgressions" (1:22a-b) implies that the way Yahweh has treated her is appropriate. We should not suppose her comment that Yahweh has "dealt harshly" with her is an ethical protest (i.e. more harshly than I deserve). She is simply asking God to deal with their evil in a manner proportionate to it (i.e. harshly). It is also noteworthy that whilst she still sees her enemies as Yahweh's tool (see 1:21b–c, 22b), *she expects Yahweh to hold them accountable for their crimes* (1:21–22).

Zion also makes an *implicit* ethical assertion about Yahweh in 1:20–22. When she turns back to address Yahweh himself for the first time since 1:11c, she calls on him for the third time to "look" at her miserable state (1:9c, 11c, 20a). Implicit in this appeal is the hope that if Yahweh were to appreciate the depth of her pain, he would act to rescue her. This hope is predicated on the idea, rooted in Israel's past relationship with Yahweh that, because he is a compassionate and faithful God, he will rescue his suffering people even if their suffering is a result of their own sin.

So, Jerusalem is somewhat conflicted in her attitude to Yahweh. Whilst she never *explicitly* accuses him of acting wrongly, her tone in the "accusation" section (1:12–16) leans in that direction. The second poem will accentuate this protest (2:20–22). However, she does acknowledge several times that she has sinned (1:14a, 18a, 19a, 20b, 22c), that Yahweh did warn her about the consequences of such behaviour (1:21c) and that Yahweh is righteous to deal with her as he has (1:18a, 22a–b). On balance, in Lam 1 *both* the narrator *and Zion* portray Yahweh as just and as justified in punishing sinful Jerusalem. However, both the narrator (1:10c) and Zion (1:12–16) have the seeds of a moral complaint against Yahweh. The second poem will accentuate this complaint into something much more explicit and angry. Lamentations never resolves this conflicted ethical assessment of Yahweh but it does provide space for the expression of ethical pain, protest and perplexity alongside more traditional expressions of piety. The faithful know *in their heads* that Yahweh's response to sin must be righteous, but often it does not *look or feel* that way and the ensuing conflict between faith and experience gives birth to the kinds of unsettled responses we see in the lament traditions.[19] Biblical laments allow room for ethical protest against Yahweh even when faith still hopes that Yahweh must indeed be righteous.

It is necessary to engage with two recent and influential writers on Lamentations at this point: Tod Linafelt and Kathleen O'Connor. Both writers draw attention to some important aspects of the text, but also, in my view, unhelpfully exaggerate the differences between the narrator and Zion in Lam 1. Linafelt argues that the narrator is too keen to keep the presentation of Zion's pain *as pain* at arms length and to focus instead on the *interpretation* of her pain as resulting from sin.[20] Zion's speech, by contrast, presents the pain simply as raw pain and defers its interpretation. "Unlike the poet in verses 1:1–11, *Zion makes little correlation between her sins and her suffering*."[21] But this claim is, at best, an exaggeration, for, as we have seen, Zion makes just as much mention of her sin as the narrator does. Linafelt makes much of the fact that Zion's first major speech makes no reference to sin (apart from 1:14, which is unpersuasively dismissed as containing a "textually very uncertain phrase"[22]). Commenting on 1:18–22, he seems to backtrack a little and notes Zion's linking of her suffering with her sin but these are only "brief allusions to guilt"[23] that are really just a "genre convention of the lament... [R]ather than making her sins the primary concern of her speeches, she admits them flatly and not altogether wholeheartedly."[24] I think that Linafelt's reading is very helpful in drawing attention to the emphasis on the presentation of pain in Zion's speeches rather than on

19. See especially C. C. Broyles, *The Conflict of Faith and Experience in the Psalms: A Form-Critical and Theological Study* (JSOTSup 52; Sheffield: JSOT Press, 1989).

20. T. Linafelt, *Surviving Lamentations: Catastrophe, Lament, and Protest in the Afterlife of a Biblical Book* (Chicago: University of Chicago Press, 2000), 44–45.

21. Ibid., 45 (italics mine).

22. Ibid.

23. Ibid., 47.

24. Ibid., 48.

confession of guilt. However, I think that he is wrong to see the narrator's focus as differing from Zion's in that respect. The narrator places no more emphasis than she does on the interpretation of the pain and does much to present her pain *as pain*. I also think Linafelt downplays Zion's admissions of guilt. That something is a genre convention does not make it an inauthentic expression of genuine feelings or beliefs. If that were the case, much of the presentation of *pain* in Lam 1 would also have to be downplayed. Responding to Linafelt's comment that "she admits [sin]...not altogether wholeheartedly," we ought to point out that the narrator's references to her transgressions are equally short, equally general, and equally embedded in a general context the main focus of which is eliciting compassion for Zion. It seems to me that the brevity, generality and compassion-seeking context of the references to sin *do* suggest that the focus is elsewhere but *not* that she is not serious or wholehearted.

O'Connor picks out an important difference in emotional tone between the narrator who observes Zion's pain *from the outside* and Zion herself who experiences it *from the inside*. However, she unconvincingly develops this insight in such a way as to set the narrator and Zion in serious tension (to the narrator's detriment):

> ...the narrator is unemotional; he coolly describes the city woman's plight and is obsessed with her lost glory... By contrast, emotion overwhelms daughter Zion... [T]he narrator...is a distant observer, an "objective" reporter who tells us what he sees, but he does not speak to her. His distance and lack of passion contribute to her abandonment... He thinks she has brought [her suffering] upon herself... Daughter Zion... absorbed in her pain, she ignores her past to speak only of the awful now from which she cannot emerge. The immediacy of her speech gives her the moral authority of the survivor and undermines the narrator's perspective.[25]

Speaking of the narrator's reference in 1:2 to "those who loved her," she comments, "When the narrator tells of the failure of Zion's lovers to comfort her, his opinion of her is clear. *She deserves no comfort, for she has brought her suffering upon herself*, and now she is alone."[26] Unlike the narrator, Zion has no interest in her loss of glory and status but only in God's awful treatment of her and her aloneness.[27] For O'Connor, the narrator's words in the *first* poem are to be resisted ethically.

---

25. O'Connor, *Lamentations*, 17–18.
26. Ibid., 20 (italics mine).
27. Ibid., 26.

Now, this antithesis between the perspectives of Zion and the narrator is too strong. First, whilst not to the same extent, Zion, like the narrator, *is* concerned with her loss of social status (1:8c, 11c). Second, it is not true that Zion "ignores her past," for she clearly thinks that she has brought this suffering upon herself. Third, suggesting that in 1:2 the narrator thinks she got what she deserved, and so has no pity on her, is to ignore the fact that the Hebrew word אֹהֲבֶיהָ is *neutral*, that it is *Zion* who uses the more morally condemning word for her illicit lovers (מְאַהֲבֶיהָ) and that the narrator is clearly seeking to elicit sympathy for Jerusalem in 1:1–11.

However, O'Connor has indeed identified a difference in emotional tone that has hermeneutical significance. Even the casual reader of Lam 1 will feel a contrast between the passionate emotion of Zion and the calmer tones of the sympathetic narrator. He sees her pain and he pities her, but arguably he does not appreciate the depths of her despair. There are some signs of passion in the narrator in the first poem. His very first "word" is the guttural cry, אֵיכָה, "Alas!" His descriptions of her suffering identify some of the key elements Zion herself draws attention to, and his implicit complaint to Yahweh in 1:10c suggests that he is moved. But when we take into account the narrator's stronger emotional tone in the *second* poem, we appreciate that there has been a notable change in him as he has stood watching Zion. In the first poem he has described Zion's lack of a comforter but, although by seeing and describing her pain he has *begun* to move into the role of a comforter, he has not sought to draw close to her nor spoken to her. In ch. 2 this changes. There the narrator, perhaps in response to Zion's focus on Yahweh's role in 1:12–15, pays almost exclusive attention to Yahweh as the angry destroyer of his own city (2:1–17). Furthermore, he himself joins her in weeping in 2:11:

> My eyes are worn out from tears;
>> my bowels churn;
>> my liver bile is poured out on the ground,
> because of the destruction of the daughter of my people,
>> because infants and babies faint,
>> in the city squares.

On top of that, in 2:13 he breaks frame and becomes a character in the story by addressing her directly in a way which indicates that he recognizes his own responsibility to comfort her and that he understands her feelings about the incomparability of her pain (1:12b):

What can I say [?] to you, to what can I liken you,
   O Daughter Jerusalem?
What can I compare to you so that I may comfort you,
   O Maiden Daughter Zion?
For vast as the sea is your destruction;
   Who can heal you?

It is important to note that this deepening emotional engagement and sympathy does not lead him to seeing her as an innocent victim. He *still* thinks that her transgressions lie behind the calamity (2:14) but his focus has shifted. So he calls to her to "cry aloud to the Lord" with much weeping for the sake of her children (2:18–19). This Zion does in 2:20–22, although interestingly in 2:20 it is not clear whether the speaker is Zion or the narrator as their words blend into one angry complaint. So, whilst I do not see a serious tension between the narrator and Zion in Lam 1 in terms of ethical assessment, I do think that he has only begun a journey of appreciating the depths of her pain and it is not until the second poem that he really sees her clearly. This is a journey of ethical transformation *which the audience are encouraged to follow*.

2. *The Potential Ethical Impact on the Readers of Lamentations 1*

a. *Human Readers*

Lamentations 1 is a poem that is crafted such that it draws out an ethical reaction from its audience. The narrator speaks directly to the implied readers and demands that they not look away from the grieving woman who sits alone. He guides the implied readers towards certain ethical evaluations of Zion, her enemies, her allies and her God. By his portrait of her sorrow he seeks to draw readers to have compassion on this most broken of women. Yet there is a development over the first two poems in his ethical-emotional appreciation of her pain and the implied readers are invited on a similar journey.

Zion speaks not to the implied readers, but to other characters in her textual world: the passers-by (1:12a) and the nations round about her (1:18b, perhaps the same group). However, the implied and the actual readers will find it hard not to place themselves in the position of those passing-by on the road. As she speaks, the difference between those bystanders and the readers subtly collapses and the text makes readers feel that she is speaking to *them*, calling *them* to see her pain, drawing out *their* sympathy, inviting *them* to act as her comforter. In other words, the readers are invited to make an ethical response to this pain-sensitizing poem. Like the narrator, she also guides readers towards certain ethical evaluations of herself, her enemies, her allies and her God. Her gut-wrenching descriptions of abuse, her deeply felt expressions of emotion, and her incessant calls for help compel readers to face her tragedy. This poem does not allow readers to turn their eyes away from the lonely woman, for every part of the textual space is filled with her sorrow: to read *this* poem *is* to confront the pain.

Indeed, the very existence and reading of the poem itself serves as an ethical response to Jerusalem's holocaust. The unknown author, by writing the poem, has made possible the ongoing remembrance of the calamity. The real readers in the Jewish and Christian communities that have preserved and used the text as Holy Scripture, are led to pay attention to her. So, the poem, by its existence, serves as an ethical response to this pain and, in its use, serves to elicit ongoing ethical responses from actual readers.

The ongoing use of the poem in subsequent generations invites the readers to engage it in the light of subsequent calamities and sufferings beyond the specific decimation described by the text itself. The experiences of later readers open up the text in new and unexpected ways and enable the sufferings of readers to be interpreted in fresh ways. Of course, readers will not feel obligated to see every aspect of their experience mirrored in the text. Different readers will engage different elements of the poem as they set it in hermeneutical dialogue with their own situations.

> Lamentations is a potent work of art. To read it is to enter into a world apart, a world created by suggestion, image and metaphor. Because it is an imagined symbolic world, it can, like all good poetry, intermingle with our real worlds to reveal, mirror, and challenge them. In this conversation between worlds, it can help us see our pain, and, by reflecting it back to us, however indirectly, it has the potential to affirm our human dignity in a first step towards healing.[28]

b. *The Divine Reader*

What commentators usually pass over in silence is *Yahweh's* ethical reader-response to Lamentations. The *primary intended audience* of a lament was not the community but *God*. Christians are used to thinking of God as the *inspirer* of Scripture and the one who *speaks to us through* Scripture, but to picture God as a *reader* of Scripture is not something

28. Ibid., 4. Interestingly, if Lamentations was written quite soon after the Babylonian destruction of Jerusalem, the original audience would have been fellow sufferers; yet the implied readers are onlookers *and not insiders*. Thus, the first *real* audiences of this poem were being drawn by the text into a different viewing position vis-à-vis *their own* sorrow. It would be interesting to explore the implications of this.

that comes naturally. However, once we realize that the primary audience was Yahweh, then we see that all the strategies employed by the author to draw the implied readers to comfort Zion were actually employed simultaneously to persuade *Yahweh* to fulfil this role.

The one observation about God-as-reader of Lam 1 that can be almost guaranteed to be made by commentators is the observation that God does *not* respond to Jerusalem's suffering in Lamentations. This is an important insight that needs holding on to, for it preserves the view from below. However, for Jewish and Christian readers, Lamentations has been framed within a bigger context and this invites fresh perspectives on texts beyond those of implied authors.[29] Of special interest is the way in which Yahweh in Second Isaiah explicitly picks up on the pleas of Lamentations and takes on the role of Zion's comforter.[30] It would be worth, on another occasion, exploring the implications of the numerous allusions to Lamentations in Isa 40–55 for a Jewish or Christian consideration of God-as-ethical-reader-of-Lamentations.

Let me end with a New Testament contribution to discussions of Yahweh-as-ethical-reader-of-Lamentations.[31] If we recognize Jesus as Israel's Messiah, the one who represents the nation of Israel, then we can recognize in his suffering and death the exilic suffering and death of Israel. This draws Jesus' cross alongside the motif of the destruction of Jerusalem, so prominent in Lamentations, and it allows us to see Jesus, in some senses, *in the role of* Zion in Lamentations. *Unlike* Jerusalem, Jesus did not sin, but bore the sins of others. However, *like* Jerusalem, Jesus was beaten, stripped naked, publicly humiliated and afflicted. *Like* Jerusalem, he felt abandoned by Yahweh in the face of pagan military oppressors. *Like* Jerusalem, he was under God's curse for covenant disobedience (Gal 3:13). For the Christian who believes that *"God* was in

29.   Hugh Pyper has objected to the way in which Lamentations, by virtue of the fact that it is a fixed text, "endlessly repeats the same words to its readers, frozen in the posture of abandonment. As a text, it cannot move to a point of new attachment" (H. Pyper, "Reading Lamentations," *JSOT* 95 [2001]: 55–69 [56–57]). Thus, the textuality of Lamentations makes it not a text of mourning but of unrelenting, psychologically harmful melancholia. This is why it is so critical to appreciate that Jewish and Christian canons have framed the way the text has been read and this is why the lack of resolution *within the book itself* does not degenerate into melancholia.

30.   See especially P. T. Willey, *Remember the Former Things: The Recollection of Previous Texts in Second Isaiah* (SBLDS 161; Atlanta: Scholars Press, 1997).

31.   For a fuller defence, see my "Prolegomena to Christian Theological Interpretations of Lamentations', in *Canon and Biblical Interpretation* (ed. C. G. Bartholomew, S. Hahn, R. A. Parry and C. Seitz; Scripture and Hermeneutics 7; Milton Keynes: Paternoster, 2006), 393–418.

Christ," this puts Lam 1 in a surprising new light. God stands not only as judge, but also as the Judge judged in Jerusalem's place. Where was God as Jerusalem wept? Not only standing above her in silence, but also standing *right beside her*, weeping with her. Not simply as one who *understands* her pain, but as one who *suffers* her pain with her. That is not a response either Jerusalem or the narrator could ever have imagined, but it does open avenues for *Christian* reflection on the ethics of Yahweh in Lamentations.

This essay has simply scratched the surface of the ways Lam 1 can begin to play a role in our own ethical formation and reflection. What I hope to have achieved is to have persuaded any doubters that laments may be a richer resource for understanding Israelite ethics and for funding contemporary theological ethics than is usually realized.

THE TORAH AND HISTORY IN PRESENTATIONS
OF RESTORATION IN EZRA–NEHEMIAH

H. G. M. Williamson

In recent years Rainer Albertz has started to question whether the term "restoration," as in the familiar phrase "exile and restoration," is suitable as a description for the developments which took place in Judah during the first half of the Persian period.[1] As he observes, the Davidic monarchy was not restored, nor did Judah regain its status as an independent state. Others have added their voices in support of this position. Philip Esler, for instance, regards the label as "inapposite" for two reasons: the length of time between the fall of Jerusalem and the rebuilding of the temple was such that it could not possibly have been a precise copy, either architecturally or in terms of its cult, and secondly the local political situation was no mere replication of the pre-exilic position.[2]

In the strictly historical terms in which this opinion is expressed and on a narrow definition of restoration, this is clearly correct. The post-exilic province of Judah was not an exact replica of the pre-exilic country of the same name. To the obvious points already mentioned might be added the further observation that it was not even geographically the same, being much reduced in size by comparison with the earlier monar-

---

1. See, for instance, R. Albertz, "The Thwarted Restoration," in *Yahwism After the Exile: Perspectives on Israelite Religion in the Persian Era* (ed. R. Albertz and B. Becking; STAR 5; Assen: Van Gorcum, 2003), 1–17.

2. P. F. Esler, "Ezra–Nehemiah as a Narrative of (Re-Invented) Israelite Identity," *BibInt* 11 (2003): 413–26 (417); see too T. Pola, *Das Priestertum bei Sacharja: historische und traditionsgeschichtliche Untersuchungen zur frühnach-exilischen Herrschererwartung* (FAT 35; Tübingen: Mohr Siebeck, 2003), 281. I shall not attempt in this essay to respond to the more radical suggestion that those who came from Babylon had no connection whatsoever with the pre-exilic population of Judah. For some preliminary discussion of the issues either way, see L. L. Grabbe, ed., *Leading Captivity Captive: "The Exile" as History and Ideology* (JSOTSup 278; Sheffield: Sheffield Academic Press, 1998).

chy, especially in the south.[3] And even in the unlikely event that those scholars were right who have sought to defend the view that the Davidic family continued in power until at least the generation after Zerubbabel,[4] that would still not compensate for the political shift from vassal state to what Gottwald has not inappropriately called the colonial status of the post-exilic province.[5]

If we then ask why the term restoration has been so widely used as a description of this period, we shall no doubt soon come to the conclusion that it is because this is the way that the main biblical sources want us to regard it. An influential group within the post-exilic province clearly saw themselves as the direct successors of the pre-exilic inhabitants of Judah both socially and religiously, and they wrote their accounts of the period in such a way as to reflect, and indeed to develop, that understanding.

3. There is general agreement on most aspects of this; see, for instance, A. Lemaire, "Populations et territoires de Palestine à l'époque perse," *Trans* 3 (1990): 31–74; C. E. Carter, *The Emergence of Yehud in the Persian Period: A Social and Demographic Study* (JSOTSup 294; Sheffield: Sheffield Academic Press, 1999), 75–113; L. L. Grabbe, *A History of the Jews and Judaism in the Second Temple Period.* Vol. 1, *Yehud: A History of the Persian Province of Judah* (Library of Second Temple Studies 47; London: T&T Clark International, 2004), 134–40; J. Sapin, "La 'frontière' judéo-iduméenne au ive s. avant J.-C.," *Trans* 27 (2004): 109–54. A recent dissenting voice is that of D. Edelman, *The Origins of the "Second" Temple: Persian Imperial Policy and the Rebuilding of Jerusalem* (London: Equinox, 2005), 209–80, who argues for a significant boundary change in the south in the mid-fifth century (though her position is in broad agreement with the consensus for the opening years of Achaemenid rule). The most significant topic of dispute concerns the area of Lod, Hadid and Ono on the north-western border; in addition to the works just cited, see too J. Sapin, "Sur le statut politique du secteur de Ono à l'époque perse," in *Lectio Difficilior Probabilior? L'exégèse comme expérience de décloisonnement: Mélanges offerts à Françoise Smyth-Florentin* (ed. T. Römer; DBATB 12; Heidelberg: Wissenschaftlich-Theologisches Seminar, 1991), 31–43.
4. See P. Sacchi, "L'esilio e la fine della monarchia davidica," *Henoch* 11 (1989): 131–48; F. Bianchi, "Le rôle de Zorobabel et de la dynastie davidique en Judée du VIe siècle au IIe siècle av. J.-C.," *Trans* 7 (1994): 153–65; A. Lemaire, "Zorobabel et la Judée à la lumière de l'épigraphie (fin du VIe s. av. n.è.)," *RB* 103 (1996): 48–57; H. Niehr, "Religio-Historical Aspects of the 'Early Post-Exilic' Period," in *The Crisis of Israelite Religion: Transformation of Religious Tradition in Exilic and Post-Exilic Times* (ed. B. Becking and M. C. A. Korpel; OTS 42; Leiden: Brill, 1999), 228–44; but cf. N. Naʾaman, "Royal Vassals or Governors? On the Status of Sheshbazzar and Zerubbabel in the Persian Empire," *Henoch* 22 (2000): 35–44, repr. in N. Naʾaman, *Ancient Israel and Its Neighbors: Interaction and Counteraction* (Collected Essays 1; Winona Lake, Ind.: Eisenbrauns, 2005), 403–14.
5. Cf. N. K. Gottwald, *The Politics of Ancient Israel* (Library of Ancient Israel; Louisville, Ky.: Westminster John Knox, 2001), 96–112.

This too is an important historical datum, not in the sense that it necessarily reflects political realities but in what is arguably the even more
important sense of telling us about their sense of self-identity. To adopt
the current jargon, I am merely calling attention to the distinction between
emic and etic approaches to this period, for a simple definition of which
we may usefully adopt Mayes's summary:

> emic approaches involve trying to find the meaning of something from a
> participant's point of view; etic approaches involve trying to find the
> cause of something from an observer's point of view. Emic involves
> meaning and description; etic involves cause and explanation.[6]

While the importance of both approaches would be immediately clear to
an anthropologist, recent discussions about the way in which historical
research into ancient Israel and Judah should be conducted suggest that it
is in danger of being undervalued. It is true that histories of Israel in the
distant and not so distant past have obviously been too narrowly emic in
approach; indeed, until the comparatively recent upsurge of evidence
from sources outside the Bible became accessible, scholars attempting to
write such a history had little choice. But now the danger in some
quarters is that the pendulum may be swinging too far in the opposite
direction. But provided we are aware of the distinction and allow each
approach to serve its proper purpose and not be forced into saying more
or less than it should, then both may be allowed to contribute to the
understanding of the past.

It is the contention of this essay that the Torah plays a central role in
the way that the writers give shape to their narrative as an expression of
restoration and that they do so in several different ways, some more
overt, and some more beneath the surface. In order to appreciate that,
however, we need first to come to some preliminary understanding of the
nature of the writing that we have in the books of Ezra and Nehemiah.

The most important point to make in this regard concerns historical
cause and effect. This is fundamental to the whole historical enterprise
because it treats both the proper sequencing of events and the explanation for them. Using the books of Ezra and Nehemiah, however, I should
maintain that it is simply not possible to construct a history of that sort.
That does not mean that what is related did not happen as told; that is a
separate issue on which opinions differ, and the present argument is fully

---

6. A. D. H. Mayes, "The Place of the Old Testament in Understanding Israelite
History and Religion," in *Understanding Poets and Prophets: Essays in Honour of
George Wishart Anderson* (ed. A. G. Auld; JSOTSup 152; Sheffield: Sheffield
Academic Press, 1993), 242–57 (245).

compatible with the somewhat conservative stance I have sought to defend on this matter elsewhere.[7] Rather, the problem is that for the most part there is simply no way in which at the historical level one source included in the books can be related to another. An etic approach, which we saw involves analysis of cause and explanation, is just not possible. The sources are rather like the pearls of a necklace. Each one is of the highest value. The trouble is, they have lost the string that is supposed to keep them together and in order.[8] The very fact that there is so much discussion precisely of chronological issues with regard to these books indicates clearly that these sources were not included as they are in order to answer the kind of historical questions which we typically pose. An historically etic approach to this material is almost bound to fail, at least so far as the writing of a historically connected account is concerned. And this is hardly surprising; on a conservative estimate the books span a period of more than a hundred years, whereas the duration of the specific events which they recount occupies only about a tenth of that time. In the terms which we would understand, one complex of events just does not lead on to another.

There is, however, sufficient evidence scattered throughout these books to indicate that the compilers did have a sense of how all this material should be held together, but that that was in the realm of divine causality. In this realm, time scarcely matters; the generations can be run together almost as one. What matters from this emic perspective is God's over-all plan for the restoration of the community. Different individuals may each contribute something towards it, but it is the realization of the whole which is finally in view, and there is no necessary indication that the actors themselves were aware of what this was. Let me list some examples.

At Ezra 6:14, the rebuilding of the temple is summarized in this way: "The elders of the Jews went on successfully with the building under the prophesying of Haggai the prophet and Zechariah the son of Iddo, and

---

7. See, for instance, my commentary *Ezra, Nehemiah* (WBC 16; Waco, Tex.: Word, 1985); idem, *Studies in Persian Period History and Historiography* (FAT 38; Tübingen: Mohr Siebeck, 2004).

8. I am reminded of some words of P. R. Ackroyd: "I have tried to penetrate the complexities of a period about which we know at one and the same time a great deal, in the sense that we have material which is relevant, and very little, in the sense that there are such gaps in our knowledge that we do not know how to fit together what we do know. If I could make any general comment on the progress of my work over these thirty years, it could very well be in Ronald Eyre's words: 'I have rearranged my uncertainties'" (*The Chronicler in His Age* [JSOTSup 101; Sheffield: JSOT Press, 1991], 157).

they completed the building according to the command of the God of Israel and the decree of Cyrus and Darius and Artaxerxes the king of Persia." Two things claim our attention here. First, the whole operation is directed by God, active through his prophets. This is unlikely to have been apparent to the Persian kings, but it comes before the reference to them in order to indicate that it is of first importance to the writer. Secondly, he here includes an anachronistic reference to all three of the Persian kings who play a major role in the history, showing that he is standing back from the usual flow of the historical continuum and regarding the whole task of temple restoration as a single event in response to "the command of the God of Israel."

Soon after this verse we reach Ezra 7, which on a conservative dating comes more than fifty years later (much more, of course, if Ezra followed Nehemiah). To a modern way of thinking, there is no direct connection between the two. It is astonishing, therefore, to find the chapter introduced casually with the words "After these things." Within the divine economy, however, Ezra's mission is regarded as the next significant step, so that theologically the remark is wholly appropriate. The same may apply to Ezra's genealogy which immediately follows, for Ezra is there called the son of Seraiah, even though, so far as we can tell, Seraiah was the high priest just before the Babylonian exile (1 Chr 5:40 [Eng. 6:14]), so that once again chronology is telescoped.

At Neh 8, the careers of the two great reformers are interwoven, as we shall see again later. Historically, it is virtually certain, in my opinion, that they acted separately, but here their work is bound together as parts of one event in the restoration of the community.

Following the account of the dedication of the walls of Jerusalem, we find the remarkable statement that "in the days of Zerubbabel and in the days of Nehemiah all Israel gave the daily portions for the singers and the gatekeepers" (Neh 12:47). This links the first and last major leaders mentioned in these books in such a way as to pass over the several generations which separated them from each other. To adapt a later rabbinic saying, there is neither before nor after in the service of God.

As a final example of this same outlook, we may refer to the lists of priests and Levites in Neh 12 which span the whole period covered by these books and which end with the unifying statement that "these served in the days of Joiakim, son of Jeshua son of Jozadak [i.e. the days of the first return] and in the days of the governor Nehemiah and of the priest Ezra, the scribe [i.e. both uniting the two reformers and associating them again with the first return]" (Neh 12:26).

I conclude this preliminary point, therefore, with the suggestion that we are being invited to regard the restoration period as a history of salvation, a way of history writing which in one sense puts these books on a par with the Torah. We are more familiar with the application of the term to the biblical descriptions of the origins of Israel. In the present instance it is no less true, however. History is governed and structured not by reference to the progress of human affairs in their relation to one another, but by the purpose of God for his people which overrules in the affairs of this world even when that is not recognized at the time by its participants.

The next point for consideration follows on well from the first one, because there is evidence that the return from Babylon to Jerusalem has been presented typologically as a second exodus.

Already in the first chapter of Ezra we find clear signs of this. Here, it is helpful to recall that the author was probably working with a selection of independent primary sources, such as the inventory of temple vessels, so that the amount of text which we can ascribe directly to his hand is less than might be supposed. It means that in terms of gauging his own outlook this concentration is quite pronounced.

First we may note verse 6: "All their neighbours aided them with silver vessels, with gold, with goods, with animals, and with valuable gifts, besides all that was freely offered." It is generally agreed that the phrasing here echoes the prominent theme of the "despoiling of the Egyptians" which is mentioned three times in the exodus narrative (Exod 3:21–22; 11:2; 12:35–36) as well as in Ps 105:37.[9]

Secondly, it is evident from a passage such as Isa 52:11–12 that the theme of transporting the sacred vessels had already become an established part of the prophetic complex of motifs which anticipated the return from Babylon as a second exodus.[10] This may be associated more widely, therefore, with the accounts of the tabernacle vessels which were carried through the wilderness, and in this connection it is of interest to note that in Num 7:84–86 a number of gold and silver vessels that were given for the dedication of the altar were presented by the "princes (נשׂיאי) of Israel," apparently one from each tribe, as in 2:3–31; 7:1–83; 34:18–28. This seems to me to provide the most plausible explanation for Sheshbazzar's enigmatic title "prince of Judah" in Ezra 1:8. Attempts

9. For the theme, see G. W. Coats, "Despoiling the Egyptians," *VT* 18 (1968): 450–57. Apart from general thematic similarities, the Ezra author has apparently added the word "vessels" to the prescriptions of the decree of Cyrus in v. 4 in order to draw the wording closer to that in the Exodus texts mentioned above, in each of which this word also occurs.

10. Contra H. M. Barstad, *A Way in the Wilderness: The "Second Exodus" in the Message of Second Isaiah* (JSS Monograph 12; Manchester: Victoria University of Manchester Press, 1989), 102–5, who interprets the כלים here as weapons.

to explain this title in political terms have never been found persuasive, and the commentaries always find themselves obliged to express considerable uncertainty. But as a title reminiscent of the first exodus, it fits naturally in its context and requires no further explanation.

Finally, the wording at the end of Ezra 1 used to describe the return from Babylon would be strange in a straightforward account: "the exiles were brought up from Babylonia to Jerusalem." I suggest that this too is to be explained as contributing to the exodus typology, because it makes use of a standard formula, as found, for instance, in Exod 33:1, where God speaks to Moses of "the people whom you have brought up from the land of Egypt unto the land which I promised to Abraham"; similar wording occurs at Gen 50:24; Exod 3:8, 17, and so on.[11]

It seems clear from this, therefore, that not only do the books conflate the scattered events of the restoration period in the manner of a salvation history, but that they present them as typologically related to the foundational salvation history of the birth of the nation itself. Historically speaking, it is likely that the return was a long drawn out and somewhat unspectacular affair. The use of typology, however, opens the eye of faith to the hand of God behind the historical process. There may not have been a restoration in the sense that Albertz has in mind, but instead it is as though the same nation has been born again, which is arguably even better!

Nor is this limited to the period of the first return. In a famous essay, Klaus Koch demonstrated that the description of Ezra's journey to Jerusalem was also presented in terms of a second exodus.[12] The language of "going up" several times in Ezra 7:6–9 is suggestive, but he drew particular attention to the connection between these verses and the next one ("because"), which suggests that Ezra determined the date for his journey by study of the Torah, the first day of the first month being, of course, the date of the passover festival (Exod 12:2), itself associated in particular with the exodus. Furthermore, he has insisted that Ezra's concern as mentioned in 8:15–20 that some Levites should journey with him is intelligible "only against the background of the order of the march through the desert after the original Exodus. In accordance with the P source (Num. x. 13ff.), there must be Levites with special tasks, as well

11. Cf. J. Wijngaards, "הוציא and העלה: A Twofold Approach to the Exodus," *VT* 15 (1965): 91–102.

12. K. Koch, "Ezra and the Origins of Judaism," *JSS* 19 (1974): 173–97. Whereas Koch considered this to be Ezra's own understanding, it is more likely, in my opinion, to be a result of the work of the book's editor, v. 10 in particular (on which an important part of the argument hangs) being probably the contribution of the latter.

as priests and laymen, with Ezra also."[13] Finally we should not forget that the later portrayals of Ezra as a second Moses confirm the results of an emic analysis which suggest that such typological correspondences were seen in these texts from early times.

This typological portrayal of the return as part of the restoration has important hermeneutical implications. Being repeated in Ezra 1 and 7–8, as well as featuring in a different way in the great prayer of Neh 9, it indicates that a second exodus is not a solitary event but a type of experience which successive generations may enjoy. Its promise and hope are not exhausted by the first group who returned, and no blame is attached to those who chose to go only later. The prospect of new life is ever open, and it confronts each successive generation with its challenge for decision. As in the New Testament (cf. Matt 20:1–16; 21:28–31; Luke 15), no virtue attaches to preceding others in responding to this challenge.

A third topic within these books brings us even closer to the centrality of the role of the Torah, namely the theme of institutional continuity. I have already acknowledged the truth of Albertz's claim that post-exilic Judah cannot be said historically to have been an exact restoration of the pre-exilic reality, yet the authors of Ezra and Nehemiah were evidently anxious to stress the extent to which there was a direct continuity between several of the important pre- and post-exilic institutions that were central to its sense of identity.

Some of the most important elements which contribute to this, it is true, fall outside our immediate concern because they reflect continuity with topics discussed in the earlier historical books of the Old Testament rather than the Torah itself, and so they will not be fully discussed here. I refer, for instance, to such matters as the genealogical identity of the people, the land in which they settled, and especially, of course, the rebuilt temple, where time and again the authors stress the extent to which with regard to its site (Ezra 3:3; 6:7 etc.), preparation (Ezra 3:7; cf. 1 Chr 22:4; 2 Chr 2:8–16), dimensions (Ezra 6:3; cf. 1 Kgs 6:2), construction technique (Ezra 5:8; 6:4; cf. 1 Kgs 6:36; 7:12), vessels (Ezra 1:7–8; 5:14–15; 6:6), personnel (Ezra 6:18; Neh 12:24, 45–46, etc.) and sacrifice (passim) it was the exact successor to the first, Solomonic temple.

As well as people, land and temple, there is another institutional point of continuity that deserves attention, and this brings us very much to the heart of our present concern because it is the book of the law itself. Gordon Wenham does not need me to tell him that the history of the formation of the Pentateuch or Torah is a complicated issue on which

13. Koch, "Ezra," 187.

agreement is unlikely ever to be reached among scholars. That, however, will not have been the concern of our authors. For them, it was the book of the law of Moses, a foundational constitution for their ancestors. The mere fact that they had it still was a direct link to the Israel of the past.

At the same time, however, circumstances had changed (as Albertz has rightly stressed), so that in many respects this law appeared no longer to be relevant to them. Not only did they not have their own king, but they were no longer even in a position to enforce every aspect of the law as they could previously when they were an independent nation. No matter how far we extend the principle of Persian adoption of local law for the regulation of local affairs,[14] at the end of the day the Jews were conscious that their lives were still lived under the jurisdiction of both "the law of your God and the law of the king" (Ezra 7:26). It would not have been surprising if the law had therefore slowly slipped into obscure and antiquarian oblivion, at least so far as its legislative aspects were concerned, and indeed, there are indications here and there in the Ezra story in particular which suggest that this process had already well and truly begun by the time that he travelled to Jerusalem.

Without going into detail at this point (since the issues become rather technical[15]), I believe that the most important thing which Ezra bequeathed to later Judaism was the start of a process, which we have all inherited, of applying a hermeneutic to these ancient prescriptions so that they could be given a contemporary application which relates very little to their original purpose, but which seeks in some way to capture and apply their underlying principle, what we sometimes call the spirit of the law. The techniques involved have been the subject of repeated and detailed scrutiny, and their links forward to post-biblical Judaism as well as to New Testament and other similar religious and literary expressions are well known in general terms even if highly complicated in detail. The point that I want to stress now, however, is that the beginning of this process in the books of Ezra and Nehemiah is a testimony of the first importance to their sense of a striving to establish continuity with an earlier embodiment of Israel. By submitting to this sacred and hallowed

14. The theory of full-blown imperial authorization has been seriously challenged of late and should no longer form a basis for speculation about the composition or promulgation of the Pentateuch; see several of the contributions to J. W. Watts, ed., *Persia and Torah: The Theory of Imperial Authorization of the Pentateuch* (SBLSymS 17; Atlanta: Society of Biblical Literature, 2001).

15. See, for instance, M. Fishbane, *Biblical Interpretation in Ancient Israel* (Oxford: Clarendon, 1985); K. L. Spawn, *"As It Is Written" and Other Citation Formulae in the Old Testament: Their Use, Development, Syntax, and Significance* (BZAW 311; Berlin: de Gruyter, 2002).

scripture, the community evidently believed that it was drawing on the same life-blood as its ancestors, even if the circumstances in which they lived had changed. The role of the written law in giving expression to continuity and so to a sense of restoration can scarcely be exaggerated.

A fourth approach to the role of the Torah in the depiction of restoration in the books of Ezra and Nehemiah may best be approached from a consideration of the overall shape of these books. As has often been observed, the three major periods with which they deal seem to be treated according to a common pattern. First there is the return of a group or an individual from Babylon to Jerusalem under the explicit authority of the king. Thus in Ezra 1–2 a large number are said to have returned following the decree of Cyrus, in Ezra 7–8 Ezra and others return after the Edict of Artaxerxes, and in Neh 1–2 Nehemiah returns after being commissioned by the king. Next, as they begin to undertake the task for which they have been sent, they encounter serious obstacles which threaten the success of the whole operation. The initial moves by the first returnees to rebuild the temple are delayed by external threats and intrigues in Ezra 3–4.[16] In the second section at Ezra 9, the obstacle is posed by the marriage of many Judean men to foreign wives, something which is perceived as threatening the integrity of the community. Thirdly, in Nehemiah the opposition comes not once but repeatedly throughout the account of the rebuilding of the wall; indeed, stereotyped references to it are the main structuring device for the Nehemiah Memoir as a whole.[17] Finally, each section ends with an account of how these obstacles were overcome and the project successfully concluded: Ezra 5–6 describes the building and dedication of the second temple, Ezra 10 reports on the resolution of the mixed marriages issue, and at the end of Neh 6 we learn of the completion of the wall-building project. Thus far, therefore, we seem to be presented with parallel accounts of the restoration of the temple, of the community and of the city of Jerusalem; what more could possibly remain to be said?

There are indications of the need for more to follow from the fact that, unlike in Ezra 1–6, the successes of Ezra 7–10 and of Neh 1–6 are not celebrated. Ezra 10 ends abruptly, while the resumption of the first person account by Nehemiah only with the dedication of the walls in Neh 12 indicates that there has been some purposeful redactional arrangement of

16. The historical problems raised by the apparent chronological displacements in Ezra 4 are well known, but need not be discussed here; all that matters for our present purpose is to note that they reinforce the interruption in the work on the temple by external interference.

17. See my *Ezra, Nehemiah*, 215, 224, 251.

material at this point. On both counts, therefore, attention comes to be focussed on Neh 8, both because it is here that Ezra suddenly and unexpectedly reappears and because it is the point at which the Nehemiah account gets broken into.

Initially we might suppose that there is to be a fourth section of the books parallel with the first three, for here too we read of a formal proclamation. This time, however, it is not a royal proclamation or authorization but rather a public proclamation of the law of God. And this observation is of major importance for our understanding of what is happening here. Just as the three royal proclamations are clearly to be understood as positive from the Judean point of view and acts of grace from a theological perspective, so too we are invited to view the Torah here as a positive act of God's grace. Despite what follows, there should be no sense that the law is presented as exclusive demand, as the condition for restoration; rather, it is a gracious provision for the life of a community which must therefore have already experienced restoration. As Childs has put it, "Ezra does not read the law in order to reform Israel into becoming the people of God. Rather, the reverse move obtains. It is the reformed people to whom the law is read."[18]

In such a situation there can be no talk of obstacles and opposition. The position that this held in the earlier sections is here filled instead by confession in Neh 9, a means of overcoming what might be seen as the otherwise insuperable obstacle of failure to follow the Torah with loyalty. And finally, in place of a narrative of the successful conclusion of a task, we find in Neh 10 the statement of recommitment by the whole community both to the law in its entirety and to a series of specific stipulations in particular. Moreover, as Duggan has recently stressed, from the confession through to the end of the pledge the narrative voice shifts to the first person as if to emphasize the direct involvement of the people as a whole.[19] At this point, then, the stage is set for a celebration of the combined work of all the previous reformers in the dedication of the walls of Jerusalem (Neh 12:27–43): Ezra and Nehemiah are both present (in the text as we have it), and the whole celebration ends up in the temple in a joyful scene whose sound could be heard from far away.

In my opinion, and for reasons that need not be elaborated here, the three chapters which make up Neh 8–10 were each originally separate

18. B. S. Childs, *Introduction to the Old Testament as Scripture* (London: SCM Press, 1979), 636.

19. M. W. Duggan, *The Covenant Renewal in Ezra–Nehemiah (Neh 7:72B–10:40): An Exegetical, Literary, and Theological Study* (SBLDS 164; Atlanta: Society of Biblical Literature, 2001).

pieces, drawn from different sources of whatever sort. This is not to say, however, as some have maintained, that their present order and position are the result of confusion or scribal accident. Despite the tensions which a close analysis can demonstrate, it is clear that they have been assembled into an intelligible whole in order to bring the preceding narrative to a theological climax, just as the dedication of the walls marks the narrative's physical climax. It has been common to label this section "Covenant Renewal." We lack direct evidence as to whether this label corresponds to any social or historical reality at this time, but in general it may be accepted as a literary designation provided we do not allow it to mislead us as to the nature of what is here being said. It is not that through this the community moves towards restoration; in that sense it is not a portrayal of restoration of the sort that we have looked at in previous parts of this essay. Rather, it indicates something of the redactor's understanding of what a restored community is like—attentive and responsive to God's gracious word, conscious of the need for constant forgiveness and grace and committed to both the letter and the spirit of the law's demand. It is the goal of restoration rather than a description of the path which leads to it.

We have now looked at several ways in which restoration is presented in Ezra and Nehemiah, at least from an emic perspective. While I have agreed that an etic evaluation would have to conclude that the label is not really appropriate, the spin, as we might say, that later inside interpreters of the community's history put on events was clearly shaped and phrased in order to present the first half of the period of Achaemenid rule as one of restoration. Does that mean, as some distinguished commentators have suggested, that this is all that needed to be said, that there was nothing more to look forward to, and that life from now on should consist of nothing other than steadfast loyalty to the cultic norms that had been re-established? In my view, that interpretation overlooks two important points[20] which strongly indicate the consciousness that even with so much achieved there remained yet further steps before restoration could be said finally to be accomplished.

Of first importance in this regard has to be the remarkable prayer included in Neh 9. I have argued elsewhere[21] that this prayer reflects the outlook of those who remained in the land during the period of the exile,

20. For a more detailed examination than is possible here, see J. G. McConville, "Ezra–Nehemiah and the Fulfilment of Prophecy," *VT* 36 (1986): 205–24.

21. See my *Studies in Persian Period History and Historiography*, 282–93. Note also M. J. Boda, *Praying the Tradition: The Origin and Use of Tradition in Nehemiah 9* (BZAW 277; Berlin: de Gruyter, 1999).

so that in many ways it was bound to present a very different point of view from that of the rest of Ezra–Nehemiah, which is so clearly dominated by the outlook of those who returned from Babylon. Nevertheless, the prayer was included by the editor responsible for what we have seen to be the climactic section of the work, so that we must include it in our account of the work's overall point of view.

Of the many things that could be said about this prayer, let me single out just two. First, there can be no doubt that one of its dominant concerns is the land as promised originally to Abraham and inherited by the generation following those who came out of Egypt. Contrary to the dominant biblical paradigm, however, we are not told that it was lost because of disobedience at the time of what we call the exile, but rather that it came under foreign domination at that time and has continued so until the time of writing. The inhabitants of the land view themselves as living in servitude to foreign kings; they feel acutely the loss of independence together with the fact that their economy is no longer under their own control but exploited to the advantage of non-native kings. Here surely is the clearest indication that restoration has not yet been fully achieved, and that for some of the very reasons that Albertz and others recognize. It is precisely in the political realm that the greatest contrast with the pre-exilic period is to be found.

Secondly, however, the prayer gives remarkable expression to a sense of openness to future change in this regard, no matter how unrealistic that might have seemed at the time. In its historical retrospect, the prayer describes the pre-exilic life in the land by use of the well-known Deuteronomic cycle of rebellion, handing over to a foreign power, cry for help and response by God in deliverance. This cycle occurs twice in its full form, in vv. 26–27 and 28. It then starts out in vv. 29–31 on a third cycle, but this time it is not completed. For several reasons it seems likely that this third description of judgment is meant to refer to the Babylonian conquest, and it is at that point, halfway through the cycle, that the long historical recital breaks off. The expected elements of cry for help and deliverance are not recorded. Instead, in a most powerful move from the point of view of intercession, the writer catches himself and his readers up into the historical continuum by actualizing the words of prayer and confession which arise from their present situation: "Now therefore, our God…do not treat lightly all the hardship that has come upon us," and so on. The description of land and people in bondage which follows is not just a cry of despair but rather a holding up before God of the situation which now exists but which repeated historical experience has taught them God is well able and willing to reverse. There is thus an intense expectation that he will again "hear from heaven" and bring deliverance, so realizing that restoration in the political realm that was so obviously lacking in post-exilic Judah's colonial status.

From this theological highlight of the book, let us turn briefly in conclusion to its ending. As many commentators have noted, the final chapter of Nehemiah is remarkably anti-climactic. The whole work seems to peter out with a whimper of minor concerns that apparently lead nowhere. The heady excitement of the dedication of the walls would be a so much better conclusion from our point of view. Why not stop there, with Jerusalem rejoicing in its restored state?

Perhaps the answer is that the writer was more of a realist than a novelist. He knew, as all of us come to learn from bitter experience, that any triumph, whether political, religious of other, does not retain its shine for long unless some way is found to translate its values and achieve-ments into the regular routines of ongoing life and activity. This is what the anthropologists call routinization,[22] and our author knew the truth of that without having first to learn the jargon. By probably reversing the historical sequence of events, in which the pledge of Neh 10 surely followed the abuses of 13, he reminds us that restoration is not a once-for-all event which can be documented and then consigned to history. It is rather a process, which may certainly have a beginning but of which it would be a mistake to say that it has an end. Just as the prayer of Neh 9 indicates that there remains more to be done in restoration from God's side, so too does Neh 13 contribute its own witness to the truth that in smaller ways the same may be said from humanity's. And for that, the guidance of the Torah is paramount.

In this essay I have tried to gather together some of the most familiar points that the books of Ezra and Nehemiah emphasize with regard to the post-exilic restoration. As we have seen, this is history told from an emic perspective; we learn of an ancient community's self-perception, which is an important historical datum in its own right, even if it poses insuper-able problems in our attempts to construct a modern scientific historical account. At the end, however, we have found some slight evidence that should equally not be ignored which suggests that even within this the writers were not unaware that restoration was not as complete as some commentators have suggested. In their own way and with their own voice, they thus join with the recently expressed concerns of modern historians who inevitably approach their subject from an etic perspective

22. Cf. K. D. Tollefson and H. G. M. Williamson, "Nehemiah as Cultural Revitalization: An Anthropological Perspective," *JSOT* 56 (1992): 41–68, repr. in *The Historical Books: A Sheffield Reader* (ed. J. C. Exum; Sheffield: Sheffield Academic Press, 1997), 322–48.

and so conclude that it is misleading to speak of this period as the restoration period without qualification. These ancient writers may not have expressed themselves with the kind of language that we use today, but all the same we should try to come to terms sympathetically with what they were attempting to achieve. The Torah was central to their self-understanding, so that in conscious as well as unconscious ways it shaped the way they thought about and gave expression to a presentation of their current political, social and religious situation. It was part of their faithfulness to what they regarded as inherited tradition that they should present an important aspect of that situation as one of restoration even while recognizing that it could not yet be considered complete.

Part IV

READING THE LAW FOR THEOLOGY

THE THEOLOGY OF PLACE IN GENESIS 1–3*

Craig G. Bartholomew

1. *Introduction*

Most of Gordon Wenham's research has focused on the Pentateuch, with ground-breaking commentaries on Genesis, Leviticus and Numbers following his doctoral work on Deuteronomy. In this essay I seek to build on that work by exploring a neglected theme, namely the theology of place in Gen 1–3. My interest in place as a biblical theme was sparked *inter alia* by my involvement in a project on a Christian theology of pilgrimage.[1] Pilgrimage is all about "holy *place*" and in order to ground pilgrimage theologically I began thinking about place in the Bible.[2] This essay develops that earlier work by focusing on place in Gen 1–3. It should be noted that this is an exercise in theological interpretation—the focus is on Gen 1–3 rather than the Canon as a whole, but the concern is theological interpretation of these chapters in relation to place.

a. *Definition*

Place is a rich, thick concept. E. S. Casey, who has published two major philosophical volumes on place, defines it as follows:

* I am delighted to contribute this essay to a Festschrift for Gordon Wenham. When I was looking for a person to supervise my doctoral research I searched for that unusual combination of a scholar who was critically rigorous while also taking the Bible seriously as Scripture. Gordon Wenham became the obvious choice, because of his fine Old Testament scholarship and his commitment to Christian theology. It was a privilege to work under his supervision and then as a colleague at the University of Gloucestershire. It is good to celebrate his gifts and considerable achievements in this Festschrift.

1. C. G. Bartholomew and F. Hughes, eds., *Towards a Christian Theology of Pilgrimage* (Aldershot: Ashgate, 2004).

2. See Bartholomew, "Journeying On: A Concluding Reflection," in Bartholomew and Hughes, eds., *Pilgrimage*, 201–15.

> To be in the world, to be situated at all, is to be in place. Place is the
> phenomenal particularization of "being-in-the-world," a phrase that in
> Heidegger's hands retains a certain formality and abstractness which only
> the concreteness of *being-in-place*, i.e., being in the *place-world* itself,
> can mitigate.[3]

Place is so fundamental to human existence that it is easy to miss. Its
reality and importance cannot however be in doubt, but its neglect and
thickness make it hard to pin down conceptually. Although space and
place are inseparable, place must be distinguished from space:

> [space] fails to capture what is specific to place, namely, the capacity to
> hold and situate things, to give them a local habitation. Such holding
> action proffers something ready-to-hand (*zuhanden*), something con-
> cretely palpable, to which attachment can be made. This palpability
> belongs properly to place and not to space.[4]

Place is central and foundational to human life and identity.[5] Casey
speaks in this respect of the human condition as one of *implacement*: "To
exist at all...is to have a place—to be *implaced*, however minimally or
temporarily."[6] "[P]lace belongs to the very concept of existence. To be is
to be bounded by place, limited by it."[7] Part of being embodied involves
being in a particular place:

> In my embodied being I am *just at* a place as its inner boundary; a sur-
> rounding landscape, on the other hand, is *just beyond* that place as its
> outer boundary. Between the two boundaries—and very much as a func-
> tion of their different interplay—implacement occurs. Place is what takes
> place between body and landscape.[8]

Place is something that humans experience, and the interplay between
humans and their contexts means that place has a "distinctively cultural
dimension."[9] "[J]ust as every place is encultured, so every culture is

---

3. E. S. Casey, *Getting Back into Place: Toward a Renewed Understanding of
the Place-World* (Bloomington and Indianapolis: Indiana University Press, 1993),
xv. He also notes that "Heidegger alone of postmodern thinkers has thematized
place, albeit fragmentarily and inconsistently"; cf. idem, *The Fate of Place: A
Philosophical History* (Berkeley: University of California Press, 1998), 11. It is not
surprising therefore that Casey uses Heidegger's terminology in defining place.

4. Casey, *The Fate of Place*, 20.

5. See K. Norris, *Dakota: A Spiritual Geography* (New York: Ticknor & Fields,
1993; 1st Mariner Books ed., Boston: Houghton Mifflin, 2001), for a fine expression
of this reality.

6. Casey, *Getting Back*, 13.

7. Ibid., 15.

8. Ibid., 29.

9. Ibid.

implaced."[10] Place is furthermore never just an individual thing, it "insinuates itself into a collectivity."[11] There is thus a social dimension to place. Implacement is an ongoing, dynamic process and being cultural and social it is also historical. "The cultural dimension of place—along with affiliated historical, social, and political aspects…this dimension contributes to the felt density of a particular place, the sense that it has something lasting to it."[12] To understand place is thus, as O'Donovan notes, to "grasp the reciprocal relation between nature and culture: geographical space mediating a possibility for human life in community; human inhabitation elevating a dead space into the character and distinctiveness of place."[13]

b. *Contemporary Relevance*
We live amidst a crisis of place. In our late-modern age we have lost that very human sense of place amidst the time–space compression[14] characteristic of "postmodernity." Place has become something that one moves through, and virtual reality is no replacement.[15] As David Lyon perceptively notes of cyberspace, "There is no place to this space."[16] Casey

10. Ibid., 31.
11. Ibid., 31.
12. Ibid., 33.
13. Oliver O'Donovan, "The Loss of a Sense of Place," *Irish Theological Quarterly* 55 (1989): 39–58 (47).
14. See D. Harvey, *The Condition of Postmodernity* (Oxford: Blackwell, 1990), and D. Lyon, *Jesus in Disneyland: Religion in Postmodern Times* (Cambridge: Polity, 2000), on this theme.
15. I am indebted to my friend Bob Walker for alerting me to the relevance of theology of place to the current discussion of "new urbanism" in North America, as North Americans have become aware of the problems with urban sprawl. See P. Katz, *The New Urbanism: Towards an Architecture of Community* (New York: McGraw–Hill, 1994); J. H. Kunstler, *The Geography of Nowhere: The Rise and Decline of America's Man-Made Landscape* (New York: Touchstone, 1993); idem, *Home From Nowhere: Remaking Our Everyday World for the Twenty-First Century* (New York: Touchstone, 1996).
16. Lyon, *Jesus in Disneyland*, 124. But cf. Casey, *The Fate*, xiv, who notes that "The comparative coziness and discreteness of such compresence…makes it a genuine, if still not fully understood, phenomenon of place." G. Ward, commenting on cyberspace, notes that "[Manuel] Castells analyses space in terms of flows, in which places and local cultures are superseded. He emphasizes that it is not placeless, but the logic and meaningfulness of place, rootedness, and an urbanism generating cities of collective memory…is absorbed into the 'flows of capital, flows of information, flows of technology, flows of organisational interaction, flows of images, sounds, and symbols'" (*Cities of God* [London and New York: Routledge, 2000], 245; citing Manuel Castells, *The Rise of the Network Society* [Oxford: Blackwell, 1996], 412).

describes our culture as *dromocratic*, that is, a speed-bound era.[17] The suffering of placelessness is not limited to refugees and those in exile; in our dromocratic society every person "on the move" suffers from place-lessness in one form or another.

Philosophically Casey tracks in detail how "space" has won over "place" in modernity so that modernism has downplayed place. Space in turn has been made subservient to time.[18] According to Casey,

> In the past three centuries in the West—the period of "modernity"—place has come to be not only neglected but actively suppressed. Owing to the triumph of the natural and social sciences in this same period, any serious talk of place has been regarded as regressive or trivial... For an entire epoch, place has been regarded as an impoverished second cousin of Time and Space, those two colossal cosmic partners towering over modernity.[19]

One can ignore place but it is unavoidable:

> We are immersed in it and could not do without it. To be at all—to exist in any way—is to be somewhere, and to be somewhere is to be in some kind of place. Place is as requisite as the air we breathe, the ground on which we stand, the bodies we have. We are surrounded by places. We walk over them and through them. We live in places, relate to others in them, die in them. Nothing we do is unplaced.[20]

Similarly, Giddens rightly notes, "the setting of interaction is not some neutral backdrop to events that are unfolding in the foreground. 'Locales' enter into the very fabric of interaction in a multiplicity of ways."[21] Heidegger characterizes the human person as *Dasein*, and a major impli-cation of this perspective is that placed-ness, dwelling, habitation are at the heart of being human.[22] The neglect of place has thus had devastating consequences. In our late-modern context we are witnessing the develop-ment of global cities in which "[P]lace no longer matters and...the only type of worker that matters is the highly educated professional."[23] The

17. Casey, *Getting Back*, xiv.
18. See Casey, *The Fate*, 75–193.
19. Casey, *Getting Back*, xiv.
20. Casey, *The Fate*, ix.
21. A. Giddens, *Problems in Social Theory* (Cambridge: Polity, 1979), 201.
22. On Heidegger and place, see Casey, *The Fate*, 243–84.
23. Saskia Sassen, *The Global City: London, New York and Tokyo* (Princeton: Princeton University Press, 1991), 6–7 (quoted by Ward, *Cities of God*, 242). In the same place Ward notes that "Severing connections with the grassroots of the people, catering for the needs of an increasingly mobile and short-stay populace, the polis becomes a panopticon surveying the international scene, speculating here and there on its future aggrandisement."

dehumanizing effect of Western urban sprawl is well documented else-where.[24] The crisis of city life is related to the concomitant crisis of rural and agrarian life.[25] Problems in both areas are symptomatic of the larger crisis of place central to late-modernity.

Harvey Cox lists and celebrates the major gifts of the modern city as anonymity and mobility.[26] Brueggemann, however, rightly notes that we suffer not so much from *anomie* but more foundationally from *atopia*:[27]

> That promise concerned human persons who could lead detached, unrooted lives of endless choice and no commitment. It was glamorized around the virtues of mobility and anonymity that seemed so full of promise for freedom and self-actualization. But it has failed… It is now clear that *a sense of place* is a human hunger that urban promise has not met…it is *rootlessness* and not *meaninglessness* that characterizes the current crisis. There are no meanings apart from roots.[28]

Place is so constituent of human being that perhaps this is one reason why it is so easily overlooked. "The present moment is a propitious one for assessing the fate of place. This is so even though there is precious little talk of place in philosophy—or, for that matter, in psychology or sociology, literary theory or religious studies."[29] Theology and biblical studies suffer a similar neglect.[30] Emphases on existentialist and "great deeds" approaches resulted in the neglect of creation, nature, land and place in most biblical theology. Brueggemann's *The Land* marked a sig-nificant reversal in this trend and encouragingly an ecological hermeneu-tic is emerging with similar concerns.[31] However, it is rare to find theo-logians and biblical exegetes working specifically with the concept of place. As will be demonstrated below, place is particularly well suited to excavate key elements of the biblical message.

24. Not least in the literature of new-urbanism, which offers an answer to the problem.
25. See W. Berry, *The Unsettling of America* (New York: Avon Books, 1977), and *What are People For? Essays by Wendell Berry* (New York: North Point, 1990); and also, for example, R. A. E. North, *The Death of British Agriculture: The Wanton Destruction of an Industry* (London: Duckworth, 2001).
26. Harvey Cox, *The Secular City* (London: SCM Press, 1965), 80–99.
27. The terminology is from Casey, *Getting Back*, xi.
28. W. Brueggemann, *The Land: Place as Gift, Promise and Challenge in Bib-lical Faith* (2d ed.; London: SPCK, 2002), 3–4 (original emphasis).
29. Casey, *The Fate*, xi–xii.
30. J. Inge, *A Christian Theology of Place* (Aldershot: Ashgate, 2003), is an important exception.
31. See N. Habel and S. Wurst, eds., *The Earth Story in Genesis* (The Earth Bible 2; Sheffield: Sheffield Academic Press, 2000).

In the second edition of *The Land*, Brueggemann acknowledges the need for a stronger emphasis on creation—indeed, the early chapters of Genesis are fundamental to a biblical theology of place, as is the Pentateuch as a whole. Significant work has been done on the theology of the Pentateuch but rarely through the prism of place, and in this essay, I examine Gen 1–3 through that prism. (Readers should note that this essay is part of a planned larger work on the theology of place.)

2. Genesis 1

the world is the house where mortals dwell
—Heidegger[32]

In recent decades considerable advances have been made in reading Gen 1 as carefully crafted literature with a polemical dimension which sets it against alternative creation stories of the ancient Near East. Gordon Wenham has contributed to this type of creative reading of Gen 1.[33] More recently ideological questions have been raised about Gen 1 and this particularly in relation to its view of humankind's relation to the earth.[34] Norman Habel's ecological reading of Gen 1 is worth noting in this respect.

Habel notes that while Gen 1:1—2:3 is cosmic in its scope its focus is clearly on the earth, and says: "the earth story at the beginning of Genesis is a dramatic account that celebrates the wonder and worth of Earth as a geophany."[35] He helpfully reads Gen 1:2 as indicating that the primordial earth is present but hidden.[36] For him, earth is the primary character of the story and the reader eagerly awaits her appearance and development; she is hidden by darkness and the waters. Genesis 1:2a indicates that she is an empty, uninhabited place. The creation of light and sky set the stage for earth to appear on centre stage. Proceeding stages describe the acti-

---

32. M. Heidegger, *Hebel der Hausfreund* (Pfullingen: Neske, 1957), 13.

33. See, e.g., G. J. Wenham, *Genesis 1–15* (WBC 1; Waco, Tex.: Word, 1987), 37; idem, "Sanctuary Symbolism in the Garden of Eden Story," *PWCJS* 9 (1986): 19–25.

34. See the celebrated article by Lynn White, Jr., "The Historical Roots of Our Ecological Crisis," *Science* 155 (1967): 1203–7; repr. in *The Care of Creation* (ed. R. J. Berry; Leicester: InterVarsity, 2000), 31–42.

35. Habel, *Earth Story*, 35.

36. Wenham, *Genesis 1–15*, 16–17, similarly says of the darkness covering the surface of the deep that "Prima facie, it is just another description of the terrible primeval waste, but it could hint at the hidden presence of God waiting to reveal himself." Wenham translates רוח אלהים (*rûaḥ ĕlōhîm*) as "wind of God" and argues that this refers to the presence of God moving over the waters.

vation of earth with plant and animal life and her illumination with the sun and moon. The emergence of earth is complete by the end of day 6— God's rest indicates the integrality of this geophany.

For Habel, however, this earth story, which he articulates in helpful and creative detail, is in stark contrast to the story of the creation of humans in 1:26–30. For Habel, "the human story (Gen. 1.26–30) violates the spirit of the Earth-oriented story that precedes it (Gen. 1.1–25)."[37] "In terms of justice for Earth, the text of Genesis 1 moves from honouring Earth by describing its revelation as a geophany, to negating Earth as a force to be overcome by humanity."[38] For Habel, it is time we restored the Earth story to its rightful place as a genuine counterpart to the human story with which the Earth story interacts in subsequent narratives in Genesis.

There are several difficulties with Habel's discernment of conflicting narratives in Gen 1. First, considerable work has been done to show that Gen 1:1–2:3 is carefully crafted literature and one would need strong arguments to subvert the literary unity of this pericope simply by removing Gen 1:26–28.[39] Secondly, despite Habel's admirable and creative attempt to draw attention to earth as a central focus of Gen 1, there is a tendency to personify "Earth" which is unhelpful. Thirdly, the whole point of Gen 1 is to present the earth as the context for human habitation, for implacement.[40] The earth is one of the major actors in the narrative but so too is the human, and one of the motifs of the narrative is how humans are to interact with the earth. Thus, it is far better to see Gen 1 as a *place* story rather than an earth story. Place, as noted, evokes human inhabitation of the earth, and in this respect helps us to see what is going on in Gen 1 far better than a renewed source criticism which uses ideological critique to discern conflicting stories. Genesis 1 portrays the earth as a *potential* place for human habitation and dwelling. As Heidegger notes, "the world is the place where mortals dwell."[41]

37. Habel, *Earth Story*, 47.

38. Ibid., 48.

39. Wenham, *Genesis 1–15*, 6, notes that, "The arrangement of 1:1–2:3 is highly problematic." But he concludes that "The careful symmetries and deliberate repetitiveness of the chapter reveal…a carefully composed introit to the book of Genesis" (p. 10, and see pp. 5–10 for context). The point is that, despite the challenges of discerning the literary structure of 1:1–2:3, it is too easy and anachronistic simply to remove 1:26–28 while reading the rest as a unity.

40. Casey, *The Fate*, notes how this is common to ancient creation narratives. This is a further argument against Habel's distinguishing of two conflicting stories.

41. "If Bachelard is right in claiming that 'all really inhabited space bears the essence of the notion of home' and that home itself is 'a real cosmos in every sense

Wenham and others have noted how, contra the *Enuma Elish* and other ancient Near Eastern creation stories, the differentiation of place that takes place during the six days of Gen 1 is all oriented towards creating a context suitable for human implacement and flourishing. The gradual differentiation of place that we find in Gen 1 is common to other creation stories. As Casey notes, "The cosmogonic gathering is in effect a formation of place. Thus, even if the beginning is characterized as a situation of no-place, the ineluctable nisus is towards place—and towards an ever increasing specificity of place, its laying out in the right...order."[42] Casey discerns three levels of place in Gen 1:

1.   the *ur*-places presupposed by the activity of God himself;
2.   the elemental regions of darkness;
3.   the formed regions of earth.

Casey's first level is theologically controversial, since he finds it hard to imagine God creating out of no-place.[43] However, if one takes seriously the distinction between Creator and creation, as does the Judaeo-Christian tradition, then speculation about the place of God is unhelpful. However, Casey is quite right to note that creation involves differentiation and that this is progressively more determinate and leads towards human inhabitation.[44] As far as Gen 1 is concerned, the move towards place is particularly strong because, contra other ancient Near Eastern creation stories, Gen 1 presents a picture of the earth being shaped into an environment that is very good for human habitation, rather than humans beings created to make the lives of the gods easier.[45] As Karl Barth notes, this is particularly true from the fourth day onwards:

> The preceding works all aimed generally at man, or rather at God's relationship with man. But from this point onwards everything aims particularly at man's interested partnership in his relationship with God. The wisdom and goodness of the Creator abound in the fact that, following the creation, establishment and securing of a sphere of human life, He wills to fashion and does fashion it as a *dwelling-place* for the man who can

of the word,' then home and cosmos alike—home *as* cosmos—result from practices of cultivation" (Casey, *Getting Back*, 175).
   42.   Casey, *The Fate*, 15–16.
   43.   Ibid., 13: "The act of creating takes place in place."
   44.   Ibid., 16: "[C]reation is a process of progressive implacement."
   45.   Cf. here section VI of the Babylonian Epic of Creation (*Enuma Elish*) where humanity is created: "They shall bear the gods' burden that those may rest," cited in W. W. Hallo and K. Lawson Younger, eds., *The Context of Scripture*. Vol. 1, *Canonical Compositions from the Biblical World* (Leiden: Brill, 1997), 400 (the translator of the Epic of Creation is Benjamin R. Foster).

recognize God and himself and his fellow-creatures, and who in the recognition of what is and occurs can be grateful and express his gratitude… The office of these lights, the heavenly bodies, is to summon him in relation to his Maker to sight, consciousness and activity.[46]

Because day and night have already been created, there is a sense in which the luminaries are redundant; however, not only are they not gods, but they are given as signs *for humankind* to demarcate seasons, days and years (1:14).[47] In this sense 1:26–30 is indeed the highpoint of 1:1–2:3, since it involves the implacement of those earthly creatures made in God's image in the home he has prepared for them. The world, as presented in Gen 1, is indeed the home prepared for them to indwell. As Heidegger notes, "The relationship between man and space is none other than dwelling, strictly thought and spoken."[48]

Thus, approaching Gen 1 through the prism of place helps us to see that earth and humankind are both central characters in the narrative, and that their interrelationship is a central motif. There remains the question of whether or not 1:26–30 affirms exploitation of the earth. Much has been written about this issue. Suffice it here to note that God, and not humankind, is the central character in the narrative, and that dominion is best understood as a royal stewardship in which humankind's role is to serve, develop and indwell the creation such that it is enhanced and God is honoured.[49] As we will note with respect to Gen 2–3, the depiction of humankind is as an earth-ling, and his/her embodiment ties humankind into the ecology of creation such that his/her role cannot be reduced to mastery and exploitation. Wallace rightly notes the significance of Gen 2:1–3 in this respect. Genesis 2:1 stresses once again the interrelatedness and completeness of the creation. "Thus Gen. 2:1–3 stands as a check

46. Karl Barth, *Church Dogmatics*, vol. 3, *The Doctrine of Creation*, part 1 (Edinburgh: T. & T. Clark, 1958), 157 (emphasis added).

47. Ibid., 160. Wenham, *Genesis 1–15*, 23, notes that what is clear about 1:14 is the luminaries' role in fixing seasons and days of cultic celebration.

48. Heidegger, "Building Thinking Dwelling," in *Basic Writings from Being and Time (1927) to The Task of Thinking (1964)* (London: Routledge, 1978; Henley: Kegan Paul, 1977), 319–39.

49. Barth, *Church Dogmatics*, 235, notes: "He [the man] thus appears as the being which must be able to and ready to serve in order to give meaning and purpose to the planting of the earth… In view of his complete integration in the totality of the created world, there can be no question of a superiority of man supported by appeals to his special dignity, or of forgetfulness not merely of a general but of the very definite control of Yahweh Elohim over man. In spite of all the particular things that God may plan and do with him, in the first instance man can only serve the earth and will continually have to do so."

against any interpretation of the role of humans in Gen. 1:28 that ignores the harmony and wholeness of all the work God has done in creation."[50] In contrast to the Akkadian and Ugaritic narratives, in which humans are created to achieve the rest of the gods by relieving them of manual labour, in Genesis humans are intended to participate in God's rest. Thus, "The seventh day is a recognition that the creation is held together by God and that God is the one on whom it is totally dependent."[51]

Genesis 1 is universal in its scope with a developing focus on the whole earth as humankind's home, whereas, as we will now see, Gen 2–3 is place-specific in its focus. As we move on to Gen 2–3, we should however note that Gen 1's universal vision of the world as a whole is place-oriented rather than space-oriented. Again, as Heidegger perceptively notes, place precedes space: "Unless we go back to the world, space cannot be conceived."[52]

3. *Genesis 2 and 3: Implacement and Displacement*

a. *Implacement*

The debate about the relationship between Gen 1:1–2:3/4a and 2–3 is well known. Source criticism identified two different creation stories, with 1:1–2:3 identified as part of P and Gen 2–3 as part of J, and scholars continue to wrestle with the relationship between the two. Indeed, the ongoing legacy of source criticism is to read the two creation stories independently of each other. Undoubtedly there are important differences between them, and undoubtedly they draw on a variety of sources, but canonically and in terms of the literary shape of Gen 1–11 it is important to inquire into the juxtaposition of these two narratives and the consequent relationship opened up between them. Childs rightly notes that:

> [I]t is equally true that the two originally different accounts have not simply been juxtaposed in Genesis as two parallel creation stories. To read them in this fashion...disregards the essential effect of the canonical shaping which has assigned the chapters different roles within the new context of the book of Genesis.
>
> The introductory formula in 2:4 makes it clear that J's account has now been subordinated to P's account of the creation. What now follows proceeds from the creation in the analogy of a son to his father...ch. 2 performs a basically different role from ch. 1 in unfolding the history of

50. Howard N. Wallace, "Rest for the Earth? Another Look at Genesis 2:1–3," in Habel and Wurst, eds., *The Earth Story in Genesis*, 49–59 (53).

51   Ibid., 58.

52.   Quoted by Casey, *The Fate*, 243.

mankind as the intended offspring of the creation of the heavens and the earth… By continuing to speak of the "two creation accounts of Genesis" the interpreter disregards the canonical shaping and threatens its role both as literature and Scripture.[53]

Certainly if we are concerned with *Reading the Law* then the question of their relationship is relevant and important in terms of the ongoing narrative.

The תולדות (*tôlĕdôt*, "generations") structure of Genesis as a literary unit is well known and it is important to note that Gen 1:1–2:3 stands outside this literary shaping, whereas Gen 2–4 is the first major section contained within a *tôlĕdôt* heading.[54] Genesis 1:1–2:3 functions therefore as an introduction to Genesis (and the Pentateuch) as a whole, whereas chs. 2–3 initiate the story that will lead on to Abraham and Israel. "The role of the *tôlĕdôt* formula in 2:4, which introduces the story of mankind, is to connect the creation of the world with the history which follows."[55] The genre of Gen 1–11 is much debated but this much can surely be said: Gen 2–3 have more of a narrative/historical function within Genesis than does Gen 1:1–2:3.[56]

In terms of the perplexing relationship between these creation stories, the concept of place is once again very helpful. I noted above that Gen 1 presents the earth as a *potential* place for humans; it is depicted as an ideal home. I also noted the progressive place differentiation. In Gen 2 this differentiation is taken a step forward. Indeed 2:4b, with its inversion of "heavens and earth"[57] to "earth and heavens," signals the shift in focus to the earth.[58] Genesis 2 becomes far more specific with its focus on Eden as the garden in which Adam and Eve are to dwell. As von Rad perceptively notes of J's account of creation, "It is altogether a much smaller area with which the narrator deals—not even the 'earth,' but the world that lies at man's own doorstep—garden, rivers, trees, language, animals, and woman."[59] "P is concerned with the 'world' and man within it, while J shows the construction of man's immediate environment and defines

53. B. S. Childs, *Introduction to the Old Testament as Scripture* (London: SCM Press, 1979), 149–50.

54. With Wenham, *Genesis 1–15*, 49, 55, 56, I take 2:4 to be a heading for what follows in Gen 2–4.

55. Childs, *Introduction*, 146.

56. See Wenham, *Genesis 1–15*, 53–55.

57. Cf. Gen 1:1; 2:1, 4a.

58. As Barth (*Church Dogmatics*, 234) notes: "The heavens are not overlooked or denied, but in this saga attention is focused on the earth."

59. G. von Rad, *Old Testament Theology*. Vol. 1, *The Theology of Israel's Historical Traditions* (Edinburgh: Oliver & Boyd, 1962), 148.

his relationship to it."[60] Yahweh Elohim plants a garden in Eden and there he places the man he had formed of dust from the ground. In this sense at least Gen 2 represents a continuation of the place differentiation in Gen 1. As Casey notes:

> When it is added…that "a mist went up from the earth and watered the whole face of the ground" (2:6) and that "God planted a garden in Eden, in the east" (2:8), we attain a still more definite degree of place-determination, one that now includes quite particular places (i.e. patches of ground) that have proper names and even cardinal directions…the movement is from less determinate to more determinate places.[61]

Thus, narratively, the move from Gen 1 to 2, rather than indicating a juxtaposition of two unrelated sources, involves a movement of progressive implacement[62] culminating in the planting of Eden as the specific place in which the earthlings Adam and Eve are to dwell.

Childs, as quoted above, is thus right in his assertion that Gen 2 connects the history of humankind with creation. But it is important to note just how illuminating place is at this point. Genesis 1 presents the world as a *potential* place for human habitation but the nature of Adam and Eve as embodied earthlings means that the human story itself must begin in a specific place, in this case Eden. As Casey notes, "*Implacement* itself, being concretely placed, is intrinsically particular."[63]

The Hebrew word for humankind in 1:26–28, namely אדם (ʾādām), already creates the closest connection between humankind and the earth, with its association with אדמה (ʾădāmāh, "ground"), although the word used for the earth as a whole in Gen 1 is ארץ (ʾereṣ). In 2:7, however, Yahweh Elohim forms ʾādām out of the ʾădāmāh, and in Eden it is out of the ʾădāmāh that Yahweh Elohim causes trees to grow which are aesthetically pleasing and nutritionally satisfying. Throughout 2:4–3:24, ʾădāmāh is used for Eden, and ʾereṣ does not occur in that sense. "Earthling" is therefore an apt description of human beings since it points clearly to the *embodied* nature of human being.[64] And embodiment and place are correlated concepts, both of which have been suppressed in modernity.

---

60. Ibid., 150.
61. Casey, *The Fate*, 14.
62. The term is Casey's; see ibid., 16.
63. Casey, *Getting Back*, 23.
64. See Carol A. Newsom, "Common Ground: An Ecological Reading of Genesis 2–3," in Habel and Wurst, eds., *The Earth Story in Genesis*, 60–72, for a perceptive account of the human beings' relationship to their environment in Eden.

Drawing upon Merleau-Ponty and the few others who have attended to the body philosophically, Casey is once again perceptive in this respect, as the following passages indicate:

> Only if explicit attention is given to the lived body in relation to its whereabouts does the importance of place in distinction to space become fully evident.[65]

> My body continually *takes me into place*. It is at once agent and vehicle, articulator and witness of being-in-place... Without the good graces and excellent services of our bodies, not only would we be lost in place...we would have no coherent sense of place itself. Nor could there be any such thing as *lived* places, i.e., places in which we live and move and have our being.[66]

> ...body and place are congruent counterparts. Each needs the other. Each suits the other...*place is where the body is*.[67]

> ...we are bound by body to be in place.[68]

Embodied human life implies specific place and the order of Gen 1–2 exemplifies this. The world as a whole is a wonderful *potential* place for human habitation, but human habitation can never straddle the whole earth; it is of necessity specific, and in Gen 2's case that means the garden which God plants, namely Eden. Place names begin to accumulate in Gen 2—Eden, Pishon, Havilah, Gihon, Tigris, and Assyria—and this again indicates the differentiation towards a specific place: "Place-names embody this complex collective concreteness despite their considerable brevity."[69]

Genesis 2 thus begins the story of human history with the specific implacement of Adam and Eve. "Here" and "there" are terms denoting place,[70] and in this respect the םש (*šām*, "there") of 2:8 is significant, carrying all the weight of implacement: "To dwell means to belong to a specific place."[71] The place in mind is "a garden in Eden, in the East." We are not told much about this garden other than that it is fertile with a variety of trees; aesthetically it is pleasing and a river flows out of it and thus we conclude that it is well irrigated. The result of this minimal information is that we easily read into Eden our own experience of

65. Casey, *Getting Back*, 46.
66. Ibid., 48.
67. Ibid., 103.
68. Ibid., 104.
69. Ibid., 23.
70. Ibid., 50–56.
71. Ibid., 109.

gardens or the Romantic notion of untamed wilderness. What should we imagine when we think of Eden?

First, we should think of a specific place. As Barth notes, "the biblical witness is speaking of a definite place on earth."[72] Wenham explores the clearly symbolic value of Eden as a place where God dwells; indeed, several features of the garden liken it to a sanctuary. However, he rightly asserts that "the mention of the rivers and their location in vv. 10–14 suggests that the final editor of Gen 2 thought of Eden as a real place, even if it is beyond the wit of modern writers to locate."[73] This is strengthened by the *tôlĕdôt* context in which chs. 2–3 occur, signalling the unfolding history of humankind.[74] Furthermore, as I have noted, the move in chs. 1–3 is from heavens and earth to earth, then to the garden. The setting in 2:5–8 indicates a Mesopotamian site for Eden.[75]

But what kind of garden is Eden? The details in ch. 2 are sparse. God plants the garden and makes all kinds of trees grow in it, trees that are good for food and aesthetically pleasing. The garden is well irrigated, an attractive prospect in the arid East. "Eden" probably derives from its homonym "pleasure, delight," indicating the abundance of provision and fertility of the garden.[76]

Benjamin notes that the legacy of a Romantic perspective is the tendency to interpret Eden as an unspoiled wilderness.[77] In his view "it is more likely that the Eden in the story of the Adam is a landscaped garden or urban masterpiece than an undeveloped wilderness or a geological wonder."[78] Tuplin, however, thinks the description of the garden of Eden is modest and in line with the other gardens mentioned in the Old

72. Barth, *Church Dogmatics*, 252.

73. Wenham, *Genesis 1–15*, 61–62.

74. E. Noort suggests that "In the stories of Gen 2–3 Paradise is not located; it is far away. But in this mythic-geographical fragment, probably a learned addition to the original text, a (partial) localization is tried"; see E. Noort, "Gan-Eden in the Context of the Mythology of the Hebrew Bible," in *Paradise Interpreted: Representations of Biblical Paradise in Judaism and Christianity* (ed. G. P. Luttikhuizen; Leiden: Brill, 1999), 21–36 (28). Noort explores the many attempts to solve the geographical problems of locating Eden and concludes that the difficulties encountered show that the author intended to offer a mystified location for Eden which demonstrates its reality as Paradise while not wanting to locate Eden in an accessible place.

75. Wenham, *Genesis 1–15*, 66.

76. Ibid., 61.

77. D. C. Benjamin, "Stories of Adam and Eve," in *Problems in Biblical Theology: Essays in Honor of Rolf Knierim* (ed. H. T. C. Sun and K. L. Eades; Grand Rapids: Eerdmans, 1997), 38–58 (43).

78. Ibid., 43–44.

Testament.[79] It is hard to be sure of the ancient Near Eastern background to ch. 2,[80] and so to decide between Benjamin and Tuplin. Gardens were an important part of the irrigation economies of Mesopotamia and Egypt; in the case of wealthy and influential persons, the garden could be expansive and generally adjoined the residence. The ancient Egyptians also cultivated gardens, orchards and parks, and wealthy families often maintained country estates where the owners could relax amidst flowers, fruit trees and ponds.[81] Within the Old Testament, Yahweh Elohim's planting of a garden may be comparable with Qoheleth's planting of vineyards, founding of gardens and parks, and creation of pools from which to water the forest of growing trees. This would fit with the royal fiction in Ecclesiastes, since such projects cohere with the description of the projects of kings in the ancient Near East.[82] That it was generally the wealthier who owned gardens affirms the monarchical dimension, albeit democratized, of the *imago dei* as presented in Gen 1.

What is clear on all accounts is that a garden was an enclosed area designed for cultivation.[83] This background casts interesting light on Eden as a place for human habitation. Rather than Gen 2 presenting an image of primitivism, it would appear to portray an area bounded, probably by walls, which is carefully landscaped and intensively cultivated with orchards and the like. It may well have included buildings—its urban connotations in the ancient Near East are particularly interesting in the light of the tendency to portray Eden as a form of primitivism.[84] Thus God, as King, a central image of God in Gen 1, plants a garden, and as the under-kings, Adam and Eve dwell in the garden, which is a royal residence.

79. C. Tuplin, *Achaemenid Studies* (Historia Einzelschriften 99; Stuttgart: Franz Steiner Verlag, 1996), 81.

80. Wenham (*Genesis 1–15*, 51–53) explores the background and concludes that the writer probably borrowed various motifs from different stories and created from them his own story.

81. See R. K. Harrison, "Garden," in *ISBE*, 2:399–400.

82. A bronze bottle from Tell Siran in Jordan lists the works of Amminidab, king of the Ammonites, which include the creation of a vineyard, a garden, and pools. Some Neo-Assyrian inscriptions mention the planting of gardens, orchards and parks as well as irrigation projects. See C.-L. Seow, *Ecclesiastes* (AB 18C; New York: Doubleday, 1997), 151.

83. Wenham, *Genesis 1–15*, 61. In the same place, he suggests that we think of a park surrounded by a hedge.

84. Contra the tendency to portray the narrative arc of Scripture as the move from a garden to a city. This also undermines Ellul's view of the city/urban life as portrayed almost wholly negatively in Scripture.

We should therefore note that Eden is here represented as a full-fledged dwelling place. According to Casey, dwelling places range across countless different styles, types, and purposes, but full-fledged dwelling places fulfil two necessary conditions: they must be constructed so as to allow for continual return, and they must possess a certain felt familiarity. Eden clearly fulfils these conditions. including that of landscape.[85]

Secondly, we should note that Eden as a dwelling place has the specific characteristics of a garden. Historically, there has been an immense variety of gardens and Casey limits his analysis to three types.[86] From his analysis, he concludes that gardens offer three special lessons of their own:

1. mood is an intrinsic feature;
2. gardens instruct us as to the expanded building potential of certain material elements, such as ground, wood, water and rock;
3. gardens offer dwelling of some sort.

Casey notes that the gardens he analyzes do not normally offer permanent dwellings,[87] but here the ancient Near Eastern background is instructive, linked as gardens are to royal residences. Clearly in Eden the dwelling is hestial (aiming at centredness) in the sense that Adam and Eve reside there.

A characteristic of gardens is *cultivation*,[88] which fits precisely with Yahweh Elohim putting Adam and Eve into Eden in order to "till it and keep it" (2:15). A possible translation of עבד (*'bd*, "till," NRSV) is to "serve,"[89] and this helpfully undermines any sense of brutal mastery over the garden. Cultivation is polysemic in its connotations and in order to find a connecting thread through its many uses Casey returns to the root of the word in the Latin verb *colere*, "to care for." "In tilling the soil we care for it by ploughing and planting in ways useful to the growing of food… We must question the presumption that building is an exclusively Promethean activity of brawny aggression and forceful imposition."[90] "We get back into place—dwelling place—by the cultivation of built places. Such cultivation localizes caring. What is for Heidegger a global feature of existent human being—namely, 'care' (*Sorge*)—is here given

---

85. See Casey, *Getting Back*, 115–16.
86. Ibid., 155–72.
87. Ibid., 169, observes that "garden-dwelling is never purely hestial."
88. Ibid., 155.
89. Wenham, *Genesis 1–15*, 67.
90. Casey, *Getting Back*, 173.

a local habitation and not just a name. We care about places as well as people so that we can say that *caring belongs to places*."[91]

The element of cultivation central to Eden again reminds us that, as in Gen 1, we are not dealing with an earth story but with a place story. "Another current in place's overflowingness is its distinctively cultural dimension. If body and landscape are the concurrent epicentres of place, this does not mean that they must be natural givens. This interpretation was as tempting to the Greeks as it remains in the modern era."[92]

Casey notes of gardens that "Even if we pause from time to time, for the most part we perambulate in gardens."[93] Gardens evoke a mood that is peculiarly suited for sociality, contemplation and reflection. This resonates with 3:8 where Adam and Eve "heard the sound of the LORD God walking in the garden at the time of the evening breeze." The garden is not just a place for the production of vegetables, fruits and herbs, but is also a place of "intimacy, meditation, and family solidarity."[94] Wenham has noted how Eden is depicted as a sanctuary[95] and this fits with the intimate relationship pictured here with God. The unusual use of Yahweh Elohim as the name for God in Gen 2 and 3 already alerts us to the relationship with God that Adam and Eve participate in.[96] The image of God walking in the garden reinforces this in the strongest way—Eden was a place of intimate relationship with God.

Thirdly, we should note that we are presented in Gen 2, as in ch. 1, with a *theology* of place. The tree of life is at the centre of the garden. In Scripture trees are a symbol of the life of God and "the tree of life is an essential mark of a perfect garden in which God dwells."[97] As Barth notes, the tree in the midst of the garden "indicates that the Garden is God's sanctuary."[98] And "While He gives man the enjoyment of the whole Garden and all its trees, by the planting of the tree of life in its midst God declares that his primary, central and decisive will is to give him Himself." Significantly for place, Barth asserts that "God grants him His own presence, i.e., Himself as the Co-inhabitant of *this place*."[99]

91. Ibid., 175.

92. Ibid., 29. And see the ensuing argument, pp. 29–33, which reinforces the weakness of Habel's attempt to portray Gen 1 as an earth story.

93. Ibid., 155.

94. Ibid., 158.

95. Wenham, "Sanctuary Symbolism."

96. J. L'Hour, J., "Yahweh Elohim," *RB* 81 (1974): 524–56.

97. Wenham, *Genesis 1–15*, 62.

98. Barth, *Church Dogmatics*, 282.

99. Ibid., 282 (emphasis added).

From this perspective, place is not fully place without the presence of Yahweh Elohim as a co-inhabitant.

It is clear from the above that approaching Gen 1 and 2 through the prism of place is fecund. It not only enables us to avoid some of the dualisms of contemporary ecological readings, but also illuminates the logical connection between Gen 1 and 2, and in the process allows us to see the centrality of place in human identity and being.

b. *Genesis 3: Displacement*

Much has been written about Gen 3. Suffice it to note here that place once again enables us to gain fresh insight into the condition of fallenness that Gen 3 portrays. The philosopher and ecologist Baird Callicott has recently presented a persuasive interpretation of what is involved in eating of the tree of the knowledge of good and evil. For Callicott, it involves *self*-consciousness such that, once aware of themselves, humans may treat themselves as an axiological point of reference. This provides a more sophisticated complement to Wenham's view that the tree stands for wisdom in the sense of autonomy[100] and as such seems to me to be correct. Once self-aware in this way, humans treat themselves "as an intrinsically valuable hub to which other creatures and the creation as a whole may be referred for appraisal. Self-consciousness is a necessary condition for self-centeredness, self-interestedness."[101]

Human identity is deeply bound up with place, as I have shown, and what is fascinating in Gen 3 is that the heart of God's judgment in the light of humans making themselves the hub of other creatures is *displacement*. Genesis 3 concludes with the damning indictment: "therefore the LORD God sent him forth from the garden of Eden, to till the ground from which he was taken. He drove out the man…" The prior judgment pronounced on the man in 3:17–19 also amounts to displacement—the man's relationship to the ground, that is, his experience of place, will be transformed. Cultivation will be in danger of radical misdirection from care to abuse. Callicott notes that the thorns and thistles which the ground will produce are indicative of ecological destruction: "With agriculture there begins the paradoxical history of human destruction of the Earth's fertility in the very search for productive land."[102]

---

100. Wenham, *Genesis 1–15*, 62–64.
101. J. B. Callicott, "Genesis and John Muir," in *Covenant for a New Creation: Ethics, Religion and Public Policy* (ed. C. S. Robb and C. J. Casebolt; Maryknoll, N.Y.: Orbis, 1991), 107–40 (123–24).
102. Newsom, "Common Ground," 70.

With the modern suppression of place and amidst our dromocratic society, it is hard to grasp the horror of this judgment. However, in the Old Testament and ancient Near Eastern context there would have been a far greater sense of the angst associated with landlessness, and, especially if Gen 2 and 3 were written around the time of the exile, then readers would have a keen sense of the pain of *this* exile, imaging as it does their being vomited out of the land of Israel and Judah (Lev 18:25–28).

Casey observes that,

> Landscape itself, usually a most accommodating presence, can alienate us. (Lyotard goes so far as to assert that "estrangement (*dépaysement*) would appear to be a precondition for landscape.") Entire cultures can become profoundly averse to the places they inhabit, feeling atopic and displaced within their own implacement. If Freud and Heidegger are correct, this dis-placement, or "displacement" as it could also be called, is endemic to the human condition in its ineluctable "uncanniness"; *Unheimlichkeit*, not being-at-home, is intrinsic to habitation itself.[103]

Genesis 1 and 2 alert us to the fact that estrangement or displacement is not, as Lyotard suggests, a precondition for landscape. However, the passage quoted rightly notes that in its fallen condition not-being-at-home is a constant challenge for human beings. "Displacement within their own implacement" captures vividly the challenge that will now face humankind. Implacement is unavoidable—it is part of the human condition—but to be at rest in their implacement will from now on be an entirely different story. This becomes apparent in Gen 4, in which humankind's relationship to the ground becomes increasingly complex. Cain's punishment, for example, is to be continually displaced.

However, among biblical scholars the relationship between Gen 2–3 and the rest of the Old Testament is disputed. Westermann concludes that,

> There is no tradition of the narrative of Gen 2–3 throughout the whole of the Old Testament, and this has impressed a number of scholars in recent times. It is not quoted and is never mentioned. It is never included in the syntheses of the acts of God (Credo). The reason for this is that Israel never considered it to be a historical incident side-by-side with other historical events. The Israelites did not think of it as a definite event to be dated at the beginning of human history, even though it remained eminently real to them.[104]

---

103.   Casey, *Getting Back*, 34.
104.   Westermann, *Genesis 1–11*, 276.

And again, "chs. 1–11 of Genesis must be regarded as a separate element of the Pentateuch, that is as a relatively self-contained unity, and not primarily as a part of 'Genesis.' It is a relatively late component."[105]

Awareness of place is again revealing at this point. Contra Westermann, as a story of displacement, Gen 2–3 is fundamental to the entire Old Testament and presupposed at every point. The quest for landedness will form the heart of the narrative that follows chs. 2–3.[106] It is evident in Cain's being condemned to wander as a displaced individual and in his attempt to build a city in order to secure implacement. And of course the issue of (re)implacement is central to the Abraham covenant, with its promise of the land which God will show to him.[107] And the rest of the Old Testament revolves in one way or another around the issue of Israel's implacement and displacement in the land of Canaan. Chapters 2–3 may indeed not be quoted or "mentioned," but once we become aware of the centrality of place in the Old Testament it becomes clear that Westermann's approach, which looks for specific allusions, is inadequate. Genesis 2–3 may be of late origin and was perhaps crafted during the exile—this may be one reason for a lack of allusions. However, in the context of the Canon as a whole, the connection between chs. 2–3 and what follows in the Old Testament is clear. Furthermore, the *tôlĕdôt* heading to chs. 2–5 does indicate that canonically speaking chs. 2–3 are—in some sense—seen as historical, however we define this more precisely, whether as saga[108] or proto-historical.[109]

4. *Conclusion*

It is, I trust, clear by now that approaching Gen 1–3 through the prism of place is remarkably fertile. In line with ecological readings, it enables us to see that the earth is a central actor but it avoids the danger of reductionism by enabling us to see that Gen 1 focuses on the interrelationship between God, earth and humankind. Genesis 1 is a *place* story, with all that that involves, and not just an earth story. And whereas Gen 1 is universal in its scope, focusing increasingly on the earth as potential place, Gen 2 begins the human story in a particular place, namely

105. Ibid., 2.
106. See Brueggemann, *The Land*, in this respect.
107. *The NIV Study Bible*, 24, notes on 12:1 that "Abram must leave the settled world of the post-Babel nations and begin a pilgrimage with God to a better world of God's making."
108. So Barth, *Church Dogmatics*, 81.
109. So Wenham, *Genesis 1–15*, 54.

Eden.[110] Despite the significant differences between chs. 1 and 2, this illuminates the logical connection between them and shows precisely how ch. 2 is subordinate to ch. 1, and confirms that 2:4 is the heading for what follows and not for what precedes.

The Pentateuch, and indeed the Canon as a whole, contains a remarkable amount of data about place, none of which can be explored here. Suffice it here to give some indications of where our examination of place in Gen 1–3 might lead. In terms of biblical theology, our examination of Gen 1–3 confirms that Brueggemann is right when he asserts that "land is a central, if not *the central theme* of biblical faith."[111] To be fair to Brueggemann, he does not limit his vocabulary to land but makes much of place as well. There is, however, as we have seen, an important distinction between earth/land and place. And it would certainly not be true to assert earth/land as the central theme of biblical faith. Elohim (Gen 1) or Yahweh Elohim (Gen 2–3) and not land is the central character and theme of Gen 1–3 and of the Bible as a whole. However, as Gen 1–3 make clear, for humans to say "God" is to be implaced, and insofar as *place* evokes—as it clearly does—the nexus God, earth/land and humankind, it would be quite right to see place as a major contender for the central theme of biblical faith, moving as Scripture does from Eden (an urban style garden) via the land of Israel and the cultic centre of Jerusalem, to the incarnate Jesus,[112] to the city of the new Jerusalem which is central to the new heavens and earth. Redemption, examined through the prism of place, will therefore have the structure of implacement–displacement–(re)implacement.[113]

In terms of biblical theology, my examination also indicates how fundamental Gen 1–3 is to the entire Canon. Creation establishes the place in which the drama of Scripture and thus of history will be enacted. The link between ch. 1 and chs. 2–3 is fundamental in this respect. Much is often made of the fact that certain elements in ch. 1, such as the *imago*

110.   In geography the tension between universal and particular remains a thorny issue. Intriguingly, Entrikin notes that "Narrative offers a means of mediating the particular–universal and the subjective–objective axes"; see J. N. Entrikin, *The Betweenness of Place: Towards a Geography of Modernity* (Baltimore: The Johns Hopkins University Press, 1991), 6. Gen 1–3 explores and relates the universal (the heavens and the earth) and the particular (Eden) precisely through narrative but always within a God-centred context.

111.   Brueggemann, *The Land*, 3 (original emphasis).

112.   See Inge, *Christian Theology of Place*, on the significance for place of Jesus as the incarnate one.

113.   Brueggemann, *The Land*, focuses extensively on the move from landlessness to landedness in the Old Testament.

dei, only occasionally recur in the Old Testament, but my exploration of these chapters through the prism of place exposes the inseparable link between these two blocks, and also between them and what follows. Canonically speaking, therefore, the biblical theologian is justified in presupposing them as integral to the ongoing drama.

My examination of Gen 1–3 casts important light on the human condition. Writing in 1958, Hannah Arendt prophetically posed the question:

> Should the emancipation and secularization of the modern age, which began with a turning-away, not necessarily from God, but from a god who was the Father of men in heaven, end with an even more fateful repudiation of an Earth who was the Mother of all living creatures under the sky?
>
> The earth is the very quintessence of the human condition, and earthly nature, for all we know may be unique in the universe in providing human beings with a habitat in which they can move and breathe without effort and without artifice.[114]

As was discussed above, we live amidst a crisis of place, a crisis which in its Aristotelian tendency to see place as a mere container is indeed in danger of repudiating the earth as our God-given place of habitation with debilitating consequences for the human condition of implacement. In his analysis of our late-modern culture, Graham Ward asserts that "Cyberspace is the outworking of modernity's dominant mode of thinking with respect to space. It is the final development in secularity... In fact cyberspace is a gnostic world-view where minds operate at a vast remove from bodies."[115] Cyberspace is not placeless, but "the logic and meaningfulness of place, rootedness, and an urbanism generating cities of collective memory...is absorbed into the 'flows of capital, flows of information, flows of technology, flows of organisational interaction, flows of images, sounds and symbols.'"[116] Ward is one among several cultural analysts who have discerned Gnosticism behind much post-modern culture and this is helpful insofar as it alerts us to the extent to which late-modern culture militates against embodiment and place and presents us with a crisis of displacement.

Genesis 1–3 provides us with a poignant critique of these cultural tendencies. In our day, a recovery of human flourishing will require a recovery of place, of the importance of locale and rootedness as Wendell

114.   H. Arendt, *The Human Condition* (Chicago: The University of Chicago Press, 1958), 2.
115.   Ward, *Cities of God*, 252.
116.   Ibid., 245, citing Manuel Castells (see above, n. 16).

Berry and many others have pointed out. This will not necessarily involve a rush to the countryside—the urbanism of Eden and the eschatology of a city deny this. However, insofar as we continue to build cities, radically new models will be required.[117] In his classic *After Virtue*, Alasdair MacIntyre concludes by noting that we do not need to wait for the barbarians to come; we are already ruled by them. As regards place, this would indeed seem to be the case. MacIntyre also intriguingly notes that we need a new Benedict. Doubtlessly a new Benedict would alert us, *inter alia*, to the importance of stability,[118] and therefore place, for human flourishing.

117. As in, for example, the New Urbanism. See also Ward's description of Manchester in *Cities of God*, 238–42.
118. For a nuanced understanding of stability, see ibid., 285–86.

THE REGAL DIMENSION OF THE תולדות־יעקב: RECOVERING THE LITERARY CONTEXT OF GENESIS 37–50*

T. Desmond Alexander

From the publication of Jean Astruc's monograph, *Conjectures sur les mémoires originaux dont il paraît que Moyse s'est servi pour composer le livre de la Genèse*, in 1753 through to the present day, scholarly interest in the sources used to compose the book of Genesis has continued unabated. The presence of oral and/or literary sources underlying the received text is assumed to be axiomatic, although recent scholarship has become much more vociferous in challenging the Documentary Hypothesis as the most satisfactorily explanation for the composition of Genesis.[1]

While attempts to identify and define the sources behind Genesis are unlikely to cease, the limited evidence available requires that every proposal must be treated as conjectural. In the light of this, efforts to explain the final redactional shape of the book of Genesis run the danger of being largely circular in nature.

* It is a special privilege to contribute this essay in honour of Gordon Wenham, who introduced me to the basics of biblical Hebrew and Pentateuchal Criticism when I was a young undergraduate at the Queen's University of Belfast. Later, with patience and wisdom, he supervised me as a post-graduate research student. Throughout this formative period of academic study he guided and shaped my thinking more than anyone else. With sincere gratitude for all that he gave me, this essay is dedicated to him in appreciation of his friendship over many years.

1. The studies of R. Rendtorff, *Das überlieferungsgeschichtliche Problem des Pentateuch* (BZAW 147; Berlin: de Gruyter, 1977), and R. N. Whybray, *The Making of the Pentateuch: A Methodological Study* (JSOTSup 53; Sheffield: JSOT Press, 1987), have been especially influential in creating a sea-change as regards modern scholarship's understanding of the composition of the Pentateuch. However, in spite of the many criticisms levelled against it, the Documentary Hypothesis still enjoys the support of some established scholars; see, for example, the recent positive appraisal of E. W. Nicholson, *The Pentateuch in the Twentieth Century: The Legacy of Julius Wellhausen* (Oxford: Clarendon, 1998).

With these cautionary observations in mind, this present essay seeks to explore the redactional structure of Gen 37–50 by focusing in particular on the concept of royalty. It will be proposed that the final editor of Genesis was heavily influenced by this concept when selecting and organising the present content of chs. 37–50.[2]

During the twentieth century a strong consensus has grown up supporting the belief that one of the major components of Gen 37–50 is the Joseph Story. With relatively minor variations, it is generally accepted that the detailed account of Joseph's life in chs. 37, 39–47 forms a continuous and unified narrative which cannot be easily sub-divided into earlier pre-existing sources.[3] While the precise limits of the Joseph Story are open to debate, it is reasonable to assume that the original account would have extended at least as far as ch. 47, which reports how the whole of Jacob's family migrated from Canaan to Egypt. This event, in large measure, forms a natural conclusion to a story which has as its starting point sibling rivalry that causes Joseph to be sold into slavery in Egypt.

Discussions of the origin of the Joseph Story have tended to focus on its distinctive style[4] and possible associations with sapiential literature,[5]

---

2. This essay does not attempt to provide a detailed reconstruction of how Gen 37–50 was composed. Such a project, if possible, lies well beyond what may be attempted in an essay of this length. Rather, the aim of this study is much more limited, seeking merely to advocate that the present composition of these chapters was influenced significantly by a special interest in the concept of royalty.

3. G. W. Coats, *From Canaan to Egypt: Structural and Theological Context for the Joseph Story* (CBQMS 4; Washington, D.C.: Catholic Biblical Association of America, 1976), provides a detailed analysis of the story, presenting a strong case for the substantial unity of 37:2–47:27 (apart from 38:1–30 and 47:13–26). Although Coats excludes all material after 47:27 from his analysis, R. E. Longacre, *Joseph: A Story of Divine Providence: A Text Theoretical and Textlinguistic Analysis of Genesis 37 and 39–48* (Winona Lake, Ind.: Eisenbrauns, 1989), sees the Joseph Story as extending to the end of ch. 48.

4. G. W. Coats, "Joseph, Son of Jacob," *ABD* 3:976–81 (980), states that a consensus supports the view that the Joseph Story is a "novella" ("a creative construction by the author" that does not "report historical events"). However, C. Westermann, *Genesis 37–50: A Commentary* (London: SPCK, 1987), 25–26, expresses reservations about the designation "novella." Commenting on the Joseph Story, he writes, "It is a work of art of the highest order; but the writer is not narrating something he himself invented; he is narrating a story of the patriarchs— his own fathers, and the fathers of his listeners."

5. The wisdom nature of the Joseph Story was first advocated by G. von Rad, "The Joseph Narrative and Ancient Wisdom," in *Studies in Ancient Israelite Wisdom* (ed. J. L. Crenshaw; New York: Ktav, 1976), 439–47. Von Rad's proposal is

both of which distance the material in Gen 37, 39–47 from the patriarch narratives in Gen 12–36. In line with this, it is widely held that the Joseph Story lacks theological links with the preceding materials.[6] Consequently, it is assumed that the Joseph Story was combined with the patriarchal narratives in order to form a bridge between Canaan and Egypt, explaining how the patriarchs of Genesis are linked to the Israelites of Exodus.[7] While concurring that the Joseph Story provides a necessary link between the patriarchal narratives and the account of the Israelite exodus from Egypt, it is surely worth asking: Does the Joseph Story serve a purpose in Genesis that goes beyond being merely a bridge between Canaan and Egypt? We shall return to this question later.

Once the Joseph Story is removed from Gen 37–50, the remaining sections are easily identified. Genesis 38 is a largely self-contained account of Judah's relationship with Tamar that concludes with the birth of twins, Perez and Zerah. Genesis 48, which could with some justification be viewed as continuing the Joseph Story,[8] reports how Joseph comes to Jacob, accompanied by his two sons, Manasseh and Ephraim, in order to be blessed by his now elderly and ill father. The theme of paternal blessing continues into Gen 49, which records the individual blessings that Jacob bestows upon his twelve sons (cf. Gen 49:28). The poetic nature of Gen 49:2–27 gives the impression that this passage is a self-contained unit within Gen 37–50, although the context for these blessings is actually provided by the events of Gen 48.[9] Genesis 49:29–50:14 records the death of Jacob, being framed by Jacob's instruction to his sons regarding his burial and its fulfilment. Two further brief episodes complete the book of Genesis. After Jacob's death, the brothers

---

strongly rejected by D. B. Redford, *A Study of the Biblical Story of Joseph (Genesis 37–50)* (VTSup 20; Leiden: Brill, 1970), 100–5. For a recent assessment, see M. V. Fox, "Wisdom in the Joseph Story," *VT* 51 (2001): 26–41.

6.   For example, Redford, *A Study of the Biblical Story of Joseph*, 247, writes, "The theological outlook of the writer of Gen 37–50 is different from that of the Patriarchal narrator. He does not mention the Covenant or the Promise, ubiquitous in the earlier chapters of Genesis. He is not interested in supplying the reader with comment on matters theological, as the Patriarchal author was."

7.   Hence the title of Coat's monograph, *From Canaan to Egypt*.

8.   Cf. R. E. Longacre, "Joseph," in *Dictionary of the Old Testament: Pentateuch* (ed. T. D. Alexander and D. W. Baker; Downers Grove, Ill.: InterVarsity, 2003), 469–77 (473).

9.   Strictly speaking there is no break in the Hebrew narrative between chs. 48–49. The events of ch. 49 follow on immediately from what is recorded in ch. 48. Having blessed Joseph and his sons, Jacob now summons all twelve of his sons and declares what will happen to them in the future.

seek Joseph's reassurance that he will not now take revenge on them for their earlier treatment of him (Gen 49:15–21). This section clearly presupposes the Joseph Story and could not have existed independently of it. Finally, Gen 50:22–26 records the death of Joseph, highlighting in the process the earlier divine oath to Abraham, Isaac and Jacob which promised that their descendants will eventually leave Egypt in order to occupy the land of Canaan.[10] Given the apparently disparate contents of Gen 38, 48–50, it is natural to ask what motivated the final redactor of Genesis to combine this material with the Joseph Story in order to compose the present narrative in chs. 37–50.

By way of addressing the questions raised at the end of the preceding two paragraphs, I want to draw attention to the largely neglected concept of royalty in Gen 37–50. The basic thesis of this essay is that the final redactor of Genesis was strongly influenced by the belief that in ancient Israel there existed two complementary traditions that associated kingship with the tribes of Judah and Ephraim, with the former eventually winning out over the latter. This belief is not only reflected in both the contents and redactional structure of Gen 37–50, but also figures prominently, as we shall see, in other books that form part of the Primary History (Genesis to Kings).

Throughout the Joseph Story the theme of royalty plays an important role. At the outset his "royal" dreams explain the antagonism of the older brothers towards Joseph and their subsequent desire to be rid of him. The royal motif also functions as an important element in the development of the Joseph Story because every new stage in the first part of the story makes the fulfilment of Joseph's dreams seem less and less likely. As Joseph descends in social status from favoured son to slave to prisoner,[11] it becomes highly improbable that his brothers will ever bow down to him. Yet, by a most remarkable turn of events, Joseph is promoted and placed in charge of the whole land of Egypt, second only to the pharaoh. When a severe and prolonged drought brings widespread famine to Egypt and the surrounding countries, Joseph's brothers are forced to travel there in search of food. Unbeknown to them, they bow down before their younger brother.[12] Eventually, when the brothers are reconciled, Joseph's

10. This alludes back to the divine speech found in Gen 15:13–16.
11. Even when Joseph is incarcerated, he is held in the prison for the "king's prisoners" (Gen 39:20; 40:1, 5).
12. The relationship between the dreams and their fulfilment is discussed by D. J. A. Clines, "What Happens in Genesis," in *What Does Eve Do to Help? And Other Readerly Questions to the Old Testament* (JSOTSup 94; Sheffield: JSOT Press, 1990), 49–66 (62–64) and L. A. Turner, *Announcement of Plot in Genesis* (JSOTSup

special standing enables his whole family to settle safely in Egypt. From Joseph's initial dreams through to the migration of his family to Egypt, royalty is a significant component within the Joseph Story.

It could be argued that the Joseph Story is solely interested in the theme of royalty for the benefit of the plot. This is certainly possible. Yet, when viewed as part of the book of Genesis as a whole, Joseph's regal connections take on a deeper significance. His dreams and their fulfilment come in the context of a family tradition that has royal expectations embedded within it. Although none of the patriarchs is actually designated a king, the theme of kingship is never far from the surface. This is reflected through events and in key divine and human speeches.

A significant number of episodes in Gen 12–25 record encounters between Abraham and regal figures. In Gen 12 Abraham meets an Egyptian pharaoh who unwittingly takes Sarai for a wife. In Gen 14 Abraham successfully rescues Lot from a raiding party of eastern kings and subsequently is welcomed back by Melchizedek, the king of Salem, and the king of Sodom. In Gen 20, paralleling earlier events,[13] Abimelech, the king of Gerar, takes Sarah to be his wife. Later, Abraham is obviously considered powerful enough for Abimelech to make a treaty with him (21:22–34) and for the inhabitants of Hebron to describe him as a "prince of God" (23:6). And although Abraham himself never assumes royal status, he is divinely promised that kings will be among his descendants (17:6; cf. 17:16), something probably alluded to in the divine oath of 22:17b–18 that Abraham's "seed" will overcome the gates of his enemies and in his "seed" all the nations of the earth shall be blessed.[14]

While Genesis narrates less about Isaac than the other patriarchs, like his father Abraham, he enters into a treaty with the king of Gerar (Gen 26:26–31). Moreover, Isaac very clearly hopes that his son will have king-like authority. This is evident from the firstborn blessing that he pronounces upon Jacob:

133; Sheffield: JSOT Press, 1990), 143–73. While Clines and Turner argue that the dreams are only partially fulfilled, they both see them as especially important for the plot of the story.

13. For a discussion of the relationship between Gen 12:10–20 and 20:1–18, see T. D. Alexander, "Are the Wife/Sister Incidents of Genesis Literary Compositional Variants?," *VT* 42 (1992): 145–53.

14. A royal interpretation of Gen 22:17b–18 is reflected in Ps 72:17; cf. T. D. Alexander, "Further Observations on the Term 'Seed' in Genesis," *TynBul* 48 (1997): 363–68.

See, the smell of my son is as the smell of a field that the LORD has blessed! May God give you of the dew of heaven and of the fatness of the earth and plenty of grain and wine. Let peoples serve you, and nations bow down to you. Be lord over your brothers, and may your mother's sons bow down to you. Cursed be everyone who curses you, and blessed be everyone who blesses you! (Gen 27:27b–29 ESV)

Although the precise nature of Jacob's authority is not specified by Isaac, his remarks clearly imply a status that would normally be associated with a powerful monarch or ruler. How else are the words "Let peoples serve you and nations bow down to you" to be understood? While this blessing is not fulfilled literally during Jacob's lifetime, the theme of kingship is later repeated when God speaks to Jacob:

And God said to him, "I am God Almighty: be fruitful and multiply. A nation and a company of nations shall come from you, and kings shall come from your own body. The land that I gave to Abraham and Isaac I will give to you, and I will give the land to your offspring after you." (Gen 35:11–12 ESV)

On this occasion, God unambiguously states that kings will be among Jacob's biological descendants.

While the number of direct references to kingship is not large, they come in important speeches and form part of a consistent picture that associates kingship with the future descendants of Abraham, Isaac and Jacob. In the light of the royal expectations found prior to Gen 37, it is hardly a coincidence that the plot of the Joseph Story should rely so heavily on the theme of royalty for its development. Since the narratives in Gen 12–36 associate kingship with the patriarchs and their descendants, the manner of Joseph's introduction in Gen 37 is significant.[15] Everything points to the ancestry of the future "royal" line being continued through him.[16]

---

15. Gen 36:31 also anticipates a time when there will be a king in Israel. Whereas the patriarchal narratives are interested in establishing clearly the ancestry of the prospective royal line linked to Abraham, Isaac and Jacob, Gen 36:32–43 reveals that the Edomite kings descended from Esau do not establish a continuous dynasty.

16. Viewed as a whole, the book of Genesis establishes a line of human ancestry that runs continuously from Adam to Jacob/Israel. The תולדות headings, in conjunction with the linear genealogies in Gen 5 and 11, structure the whole of Genesis around this unique family line. For a fuller discussion of this line, see T. D. Alexander, "Genealogies, Seed and the Compositional Unity of Genesis," *TynBul* 44 (1993): 255–70; idem, *From Paradise to the Promised Land: An Introduction to the Pentateuch* (2d ed.; Carlisle: Paternoster, 2002), 101–13.

The opening section of the Joseph Story is dominated by the two dreams which Joseph describes to his family.[17] Joseph's dreams are obviously interpreted by his brothers as signalling his unique royal status. Their response to his first dream emphasizes this: "Are you indeed to reign over us? Or are you indeed to rule over us?" There can be no doubting the intensity of the brothers' reaction to Joseph's dreams.[18] Read against the background of Gen 12–36, these dreams unambiguously indicate that Joseph will be the one through whom the patriarchal "royal" line will continue.

However, even before Gen 37:5–11 reports Joseph's dreams and his family's reaction to them, Joseph's special standing has already been signalled. Favoured by his father over all his brothers, Joseph is given a special cloak. While the precise nature of this garment is unclear, it is noteworthy that the Hebrew term used to denote it comes only once elsewhere in the Old Testament (2 Sam 13:18). On this occasion it refers to a robe associated with the king's daughters. Might this suggest that Joseph was dressed by his father like a "prince"? Although we cannot be certain, this possibility fits well with other proposals regarding Gen 37:2–4. Hamilton suggests that the Hebrew syntax of v. 2 could indicate that Joseph was shepherding his brothers.[19] And Lowenthal suggests that the unusual Hebrew expression בֶן־זְקֻנִים in 37:3 denotes a "born leader."[20] Joseph's leadership quality is possibly also reflected in his willingness to report to his father the inappropriate behaviour of his brothers (Gen 37:2). While these readings are not required to establish Joseph's royal credentials, the dreams being sufficient, due consideration should be given to them in the light of the acknowledged artistry of the Joseph Story.

The preceding observations strongly suggest that the regal dimension of the Joseph Story is a natural continuation of the theme of royalty found in the patriarchal narratives of Gen 12–36. This possibility is

---

17.   This pair of dreams indirectly prepares for the dreams, also in pairs, which are recorded later in chs. 40 and 41. Since dreams are used as a medium of revelation in Gen 37 prior to Joseph's enslavement, his ability to interpret first the prisoners' and then the pharaoh's dreams comes as no surprise within the story.

18.   The use of infinitive absolutes in both of the brothers' questions in Gen 37:8 underlines the emphatic way in which they challenge Joseph.

19.   V. P. Hamilton, *The Book of Genesis: Chapters 18–50* (NICOT; Grand Rapids: Eerdmans, 1995), 406; cf. R. Pirson, *The Lord of the Dreams: A Semantic and Literary Analysis of Genesis 37–50* (JSOTSup 355; London: Sheffield Academic Press, 2002), 28–30.

20.   E. I. Lowenthal, *The Joseph Narrative in Genesis: An Interpretation* (New York: Ktav, 1973), 167 n. 7.

reinforced when we consider how the motif of the firstborn is handled in Gen 12–50. Running throughout chs. 12–36, we repeatedly see the birthright of the firstborn being given to a younger brother through whom the central family line of Genesis is traced and to whom the divine promises are reaffirmed.[21] I shall argue below that this pattern continues through into chs. 37–50.

To a large extent the plot of the Abraham narrative develops around events associated with the inability of Abraham and Sarah to have children.[22] While the divine promises and assurances given in Gen 12–15 point to the childless couple having many descendants, the lack of any progress eventually causes them to pursue an alternative approach. Following ancient Near Eastern protocol, Abraham takes Sarah's Egyptian maidservant, Hagar, as a second wife, in order that she may be a proxy for Sarah.[23] In due course a son, Ishmael, is born. While initial indications suggest that Ishmael is the promised son,[24] Yahweh subsequently appears to Abraham and announces that Sarah will have a son of her own, Isaac, through whom the divine promises will be fulfilled (Gen 17:19–21; cf. 21:12). While Abraham displays some reluctance to by-pass his eldest son, Ishmael, in favour of Isaac (17:18; 21:11), the events of Gen 21–22 emphasize Isaac's status as Abraham's "firstborn" son. Later, in 26:2–5, God appears to Isaac and confirms that he is the heir to the promises made to Abraham.

The account of Jacob's rise to prominence over his older twin brother Esau is especially intriguing. The struggle between them begins even before they are born; at this stage a divine oracle announces that the older shall serve the younger (Gen 25:23). The ensuing narrative develops this motif through a fascinating collection of incidents. A hungry Esau sells his birthright to Jacob for a bowl of stew (25:29–34). At his

21. Various studies have picked up on the motif of the eldest son being overshadowed by a younger brother; e.g., J. Goldin, "The Youngest Son or Where Does Genesis 38 Belong," *JBL* 96 (1977): 27–44; E. Fox, "Stalking the Younger Brother: Some Models for Understanding a Biblical Motif," *JSOT* 60 (1993): 45–68; F. E. Greenspahn, *When Brothers Dwell Together: The Preeminence of Younger Siblings in the Hebrew Bible* (New York: Oxford University Press, 1994).

22. For an outline of the plot of the Abraham narrative, see T. D. Alexander, *Abraham in the Negev: A Source-Critical Investigation of Genesis 20:1–22:19* (Carlisle: Paternoster, 1997), 102–10.

23. Cf. K. A. Kitchen, *On the Reliability of the Old Testament* (Grand Rapids: Eerdmans, 2003), 325–26.

24. Although Hagar has fled from Abraham's household, she is sent back by the angel of Yahweh. Undoubtedly, this was interpreted by Abraham as indicating that Hagar's son would be his heir (cf. Gen 17:18).

mother's instigation Jacob pretends to be Esau in order to obtain the paternal blessing of the firstborn (27:1–40). Esau's subsequent hatred of Jacob causes the latter to abandon his immediate family and seek refuge with his father's relatives in Paddan Aram. In exile, Jacob marries, has children and becomes wealthy as a result of God's presence and blessing. Years later Jacob returns to Canaan and is movingly reconciled with his brother (33:1–17). However, whereas Esau chooses to live in the region of Edom, Jacob settles in Canaan, occupying part of the land divinely promised to his grandfather Abraham and his father Isaac (33:16–20).

The patriarchal narratives, undoubtedly, give prominence to the theme of a younger brother replacing the firstborn. Significantly, running in tandem with this motif in Gen 12–36 is the theme of divine blessing. From the call of Abraham in 12:1–3 through to Jacob's sojourn in Paddan Aram, God's blessing is consistently and principally associated with the son who receives the status of firstborn. Moreover, blessing is mediated by the firstborn to others.[25]

In the light of the attention given to younger brothers receiving the rights and privileges of the "firstborn" within Gen 12–35 and the implications that this has for the theme of divine blessing, various aspects of Gen 37–50 require further consideration.

While Gen 37 does not state explicitly that Joseph is designated the "firstborn" by his father, his preferential treatment suggests that Jacob will probably do this in the future, if he has not already done so. Joseph's promotion over his brothers may have been prompted by the inappropriate relationship of Reuben, Leah's eldest son, with his father's concubine, Bilhah (Gen 35:22). This event probably persuaded Jacob that the status of firstborn should be removed from Reuben,[26] and, since Joseph is

---

25. The very close connection in Gen 25–35 between "firstborn" and "blessing," involving the Hebrew roots בכר and ברך, is demonstrated by M. A. Fishbane, "Composition and Structure in the Jacob Cycle (Gen 25:19–35:22)," *JJS* 26 (1975): 15–38.

26. Reuben may have been attempting to consolidate his position as firstborn (cf. 2 Sam 16:20–22 where Absalom expresses his contempt for his father David by going into his father's concubines). Later, in Gen 49:2–3, Jacob clearly refers to Reuben's actions when he states: "Reuben, you are my firstborn, my might, and the firstfruits of my strength, preeminent in dignity and preeminent in power. Unstable as water, you shall not have preeminence, because you went up to your father's bed; then you defiled it—he went up to my couch!" (ESV). The second half of Jacob's remarks implies that the firstborn status of Reuben has been taken from him due to his earlier actions. Reuben's rejection is picked up in 1 Chr 5:1, which affirms that the birthright of the firstborn is transferred to Joseph: "The sons of Reuben the firstborn of Israel (for he was the firstborn, but because he defiled his father's couch,

the eldest son born to Jacob's favourite wife, Rachel, his father may have been tempted to make him the "firstborn." While there are strong hints that Joseph will receive from his father the blessing of the firstborn, his "untimely death" prevents this from occurring.[27] Later in Egypt, however, when the entire family is again together, Joseph probably obtains the firstborn blessing when Jacob "adopts" his two sons.[28] By "adopting" Manasseh and Ephraim as his own, Jacob ensures that Joseph will receive through them a "double portion" of the patriarch's inheritance, the share normally allocated to the firstborn.[29]

The idea of Joseph being given the birthright of the firstborn is consistent with how he is pictured mediating divine blessing to others. This is highlighted in Gen 39, especially in connection with Potiphar's household (39:5). The narrator underlines that Yahweh was with Joseph and gave him success in all he did (39:3). A similar scenario follows soon afterwards when Joseph is confined with the "king's prisoners" (39:23). These events anticipate future developments in the story, revealing that Joseph's administrative success is due to God's presence with him. In time, Joseph's prowess as "governor" of Egypt will result in people from different nations being rescued from the ravages of a prolonged and severe famine. The international benefits that flow from Joseph's leadership resonate with the earlier divine promises to the patriarchs that speak of nations being blessed through Abraham and his seed (Gen 12:3; 18:18; 22:18; 26:4; 28:14; cf. 27:29).[30]

his birthright was given to the sons of Joseph the son of Israel, so that he could not be enrolled as the oldest son; though Judah became strong among his brothers and a chief came from him, yet the birthright belonged to Joseph), the sons of Reuben, the firstborn of Israel: Hanoch, Pallu, Hezron, and Carmi" (ESV).

27. This paternal blessing is normally given towards the end of the father's life, as reflected in Gen 27 and 48–49.

28. R. de Hoop, *Genesis 49 in Its Literary and Historical Context* (OtSt 39; Leiden: Brill, 1999), 333–39, offers an anti-Joseph reading of the "adoption" of Manasseh and Ephraim by Jacob. His interpretation, however, is very much at odds with how others have taken this account. Nor does it sit comfortably with his own suggestion that Gen 47:31 is best understood as indicating that Jacob bowed down to Joseph, the head of the tribe; cf. R. de Hoop, "'Then Israel Bowed Himself' (Genesis 47:31)," *JSOT* 28 (2004): 470–74.

29. This is noteworthy because it stands at odds with the requirement of the "Book of the Law," recorded in Deut 21:15–17, that the firstborn son of an "unloved" wife should not be passed over in favour of the firstborn son of a "loved" wife.

30. While it would be mistaken to suggest that Joseph's actions bring to fulfilment the earlier divine promises of blessing for the nations of the earth, his role as saviour of many lives is surely significant (Gen 50:20; cf. 47:25).

While Joseph's status as the firstborn is reflected in various ways throughout Gen 37–50, we should also observe how the firstborn motif figures prominently in two other settings within these chapters. First, when the elderly Jacob blesses Manasseh and Ephraim, he deliberately puts the younger ahead of the older. The narrator highlights this by describing Joseph's objection and Jacob's insistence that he has deliberately chosen to do this (Gen 48:13–20). While the implications of Jacob's action are not developed in Genesis, it seems indisputable that he intends the birthright of the firstborn to move from Joseph to Ephraim, rather than Manasseh. Given the wider literary context, Jacob's blessing of Ephraim as the firstborn implies that the anticipated line of kingship, linked to the patriarchs and then Joseph, will continue through Ephraim and his descendants.

Secondly, given the unusual frequency of instances in Gen 12–50 when a younger brother is promoted over older siblings in order to be given the status and privileges of the firstborn, we should also observe that the concluding verses of Gen 38 provide yet another example of this occurring. On this occasion, as Tamar is giving birth, Zerah is pushed aside by his twin brother Perez. Although the attentive midwife has attached a scarlet cord to Zerah's arm so that he may be clearly identified as the firstborn, his twin brother Perez breaks out before him. While the bizarre nature of this birth might well explain its inclusion in Genesis, a more significant reason may be the fact that the royal house of David traced its ancestry back to Perez (cf. Ruth 4:18–22). If, as this essay proposes, the theme of kingship is important to understanding the redactional structure of Gen 37–50, the account of Perez's birth would most certainly merit inclusion.

The preceding observations suggest that the editor of Gen 37–50 was interested in identifying the "firstborn" of both Joseph and Judah. This parallels the prominence given to both Judah and Joseph in Gen 49. A swift reading of the chapter reveals that the blessings pronounced by Jacob upon these two sons are significantly longer and more positive than those bestowed upon their brothers.[31] That this should be true of

31. Almost half of the speech Gen 49:3–27 is given over to Judah and Joseph. The interpretation of Jacob's speech presents a considerable challenge. The more speculative discussion of de Hoop, *Genesis 49 in Its Literary and Historical Context*, should be contrasted with the approaches of Westermann, *Genesis 37–50*, 222–44; N. M. Sarna, *Genesis* (The JPS Torah Commentary; New York: The Jewish Publication Society of America, 1989), 332–46; V. P. Hamilton, *The Book of Genesis: Chapters 1–17* (NICOT; Grand Rapids: Eerdmans, 1990), 644–87; G. J. Wenham, *Genesis 16–50* (WBC 2; Dallas: Word, 1994), 468–87; and K. A. Mathews, *Genesis 11:27–50:26* (NAC 1B; Nashville, Tenn.: Broadman & Holman, 2005), 883–910.

Joseph is hardly surprising. From early in Gen 37 through to Gen 48, he has been by far the principal character in the narrative. The prominence given to Judah is more surprising, although not entirely inconsistent with what has been revealed prior to ch. 49.[32]

Thus far I have restricted my observations to the book of Genesis. My overview of chs. 37–50 suggests that the final editor was concerned to highlight how the theme of royal descend, found in the patriarchal narratives of Gen 12–36, is linked to Joseph and through him to his son Ephraim. Alongside this, although less prominently, attention is drawn to Judah's family, with Perez being picked out for special mention.

When we move beyond Genesis into the rest of the Primary History, we discover that the descendants of both Ephraim and Judah are frequently presented as standing apart from their fellow Israelites by providing positive examples of leadership. For example, of the twelve spies who report back on their reconnaissance of Canaan, only Caleb, a Judahite, and Joshua, an Ephraimite, speak optimistically about taking possession of the land. In time, after the death of Moses, Joshua is appointed leader of the Israelites and demonstrates exceptional ability, enabling the Israelites to overcome their opponents as they enter the land of Canaan. Later, when the heads of the Israelite clans come to allocate a portion of Canaan to each tribe, it is apparent that the tribes of Judah and Ephraim have already taken the lead in occupying territory west of the River Jordan. Of the nine-and-a-half tribes still to be given land, a clear distinction is drawn between those who have already settled (i.e. Judah, Ephraim and the half tribe of Manasseh; see Josh 15–17) and those who are allocated land by lot on the basis of a survey that includes territory which has not yet been taken over by the Israelites (i.e. Benjamin, Simeon, Zebulun, Issachar, Asher, Naphtali, Dan; see Josh 18–19).

The books of Joshua, Judges and Samuel, however, provide an interesting picture of how tribal leadership shifts gradually, but noticeably, from Ephraim to Judah. While Joshua's role as Moses' successor clearly underlines the importance of the tribe of Ephraim, when it comes to the division of the land of Canaan, attention is focused first on Judah (Josh 15) and then on Ephraim (Josh 16–17).[33] This pattern continues into the

---

32. Cf. R. J. Clifford, "Genesis 38: Its Contribution to the Jacob Story," *CBQ* 66 (2004): 519–32; and B. Smith, "The Central Role of Judah in Genesis 37–50," *BSac* 162 (2005): 158–74.

33. Judah is not only mentioned first, but the territory assigned to Judah is outlined in more detail. This, alongside the "wholehearted" portrayal of Caleb, subtly points to Judah being more committed than Ephraim. Further evidence for the greater zeal of Judah comes when Simeon is allocated territory within Judah's borders (Josh 19:1).

book of Judges where Judah is clearly presented as taking the lead (Judg 1:1–20), with the Ephraimites being somewhat less enthusiastic about overcoming Canaanite opposition (Judg 1:22–26, 29, 35).

Viewed side by side, the books of Joshua and Judges provide strongly contrasting portraits of the leadership displayed by first Joshua and then his descendants. Whereas Joshua is placed on a par with Moses,[34] the description of Ephraimite leadership in Judges is far from positive. The most obvious example of this comes in Judg 12 where the Ephraimites belligerently challenge Jephthah, a Gileadite, for having gone to war without them. As Jephthah's rebuke reveals, in spite of being asked, the Ephraimites had refused to come to the aid of the Gileadites (Judg 12:2). Although they wanted to be recognized as the leading tribe, the Ephraimites were not willing to undertake the associated responsibilities. In the inter-tribal conflict that followed, 42,000 Ephraimites were slaughtered (Judg 12:6), a strong indication that the tribe was not following in the footsteps of Joshua.

While the book of Judges presents all of the tribes of Israel as being in moral and spiritual decline, it could be argued that a contributing factor to this state of affairs is the Ephraimites' failure to provide suitable leadership. While God raises up a series of judges to deliver the Israelites from their enemies, the judges themselves increasing reflect the failings of the people at large.[35] Against this background, the epilogue to Judges underlines the social chaos within Israel, hinting through the refrain, "In those days there was no king," that improvements might come with a monarchy.[36] In the light of this, it is noteworthy that the epilogue brings together characters from the tribes of Judah and Ephraim, with the members of the latter tribe being portrayed in the least favourable light. For example, Micah, an Ephraimite, is presented as disregarding the covenant obligations encapsulated in the Decalogue (Judg 17:1–13). The callous attitude of the Levite from Ephraim towards his estranged Judah-

---

34. Like Moses, Joshua is also called a "servant of Yahweh" after his death (Josh 24:29; cf. Deut 34:5).

35. The distinctive cyclical structure of the book of Judges creates a picture of a downward spiral, with each successive judge being less effective in maintaining covenantal loyalty to Yahweh. Cf. D. W. Gooding, "The Composition of the Book of Judges," *EI* 16 (1982): 70–79; B. G. Webb, *The Book of the Judges: An Integrated Reading* (JSOTSup 46; Sheffield: JSOT Press, 1987); G. J. Wenham, *Story as Torah: Reading the Old Testament Ethically* (OTS; Edinburgh: T. & T. Clark, 2000), 45–71.

36. The use of this refrain in Judg 17:6; 18:1; 19:1; 21:25 assists in setting the epilogue apart from the preceding cycles, which all centre on particular judges.

ite wife results in a conflict that decimates the tribe of Benjamin (Judg 19:1–21:25).

The overall picture in Joshua and Judges is of Ephraimite leadership declining irreversibly after the death of Joshua. This continues through into the book of Samuel, which begins by noting how the priesthood at Shiloh, in the tribal region of Ephraim, has also become corrupt. Such is the state of affairs that Yahweh himself permits the Philistines to capture the ark of the covenant.[37]

Against the background of Yahweh abandoning the tribe of Ephraim, a monarchy is established in Israel. While Saul, a Benjaminite,[38] is the first to be anointed king, he falls from grace to be replaced by David, the youngest of Jesse's sons.[39] When David eventually transports the ark to Jerusalem, kingship is firmly associated with the tribe of Judah.

The general picture sketched briefly above is captured in poetic language by the author of Ps 78:60–72:

> He (God) forsook his dwelling at Shiloh, the tent where he dwelt among mankind, and delivered his power to captivity, his glory to the hand of the foe. He gave his people over to the sword and vented his wrath on his heritage. Fire devoured their young men, and their young women had no marriage song. Their priests fell by the sword, and their widows made no lamentation. Then the Lord awoke as from sleep, like a strong man shouting because of wine. And he put his adversaries to rout; he put them to everlasting shame. He rejected the tent of Joseph; he did not choose the tribe of Ephraim, but he chose the tribe of Judah, Mount Zion, which he loves. He built his sanctuary like the high heavens, like the earth, which he has founded forever. He chose David his servant and took him from the sheepfolds; from following the nursing ewes he brought him to shepherd Jacob his people, Israel his inheritance. With upright heart he shepherded them and guided them with his skillful hand (ESV).

Two major contrasts are drawn in the final section of the psalm between (a) God rejecting the tribe of Ephraim and choosing David and (b) God abandoning Shiloh as his dwelling place in favour of Mount Zion. From

---

37. The impact of this event is captured succinctly in the name which Phinehas' dying wife gives to her newborn son: Ichabod (1 Sam 4:19–22).

38. The choice of Saul as king is unexpected, especially in the light of how the tribe of Benjamin is almost annihilated due to the actions of the men of Gibeah (see Judg 19–21). There is, however, a tendency on the part of God to choose the one least favoured by others. It may also be significant that close links existed between the tribes of Ephraim, Benjamin and Manasseh, as reflected in Num 2:18–24 and Ps 80 (see esp. v. 2).

39. This is a further example of the custom of primogeniture being set aside in favour of a younger son.

what is said, we may reasonably infer that the leadership of the nation, which was formerly linked to the tribe of Ephraim, is now transferred to David, a Judahite.[40] Confirmation of this comes through the successful relocation of the ark of the covenant to Jerusalem.

In the light of this bigger picture of national leadership passing from Ephraim to Judah, the present redactional structure of Gen 37–50 becomes much clearer. First, the Joseph Story associates kingship with Joseph and his future descendants. When Jacob promotes Ephraim over Manasseh, this signals that leadership in the future will come through the Ephraimites. In due course this becomes a reality when Joshua succeeds Moses as head of the nation and successfully guides the Israelites into the promised land, establishing Shiloh as the location for Yahweh's temple. However, although leadership of the nation continued to be linked to Ephraim, after the time of Joshua the Ephraimites gradually fail to fulfil this responsibility. In the end, they are replaced by the tribe of Judah.

Second, by incorporating the unexpected account of Judah's relationship with Tamar into the Joseph Story,[41] the editor provides an important hint that the line of Judah will play a part in the outworking of the family line that moves from Abraham to Isaac and then to Jacob. Two distinctive features of Gen 38 point in this direction. (a) The narrative begins by focusing on problems concerning the continuation of Judah's family line. The report of Er's death and the failure of Onan to raise up "seed" for his brother, consequently leading to his own death, recalls earlier episodes in Genesis where the future of the family line faces major problems. In the

40. Although Ps 78 indicates that the tradition of Ephraimite leadership is pre-Davidic, its influence may be seen in the establishment of Jeroboam, an Ephraimite, as ruler of the northern kingdom in opposition to Solomon's son, Rehoboam. Jeroboam may have more easily gained the support of the ten tribes due to the existence of a tradition that linked leadership to the tribe of Ephraim. This ancient tradition may also be the source of the much later Jewish belief that a second messiah would come from the line of Joseph/Ephraim (*b. Suk.* 52a; cf. J. Jacobs and M. Buttenwieser, "Messiah," in *JE* 8:505–12 [511–12]; and H. L. Ginsberg, D. Flusser, G. J. Blidstein, J. Dan and L. Jacobs, "Messiah," in *EncJud* 11:cols. 1407–18 [1411]).

41. The widely held assumption that Gen 38 has been inserted into a pre-existing Joseph Story may need to be revised. As noted by Clifford, "Genesis 38: Its Contribution to the Jacob Story," 519–32; and Smith, "The Central Role of Judah in Genesis 37–50," 158–74, Gen 38 has an important bearing on the reader's perception of Judah. The transformation of Judah's character, which comes to a climax in his comment regarding the righteousness of Tamar (Gen 38:26), is important for the larger Joseph Story. Judah, who displays little concern for the life of Joseph in ch. 37, is later willing to sacrifice his own well-being for that of Benjamin, in the process delivering one of the longest human speeches recorded in Genesis (Gen 44:18–34).

light of previous accounts, the attentive reader of Genesis might well suspect that Judah's line will yet play an important role in the story. (b) This expectation is reinforced when the births of Zerah and Perez are reported. The ousting of the "firstborn" by a "younger" brother is especially noteworthy given the larger context in which it is placed. Having observed other examples of the primogeniture principle being overturned, a sensitized reader of Genesis would automatically suspect that the birth of Perez is significant.[42]

Third, although the insertion of the Judah–Tamar episode into the Joseph Story goes a little way to highlighting the future importance of the line of Perez, confirmation regarding this comes through the inclusion of the blessings listed in Gen 49. Here, perhaps with an element of surprise given the emphasis on Joseph's regal status in Gen 37–48, Judah is clearly associated with kingship.[43] Since, however, the content of Joseph's blessing in 49:22–26 is not incompatible with future leadership,[44] it remains possible that kingship may descend from either Judah or Joseph. It is, therefore, no surprise that initially the ancestry of the anticipated royal line is linked to Ephraim.

Fourth, as I noted earlier, Gen 50 concentrates largely on reporting the deaths of both Jacob and Joseph. As in the preceding תולדות sections of Terah (11:27–25:11) and Isaac (25:19–35:29), the burial reports of the main participants in Gen 37–50 provide a fitting conclusion to these chapters. However, we should also observe that Gen 50 contains elements that anticipate the continuation of the story. Thus, Joseph's final words look forward to the return of the Israelites from Egypt to the land of Canaan in fulfilment of God's promises to the patriarchs.

42. From a much later perspective, the account of Perez's birth could also be interpreted as symbolic of how the tribe of Judah breaks out in front of the tribe of Ephraim, which was clearly viewed as being the firstborn line.

43. The debate in modern scholarship regarding the ambiguity of the "royal" dimension of Jacob's blessing of Judah should be noted. The fact that scholars may argue for and against a royal interpretation of this passage allows for the possibility that something similar could have occurred in ancient Israel. With hindsight it is easy to suggest that Jacob's words anticipated the royal line of David. Given, however, the status of Joseph at the time of Jacob's death, it is understandable why future leadership was linked to his descendants.

44. The content of Jacob's blessing of Joseph in Gen 49:22–26 is compatible with kingship belonging to Joseph's ancestry. Apart from the repeated emphasis on "blessing," which is very much a feature of the anticipated royal line in Genesis, Jacob's final words concerning Joseph may easily be understood as having regal/leadership connotations. Although the expression נזיר אחיו is open to various interpretations (e.g. "set apart from his brothers"; "the prince among his brothers"), all of these are compatible with expectations of royalty.

While of necessity these observations regarding the redactional structure of Gen 37–50 have been drawn with broad brush strokes, they are
sufficient to suggest that the final editor of Genesis was particularly interested in the concept of royalty. Viewed within its larger literary context,
either the book of Genesis or the Primary History, the regal dimension of
the תולדות יעקב not only makes a significant contribution towards
explaining the content and arrangement of the materials that comprise
Gen 37–50, but it also integrates these chapters more fully with the patriarchal narratives in Gen 12–36, revealing that the תולדות יעקב is more
than simply a bridge between Canaan and Egypt. Any attempt to explain
the present composition of Gen 37–50 must take into account the manner
in which these chapters associate the future leadership of the nation of
Israel with the descendants of Joseph and Judah.

ON LEARNING SPIRITUAL DISCIPLINES: A READING OF EXODUS 16

R. W. L. Moberly

1. *Introduction*

The book of Exodus, whose content is in so many ways foundational for Israel's life with God, is a constant challenge to its interpreters. Since it is the only book of the Pentateuch that has not been extensively commented upon by Gordon Wenham, I hope that it will be appropriate, in the context of honouring an old and esteemed friend, to complement his fine pentateuchal work with a brief study of a famous Exodus narrative, the story of the manna in Exod 16.

The context of the story is that it is the first extended sequence about Israel's life in the wilderness subsequent to their deliverance from Egypt and prior to their coming to Sinai. As will be seen, in this context the story is, unsurprisingly, to do with Israel's new identity as the people of YHWH, and what it means for them to learn to live as such a people.

2. *Exposition of Exodus 16*[1]

[1] The whole congregation of the Israelites set out from Elim; and Israel came to the wilderness of Sin, which is between Elim and Sinai, on the fifteenth day of the second month after they had departed from the land of Egypt. [2] The whole congregation of the Israelites complained against Moses and Aaron in the wilderness. [3] The Israelites said to them, "If only we had died by the hand of the LORD in the land of Egypt, where we sat by the fleshpots and ate our fill of bread; for you have brought us out into this wilderness to kill this whole assembly with hunger."

The scene is set.[2] A month and a half after departing from Egypt, Israel is in an unwelcome place. If it is right to see significance in the geographical

---

1. For convenience I have used the NRSV translation.
2. I offer a reading of the text in its received form in the MT. Documentary analysis tends to ascribe the narrative to P, with elements either of J and/or of redactional

detail,[3] part of the problem with the wilderness of Sin appears to be that it is set between two much more desirable places: on the one hand Elim, whence they had just departed (15:27), whose twelve springs of water and seventy palm trees (the numbers being symbolically suggestive[4]) are surely meant to make it sound like a wonderful place to stay when in desert regions;[5] and on the other hand Sinai, the mountain of God, where Israel will enter into covenant with YHWH. Other places (and, implicitly, times) may be fine; but here and now is awful. Apart from this possible

development, but such analysis is less heuristically illuminating here than in some other narratives (for details see Brevard Childs, *Exodus* [OTL; London: SCM Press, 1974], 274–83; Antony Campbell and Mark O'Brien, *Sources of the Pentateuch: Texts, Introductions, Annotations* [Minneapolis: Fortress, 1993], 41–43, 144; though see now a differing approach in Antony Campbell and Mark O'Brien, *Rethinking the Pentateuch: Prolegomena to the Theology of Ancient Israel* [Louisville, Ky.: Westminster John Knox, 2005]). That there are some unevennesses in the narrative—repetitions, gaps, unclear sequence—is unarguable; the real, and unresolved, difficulty is to determine which kind of conceptuality best enables the interpreter to comprehend such features.

3. Prior to the development of attention (within the last thirty years or so) to the narrative art/poetics of Old Testament storytelling, commentators generally resisted finding significance in such details: for example, "this is no more than a reference to [P's] list of stopping places" (Martin Noth, *Exodus* [trans. J. Bowden; OTL; London: SCM Press, 1962], 133); though, to be sure, my proposal here is primarily a reading strategy that utilizes a possible inference from the text.

4. Traditional Jewish interpretation regularly construed the twelve springs as being for each of the twelve tribes, while the seventy palm trees were for each of the seventy elders; so, for example, Rashi, though Ibn Ezra was dismissive: "there is no need for this kind of thing. For the 12 springs and the 70 trees were not created at this moment for Israel" (Michael Carasik, *The Commentators' Bible: The JPS Miqra'ot Gedolot: Exodus* [Philadelphia: The Jewish Publication Society of America, 2005/ 5765], 121).

5. As often pointed out, this depiction seems to presuppose a rather smaller number of Israelites than is the case in those passages which specifically enumerate, for example, "six hundred thousand men...besides children" (Exod 12:37), which leads to suppositions of some two million people all told. If, as seems not unlikely, the numbering of Israel is from a context subsequent to that of the Exodus and has been superimposed upon the Exodus narrative, it is important not to read the text woodenly without recognition of its peculiar character. In other words, the twelve springs and seventy palm trees should be imagined as a place of general refreshment for all, not a cause of contention as it would be if only a small proportion of the people could get access to the water and shade. For a discussion of the problem of large numbers, see Gordon Wenham, *Numbers* (TOTC; Leicester: InterVarsity, 1981), 60–66. Although Wenham does not himself favour the construal of the numbers as "the population of a later age," it still seems to me to be probably the least unsatisfactory solution.

"grass is greener..." implication, there is also the straightforward implication that just as soon as the journey becomes difficult Israel complain
("murmur," לוּן, a keynote in Israel's wilderness wanderings), and readily
view their leaders suspiciously, indeed in the worst possible light. Any
moral and spiritual fibre is conspicuous solely for its absence.

Moreover the content of their complaint is remarkable.[6] Entirely gone
is any sense of YHWH's deliverance of Israel with the prospect of giving
them a better place to live in which YHWH's deliverance will be remembered and celebrated in various ways (Exod 12–15). Rather, they seem to
take it for granted that death is all that awaits them, in which case they
would prefer at least to have had stomachs full rather than empty at their
end; and so they would rather have died in Egypt before ever setting out.
This is not a good advertisement for the power of Israel's memory!
YHWH's deliverance seems simply to be forgotten, while their time in
Egypt is entirely misremembered as a place not of oppression (Exod
1:13–14; 5:1–23) but of the kind of plenty which, had it been available,
would have been available only, one imagines, to the Egyptians and not
to their Hebrew slaves.

Thus the people are utterly immature, with a grossly distorted perception of their situation. As Childs puts it, "the people's complaint is not a

---

6. The people speak, and YHWH subsequently appears to respond, as though they
were without the numerous livestock which they are said to have had on leaving
Egypt (Exod 12:38) and still have in subsequent narratives (17:3, Num 20:4; 32:1). It
is, of course, perfectly possible to read the text as though these were presupposed:
"Like all pastoralists, they were very loath to slaughter their own beasts (cf. Num
11:22), which was the only alternative to a diet of milk and cheese in the desert"
(Alan Cole, *Exodus* [TOTC; London: Tyndale, 1973], 130); "Those of the Israelites
who possessed cattle certainly had no reason to complain about the lack of food; but
we may easily assume that there were not a few among the people who had no cattle,
whilst actual bread, such as they were accustomed to eat in Egypt, none of them
had" (U. Cassuto, *A Commentary on the Book of Exodus* [trans. Israel Abrahams;
Jerusalem: Magnes, 1967], 189). The persuasiveness of such explanations depends
upon one's overall conception of the genre, and coherence, of the combined narratives in sequence. Moreover, there are other comparable imaginative difficulties in
the narratives of Exodus and Numbers, when particular texts speak of something
regular (e.g. Moses' shining face, Exod 34:29–35) about which other texts seem
unaware. So, with regard to the manna, Propp observes: "In the rest of the Torah,
whenever the people rebel against Moses and God, we must imagine them rising in
the morning, collecting their daily Manna and—incredibly!—complaining" on
which he comments, "Their wonder and gratitude grow dull by familiarity" (*Exodus
1–18* [AB 2; New York: Doubleday], 599). Propp's comment is fair enough. Nonetheless, to read the text with total imaginative seriousness should not entail rationalizing moves that in fact lead one away from the specific dynamics of the various
stories.

casual 'gripe,' but unbelief which has called into question God's very
election of a people."[7] Or as Brueggemann puts it, "The seductive
distortion of Israel is that, given anxiety about survival, the immediacy
of food overrides any long-term hope for freedom and well-being.
The desperate, fearful choice that Israel voices in this contrast is reminiscent of Esau, who was willing to forego his birthright for immediate
satisfaction in food (Gen 25:29–34)."[8] So what will YHWH and Moses
do?

> [4] The LORD said to Moses, "I am going to rain bread from heaven for
> you, and each day the people shall go out and gather enough for that day.
> In that way I will test (נסה) them, whether they will follow my instruction
> (תורה) or not. [5] On the sixth day, when they prepare what they bring in,
> it will be twice as much as they gather on other days."

YHWH communicates to Moses an astonishing undertaking. If food is
what Israel want, food is what they will get.[9] He will make bread fall like
rain from the skies. Although this could depict just one particular down-
pour, the words that follow make clear that this will become a regular,
daily phenomenon with a particular significance. The principle of daily
collection, which will be amplified later, is here spelled out in a general
formula for a daily task (דבר יום ביומו, "the matter of a day in its day,"
as in the requirement to produce a specified number of bricks each day,
Exod 5:13, 19); though it is also made clear that when the end of the
week comes, arrangements will be different.

The purpose of this—which is articulated for Moses' understanding,
and is not necessarily what he is to communicate to the Israelites for their
understanding—is a testing (נסה) of Israel. What kind of test is it? On
first reading one might perhaps think that it is a test simply designed to
ascertain whether or not Israel will do what they ought to do (analogous
perhaps to a test of students to ascertain whether or not they have learned
the prescribed paradigm of, say, the Piel of *lamed–he* verbs). But this is
hardly likely, other than perhaps in part. The opening depiction of Israel
(vv. 2–3) makes overwhelmingly likely that such a test would be failed,
as indeed it is (v. 20); and there would be no constructive point in repeating such a test every day. Analogous use of נסה makes clear, however,

---

7. Childs, *Exodus*, 285.

8. Walter Brueggemann, "The Book of Exodus," in *The New Interpreter's Bible*
(ed. L. Keck et al.; Nashville: Abingdon, 1994), 1:675–981 (812).

9. I assume that "bread" (לחם), as used both by the Israelites (v. 3) and by YHWH
(v. 4), is a generic term for basic food; though this is of course contestable, not least
in relation to one's interpretative decision about Israel's livestock (above, n. 6).

that the test has an intrinsic pedagogic dimension.[10] This is clearest in the comment on the manna story in Deut 8:2–3, 5 where initial language (v. 2), very similar to Exod 16:4b, is followed by a statement of purpose (v. 3b), "...in order to make you understand that one does not live by bread alone, but by every word that comes from the mouth of the LORD"; and there is also a generalizing summary of the wilderness period as a time when (v. 5b), "...as a parent disciplines a child so the LORD your God disciplines you." Thus, although the precise nuances of "test" in Exod 16 will need to emerge from the developing narrative, there is good reason to see the test as formative, as contributing to the shaping of Israel into the people that God wants them to be.

> [6] So Moses and Aaron said to all the Israelites, "In the evening you shall know that it was the LORD who brought you out of the land of Egypt, [7] and in the morning you shall see the glory of the LORD, because he has heard your complaining against the LORD. For what are we, that you complain against us?" [8] And Moses said, "When the LORD gives you meat to eat in the evening and your fill of bread in the morning, because the LORD has heard the complaining that you utter against him—what are we? Your complaining is not against us but against the LORD."

Moses says nothing about what is to happen as a test. Rather, he seeks to renew Israel's awareness of YHWH by depicting what is to happen, the bread from heaven, as enabling Israel's knowledge of YHWH as deliverer and as a provision which is, apparently, tantamount to seeing divine glory. Moses states and reiterates that Israel's complaining against Moses and Aaron (vv. 2, 3b) is really a complaining against YHWH; but YHWH will meet this complaining graciously.[11]

> [9] Then Moses said to Aaron, "Say to the whole congregation of the Israelites, 'Draw near to the LORD, for he has heard your complaining.'"
> [10] And as Aaron spoke to the whole congregation of the Israelites, they looked towards the wilderness, and the glory of the LORD appeared in the cloud. [11] The LORD spoke to Moses and said, [12] "I have heard the complaining of the Israelites; say to them, 'At twilight you shall eat meat, and in the morning you shall have your fill of bread; then you shall know that I am the LORD your God.'"

---

10. For general discussion of נסה, see my *The Bible, Theology, and Faith: A Study of Abraham and Jesus* (Cambridge: Cambridge University Press, 2000), 97–107.

11. This is, of course, different from the characteristic tone in Numbers where, in stories comparable to those in Exodus, Israel suffers sharply from the divine anger. The difference appears to be the intervening gift of תורה (Torah) at Sinai, with the accompanying assumption that post-Sinai the stakes are higher: "much is expected of those to whom much is given" (cf. Luke 12:48).

In this continuation of Moses and Aaron addressing Israel[12] one difference seems to be a possible shift in location ("near to the LORD"), though what is envisaged is unclear.[13] In any case, the appearance of YHWH's glory—perhaps their looking towards the wilderness is to be imagined as looking towards Sinai and seeing YHWH's presence there, or coming from there (cf. Exod 24:15–18)—leads to an instruction to Moses to tell the people specifically what is to happen, whose purpose is to renew their existential awareness of YHWH.

> (13) In the evening quails came up and covered the camp; and in the morning there was a layer of dew around the camp. (14) When the layer of dew lifted, there on the surface of the wilderness was a fine flaky substance, as fine as frost on the ground.

Although the quails come and provide "meat" (בשׂר), as distinct from "bread" (לחם), in accordance with what YHWH had said (v. 12), they play no further role in the story, and indeed, if they continued, would implicitly diminish the importance and significance attached to the bread. Within the story, therefore, the quails are presumably to be imagined as a one-off gift,[14] unlike the recurrent daily bread.[15] It is this bread, which somehow comes with the dew, that is now the entire focus of interest.

12. The logic of the narrative sequence in vv. 6–12 is more puzzling and seemingly less well ordered than elsewhere in the story. Unsurprisingly, numerous explanations in terms of traditio-historical and redactional complexity have been offered, frequently in terms of textual displacement (that vv. 9–12 should precede vv. 6–8). I do my best with the received form; in which perspective it becomes attractive, for example, to follow Benno Jacob's proposal that the verb in v. 11 should be construed as pluperfect, and that those later divine words were thus part of the original divine address, in relating which "Moses simply mentioned the rest later" (*The Second Book of the Bible: Exodus* [trans. Walter Jacob; Hoboken, N.J.: Ktav, 1992], 442, 444, 449; though see Propp's philological criticism of this, *Exodus 1–18*, 594). But I see no point in lingering over difficulties here, for this section is still preliminary to the story's main concerns.

13. A reference to the tent and ark would be a natural implication in a later context. Although in this pre-Sinai context the tent and ark are not yet available, their presence seems presupposed in the addenda at the end of the story (vv. 33–34). However, these addenda have no chronological specification and so could envisage a post-Sinai context despite their present pre-Sinai placement.

14. Not quite "manna with a side dish of quail," though it's a nice thought (Thomas W. Mann, *The Book of the Torah: The Narrative Integrity of the Pentateuch* [Atlanta: John Knox, 1988], 96).

15. This is also the implication of Num 11:4–35 where it is the recurrence of nothing but manna that makes the Israelites long for meat.

(15) When the Israelites saw it, they said to one another, "What is it?" [*or* "It is manna" (Heb. הוא מן)] For they did not know what it was. Moses said to them, "It is the bread that the LORD has given you to eat."

The first thing about YHWH's provision is that Israel has no idea what to make of it. As Deut 8:3 puts it, drawing out its unprecedented nature, it is something "with which neither you nor your ancestors were acquainted." It fits no existing category within Israel's knowledge and experience. Although Moses explains that it is the promised bread, its intrinsic strangeness is memorialized in its name. For the Israelites' question is made to involve a wordplay between מה ("what?") and מן (the name that the substance is given, v. 30, in English "manna"). The new way of living which Israel is to learn involves accustoming themselves to the strange and unfamiliar.

(16) "This is what the LORD has commanded: 'Gather as much of it as each of you needs, an omer to a person according to the number of persons, all providing for those in their own tents.' " (17) The Israelites did so, some gathering more, some less. (18) But when they measured it with an omer, those who had gathered much had nothing over, and those who gathered little had no shortage; they gathered as much as each of them needed.

Moses passes on directions from YHWH. An initial "as much as each of you needs" (איש לפי אכלו), sounds like an invitation to gather according to the extent of their appetite. But this is followed by a qualifier: each person is to have a particular specified amount, an omer, and the variation between what people gather is to correspond to the varying numbers of people in the households within the tents (e.g. "collect four omers for a household of four, six omers for a household of six"). When these are read together, along with the narrative note that an omer for measuring did not accompany the act of collecting, it seems that "an omer per person" is to be taken as Moses' rough guide as to the appropriate amount that will meet a person's need.

There is some unclarity as to the precise sense of v. 18, in terms of how the amount collected, which was estimated by those collecting, related to precise need. Is it the case that, however much or little was collected, YHWH tacitly superintended the process in such a way as to ensure that parity per individual person was the result?[16] Or is it the case that what was gathered was pooled and then redistributed in appropriate amounts, YHWH's tacit superintending having ensured the right overall

16. So, for example, Rashi; see Carasik, *The Commentators' Bible*, 127.

amount?[17] Either way, the point appears to be that the bread from heaven comes in precisely the quantity people need, however much or little they collect; the strong and energetic are not privileged over the weak and frail, or the greedy over the abstemious.[18] They exercise their varying abilities, and their varying needs are equally met. Here is the archetypal original of those words that arguably, more than any others, won many followers over to Karl Marx: "From each according to their ability; to each according to their need."

> [19] And Moses said to them, "Let no one leave any of it over until morning." [20] But they did not listen to Moses; some left part of it until morning, and it bred worms and became foul. And Moses was angry with them. [21] Morning by morning they gathered it, as much as each needed; but when the sun grew hot, it melted.

To go out every day to collect could seem like a chore that needs to be eased. Why not collect extra on one day, and keep it, so that one does not need to go out the next (but rather have a lie-in, or whatever)? Yet Moses rules this out. YHWH's bread is not the sort that can be kept overnight, but can only be collected afresh each new day. Unsurprisingly, some doubt this and try to store the bread overnight anyway. They discover that this cannot be done, for the bread goes off badly (or, if left on the ground, it melts and so becomes unavailable). Again unsurprisingly, Moses is angered at their reluctance to trust him and take him at his word.

In this depiction the heavenly bread is resistant to one of the most basic of human urges: to save up and hoard. It is part of YHWH's new way, into which Israel is being inducted, in which familiar categories of understanding and yardsticks of behaviour are replaced. YHWH's principle is that Israel's bread must each day be provided anew and collected anew. The implicit sense is of a need to appropriate the divine gift always in the present, in the here and now. Israel indeed are to know what YHWH has done for them in the past, which is the basis for what they do in the present; yet they cannot, as it were, live off the past but must appropriate the implications of the past through a pattern of living that is renewed each new day.

> [22] On the sixth day they gathered twice as much food, two omers apiece. When all the leaders of the congregation came and told Moses, [23] he said to them, "This is what the LORD has commanded: 'Tomorrow is a day of

17. So, for example, Calvin, *Mosis Reliqui Libri Quatuor in Formam Harmoniae: Comm. in Exod.* (Calvini Opera XXIV; Brunswick: C. A. Schwetschke, 1882), 172.

18. "The wondrous reality about the distribution of this bread is that their uncompetitive, non-hoarding practice really does work, and it works for all!" (Brueggemann, "Exodus," 813–14).

solemn rest, a holy sabbath to the LORD; bake what you want to bake and boil what you want to boil, and all that is left over put aside to be kept until morning.'" [24] So they put it aside until morning, as Moses commanded them; and it did not become foul, and there were no worms in it. [25] Moses said, "Eat it today, for today is a sabbath to the LORD; today you will not find it in the field. [26] For six days you shall gather it; but on the seventh day, which is a sabbath, there will be none." [27] On the seventh day some of the people went out to gather, and they found none. [28] The LORD said to Moses, "How long will you refuse to keep my commandments and instructions? [29] See! The LORD has given you the sabbath, therefore on the sixth day he gives you food for two days; each of you stay where you are; do not leave your place on the seventh day." [30] So the people rested on the seventh day.

The principle and practice of daily provision, daily collection, and no hoarding have been established. So now it is possible to introduce an exception. On the sixth day the principle and practice change. In accordance with YHWH's initial words to Moses (v. 5), the people gather a double amount. When their leaders come to tell Moses that they have done this, Moses explains what they are to do. This can be understood in two ways. Either one assumes that Moses has told the Israelites that they will collect more on the sixth day, and when the leaders report to Moses for directions as to what to do with it all (given the established constraints) Moses then explains the principle of sabbath. Alternatively, as Childs puts it, "The people are not informed of the plan. They go blissfully out on the sixth day, gathering a day's portion as usual, and to their amazement, they gather twice the normal amount, two omers apiece. When they come to Moses, he exploits their surprise to instruct them in the nature of the sabbath."[19] Although this latter is more dramatic, the Hebrew says nothing about amazement or surprise,[20] and so I think the former reading is probably closer to the text. Either way, Moses explains that because the following day is holy, a sabbath, they can do the very thing that they cannot do on all other days: prepare the food, keep it overnight, and eat it fresh the next day. Indeed, as Moses says subsequently, on the seventh, holy day the bread is not given by God to be available for collection.

19. Childs, *Exodus*, 290.
20. If surprise were intended the Hebrew would surely read something like: ויהי ביום הששי לקטו לחם וימדו בעמר והנה משנה שני העמר לאחד. The use of והנה, which serves to shift the perspective from that of the narrator to that of the character within the story, is a common idiomatic way of indicating that something remarkable or surprising is being seen; cf. Gen 8:11; 22:13; 24:15; 25:24; 26:8; 28:12, 13; 37:7, 9, etc.

Certain Israelites, true to form, yet again refuse to take Moses' word
for it. They go out to look for the bread, just as previously they tried to
avoid having to go out for it. In place of Moses' anger comes YHWH's
rebuke. And YHWH reiterates and expands what Moses had said previously about the special status of the sabbath, which is such that double
bread comes on the sixth day to enable rest without lack on the seventh.

> [31] The house of Israel called it manna; it was like coriander seed, white,
> and the taste of it was like wafers made with honey. [32] Moses said, "This
> is what the LORD has commanded: 'Let an omer of it be kept throughout
> your generations, in order that they may see the food with which I fed
> you in the wilderness, when I brought you out of the land of Egypt.'" [33]
> And Moses said to Aaron, "Take a jar, and put an omer of manna in it,
> and place it before the LORD, to be kept throughout your generations." [34]
> As the LORD commanded Moses, so Aaron placed it before the covenant,
> for safe keeping. [35] The Israelites ate manna for forty years, until they
> came to a habitable land; they ate manna, until they came to the border of
> the land of Canaan. [36] An omer is a tenth of an ephah.

The story of the bread from heaven, and what Israel was to learn thereby,
is complete. So the narrative changes mode, and offers a number of
explanatory comments. First (v. 31), there is a note about the bread itself,
its name, appearance and pleasant taste. Secondly (vv. 32–34), a speci-
men of manna is to be kept as a holy object,[21] beside the ark,[22] which will
remind subsequent generations of YHWH's provision in the wilderness.[23]
Thirdly (v. 35), there is a note about the duration of the manna for the
whole of the wilderness period, but its cessation when Israel was about
to enter the promised land, when YHWH's normal mode of provision
became the food that grew in the land (Josh 5:12). Finally (v. 36), a note
(perhaps originally a marginal gloss to v. 16 or v. 18, subsequently
included in the text at this point where it does not break the flow?)

---

21. How an omer's quantity of manna is able to be preserved, when usually the
manna decays overnight, is not specified (just as there is no explanation as to how it
could be baked or boiled on the sixth day, even though generally it melted in the
sun's heat). Perhaps one should assume that, given the variable nature of the
manna's durability in relation to the sabbath, then if YHWH commands that manna be
kept then manna becomes keepable.

22. The Hebrew of v. 34, לפני העדות, is rendered "before the covenant" by NRSV.
Propp usefully observes, "ʿēdut is often, as here, an elliptical or metonymic reference
to ʾărōn hāʿēdût 'the Covenant Ark'" (*Exodus 1–18*, 599).

23. Stephen Geller interestingly sees a concern to connect the manna with the
"bread before the Presence" so as to interpret such bread not as food to be consumed
by the deity but as a symbol of divine provision for Israel ("Manna and Sabbath: A
Literary-Theological Reading of Exodus 16," *Int* 59 [2005]: 5–16 [12]).

explains the quantity of manna that is represented by an omer (on the assumption that one knows how much an ephah is!).

3. *The Significance of the Story Within the Wider Christian Canon*

On any reckoning this story of the bread from heaven is remarkable, and raises some basic issues about the nature of life for Israel as the people of God.

Understanding of the manna, and of the differing ways in which it is encountered by Israel, is clearly not greatly helped by attempts to rationalize the manna in terms of some "natural" phenomenon of wilderness life (beyond establishing that the story has local colour in terms of conditions in the Sinai).[24] For the explanatory "success" of such approaches is in inverse proportion to their ability to account for what the text actually says, most obviously in relation to the difference on the sixth and seventh days.[25] Rather, the manna appears to function as a symbolic concretization of divine grace—which finds and nourishes people irrespective of their varying abilities, which forms recalcitrant people into better patterns of living, which encounters people in ways that vary according to circumstance, and which is designed to enable people to appropriate the rhythm of God's own being and action (if one may generalize the text's concern for the sabbath through resonance with Gen 2:1–3).[26]

24. Rationalizing tendencies have the ancient precedent of Josephus: "It is a mainstay to dwellers in these parts against their dearth of other provisions, and to this very day all that region is watered by a rain like to that which then, as a favour to Moses, the Deity sent down for men's sustenance" (*Ant.* 3:31 [trans. H. St. J. Thackeray LCL]).

25. For a succinct account of the nature of the manna that is produced naturally in the Sinai peninsula, and of the similarities and the differences between it and the biblical manna, see S. R. Driver, *The Book of Exodus* (Cambridge Bible for Schools and Colleges; Cambridge: Cambridge University Press, 1911), 153–54. Childs valuably situates Driver and issues of rationalization in a history of interpretation and patterns of thought from Ibn Ezra onwards (*Exodus*, 298–99).

26. Fretheim, in discussing this issue, expresses the concern that "If the provisions of God in the wilderness are all subsumed under the extraordinary or miraculous, then the people of God will tend to look for God's providential care only in that which falls outside the ordinary. The all too common effect of this is to absent God from the ordinary and everyday and to go searching for God only in the deep-sea and mountaintop experiences. Consequently, the people of God will not be able to see in the very ordinariness of things that God is the one who bestows blessings again and again" (Terence Fretheim, *Exodus* [IBC; Louisville, Ky.: John Knox, 1991], 182).

A striking inner-biblical commentary is provided by Deut 8:3: "He humbled you by letting you hunger, then by feeding you with manna, with which neither you nor your ancestors were acquainted, in order to make you understand that one (הָאָדָם) does not live by bread alone, but by every word that comes from the mouth of the LORD." The story is seen to be about learning a fuller understanding of human life. Humanity (אָדָם) is indeed material and dependent upon food; but that humanity is more than material, and finds its true sustenance in the moral and spiritual realm through obedient relationship to YHWH, is a lesson that needs to be learned—even though this lesson may at least initially be unwelcome ("humbled you," "let you hunger") and may take one beyond the familiar and recognizable. Moreover, a key presupposition of the Deuteronomic interpretation is that the significance of the story is not restricted to Israel's time in the wilderness (the only time they were fed by manna, which ceased when they could be sustained by produce in the promised land, Josh 5:12), but is of enduring significance even when circumstances change.

Within its own frame of reference the story focuses upon what might be called a "discipline of daily living" in a way that incorporates the differing patterns of work and rest. The need to start each day with collecting fresh manna readily becomes metaphorical for wider patterns of starting each day through deliberate engagement with God: one thinks of the testimony of the servant of YHWH whose work of sustaining others is rooted in his own receptiveness to YHWH each morning (Isa 50:4), or of the testimony of the appallingly afflicted man who yet affirms that YHWH's mercies are "new every morning" (Lam 3:1, 22–23). Of course, such a metaphorical move does not so readily do justice to the difference of the sixth and seventh days (unless one wishes to propose that engagement with God is not needed on the seventh day!); that difference is suggestive rather of divine provision in ways that should diminish human anxieties as to how they will be provided for if they do not unceasingly work for it themselves.

Within the Christian Bible as a whole, perhaps the weightiest resonance is with the clause of the Lord's Prayer, "Give us this day our daily bread."[27] The interpretation of the rare Greek word rendered as "daily" (*epiousios*) has from ancient times been influenced by the story of the

---

Yet although Fretheim's concern is in itself entirely valid, I am not sure that it is the most helpful emphasis in seeking to understand Exod 16. For the point of the text, at least in part, is that divine grace reconstitutes the ordinary and everyday.

27.   This is the familiar liturgical form, taken from Matt 6:11; this is not the context to discuss the relationship between Matt 6:11 and Luke 11:3.

manna.[28] Whatever the precise etymology of *epiousios*, the canonical resonance remains strong and is suggestive of reading "daily bread" in a metaphorical way to include whatever is needed for sustaining life in ever-renewed openness to God within the disciplines of grace.[29] There is also the extensive Johannine reconstrual of the story in terms of Jesus as the living bread of God (John 6:31–58), which in a different way encourages a searching imaginative and metaphorical engagement with the biblical text.

4. *The Genre of Exodus 16*

If the story of Exod 16 has been to some extent understood, we may finish with the question of what kind of material the story is.[30] Here we encounter at least two difficulties. On the one hand, any particular category—history, myth, legend, saga, folktale, etc—tends to be used in so many ways that without further careful definition it signifies little. On the other hand, people sometimes fix on particular terms and then employ them rhetorically and polemically in ways that lose sight of those specifics of the text which give rise to the use of the term in the first place.

One sophisticated modern attempt to handle this issue, at least in general terms, has been the German articulation of a difference between *Historie* and *Geschichte*. As David Jasper conveniently summarizes:

> *Historie* is a description of how events actually happened; *Geschichte* is a description of what events *mean*, both to those who first experienced them and to us now. In other words, *Geschichte* is also concerned with contemporary present-day experience. History is not just about the past; it is also about the present.[31]

28. See, for example, W. D. Davies and Dale C. Allison, *The Gospel According to Saint Matthew* (ICC; Edinburgh: T. & T. Clark, 1988), 1:607–10.

29. Ulrich Luz interestingly resists this on the grounds that it "does not agree with the intention of the text" and (implicitly) gives insufficient weight to "the strong rooting of this petition in the situation of the poor" (*Matthew 1–7* [trans. Wilhelm C. Linss; Minneapolis: Fortress, 1989], 383). But even if this be granted for the likely meaning of the words in the context of Jesus' ministry, it does not necessarily resolve the question of meaning when the words are contextualized within the total canon of Christian Scripture; difference of context can appropriately engender difference of meaning.

30. Commentators sometimes start with the question of genre. But it seems to me best to be handled once one has worked with the text in detail; though of course such a sharp distinction is to some extent artificial since exegesis will regularly depend upon provisional judgments as to the nature and genre of the text.

31. David Jasper, *A Short Introduction to Hermeneutics* (Louisville, Ky.: Westminster John Knox, 2004), 93.

In addition to the extensive use of this distinction by Karl Barth—"not all history is 'historical'" (*Nicht alle Geschichte ist historisch*)[32]—one well-known exposition is by von Rad in his introduction to his Genesis commentary, where he speaks of the Genesis narratives as "sagas" whose characteristics are to be understood in terms of the nature of *Geschichte* as distinct from *Historie*. Although von Rad is writing specifically about Genesis, the generalizing way in which he writes suggests that he would have considered much of what he says to be applicable also to a narrative such as Exod 16:

> [Saga] is the form favoured by a people for depicting its early history...
> In its sagas a people is concerned with itself and the realities in which it finds itself... For there is another history that a people makes besides the externals of wars, victories, migrations, and political catastrophes. It is an inner history, one that takes place on a different level, a story of inner events, experiences, and singular guidance, of working and becoming mature in life's mysteries; and for Israel that meant a history with God...
> There is often an entire world of events—actual, experienced events!— enclosed in a single saga. The saga, therefore, has a much higher degree of density than has history (*Historie*)... At the beginning, the saga in most cases certainly contained a "historical" fact as its actual crystalliz- ing point. But in addition it reflects a historical experience on the relevant community which extends into the present time of the narrator...
> In ancient Israel the principal power in the forming of saga was faith. In any case, we do not have a single saga that has not received from faith its decisive stamp and orientation. In every instance the degree of this revi- sion, stamp and orientation is completely different.[33]

There is, of course, much in such an account with which one can, in one way or other, argue. But on any reckoning one needs some way of giving an account of narratives which combine at least three characteristics: they are set in a particular historical context of foundational significance, they read opaquely to the contemporary ancient historian, and they function in terms of high levels of existential and archetypal resonance.

---

32. *CD* III/1, 61–94 (p. 80)/*KD* III/1, 87. Barth is writing with reference to the genre of the creation narratives of Genesis. He goes on to express himself robustly on the subject of reductive attitudes towards such biblical material: "We must dismiss and resist to the very last any idea of the inferiority or untrustworthiness or even worthlessness of a 'non-historical' depiction and narration of history. This is in fact only a ridiculous and middle-class habit of the modern Western mind which is supremely phantastic in its chronic lack of imaginative phantasy, and hopes to rid itself of its complexes through suppression" (p. 81).
33. Gerhard von Rad, *Genesis* (trans. John Marks; 3d ed.; London: SCM Press, 1972), 33, 34, 35.

Von Rad's account, whatever its deficiencies, remains of real value as an articulation of this phenomenon, and enables us perhaps at least to begin to have the right kind of categories for doing justice both to a text such as Exod 16 in its own right and to insights of modern thought.

5. *Postscript*

Much contemporary Christian faith struggles to know what to make of the Old Testament, and the strategies of ignoring and/or deploring are all too well practised. To be sure, there are real and substantive difficulties in knowing how best to understand and appropriate its content—hence the vocation of the Christian Old Testament scholar. It is a pleasure to submit this small contribution to the task in honour of a scholar who has made a substantial contribution.

THE WEEK THAT MADE THE WORLD:
REFLECTIONS ON THE FIRST PAGES OF THE BIBLE

Robert P. Gordon

If this volume were to include a *tabula gratulatoria* it would properly contain not only a long list of appreciative academic colleagues of Gordon Wenham but also the names of many who approach the Bible primarily as Scripture and whose understanding of its message owes much to his gifts as an interpreter of the biblical text. Any volume by, or for, Gordon is bound to attract readers in this second category, and it is partly with them in mind that this reflection on early Genesis is written.

As the Dead Sea texts and their container jars remind us, the arranging of the books of the Old Testament in a fixed (or "canonical") order came as a secondary development in their transmission. With the advent of "canon" and then the codex, the book of Genesis more formally took up its logical position at the head of the books of the Old Testament. The account of beginnings in the early chapters of the book has naturally been the focus of special attention over centuries, and the more so for those who, like Augustine of Hippo, reckoned that Gen 1 provided information not only about beginnings but also, because of the periodization represented by the biblical "days," about the course of subsequent human history, or even the eschaton itself.[1] Inevitably, too, many people's impressions of the Bible as a whole are determined by their impressions of its first pages, whether these are formed through actual acquaintance with the text or come about as a result of public discussion of cosmic and human origins and of the Bible's perspectives on these important matters. In these circumstances, it is particularly important that those who claim to identify with "the biblical position" on beginnings do justice to what the text is seeking to communicate and do not express their commitment

---

1. See P. Kapusta, *Articulating Creation, Articulating Kerygma: A Theological Interpretation of Evangelisation and Genesis Narrative in the Writings of Saint Augustine of Hippo* (European University Studies XXIII/804; Frankfurt: Lang, 2005), 205–9.

by imposing their own schemes upon it. Otherwise, it becomes necessary for Genesis to be defended against its defenders.

1. *Environing Issues*

Before discussing "the week that made the world," it will be useful to consider three "environing issues" that should be taken into account in any such discussion. The first is that of the Bible generally in relation to science, and in particular the role of Genesis in relation to origins. It appears self-evident that the business of Scripture is not to convey scientific knowledge, and that to judge its truth-claims by the criterion of scientific awareness is a category error. Since our concern here is with origins, and no one has an eyewitness contribution to make to the subject, it will be helpful if the same basic point can be made with reference to observable phenomena—in this case human physiology. The Old Testament has much to say about humans as sentient beings who think, plan, remember and forget and do all sorts of things that we associate with brain function. But on the role of the brain in relation to all this cerebration the Old Testament is silent. Indeed, functions that we now associate with the brain are attributed by biblical writers to other bodily organs, so that a psalmist may enthuse about the nocturnal instruction that he receives from his kidneys[2] (Ps 16:7), while the "heart" is commonly identified as the seat of volition and wisdom (e.g. 1 Sam 13:14; Prov 23:15). Consequently, statements about the Bible in relation to science should consider both what is said and what is not said, if a fully rounded account is to be achieved. Specifically in relation to cosmic origins, Rabbi Louis Jacobs has fairly claimed that Israel developed no cosmology of its own.[3] That is not at all to deny that there are features and emphases that are unique to Genesis (in particular), but it is to say that the building blocks of the biblical creation narratives correspond in significant respects to creation traditions in the surrounding cultures. In that case, showing what the biblical writers do with such traditions, and thence defining the purpose of their own account of beginnings, becomes an especially important task.

The second "environing issue" is that of the archaeology and history of the ancient world and the ways in which these should affect our approach to the biblical data. As is well-known, Archbishop James Ussher calculated on the basis of the biblical data that creation took place

2. Translated "heart" in NIV.

3. L. Jacobs, "Jewish Cosmology," in *Ancient Cosmologies* (ed. C. Blacker and M. Loewe; London: Allen & Unwin, 1975), 66–86 (66).

in the year 4004 B.C.E., and essentially this position is adopted by a substantial number of modern adherents of the Bible who subscribe to "young earth" theories, given that nowadays it is often surmised that the genealogies of early Genesis are selective and that it is allowable to push the creation date back by a few thousand years. At the same time, archaeologists and historians of the Near East find evidence of early attempts at writing in southern Mesopotamia in the mid-fourth millennium at centres such as Uruk and Kish, talk of an "early dynastic period" in Sumer in the first half of the third millennium, and reconstruct the history of the Akkadian dynasty of Sargon, later in the same millennium. Since all this is preceded by evidence of human settlement and development in "prehistoric" times, the inadequacy of the 4004 calculation is clear, and not because Ussher got his sums seriously wrong—he was one of the most learned and able men of his time—but because the data were being pressed beyond what they can bear. Given that Adam lived for 930 years, according to Gen 5:5, we should expect, if strictly following the Ussher calculation (or minor variations of it), to find autograph evidence of Adam's own literary activity. Indeed, the absence of it could be worrying!

Thirdly, traditional (by now) source criticism attributes Gen 1:1–2:3 (4a) to a priestly writer who provided an introduction to the great national account of Israel's history that began with the supranational perspective of Gen 2–3 on the creation and subsequent "fall" of the first humans. There are indeed good grounds for identifying two originally independent but now complementary creation narratives in Gen 1–2, and the recognition brings positive exegetical gains with it. Moreover, we can benefit from this kind of critical insight without courting the condemnation of the late Abba Eban who, describing his classes in Old Testament study at Cambridge in the 1930s, noted that "the obsessive puzzle 'Who wrote it?'" tended to take precedence over the more important question, "What is the writer trying to say?"[4]

2. *Fashioning and Fiat*

It is a commonplace observation that Gen 1 is free of the mythological elements that feature in other Near Eastern accounts of creation and that are encountered in the more poetical parts of the Old Testament. These come mainly in the poetry of the psalms (Pss 74:13; 89:11 [10]), the prophets (Isa 27:1; 51:9) and the book of Job (9:13; 26:12–13), in passages celebrating the victory of God over primeval forces that opposed him in creation and that typify opposition to his universal kingship in the

---

4.   Abba Eban, *An Autobiography* (London: Weidenfeld & Nicolson, 1978), 16.

present order. The derivation of תהום ("the deep") in Gen 1:2 from the name of the Babylonian monster Tiamat, whose body Marduk split in two to make the sky and the earth, is rightly questioned on philological grounds, and in any case the תהום of Gen 1 appears to be no different from its other Old Testament occurrences where it simply denotes an expanse of water. Again, the great sea creatures that might have had mythological significance attached to them are simply creations of the fifth day, in company with the other maritime creatures and the birds of the air (1:20–22). There is, then, no combat myth underlying the creation sequence in Gen 1; the chapter is about a week of six days of making and fashioning, climaxed by a sabbath of rest from labour.

To the question "Are the days of Genesis 1 literal days?" the answer has to be in the affirmative, though that is only the beginning of the answer. The poetic statement in Ps 90:4 about a thousand years in God's sight being "like yesterday when it is past" affords no basis for thousand-year days nor any direct evidence that "day" in Gen 1 should be taken as other than literal—quite apart from what such elongated days might do for symbiosis in the developing creation. If such lengthening of days is to be read into the text, for example to create space for geological or human biological development, the repeated "there was evening and there was morning" sounds an improbable way of representing, or partly representing, the great geological periods as usually envisaged.

Of the four modes of creation characteristic of ancient Near Eastern creation accounts—combat, fashioning, begetting and fiat—we have so far noted only two, viz. combat, of which there is no evidence in Genesis, and fashioning (or making). Creation by fiat is also clearly present in Gen 1, and is often cited as the characteristic and distinguishing mode of divine activity in creation, for it conveys impressively the idea of effortless divine power at work, as in Ps 33:6, 9: "By the word of the Lord the heavens were made, and all their host by the breath of his mouth... For he spoke and it came to pass; he commanded and it stood firm." This comes in a communal hymn of praise, in which the trustworthiness of the divine word in general is first celebrated (vv. 4–5) and then the role of that word already at creation is introduced. Indeed, it is in the Psalter that the best reiteration of "creation by word" is found, in Ps 148:5–6 ("Let them praise the name of the Lord, for he commanded and they were created. He set them in place forever and ever; he established a decree that will never pass away"; cf. Ps 104:7). On the other hand, fiat creation is not represented in Gen 2:4–25, and it features little in the creation passages in Job and Isa 40–55, this latter under-representation being the more significant to the extent that we accept Fishbane's conclusion that within Isa 40–55 there is "aggadic transformation" of the creation tradi-

tion in Gen 1:1–2:3.[5] Thus, whereas the idea of fiat creation could have
been invoked to express the superiority of Israel's God as creator and
sustainer of the world, it plays no part in the creation doctrine of Isa 40–
55. By contrast, the divine command effects the return of exiles (43:6–7)
and other developments associated with return (44:26–28). Creation-by-
word has been claimed for 48:13,[6] though the text mentions fashioning first, and appears to be referring to God's existential control of the
heavens and the earth, which "stand up" to do his bidding when he calls
(cf. 40:26).[7] This attentiveness of the physical creation to God's bidding
may be intended to contrast with the questionable response of God's own
people (vv. 1, 12). In point of fact, the normal creation discourse of Isa
40–55 is that of fashioning (40:26, 28; 42:5; 45:7–8, 12, 18; 48:13;
51:13, 16), which language extends to God's creation of Israel (43:1, 7,
15, 21; 44:2, 24; 45:11; 46:4) and of the events by which he would bring
about its restoration (41:18–20; 48:6–7).

Fiat creation is therefore not unique to Gen 1, while at the same time it
is only occasionally represented elsewhere in the Old Testament. Nor is
it a uniquely biblical idea, inasmuch as something analogous is expressed
in the Memphite "theology of creation" in ancient Egypt, according to
which "all the divine order really came into being through what the heart
thought and the tongue commanded."[8] The extant copy of the text in
question is dated to ca. 700 B.C.E., but on philological and geopolitical
grounds it has been suggested that the original predated the copy by as
much as two millennia.[9] Now the point of once more citing this possible
Egyptian parallel in this discussion is simply to reinforce our impression
that fiat language is not the only, or even the main, conceptual contribution to the depiction of God as creator in Gen 1. There the use of fiat
language is particularly appropriate in relation to light (1:3), and it might
even be argued that the subsequent use of "let there be" in relation to the

5. M. Fishbane, *Biblical Interpretation in Ancient Israel* (Oxford: Clarendon,
1989), 322–26 (326).

6. C. Westermann, *Isaiah 40–66: A Commentary* (trans. D. M. G. Stalker;
London: SCM Press, 1969), 201.

7. The significance of the participles in both 40:26 and 48:13 should, properly,
be discussed in relation to the "creation" or "doxological" participles in other Old
Testament passages where creative acts of God are described participially (cf. Amos
4:13; 5:8; 9:6). Even so, the act of "fashioning" is mentioned first in Isa 48:13,
whereas in Gen 1 all "fashioning" takes place in consequence of the prior fiat.

8. See *ANET*, 5; R. J. Clifford, *Creation Accounts in the Ancient Near East and
in the Bible* (CBQMS 26; Washington, D.C.: Catholic Biblical Association, 1994),
106–7, 110–12, 114.

9. So J. A. Wilson in *ANET*, 4.

firmament (v. 6) and the heavenly lights (v. 14), as also the comparable usage in vv. 9, 11, 20 and 24, is influenced by the fiat of the first day.[10]

Consistently with the idea of God's fashioning of the world, we have allusion in the expression וּבֹהוּ תֹהוּ (1:2)—traditionally rendered "without form and void"—to the raw material out of which the earth was made. The expression relates to the earth in particular, for this is truly a geocentric and, for that matter, anthropocentric universe of "heavens and earth" that is depicted: only the earth is described in relation to its pre-ordered state. *Creatio ex nihilo* is not explicitly stated in Gen 1, though fiat creation and creation-from-nothing go very well together, and an apparently *ex nihilo* inference was drawn in later times (cf. 2 Macc 7:28; Heb 11:3). So, because of the existence of the unordered earth and waters at the stage represented by 1:2, it is not necessary for the land and seas to be "made" on the third day; what is required is that a separation takes place between the two (1:9).[11]

However, it is in the use of verbs for fashioning and making, in both creation narratives within Gen 1–2, that the workman character of the creator becomes most apparent. The verb בָּרָא (*bara'*, "create," 1:1, 21, 27; 2:4) is used, as also are עָשָׂה (*'asah*, "make," 1:7, 16, 25, 26, 31; 2:2, 3, 4) and יָצַר (*yaṣar*, "form," 2:7, 8, 19). Likewise, בָּנָה (*banah*, "build") is used for the creation of Eve, in 2:22. As is well-known, בָּרָא, when referring to making or creating, has only God as subject, whence it has sometimes been inferred that this creating must have been *ex nihilo*, and that, indeed, בָּרָא is a non-anthropomorphic usage. There are, however, instances of a בָּרָא meaning "cut, cut out," and, whatever etymological distinctions are entertained by modern lexicographers, the non-anthropomorphic nature of בָּרָא ("create") may not have been so obvious to biblical writers. It is בָּרָא that frames the first creation narrative of Gen 1:1–2:3, partly with the help of the felicitous wordplay at the beginning, in אֱלֹהִים בָּרָא בְּרֵאשִׁית ("In the beginning God created"), which is matched by לַעֲשׂוֹת אֱלֹהִים בָּרָא אֲשֶׁר ("which God had created and made") in 2:3.[12] Since בָּרָא belongs with fashioning rather than fiat, the emphasis within the narrative on fashioning is appropriately expressed in this "inclusion."

The creator's observance and hallowing of the sabbath at the end of "the week that made the world" (2:2–3) is also appropriate to fashioning

---

10. At the same time, the idea of light being "formed" (יָצַר) is perfectly at home in Old Testament diction (see Isa 45:7); there was more than one possible way to phrase Gen 1:3.

11. Cf. G. J. Wenham, *Genesis 1–15* (WBC 1; Waco, Tex.: Word, 1987), 20.

12. The same applies if the first narrative is terminated at 2:4a, since this ends with בְּהִבָּרְאָם ("when they were created").

in a way that does not apply to fiat creation. It is as a workman or artificer that God exerts himself and takes his sabbath rest in 1:1–2:3, and though ideas of recovery and refreshment are not explicit in the verb שבת in 2:2, it is different at Exod 31:17:

> It is a sign forever between me and the people of Israel, for in six days the Lord made heaven and earth, and rested on the seventh day and *was refreshed* (וינפש).

This is a quite expressive anthropomorphism in Exod 31, and too much for NIV, which satisfies itself with "and rested." The truer rendering is already found in AV "and was refreshed," and in modern versions such as REB ("and refreshed himself") and NRSV ("and was refreshed"). There are two other occurrences of the verb נפש, which even NIV is happy to translate by "refresh." In Exod 23:12, the purpose of the sabbath commandment is that slaves and aliens living within the Israelite community may "refresh themselves." Again, in 2 Sam 16:14, David and his people, who have been forced to evacuate Jerusalem because of Absalom's uprising against his father, arrive at their destination exhausted, and so David "refreshes himself." The picture in Exod 31:17 is therefore of a workman who exerts himself in his toil and afterwards needs time for refreshment. Its strongly anthropomorphic character becomes all the clearer when put alongside the assertion in Isa 40:28 that the creator of the ends of the earth does not grow tired or weary.

3. *Creation and Sanctuary*

The depiction of God as workman in Gen 1–2 also explains satisfactorily the resonances that exist between the concluding comments on the creation sequence in 1:31–2:3 and the account of the completion of the tabernacle in Exod 39. One explanation of this correspondence is that creation is viewed as a sanctuary in Gen 1–2: God is making a cosmos fit for his presence just as the tents and temples of the historical period were constructed as his dwelling-places on earth. Such a reading of creation in Genesis may work better in chs. 2–3, where there are elements redolent of the sanctuary traditions of the Old Testament (cf. 2:12 [gold, onyx; strictly, in the land of Havilah]; 3:24 [cherubim on guard]), but less obviously in ch. 1. More probably the creation–tabernacle correspondence arises because creation is being treated as a building.[13] Indeed, the term most frequently used for acts of creation in Mesopotamian creation

---

13. Cf. V. Hurowitz, *"I Have Built You an Exalted House": Temple Building in the Bible in Light of Mesopotamian and Northwest Semitic Writings* (JSOTSup 115; Sheffield: JSOT Press, 1992), 242 (including n. 2).

texts is the verb *banû*, one of whose basic meanings is "build." The
Hebrew cognate does not occur in Gen 1, although it is used for the creation of Eve, whom God "builds" (בנה) from Adam's "rib" (צלע, otherwise a topographical and architectural term) in 2:22. Creation-as-build-
ing is, in any case, a familiar theme in such a passage as Job 38:1–7 (cf.
Ps 104:5). The formal notice of completion, the inspection of the work
and the pronouncement of blessing are features shared by our creation
and tabernacle passages: the heavens and earth were completed (Gen
2:1)//the work on the tabernacle was completed (Exod 39:32); God saw
all that he had made and it was very good (Gen 1:31)//Moses inspected
the work and saw that they had done it just as the Lord had commanded
(Exod 39:43); God blessed the seventh day and hallowed it (Gen
2:3)//Moses blessed [the people] (Exod 39:43). Other texts and occurrences of key terms confirm that it is because creation is seen as building
construction work that there are parallels with the tabernacle account.[14]
The verb כלה ("be complete, finished"), occurring in Gen 2:1, 2 and
Exod 39:32, is also used to mark the completion of the Solomonic temple
in 1 Kgs 6:38; 2 Chr 8:16, and of the temple and royal palace in 1 Kgs
9:1, while, at the ceremony marking the completion of the temple,
Solomon blesses "all the congregation of Israel" (1 Kgs 8:13–14).

It is as builder and master craftsman, and—as we might say—as
inspector of buildings, that God reviews his work on each of the days of
creation, pronouncing the result "good," and cumulatively "very good."
As we have already noted, Moses similarly made his inspection and confirmed that the construction of the tabernacle was completed as specified
(Exod 39:43). And so also it may be with the city and tower of Babel
when the divine inspector comes down ahead of completion and undoes
the whole project (Gen 11:5). In context, the visit is a judgment visita-
tion, but it is precisely the element of routine inspection of the building
project, imposed ahead of time, that finds the builders out and puts an
end to their plan. An especially close parallel to Gen 1 is provided by the
glimpse of the cooperative member who helps in the manufacture of the
idol in Isa 41:7 and who declares of the soldering, "It is good." Recent
emphasis on the idol-maker, and not just the idol itself, functioning as a
counterpart to God in Isa 40–48 makes the comparison with Gen 1, if
anything, more appropriate.[15] Isaiah 41:7 is not about building as such,

14. This need not exclude such a further possibility as that the worship of the
tabernacle is regarded as a goal of the original creation—an idea sometimes explored
within the context of the priestly Pentateuchal strand.

15. K. Holter, *Second Isaiah's Idol-Fabrication Passages* (BBET 28; Frankfurt:
Lang, 1995).

but it is in adjacent territory, and although we may read deeper insights
into "good" and "very good" in Gen 1—for example, as countering dual-
istic ideas of creation—the divine pronouncement operates at a lowlier
level, expressing the divine artificer's satisfaction with what he has made.

There are good grounds, therefore, for being explicit about God as
workman in Gen 1 and for viewing the construct of the creation week in
that light. As the creative acts are arranged within this framework, the
oft-noted internal correspondence of the first three days to the second
triad in terms of habitat (days one to three) and inhabitants (days four to
six) comes into play. While, however, it would make sense in an ordered
creation sequence to prepare the habitat in advance of the inhabitants,
this cannot be the last or profoundest comment on this feature of Gen 1,
since, for example, the earth is bringing forth plants and fruit trees
already on the third day, in advance of the creation of the sun on the
fourth day. Only by special pleading, in particular by appealing to special
properties of the light that appears on the first day, can such a sequence
be understood. Rather, it is simply the idea of orderly procedure on the
part of the workman God that is represented in these two parallel panels.
There is further evidence of the artificial nature of the working week construct in the fact that no fewer than eight major creative "moments" are
divided among the six days, with the differentiating of land and sea and
also the appearance of vegetation on the third day, and the creation of both
animals and humans on the sixth day: "the eight works of creation are
prompted by ten divine commands and executed on six different days."[16]

So, we have creation completed within a working week—and yet there
is more to the Genesis narrative than a blow-by-blow, or daybook,
account of how it happened. Nevertheless, advocates of a literalist interpretation will counter that Exod 20:11 is a roadblock to this kind of
"narrative theological" approach to the passage: "For in six days the
Lord made the heavens and the earth, the sea and all that is in them, but
rested on the seventh day." Does not this statement in the Decalogue
assume a literal six-day creation? Perhaps so, or perhaps this alternative
grounding of the sabbath law—alternative, since the version of the
sabbath law given in Deut 5:12–15 relates the sabbath provision to the
Israelites' experience as slaves in Egypt—is more in the nature of a
reading off from the narrative tradition on creation. And if this seems to
be introducing circularity into the discussion, by suggesting that a human
working week has been used to provide a structure for the account of the
divine acts of creation and subsequent "resting," which in turn is cited as
prescriptive for human society under the Mosaic law, perhaps our earlier

16. Wenham, *Genesis 1–15*, 6.

observation of God "refreshing himself" becomes relevant. For if God does not need to refresh himself but is said to do so, then it is plain that such language is used in consideration of humans who do have such need. In other words, the prior need of human slaves and others to be refreshed on the sabbath, as in Exod 23:12, determines the exact use of language in relation to the needs of God as creator, in Exod 31:17. So, in a not dissimilar way, it appears that the human experience of the working week has provided the construct within which the divine acts of creation and cessation from work are presented. The first actual mention of sabbath in the historical period comes in Exod 16 in connection with the manna provision in the wilderness, when a double supply comes on the sixth day of the week because "[t]omorrow is to be a day of rest, a holy sabbath to the Lord" (v. 23).

4. *Purpose and Polemic*

The question of purpose in relation to meaning in texts is basic, since, if adequate purpose can be defined for a piece of literature, this has obvious implications for any further attempts to define the underlying "purpose," insofar as such can be discovered. What, then, is the purpose of Gen 1:1–2:3, the first of the two "creation narratives," if calculation and historical reconstruction in the Ussher mode are judged to make inappropriate use of genealogical and related data in the Old Testament? We can acknowledge with Gerhard von Rad that, even if the primary purpose of Gen 1 is not to transmit scientific knowledge, the chapter presents a kind of ancient science,[17] for example in the way that it deals in "kind" (or species) and order. In one respect, of course, Archbishop Ussher's approach was right in what it assumed and implied about purpose, for the so-called "protohistory" of Gen 1–11 is of a piece with the patriarchal narratives that follow it; there is no seam marking a transition from one kind of text or literary form to another. Rather, Genesis presents us with an historical continuum that runs on from creation, fall and flood to Abraham as the first of the patriarchs and ancestors of the people of Israel. The editorial device of the תולדות formulae in Genesis, in 2:4; 5:1; 6:9; 10:1; 11:10, 27 *and* in 25:12, 19; 36:1, 9; 37:2, makes its contribution in this regard, prefacing the second creation narrative in the same way as it does the several family histories of the patriarchal chapters and so reinforcing the sense of a continuous weld of the history of the world from creation to the patriarchs and onwards that is initiated in Gen 1. In

---

17. G. von Rad, *Genesis: A Commentary* (trans. J. Bowden; rev. ed.; London: SCM Press, 1972), 66.

other words, cosmogony is a part of biblical history, and this history has a strong linear and ultimately purposive character.

Discussion of purpose very soon draws us into consideration of genre, since purpose can scarcely be defined without reference to genre. However, genre is not a panacea for all the problems raised by "purpose." The question, "Whose genre?," is particularly apposite when we are discussing the Old Testament, since it is all too easy for the modern critic to impose his or her set of questions and categories upon an ancient text. As it happens, the subject of motive and intention has been addressed by Mark Brett, specifically in relation to Gen 1.[18] Basically, Brett makes a distinction between the two. Motive describes the occasioning circumstances in which a text was written—to cheer up Babylonian exiles, to clarify the context in which certain developments took place, and so on. Communicative intention is different, in relating more directly to the text and the communicative indications within it, and the search for these is legitimate and soundly based. Brett also highlights "conversational implicature" as a useful tool in interpreting the text. This relates to the possible, but never wholly explicit or definite, implications of what is said or written. The implication that we recognize as possible may be present, but we cannot be certain. We can sense "conversational implicature" at work in certain apparently polemical undercurrents in the creation narratives in Gen 1–2.

Now, so far as outright intention, or purpose, is concerned, it is widely accepted that polemic and satire are embedded in the Genesis "protohistory." The polemic is against certain beliefs and associated practices that were rejected by the prophetic religion of Israel. Clear examples of such polemic are found in Gen 6 and 11. The notion that cohabitation between gods and humans can produce superheroes is derided in 6:1–4 (8), where the coming together of the two results not in a super-breed but in the limiting of the human lifespan and in the judgment of the flood. The Babel narrative of 11:1–9 lampoons Babylonian pretensions to greatness, turning the Babel-builders' efforts at consolidation and self-aggrandizement into confusion and dispersal, and even making mocking repetition of their rallying-call as God rouses himself to descend and confound their enterprise.

However we interpret Gen 1–2, therefore, our approach must make room for the possibility of polemic in the narratives. But polemic sits awkwardly with a more literalistic reading of these chapters—though it should be obvious that what I am advocating in this study is, in the first instance, a literal reading of the text. In this connection, the incongruity

18. M. G. Brett, "Motives and Intentions in Genesis 1," *JTS* n.s. 42 (1991): 1–16.

of having the heavenly lights that are made in order to govern day and night appear only on the fourth "day," in 1:14–19, is worthy of inspection, as was recognized already in antiquity. In explanation, it is frequently asserted that this placement of the heavenly bodies represents their demotion from the status of deities—as they were widely regarded in the Near East—to mere luminaries whose light is subsidiary to a greater light created at the very beginning of creation (1:3). And without doubt, there are grounds within 1:14–19 for thinking in terms of polemic. It is a commonplace to note that the actual names of the two principal luminaries, representing as they would the gods thought to be manifest in the physical phenomena, are not mentioned: they are merely "the greater light" and "the lesser light" (1:16). This omission is all the more noticeable when taken against the background of several namings in the chapter (day and night, v. 5; sky, v. 8; earth and seas, v. 10).[19] Moreover, the mention of the creation of the stars, representing the heavenly "host" venerated throughout the Near East, is relegated to the status of an afterthought—"and the stars" (v. 16)—as if to put them in their merely functional place. Thus, independently of the issue of delayed placement on the fourth day, there is good reason to think of a polemical handling of the heavenly bodies in 1:14–19.

A question then arises as to the significance of this polemic for the interpretation of Gen 1 more generally. A simple narrative approach attributes the placement of the heavenly bodies, and the manner in which they are introduced, partly to polemical intent. The heavenly bodies are not deities, and their allocation to the fourth day is simply in keeping with the internal correspondence of days one to three and days four to six, as noted above: the luminaries of day four correspond to the light of day one. Six-day creationism, on the other hand, must either disregard the polemical factor, or must indulge in some strange reasoning in order to accommodate it, for in this case if polemic is involved then it must have been a factor in the original intention of the creator when he planned the universe. In other words, because human beings were eventually going to believe that the earth and other planets derive in one way or another from the sun—per tidal theory, accretion or some such process—God sought to subvert their theorizing by postponing the creation of the heavenly bodies until the fourth day. (The moon and the stars were drawn in, perhaps gratuitously, but we shall eschew unnecessary complication in this discussion.) An ancient version of this approach is presented by Theophilus of Antioch who, in his *Apology* addressed to his friend Autolycus, represents both absolute literalism and polemic:

19. Naming, or calling by name, has a different significance in Isa 40:26.

> On the fourth day the luminaries came into existence. Since God has fore-knowledge, he understood the nonsense of the foolish philosophers who were going to say that the things produced on earth come from the stars, so that they might set God aside. In order therefore that the truth might be demonstrated, plants and seeds came into existence before the stars. For what comes into existence later cannot cause what is prior to it.[20]

Theophilus thus is willing to combine polemic with literalism in his own version of God planting the dinosaurs to fool the rationalists. Such approaches, with their hints of supralapsarianism, disregard the obvious circumstance that the biblical text itself has an historical context and that in Gen 1 the biblical writer responds to this in the way that biblical writers commonly do. There is no suggestion that the very ordering of creation anticipates the defection of those to whom the stewardship of the earth was entrusted.

5. *Creation and Coherence*

If the first creation narrative uses the working week as the frame upon which to construct its account of creation, then the coherence of the two creation narratives in Gen 1–2 exists at a different level from that of merely literal correspondence. Old Testament scholarship has long judged that in the separate designations for the creator, as "God" in 1:1–2:3 and "Lord God" in 2:4–25, as well as in the obvious perspectival differences in the respective narratives, we may have an indication of the separate origins of the two. But to portray them as two alternative, or even rival, accounts of creation, or as relating to two distinct sets of human subjects—as did Isaac de La Peyrère, who thought that ch. 1 referred to humanity in general and ch. 2 to the Jewish people[21]—is wide of the mark. Since the second narrative more or less starts where the first leaves off, with the creation of the man/Adam and his placing in the garden prepared for him, the two narratives dovetail to a considerable degree even while they exhibit their own special features and emphases. It is in these circumstances a work of exegetical supererogation to make one narrative conform to the event-sequencing of the other, whether it is the introduction of plant life *vis-à-vis* the creation of humans (plants preceding human beginnings in ch. 1, following in ch. 2), or the creation

20. Text and English translation in R. M. Grant, *Theophilus of Antioch Ad Autolycum* (Oxford: Clarendon, 1970), 50–51.
21. See A. Grafton, *Defenders of the Text: The Traditions of Scholarship in an Age of Science, 1450–1800* (Cambridge, Mass.: Harvard University Press, 1991), 204–13 (205).

of the animals *vis-à-vis* humans (animals created first in ch. 1, created after the man in ch. 2). These "tensions"—which can be relieved but partly and superficially by distinguishing among plant types in the one case and by introducing a pluperfect in 2:19 in the other (cf. NIV, "Now the Lord God had formed")—only exist if we misuse our narratives. And if we need not risk distortion in order to defend the creation narratives, neither do we need to exaggerate their literary qualities or scientific insight. What they say and the way they say it are unique, and at the same time both simple and sophisticated, and best appreciated against the background of the world in which they were written, as both "inspired" and "inspiring" statements about God's world and the people whom he has placed in it.

I am most grateful for this opportunity to pay tribute to Gordon Wenham's very special contribution to biblical scholarship in the church and in the academy.

Part V

READING THE LAW AND HISTORY

GOING DOWN TO SHEOL: A PLACE NAME AND ITS WEST SEMITIC BACKGROUND

Richard S. Hess

The Bronze Age was a time when many deities were identified in the West Semitic world. At thirteenth-century Ugarit, for example, one estimate indicates some 240 names and epithets of different deities recognized in the texts.[1] The other Middle and Late Bronze Age archives of this region, along with the less productive Early Iron Age sources and the biblical traditions, all provide additional attestations of many of these and other deities. Some names are well known and have a long and secure pedigree. These include major deities such as El, Asherah, Baal, and Dagan. Others are controversial as to their attestations and reflect issues with the spelling and vocalization in different periods or with the existence of the name as a divine name versus its use as a personification of a natural force. Two examples of this would be Reshef and Debir, who appear as deities of plague at Ugarit but function as personified forces that accompany Yahweh in the Hebrew Bible (Hab 3:5). Finally, there are of course the majority of deities whose names occur once or twice at Ugarit or Emar or elsewhere, and are known only by their names in those appearances.

Deities whose names reflect some controversy are ones of most interest for this study. Our focus here will be to look at examples of a deity who was known in the Late Bronze Age archives already mentioned and for which there is some evidence that it was also known in the world of ancient Israel, though perhaps not as a deity. We will consider the divine name behind the biblical place of the dead, Sheol. A review of this name in Late Bronze Age religious texts and in personal names will raise questions about the continuity of the deity between the cultures of the West Semitic world.

---

1. G. del Olmo Lete, *Canaanite Religion: According to the Liturgical Texts of Ugarit* (trans. W. G. E. Watson; Bethesda: CDL Press, 1999), 78.

1. *The Hurrian Connection*

The use of the term Sheol (שׁאוֹל) in the Hebrew Bible to describe the realm of the dead has been identified with a West Semitic deity mentioned in the thirteenth-century Emar texts. The name appears in two *kissu* festivals that prescribe offerings for different deities during a sequence of several days.[2] The name of the deity appears three times in two ritual texts, written as ᵈšu-PI-la, and read by the editor of the text, D. Arnaud, as ᵈšu-wa-la.[3] Singers perform for Shuwala in both texts, and at one point the deity receives a sheep as an offering. Arnaud identifies Shuwala as Sheol. De Moor has observed the textual connection and, for him, the identification of Shuwala with Ereshkigal, the goddess of the underworld and spouse of Nergal.[4] Whether this identification can be demonstrated from the text is not clear. However, Shuwala's association with underworld deities does seem established, as will be argued below.

Shuwala probably had an antecedent in the Hurrian cultural sphere as *šu-u-wa-a-la*, the husband of Nabarbi.[5] They appear together in various Hurrian texts.[6] In the fourteenth-century B.C.E. treaty between the Hittite sovereign Suppiluliuma and the Mitannian Shattiwazi, Nabarbi appears in the god list as a Hurrian deity.[7] Because Mitanni is located in northern Syria and across the border in Turkey, this provides further evidence for both Nabarbi and Shuwala as originating in the region of the Ḫabur river

2. *Kissu*, perhaps related to *kissû*, "throne," may celebrate the enthronement and sovereignty of each of the deities as ruler over their respective realms. See D. Fleming, "Two *kissu* Festivals," in *The Context of Scripture*. Vol. 1, *Canonical Compositions from the Biblical World* (ed. W. W. Hallo and K. L. Younger, Jr.; Leiden: Brill, 1997), 442–43.

3. D. Arnaud, *Recherches du Pays d'Aštata. Emar VI*. Tome 3, *Textes sumériens et accadiens* (Paris: Editions Recherche sur les Civilisations, 1986), texts 385.23; 388.6, 57.

4. J. C. de Moor, "Lovable Death in the Ancient Near East," *UF* 22 (1990), 233–45 (239).

5. E. Laroche, "Glossaire de la langue Hourrite. Deuxième partie (M–Z, Index)," *Revue Hittite et Asianique* 35 (1997): 163–322 (174, 245).

6. For the dozens of occurrences, see B. H. L. van Gessel, *Onomasticon of the Hittite Pantheon. Part I* (Handbook of Oriental Studies 33; Leiden: Brill, 1998), 417–19; *idem, Onomasticon of the Hittite Pantheon. Part III* (Handbook of Oriental Studies 33; Leiden: Brill, 2001), 330.

7. E. Laroche, *Catalogue des textes hittites* (Paris: Klincksieck, 1971), number 51 (reverse ll. 54–58); English translation in G. Beckman, *Hittite Diplomatic Texts* (ed. H. A. Hoffner; SBL Writings from the Ancient World Series 7; Atlanta: Scholars Press, 1996), 43.

valley.[8] If so, the Hurrian background fits comfortably within the context of the inland Syrian city of Emar and the large percentage of Hurrian personal names attested there. Shuwala corresponds to the Mesopotamian Ninurta, the god of agriculture. It has been suggested that his name is a shortened form of Shuwaliyatt, with the meaning "pure brother of the storm god."[9]

Is the identification of Shuwala with Sheol correct? On the surface, there is little in the Hurrian and Hittite texts to suggest such an identification. However, at Emar the ritual of text number 385 pairs Shuwala with U.GUR as recipients of the music of the temple singers. U.GUR is associated with the divine name dU-ku-ru-un in an Emar god list.[10] More significantly, a deity whose name is spelled in this manner is identified with Nergal, the Mesopotamian god of the underworld, in texts from Samarra and from the Hittite capital of Boghazkoy.[11] Further, this text mentions these deities in the context of an offering to Ereshkigal, the queen of the underworld.[12] Thus the association of Shuwala with deities of the underworld at Emar seems to be established.

However, this is a different picture of Shuwala from that found with the Shuwala of the Hittite and Hurrian sources, who is connected with Ninurta and agriculture. Perhaps this represents a different aspect of Shuwala. Perhaps an alteration in the deity and his attributes has taken place. If this proves to be the origin behind the place name, Sheol, then the suggested etymology that connects it with the Semitic root, $š^cl$, and with the meanings, "inquire" and "call to account," must be secondary.[13]

---

8. V. Haas, "Nabarbi," in *Reallexikon der Assyriologie* (ed. E. Ebeling *et al.*; Berlin: de Gruyter, 2001), 9:1–2.

9. E. Laroche, *Recherches sur les noms des dieux hittites* (Paris: G.P. Maisonneuve, 1947), 60; H. G. Güterbock, "The God Šuwaliyat Reconsidered," *Revue Hittite et Asianique* 68 (1961): 1–18 (15).

10. D. E. Fleming, *The Installation of Baal's High Priestess at Emar* (HSS 42; Atlanta: Scholars Press, 1992), 139 n. 222.

11. Ibid.; C. Rüster and E. Neu, *Hethitisches Zeichenlexikon. Inventar und Interpretation der Keilschriftzeichen aus den Boğazköy-Texten* (Studien zu den Boğazköy—Texten Beiheft 2; Wiesbaden: Harrassowitz, 1989), 223 sign number 261.

12. Shuwala and Ugur occur on l. 23 of Emar text 385. Ereshkigal occurs on l. 27.

13. For a review of these and other etymological proposals, sometimes identified with necromancy and more recently with a place of punishment as a result of judgment, see K. Sponk, *Beatific Afterlife in Ancient Israel and in the Ancient Near East* (AOAT 219; Neukirchen–Vluyn: Neukirchener Verlag, 1986), 66–67; T. Lewis, *Cults of the Dead in Ancient Israel and Ugarit* (HSS 39; Atlanta: Scholars Press, 1989), 104–17; R. Rosenberg, "The Concept of Biblical Sheol Within the Context of the Ancient Near East" (Ph.D. dissertation, Harvard University, 1980).

This would explain the lack of an explicit connection of the name Sheol with these actions in the Bible.

2. *The Linguistic Connection*

If Shuwala is indeed associated with the underworld, is there any possible connection with the word, Sheol, as found in the Bible? The first and last consonants of both names agree. There remains the question of the middle consonant. In Hebrew, the *ʾaleph* fills this slot, whereas in the Akkadian syllabic cuneiform script, the middle sign used is that of PI. Now, the PI sign can be read as *pi*. It can also be read as *wa*, *wi*, and *wu*, and as *ya*, *yi*, and *yu*. Examples of this sign read most frequently as *wa*, but also as *ya* and *yu*, have been identified in texts found at Emar.[14]

However, even though the PI sign can be read in a variety of ways, none of these suggests that it would indicate an *ʾaleph*, something necessary for the Sheol of the Bible. Nevertheless, it is true that *ʾaleph* may not be represented by any sign in the cuneiform script, especially as it is used in West Semitic archives, whether at Emar or elsewhere.[15] According to Durand, the substitution of a glide such as the PI sign for an *ʾaleph* may represent a distinctive Emarite dialect or pronunciation.[16] If the *ʾaleph* is not represented in the cuneiform script, then the *wa* phoneme can act as a glide between the adjacent *u* and *a* vowels. This phenomenon is known throughout various periods of Akkadian.[17] It occurs at Emar particularly with the third person singular oblique personal pronoun, *šu-wa-ti* or *šu-wa-tu*.[18]

If the *ʾaleph* presents no difficulty, is there any basis for the vocalic difference between Shuwala and Sheol? While this sort of vocalization is not common, similar forms with this vowel alteration are attested elsewhere. For example, the Amorite personal name *zu-ba-la-an* becomes

14. J. Ikeda, "A Linguistic Analysis of the Akkadian Texts from Emar: Administrative Texts" (Ph.D. dissertation, Tel-Aviv University, 1995), 278; E. J. Pentiuc, *West Semitic Vocabulary in the Akkadian Texts from Emar* (HSS 49; Winona Lake: Eisenbrauns, 2001), 211.

15. For Emar, see Pentiuc, *West Semitic Vocabulary*, 217. For elsewhere, see D. Sivan, *Grammatical Analysis and Glossary of the Northwest Semitic Vocables in Akkadian Texts of the 15th–13th C.B.C. from Canaan and Syria* (AOAT 214; Kevelaer: Verlag Butzon & Bercker; Neukirchen–Vluyn: Neukirchener Verlag, 1984), 53, 194–202.

16. Pentiuc, *West Semitic Vocabulary*, 175.

17. W. von Soden, *Grundriss der Akkadischen Grammatik* (Analecta Orientalia 33/47; Rome: Pontificium Istitutum Biblicum, 1969), 22 §21 h.

18. Ikeda, *A Linguistic Analysis*, 44, 59.

the personal name *z^ebul* in the book of Judges and the tribal name *zebûlûn*.[19] At Ugarit, the personal name ᵈIM-ᵈšu-la-mu contains in its second element a form of the *šlm* root that often appears in Hebrew as *šālôm*.[20] This corresponds to the vocalization change and pattern between Shuwala and Sheol, without the pretonic lengthening of the first vowel. At Emar itself there are the common noun forms *ku-ba-du*, *ku-ba-dì*, and *ku-ba-di₁₂*.[21] These may be compared with the Hebrew *kābôd*. Thus there are comparative West Semitic forms, both common nouns and proper names, that exhibit a similar vocalic change.

3. *The Proper Name Connection*

If it is linguistically possible that Shuwala is related to the biblical Sheol, is it likely? It is true that we are dealing with a divine name at Emar and a place name in the Bible. While biblical Sheol is personified in a number of texts, it nowhere can be clearly identified as a divine being. Rather, it is personified as Sheol who brings affliction (Hos 13:14), swallows his victims (Prov 1:12), and has an insatiable appetite (Prov 27:20; 30:15–16; Isa 5:14; Hab 2:5). In all this Sheol resembles the Ugaritic god of death, Mot, but nowhere is Sheol recognized as a person outside of poetic and clearly metaphorical contexts.[22]

If Sheol is a place name, is it appropriate to assume that it could derive from a divine name such as Shuwala? In fact, there are many examples of divine names in the Late Bronze Age that are attested as place names. Astarte, found at Ugarit and elsewhere as a goddess, occurs in the place names of Ashtaroth and Ashteroth-Karnaim, known in the Bible and possibly earlier. Indeed, the same site may be identified in an Ugaritic mythological text.[23] Like Sheol, whose location is often described in texts

19. M. P. Streck, *Das amurritische Onomastikon der altbabylonischen Zeit*. Band 1, *Die Amurriter. Die onomastische Forschung. Orthographie und Phonologie. Nominalmorphologie* (AOAT 271/1; Münster: Ugarit-Verlag, 2000), 331.

20. Sivan, *Grammatical Analysis*, 87, 274, for this and similar forms of personal names with the same vocalization.

21. Pentiuc, *West Semitic Vocabulary*, 241.

22. T. Lewis, "Dead, Abode of the," *ABD* 2:103; H. M. Barstad, "Sheol," in *Dictionary of Deities and Demons in the Bible* (ed. K. van der Toorn, B. Becking, and P. W. van der Horst; 2d ed.; Leiden: Brill; Grand Rapids: Eerdmans, 1999), 768–70; P. S. Johnston, *Shades of Sheol: Death and Afterlife in the Old Testament* (Apollos; Downers Grove, Ill.: InterVarsity, 2002), 69–85.

23. Dennis Pardee, *Ritual and Cult at Ugarit* (SBL Writings from the Ancient World; Atlanta: SBL, 2002), 194, 205. The text is RS 24:252, with the place

that reach beyond the natural world, this place name, which has its origin in the goddess Astarte, also occurs in texts populated with gods and goddesses. Elsewhere, the divine sun, Shemesh, appears in the place name, Beth Shemesh (Josh 15:10) and the moon deity Yearḥ can be found in the name of the well-known site of Jericho. The divine name Baal, so prominent in major myths at thirteenth-century B.C.E. Ugarit, becomes attached to several clan names that are remembered as the names of Israelite settlements: Baal-Shalishah (2 Kgs 4:42); Baal-Perazim (2 Sam 5:20); and Baal-Tamar (Judg 20:33).[24] These and other place names compounded with Baal are remarkable because they are not attested in Palestine before the beginning of the Iron Age. Thus there seems to be a development in the use of the name Baal, from the divine name to a point where it could be used as a place name. Also significant is the appearance of the goddess Anat, who is well known at Ugarit as a warrior. Her name is preserved in Jeremiah's home town of Anathoth, as well as in other place names.[25] She is of special note in our survey because Anat does not occur as a divine name by herself in the Hebrew Bible. She is remembered only in place names and possibly in the personal name Shamgar ben-Anat.[26] Again, this resembles Sheol who no longer occurs as a divine name in the Bible, but only as a place. Thus in every way the development from the Late Bronze Age Emar Shuwala as a divine name to Sheol as a biblical place name finds parallels.

As we have seen in the case of Anat, this goddess can appear prominently in the mythological literature of Ugarit, yet she has no role as a goddess in the biblical corpus. Anat does, of course, reappear in the late fifth-century archive of the Jewish colony at Elephantine in Egypt. There her name is compounded with that of other deities to produce additional divine names revered by people at Elephantine. There may be a variety of reasons for this, related to the different types of literature, the theological views of the people who wrote the literature, and the differences in culture and the values of that culture. The point here is that arguments

Ashtaroth mentioned in the first three lines. It also occurs in other myth texts from Ugarit.

24. P. D. Miller, *The Religion of Ancient Israel* (London: SPCK; Louisville, Ky.: Westminster John Knox, 2000), 66.

25. N. H. Walls, *The Goddess Anat in Ugaritic Myth* (SBLDS 135; Atlanta: Scholars Press, 1992); J. Day, *Yahweh and the Gods and Goddesses of Canaan* (JSOTSup 265; Sheffield: Sheffield Academic Press, 2000), 132–33.

26. Judg 3:31; 5:6. For a survey of other Late Bronze and Early Iron Age appearances and the view that ben-Anath, "son of Anat," represents a warrior class, see R. S. Hess, "Israelite Identity and Personal Names in the Book of Judges," *Hebrew Studies* 44 (2003): 25–39.

that Shuwala was an obscure deity who could not have developed into the customary biblical term for the underworld cannot have significance from the standpoint of known custom in the ancient Near East.

4. *Methushael*

It is therefore appropriate to conclude that the name Shuwala could and very possibly did develop into the name Sheol in Iron Age Israel and in the Hebrew Bible. There remains the question of an additional connection with the Bible. In the line of Cain in Gen 4, the father of Lamech in v. 18 is designated as Methushael. The analysis of this name has generally recognized that it consists of two elements. The first element, $m^e t\hat{u}$, is normally interpreted as a West Semitic vocable for "man," "person," or here "devotee." In many West Semitic personal names this term occurs as the first element of a two-element name where a construct relationship between the two elements creates the form, "devotee of X."[27] X is the second element and is normally a divine name.

This formal illustration itself should raise doubts about some attempts to interpret Methushael as the initial $m^e t\hat{u}$ element followed by the relative *ša* and the term for "god," *ʾil*. This would yield the sense, "devotee of a god" or "devotee of El." To add to the doubt regarding such an interpretation, one may suggest two more objections. First, despite the opinion of some, there is no evidence for this name in either West Semitic or in its Akkadian equivalent (*mutu-ša-ili*). Second, there is no clear evidence for any West Semitic three-element name with the relative *ša* forming part of that name.[28] Thus there are likely two elements in this personal name. It is possible that the second element is based on the root, *šʾl* ("to ask"), but there are few names constructed with this root. Further, the structure of the name would presuppose a divine name in the second slot.

The common interpretation for this name assumes the close similarity of a number of names in the lines of Cain and of Seth, in Gen 4 and 5. Using this argument, Methushelah ($m^e t\hat{u}šelah$) becomes identified with Methushael. The scholars who hold to this view usually go on to assert

27. For examples of this name form, including names as early as eighteenth-century B.C.E. Mari and as late as thirteenth-century Ugarit, see R. S. Hess, *Studies in the Personal Names of Genesis 1–11* (AOAT 234; Kevelaer: Butzon & Bercker; Neukirchen–Vluyn: Neukirchener Verlag, 1993), 44 n. 112; S. C. Layton, *Archaic Features of Canaanite Personal Names in the Hebrew Bible* (HSM 47; Atlanta: Scholars Press, 1990), 67.
28. Hess, *Studies*, 43–44; Layton, *Archaic*, 70–71.

that the similarity of some names in the two lists demonstrates that both
genealogies derived from a single source. Further, because Methushelah
is often perceived as easier to analyze, the assumption is made that
Methushael is a corrupted and derivative form of Methushelah.[29] This
hypothesis is certainly possible, but it cannot be demonstrated as fact nor
should it be assumed as the preferable explanation. The reason for this
lies in the often overlooked parallel that exists between the earlier
antediluvian list of kings on the Sumerian king list and the corresponding
apkallu or cultural innovators who each mirror one of the kings on the
list.[30] When these lists are compared, it is clear that some of the names of
the kings correspond closely to those of the *apkallu*. Yet the evidence
suggests separate origins for these lists. If one compares these two earliest lists of antediluvian figures to the two antediluvian genealogies of
Gen 4 and 5, there are significant parallels. While the king list and that of
the *apkallu* take different forms, it remains significant that the line of
Cain in Gen 4 resembles that of the cultural founders who are the *apkallu*.
In both, significant cultural inventions are attributed to each member of
the list. Both the line of Cain and that of the *apkallu* end at or before the
flood and do not continue after it. On the other hand, the line of Seth in
Gen 5 and that of the kings listed on the Sumerian king list both have
incredibly large numbers attached to their lives or reigns and in some
sense continue after the flood. As with flood stories and other literature
shared between Mesopotamian traditions and myths and those found in
Gen 1–11, so the genealogies of Gen 4 and 5 may reflect a shared tradition with the lists of the *apkallu* and the antediluvian kings. If so, then
assumptions about the common origin of both biblical genealogies must
be set aside, especially when based solely upon an argument of some
similarity in the names. Such similarity is found in the earlier Sumerian
sources but is not considered proof for the common origin of both lists
there.

For these reasons it is premature to assume that the name Methushael
must have evolved from Methushelah. Rather, it needs to be examined
on its own. In light of the above evidence, the second element of Methushael should be considered as a viable candidate for an association with

29. Cf., e.g., Barstad, "Sheol," 769; Layton, *Archaic*, 72.
30. For background to the following discussion and full bibliography of sources,
see R. S. Hess, "The Geneaologies of Genesis 1–11 and Comparative Literature," in
*"I Studied Inscriptions from before the Flood": Ancient Near Eastern, Literary, and
Linguistic Approaches to Genesis 1–11* (SBTS 4; ed. R. S. Hess and D. T. Tsumura;
Winona Lake, Ind.: Eisenbrauns, 1994), 58–72; reprint of "The Genealogies of
Genesis 1–11 and Comparative Literature," *Bib* 70 (1989): 241–54.

Sheol or its related forms in the West Semitic world. This is all the more credible insofar as a connection with Shuwala, a divine name, is recognized. This is because, as already observed, the slot occupied by the second element of this form of personal name normally requires a divine name.

Given these considerations, we should be predisposed to find in Methushael a remnant of the name of the underworld deity that elsewhere in the Bible occurs as the place name Sheol. However, the question remains as to how the long *a* and long *e* vowels can be explained. This is different from the vocalization of both Shuwala and Sheol. We have already seen how the second element of the personal name ᵈIM-*šu-la-mu* appears as *šālôm* in Hebrew. A divine name with the same consonants, Shalem, is found as a known deity throughout the Middle and Late Bronze Ages. The name represents the goddess associated with the evening star in myths from Ugarit. Such a name has also been identified in the place name of Jerusalem as attested as early as the Egyptian Execration texts of the first part of the second millennium B.C.E. In the fifteenth century it is vocalized as *–sa-li-im* in the Amarna texts from Jerusalem. It may also be found as an element in the personal names, Solomon and Absalom. Unfortunately, it is impossible to know for certain because these elements could also derive from the *šlm* root. The absence of certainty regarding the biblical names is not crucial, however, because the divine name is attested widely. As *–šu-la-mu* became *šalim*, so *šu-wa-la* could become *-shael*. This example demonstrates that such vocalizations of divine names did exist in the West Semitic world.

We may therefore suggest that the Shuwala of Emar was an underworld deity who enjoyed some recognition at that city and may have been related to the Mesopotamian Ninurta. This Shuwala had a common origin with the place name of Sheol in the Hebrew Bible. Further, there may well have been some connection between Sheol and the second element of Methushael, the father of Lamech in Gen 4:18.

THE TABLETS IN THE ARK

Alan Millard

According to Exod 24:12, God said he would give to Moses "the tablets of stone with the law and commandments I have written for their [the Israelites'] instruction." On the basis of Exod 34:28, "Moses wrote on the tablets the words of the covenant—the Ten Commandments," and of Deut 10:4, "The Lord wrote on these tablets what he had written before, the Ten Commandments," the contents of the tablets have been undisputed. Recently, in his study of the formation of the Bible in the light of the history of writing, W. Schniedewind, after analysing Exod 24 and other passages, has concluded that "the tablets were engraved with the divine instructions for building God's tabernacle."[1] He observes that "the words used to describe the initial revelation on Sinai...have to do with *speaking*, not with *writing*. They have to do with *orality*, not with *textuality*." He adds, "It is a truly astonishing observation that writing has no role in the revelation at Mount Sinai in Exod 19. Writing has no role in the so-called Covenant Code in Exod 21–23. Somehow the story of the revelation in Exod 19–23 seems unaware that the Torah is a text." Only in Exod 24:4 "as almost an afterthought...the narrator notes that Moses himself wrote these things down."[2]

To support this novel interpretation Schniedewind analyses the structure of Exod 24 and calls upon some ancient Near Eastern texts. The following paragraphs offer a different interpretation, favouring the traditional understanding of the content of the tablets, also in the light of ancient Near Eastern texts.

1. *Syntax and Context of Exodus 24*

For more than a century, Old Testament scholarship has accepted that Exod 24 is a composite, in which vv. 1 and 9–11 belong together and

---

1. W. M. Schniedewind, *How the Bible Became a Book: The Textualization of Ancient Israel* (Cambridge: Cambridge University Press, 2004), 131.
2. Ibid., 121–22.

vv. 2–8 form a section within which vv. 4–8 seem to be an addition. Other divisions have been proposed. Yet throughout that period, no consistency has existed among exegetes over the attribution of the sources delineated within the chapter, as Schniedewind's discussion shows.[3] He follows the usual analysis, finding, for example, a contradiction between vv. 1 and 9, which tell of Moses and others ascending the mountain and v. 2 in which only Moses may go up.

Exodus 24 has "an unusual opening," B. S. Childs commented, which "does not appear to attach smoothly to what precedes," observing that M. Noth had argued "that a whole section must have fallen out." The difficulty is said to lie in the absence of a subject for the verb, "he said" (ויאל־משה אמר). Here recent syntactical studies of Hebrew narrative prose bring a fresh perspective which removes the problem Western logic perceives, permitting the verses to be read as a reprise to an earlier section of Exodus and as background to the following report. Attention to the Hebrew text and its immediate and wider context within the Bible, when given priority over traditional literary or historical criticism, can make the exegetes' path straight! Gordon Wenham in his commentary on Genesis wisely aimed "to discuss first what is certain, namely the present form of the text, before tackling the less certain issues of sources and their redaction."[4] The opening of v. 1 with *waw* and a noun clause followed by a *qatal* verbal form, shows that vv. 1 and 2 are circumstantial, and it is the *wayyiqtol* verb starting v. 3 which begins the main narrative (v. 1, ואל־משה אמר; v. 2, ונגש משה ; v. 3, ויבא משה ויספר לעם). Verses 1 and 2 can be seen to refer back to 19:24, the command that Moses and Aaron ascend the mountain, given prior to the proclamation of the Law and the Covenant of chs. 20–23.[5] Before he could fulfil that command, Moses had to present the terms of the covenant to Israel and it is clear from the process of covenant-making that Moses could not go up the mountain with the representatives of the people to see their suzerain until he had announced the terms of the covenant and the Israelites had accepted them. Many commentators, like Childs and including

3. Ibid., 121–28. Compare S.R. Driver, *Exodus* (CBSC; Cambridge: Cambridge University Press, 1911), 251–56; B. S. Childs, *Exodus* (OTL; London: SCM Press, 1974), 499–502.

4. G. J. Wenham, *Genesis 1–15* (WBC 1; Waco, Tex.: Word, 1987), xxxvi.

5. See A. Niccacci, "Basic Facts and Theory of the Biblical Hebrew Verb System in Prose," and "Workshop: Narrative Syntax of Exodus 19–24," in *Narrative Syntax and the Hebrew Bible: Papers of the Tilburg Conference 1996* (ed. E. van Wolde; BIS 29; Leiden: Brill, 1997), 167–202 (188), 203–28 (222–25), and A. Talstra, "Workshop: Clause Types, Textual Hierarchy, Translation in Exodus 19, 20 and 24," in van Wolde, ed., *Narrative Syntax*, 118–32 (130).

Schniedewind, contrast the naming of Aaron, Nadab, Abihu and seventy
elders in the command of 24:1 with the naming of Aaron alone beside
Moses in the command of 19:24. Yet 24:1 can be read as a simple expansion of 19:24, preparing for the event of 24:9, 10, when all of them
"beheld God," their suzerain. As ordinary human beings, no Israelite
could do that unless they had accepted the suzerain's terms; only Moses
as mediator, "a priest before the high priest was ordained" as Gordon
Wenham has described him,[6] was allowed near God before that moment.
Therefore, it is essential that the actions of vv. 3–8 in which Israel ratifies
the agreement and the people bind themselves to it in a solemn ritual
precede her representatives' ascent to the divine presence; there is no
lack of unity between vv. 1 and 2 and the following verses, vv. 1 and 2
set the scene. Referring vv. 1 and 2 back to 19:24 is preferable syn-
tactically to reading them as a direct sequel to 23:33, as T. D. Alexander
has done in his laudable attempt to demonstrate the unity of chs. 19–24.[7]

In order that there should be no dispute about the stipulations the
people had accepted, Moses recorded them on a scroll, but it was only
after the people had accepted them that he did so, and then read the
words to the people, ensuring that he had recorded them correctly. That
book should later play a decisive role as a witness in determining
whether or not Israel has remained faithful to the agreement. The book
could travel with the people; the stone pillars erected at the foot of
Mount Sinai could not. It was not until those actions had been carried
out, with everything due from Israel's side having being completed, that
Moses and his colleagues could approach God without fear, knowing that
he, their suzerain, would receive them as his willing and obedient
vassals. Verse 11 emphasizes his acceptance of them, signalled by their
liberty to eat and drink in his presence, presumably from provisions he
supplied. Thereafter, Moses, the mediator, could approach closer to God.
There is no contradiction between v. 1, commanding Moses and others
to "go up and worship from a distance," and v. 2, commanding Moses
alone to approach God, for there is a gradation, as already observed by
S. R. Driver (*pace* Schniedewind), nor does "Moses again go up the
mountain" in v. 11, as Schniedewind asserts, for that verse is simply the
fulfilment of v. 2. That is the point when Moses would be given the text
God had written on the two stone tablets. Only when both sides had
accepted the terms were the formal, written, texts prepared and oaths

6. G. J. Wenham, *The Book of Leviticus* (NICOT; Grand Rapids: Eerdmans, 1979), 132.
7. T. D. Alexander, "The Composition of the Sinai Narrative in Exodus XIX 1–XXIV 11," *VT* 49 (1999): 2–20.

sworn. Before presenting the terms of the covenant to the Israelites, Moses had climbed Mount Sinai more than once to establish the method of communicating the covenant and the preparations for it.

2. *Exodus 24 and Ancient Covenant Contexts*

Exodus 24 and adjacent chapters give an account of the making of the covenant between God and Israel. They present a narrative which contains the text of the agreement, but are not themselves a treaty text. From the ancient Near East there survive numerous texts of treaties, but no complete narrative reports of their making, like Exodus, as D. R. Hillers observed.[8] Nevertheless, setting the Egyptian and cuneiform sources beside the biblical may bring clearer understanding of the latter.

In the case of God and Israel, the two parties were close enough for Moses to convey messages quickly from one to the other. When greater distances were involved, agreeing the terms of a treaty could be a prolonged process, with messengers travelling several times between one partner and the other. The correspondence of Ramesses II and the Hittites gives hints of that[9] and letters from Mari, five centuries earlier, illustrate how differences had to be resolved.[10] In one Mari letter, King Shamshi-Adad informs his son, Yasmah-Adad, "The ruler of Eshnunna has written to me about the treaty. There is one matter I have removed from the tablet of the oath by the gods. I have sent to Eshnunna. The people of Eshnunna are objecting and, until now, nothing new has reached me." Another letter, from one of two of the envoys Zimri-Lim, king of Mari, sent to Babylon, tells of a problem they faced:

> I have arrived in Babylon and set out the whole matter before Hammu-rabi. I have taken up the question of a pact with him, but there is a blank refusal over Hit. He has tried to argue against me, but, without agreeing, I have managed the affair as desired. By resisting him, I have brought him round. Hit is no longer in dispute.[11]

8. D. R. Hillers, *Covenant: The History of a Biblical Idea* (Baltimore: The Johns Hopkins University Press, 1969), 39.

9. E. Edel, *Die ägyptisch-hethitische Korrespondenz aus Boghazköi in babylonischer und hethitischer Sprache* (ARWAW 77; Opladen: Westdeutscher, 1994).

10. See D. Charpin, "Les représentants de Mari à Babylone (I)," in *Archives épistolaires de Mari*, I/2 (ed. D. Charpin et al.; ARM 26; Paris: Editions Recherche sur les Civilisations, 1988), 139–66 (144–47, 153).

11. G. Dossin, *Archives royales de Mari*. Vol. 1, *Lettres* (TCL 22; Paris: Geuthner, 1946), no. 37; C.-F. Jean, *Archives royales de Mari*. Vol. 2, *Lettres* (TCL 23; Paris: Geuthner, 1941), no. 77. Fresh translations, incorporating advances in understanding the Mari documents, are given by J.-M. Durand, *Documents épi-*

In the first millennium B.C.E. Assyrian treaties also involved negotia- tions. A letter from an official to Sargon II reports on treaty-making moves with tribes in western Iran and a letter from Esarhaddon's crown prince states, "Having listened to one another, the king of Elam and the king of As[syria] have made peace with one another at Marduk's com- mand and become treaty partners." Later, Ashurbanipal sent trusted courtiers with a "treaty tablet" (*tuppi adê*) for the governor and people of Uruk in Babylonia to accept.[12]

Oaths concluded treaties, usually taken by the junior partners, the gods named as witnesses being invoked to punish the treaty-breaker. The Mari documents supply some examples of oath texts with the junior partner's words, "I swear that, so long as I live, I will not sin against…" and the oaths are followed by the specific obligations.[13] At Mount Sinai the Israelites promised "We will do everything the Lord has said" before the laws were spoken (19:8), then after Moses had told them to the people (24. 3) and again, after the covenant ceremony (24:7). Whether or not the people repeated all the laws as part of their oath, like the vassal kings in the Mari documents, is not stated.

Treaties share several basic features with ordinary legal contracts of the ancient Near East in which the parties often bound themselves by oath in the presence of witnesses and the written document was determi- native should a dispute arise. There are a few deeds that report the parties eating together after concluding the contract, such as a sale of land,[14] and that is a feature of some agreements in the Bible, as, for example, those

stolaires du palais de Mari, vol. 1 (LAPO; Paris: Cerf, 1997), 431–32 no. 280, 448– 50, no. 287.

12. F. Reynolds, *The Babylonian Correspondence of Esarhaddon* (SAA 18; Helsinki: Helsinki University Press, 2003), 7–9 no. 7; A. Fuchs and S. Parpola, *The Correspondence of Sargon II, Part III: Letters from Babylonia and the Eastern Provinces* (SAA 15; Helsinki: Helsinki University Press, 2001), 60–61 no. 90; R. F. Harper, *Assyrian and Babylonian Letters* (Chicago: Chicago University Press, 1892– 1914), no. 539, see S. Parpola, *Letters from Assyrian Scholars to Esarhaddon and Ashurbanipal* (AOAT 5/1; Neukirchen–Vluyn: Butzon & Bercker, 1983), 463, no. 56.

13. F. Joannès, "Le traité de vassalité d'Atamrum d'Andarig envers Zimri-Lim de Mari," in *Marchands, Diplomates et Empereurs*: *Etudes sur la Civilisation mésopotamienne offertes à Paul Garelli* (ed. D. Charpin and F. Joannès; Paris: Recherche sur les Civilisations, 1991), 167–77, translated as no. 291 in J.-M. Durand, *Documents épistolaires*, 453–54, cf. nos. 290, 292.

14. For example, an early Old Babylonian text from Mari; see J.-M. Durand, "Sumérien et akkadien en pays amorite. I. Un document juridique archäique de Mari," *MARI* 1 (1982): 79–89; G. Boyer, *Textes juridiques* (ARM 8; Paris: Imprimerie Nationale, 1958), no. 13, see 328.

made between Isaac and Abimelech (Gen 26:30), Jacob and Laban (Gen 31:54). The vassal's privilege of eating at his suzerain's table or in his presence is mentioned occasionally in other sources, such as Sargon of Assyria's acknowledgment of his Mannaean vassal Ullusunu.[15]

3. *Treaty Texts, Oral or Written?*

Schniedewind insists that *torah*, "teaching, instruction," originally implied exclusively oral activity and that sense holds in Leviticus and Numbers. Orality, he maintains, is to be expected in early Israelite tribal society. Consequently, he treats v. 4 of Exod 24, which tells of Moses writing the words of God, as an insertion from "the final editing of the Bible...probably taking place in the late Persian or Hellenistic period."[16] His astonishment at the absence of references to writing in Exod 20, 21– 23 should be weighed against the occurrences of references to writing in surviving copies of ancient Near Eastern treaties. While some of them refer at the beginning to "this treaty tablet," in most examples the written document is not mentioned until near the end where the clauses concerning the preservation and reading of the text and lists of deities "named on this tablet" occur. The texts are presented as wholly oral pronouncements; as D. J. McCarthy noted, "The bulk of the vassal treaty is actually a proclamation."[17] The suzerains address their vassals in the Hittite treaties, in others of the same period, for example from Alalakh, in Neo-Assyrian treaties and in the Aramaic Sefire treaties.[18] Whether or not the vassals or their ambassadors were present at the suzerain's court to hear the stipulations, they would take written versions home with them. Although incomplete, one large tablet found in Mari evidently expressed the terms King Zimri-Lim of Mari had accepted from his overlord, the king of Eshnunna, and the tablet almost certainly was written in Eshnunna, east of the Tigris.[19] In the case of Israel, the people were able to

15. B. R. Foster, *Before the Muses* (3d ed.; Bethesda, Md.: CDL Press, 2005), 794.

16. Schniedewind, *How the Bible Became a Book*, 126.

17. D. J. McCarthy, *Treaty and Covenant: A Study in Form in the Ancient Oriental Documents and the Old Testament* (2d ed.; AnBib 21A; Rome: Pontifical Biblical Institute, 1981), 253.

18. Translations by R. S. Hess for Alalakh, "The Agreement Between Ir-Addu and Niqmepa," and by J. A. Fitzmyer, "The Inscriptions of Bar-Gaʾyah and Matiʾel from Sefire," in *The Context of Scripture*, vol. 2 (ed. W. W. Hallo and K. L. Younger; Leiden: Brill, 2000), 329–31, 213–17. For the Neo-Assyrian treaties see E. Reiner's translation in *ANET*, 533–41.

19. D. Charpin, "Un traité entre Zimri-Lim de Mari et Ibâl-pî-el d'Esnunna," in Charpin and Joannès, eds., *Marchands, Diplomates et Empereurs*, 139–66 (141).

hear the terms at Sinai, so there was no need for writing until the agreement was concluded, when Moses, as D. R. Hillers expressed it, read
"the final and binding assent."[20]

If Moses and the Sinai covenant are placed in the thirteenth century
B.C.E., as seems most likely,[21] could the text have been committed to
writing at that time? Were the early Israelite tribes ignorant of all scripts?
While cuneiform was used in most parts of the Levant for documents of
every kind, including treaties, during the Late Bronze Age, and Egyptian
was probably as widely used in the south, the number of surviving
examples from Canaan is small.[22] Beside the long-established scripts, the
Canaanite "alphabet" was taking root. The regrettable fact, from our
perspective, that it, like Egyptian, was most often written on perishable
surfaces, papyrus, leather or wax-covered wooden tablets, means that
only meagre specimens of it are recovered, written on ostraca or
scratched on stone and metal objects.[23] The lack of texts should not be
interpreted as evidence that little writing was done—analogies from
other periods and places warn against that (e.g. leather was used as a
writing material for Aramaic in the Persian empire, but only in Egypt and
Afghanistan have conditions allowed some sheets to survive[24]). Israel's
"early tribal society" was not so isolated from other societies that a few
of its members could not be aware of, and adopt, the Canaanite script,
even before they had settled in the Promised Land. If they were in the
wilderness, the Israelites were able to communicate with other people,
and in Canaan they mixed with the local population among whom writing was current. Again, the paltry examples of the script available in
modern times should not lead anyone to suppose that writing longer texts
was impossible. There is no reason why book-length compositions

20. Hillers, *Covenant*, 57.
21. See the arguments set out by K. A. Kitchen, *On the Reliability of the Old
Testament* (Grand Rapids: Eerdmans, 2003), 307–10.
22. A. Horowitz, T. Oshima, and S. Sanders, *Cuneiform in Canaan: Cuneiform
Sources from the Land of Israel in Ancient Times* (Jerusalem: Israel Exploration
Society, 2006).
23. See A. Millard, "The Knowledge of Writing in Late Bronze Age Palestine,"
in *Languages and Cultures in Contact: At the Crossroads of Civilizations in the
Syro-Mesopotamian Realm—Proceedings of the 42nd RAI* (ed. K. van Lerberghe
and G. Voet; Leuven: Peeters, 1999), 317–26.
24. G. R. Driver, *Aramaic Documents of the Fifth Century B.C.* (Oxford: Clarendon, 1954), re-edited by B. Porten and A. Yardeni, *Textbook of Aramaic Documents
from Ancient Egypt. A, Letters* (Jerusalem: Hebrew University, 1986); S. Shaked, *Le
satrape de Batcriane et son gouverneur. Documents araméens du IVe s. avant notre
ère provenant de Bactriane* (Persika 4; Paris: de Boccard, 2004).

should not have been contained on papyrus scrolls; the Ten Commandments and the Book of the Covenant (if Exod 21:1–23:19) would have fitted easily on to a short scroll.[25] At a later date, in the seventh century B.C.E., another tribal society, the nomadic Arab tribe of Qedar and its ruler, entered into a treaty with Ashurbanipal of Assyria, presumably holding their own written copy.[26]

The two tablets placed in the Ark were tablets of stone, not of clay, like the normal cuneiform tablets. In a book which has achieved prominence in certain circles, G. Garbini asserted. "There were no tablets of this kind in the ancient Near East; there were no fairly small stone tablets, written on both sides and containing a fairly long text…," and he continued with the further assertion that the Israelite writer had cuneiform tablets in view, but since they had disappeared from Egypt and Palestine by the end of the thirteenth century B.C.E., he was evidently writing at a time when cuneiform tablets would have become familiar to Israelites, the time of the Babylonian exile.[27] Yet Egyptians used both sides of stone flakes (ostraca) for writing exercises, sometimes of considerable length, and many of the "Proto-Sinaitic" inscriptions were scratched on rock surfaces and a few on stone stelae or panels (although only on one side).[28] Garbini assumes that Israelites could not distinguish between clay and stone and overlooks the likelihood that cuneiform tablets continued in use in the Levant a little later than the thirteenth century B.C.E. (see n. 22), discounting any possibility that the Pentateuch might reflect customs of that date (if cuneiform tablets had been in view!).

4. *Preserving the Documents*

Preservation of texts was always a matter of concern. The invention of writing soon demanded a means of storage for all but the most ephemeral

25. A. Millard, "Books in the Late Bronze Age in the Levant," in *Past Links: Studies in the Languages and Cultures of the Ancient Near East—Essays in Honor of Anson Rainey* (ed. S. Izre'el, I. Singer, and R. Zadok; IOS 18; Winona Lake, Ind.; Eisenbrauns, 1998), 171–81.

26. S. Parpola and K. Watanabe, *Neo-Assyrian Treaties and Loyalty Oaths* (SAA 2; Helsinki: Helsinki University Press, 1988), 68–69. For Qedar, see I. Eph'al, *The Ancient Arabs: Nomads on the Borders of the Fertile Crescent, 9th–5th Centuries B.C.* (Jerusalem: Magnes, 1982), 142–69, 223–27.

27. G. Garbini, *History and Ideology in Ancient Israel* (London: SCM Press, 1988), 104, cf. xiii.

28. See B. Sass, *The Genesis of the Alphabet and Its Development in the Second Millennium B.C.* (AeUAT 13; Wiesbaden: Harrassowitz, 1988), 10.

documents. Nothing is known of the methods adopted in the earliest stages, but cuneiform texts from ca. 2300 B.C.E. onwards were garnered in various ways. At Ebla, in the royal archive room, tablets lay on shelves. Cylindrical clay labels from the Third Dynasty of Ur list administrative tablets held in baskets, and others from slightly later include literary compositions.[29] In the reign of Tiglath-pileser I of Assyria (ca. 1114–1076 B.C.E.), large jars were inscribed before firing with the types of records they would contain.[30] From the Hittite capital Hattusa, there are tablets listing texts and similar ones have been found at Assur and, from the seventh century B.C.E., at Nineveh.[31]

The Late Bronze Age archives at Assur include a list of the contents of a store-room belonging to a royal official late in the thirteenth century B.C.E. and among the items listed are several boxes or baskets (*quppu*) of tablets recording debts and matters concerning property.[32] Tablets from the same time, found at Emar on the mid-Euphrates, include several legal deeds that specify the deposit of the tablets in the owner's basket or box, for example, "a complete document has been put in PN's box" (*pisannu* "box," has before it either the determinative sign for an object of reed— *g i*—or of wood—*giš*). There is also a label from Emar for a basket of tablets.[33] In every case, the containers held documents of legal or administrative significance.

29. For administrative examples, see P. Steinkeller, "Archival Practices at Babylonia in the Third Millennium," in *Ancient Archives and Archival Tradition: Concepts of Record-Keeping in the Ancient World* (ed. M. Brosius; Oxford: Oxford University Press, 2003), 37–58 (48–49).

30. See O. Pedersén, *Archives and Libraries of the Ancient Near East 1500–300 B.C.* (Bethesda, Md.: CDL Press, 1998), 84. For literary texts, see W. W. Hallo, "On the Antiquity of Sumerian Literature," *JAOS* 83 (1963): 167–76 (169); A. Shaffer, "A New Look at Some Old Catalogues," in *Wisdom, Gods and Literature: Studies in Assyriology in Honour of W. G. Lambert* (ed. A. R. George and I. L. Finkel; Winona Lake, Ind.: Eisenbrauns, 2000), 429–36.

31. H. A. Hoffner, "Archive Shelf Lists," in *The Context of Scripture*. Vol. 3, *Archival Documents from the Biblical World* (ed. W. W. Hallo and K. L. Younger; Leiden: Brill, 2002), 67–69; Hallo, "Antiquity of Sumerian Literature," 169; S. Parpola, "Assyrian Library Records," *JNES* 42 (1983): 1–29.

32. See J. N. Postgate, *The Archive of Urad-Šerūa and His Family: A Middle Assyrian Household in Government Service* (Pubblicazioni del progetto "Annalisi elettronica del cuneiforme," Corpus Medio-Assiro; Rome: Roberto de Nicola, 1988), 106–19.

33. See D. Arnaud, *Recherches au Pays d'Aštata. Emar*, IV.3 (Textes sumériens et accadiens, Texte; Paris: Recherche sur les Civilisations, 1986), 99–101 no. 90.16–17, 70 no. 62 (label).

The written text of a treaty was the indisputable record of the agreement and a witness that could be consulted in a case of disloyalty, real or
alleged. Consequently, the text was a highly important document which
should be carefully preserved. The parties to a parity treaty would
exchange their copies of the terms, as in the case of Ramesses II and
Hattusili III.[34] In a vassal-treaty, the suzerain would dictate the terms,
making one or more copies for himself and for his vassal. The parity
treaty between Ramesses II and Hattusili was engraved in cuneiform on
tablets of silver for each party and the copies exchanged. Ramesses had
an Egyptian translation of the treaty carved on the walls of the temple of
Amun at Karnak and of the Ramesseum,[35] while Hittite scribes copied
the Egyptians' Akkadian version on clay tablets.[36] In both cases, the
royal seals impressed or engraved on the silver were carefully described.
The treaty documents were placed under the protection of the gods who
were invoked in the agreement. In letters to Hittite dignitaries, Ramesses
states, "The written version of the oath which [I made] for the Great
King, the King of Hatti, my brother, has been set at the feet of [the
Storm-god] and before the Great Gods. They are witnesses [to the words
of the oath]" and the copy sent from Hatti had been placed at the feet of
the gods of Egypt.[37] The silver tablets of Ramesses and Hattusili have
disappeared, as has the iron tablet mentioned in a treaty between
Tudhaliya IV and Ulmi-Teshub of Tarhuntassa concluded about 1235
B.C.E., but a happy discovery at Boghazköi has made available an example of a treaty text engraved on a bronze tablet. It is a pact made between
Tudhaliya IV and Kurunta of Tarhuntassa in Cilicia.[38] The treaty concludes, "This document is made in seven copies... One tablet is to be
placed in the presence of the Sun-goddess of Arinna, [five before other
deities]. And Kurunta, king of the land of Tarhuntassa, has one tablet."
Other treaties include similar notices of deposition. In the treaty between
Suppiluliuma the Hittite and Shattiwaza of Mitanni (ca. 1350 B.C.E.), it is
stated, "A duplicate of this tablet [the one found in the suzerain's archive
at Boghazköi] is deposited before the Sun-goddess of Arinna... And in
the land of Mitanni a duplicate is deposited before the Storm-god...of
Kahat."[39] The prescriptions in those and other treaties that the vassals

34. E. Edel, *Der Vertrag zwischen Ramses II. von Ägypten und Ḫattušili III. von
Ḫatti* (WVDOG 95; Berlin: Mann, 1997); G. Beckman, *Hittite Diplomatic Texts* (2d
ed.; SBLWAW 7; Atlanta: Scholars Press, 1999), 96–100.
35. J. A. Wilson in *ANET*, 199–201.
36. Beckman, *Hittite Diplomatic Texts*, 96–100.
37. Ibid., 130–31 (Ramesses to the king of Mira).
38. Ibid., 109–13 para. 14 (Ulmi-Teshub treaty), 114–23 (bronze tablet).
39. Ibid., 46 para. 13, cf. 51 para. 8, 111 para. 5, 123 para. 28, 7 copies.

should read the treaties regularly imply that they had access to copies. For example, the Hittite king Muwatalli II (ca. 1300 B.C.E.) instructs his vassal, "Furthermore, this tablet which I have made for you, Alaksandu, shall be read out before you three times yearly, and you, Alaksandu, shall know it."[40] Prohibitions on altering them carry the same implication. Centuries earlier, in the Mari archive, there is evidence of the vassal Zimri-Lim holding a copy of his treaty with the king of Eshnunna (see above).

5. *Ten Commandments or Tabernacle Designs?*

The Near Eastern treaties of the second millennium B.C.E., with their references to the texts being preserved in temples, offer very close analogies to the deposit of the two Tablets of the Law in the Ark, but there is a natural objection, which Schniedewind raises, that those tablets could not be read if they were sealed in the box, whereas, "if the tablets contained the building plans for the tabernacle, their purpose had been served once the tabernacle was constructed...they could be sealed within the ark as evidence...that the dwelling of God on earth was built through divinely revealed and inscribed plans."[41] He observed that there are ancient Near Eastern parallels to the divine plan for the Tabernacle, but did not examine the documents to discover whether or not any of them were concealed in the heart of a shrine. In fact, many of the Mesopotamian texts concerning temple building that can be read today were inscribed on clay tablets or cylinders and hidden from the eyes of their contemporaries, buried in the foundations of the structures in order for future generations to read them and laud their predecessors when the temples they had built needed repair.[42] Most well known are the two clay cylinders written for Gudea of Lagash (ca. 2100 B.C.E.), each over half a metre high. They report the instructions the god Ningirsu gave to Gudea for the erection of his temple and Gudea's fulfilment of them. It is impossible to know whether the cylinders stood in the temple, or in its foundations. Some other building inscriptions were displayed in temples (e.g. Nabonidus' Harran stelae). Perhaps most similar to the tablets in the Ark is the stone tablet found in a clay box at Sippar. The tablet relates the history of the temple of Shamash and its neglect until the reign of Nabu-apla-iddin (ca.

40. Ibid., 91 para. 16 and 81 para. 28, cf. 46 para. 13 ("shall be read repeatedly, for ever").
41. Schniedewind, *How the Bible Became a Book*, 131.
42. See V. Hurowitz, *"I Have Built You an Exalted House": Temple Building in the Bible in the Light of Mesopotamian and Northwest Semitic Writing* (JSOTSup 115; Sheffield: JSOT Press, 1992).

870 B.C.E.) who rebuilt it. At that time a priest found a model of an image of Shamash and so a new statue of the god was created. The clay box was prepared to contain the tablet after it was discovered in the reign of Nabopolassar (625–605 B.C.E.) and was possibly buried within the temple, but if so, it was not intended for contemporary readers.[43]

The treaty tablets kept in ancient temples were, presumably, not readily accessible, certainly only priests could view the versions carved on temple walls in Egypt. On the other hand, as the Hittite tablets cited make clear, vassals could consult copies of their treaties, one, at least, being specifically kept in the vassal's palace, and those Hittite tablets were housed in the archives of the capital. The discovery of a tiny piece of a cuneiform tablet bearing lines connected with the Hittite treaty at the site of Ramesses II's palace at Avaris, Pi-Ramesse, suggests copies were available in the chancery.[44] The copy that Moses wrote, which, according to Exod 24:4, contained "everything the Lord had said," that is, "the Lord's words and laws" mentioned in v. 3, could thus have served as the accessible exemplar from which Israelite scribes would make other copies.

The deposit of the stone tablets in the Ark, which was then placed in the holiest part of the Tabernacle, is exactly like the deposit of ancient treaty texts in the presence of the gods. The Ark was a wooden box, most suitable for the mobile circumstances of the wilderness. Its lid had a special function, for it concealed the tablets from view and so symbolically prevented them from having immediate effect on any Israelite who broke their terms. The penalty for the frequent infractions of individuals could be averted by penitence and sacrifice, as the regulations of Leviticus specify, but national disloyalty should bring rejection by the suzerain. The unique ritual of the Day of Atonement (Lev 16), provided to avert that, involved pouring blood over the lid, in effect countering the force of the oath to which the tablets within the box were witness.[45] The lid was meaningless apart from the box and neither had any significance without the contents of the box, the tablets of the covenant.

Now we have seen that Israel's leaders were able to enjoy God's presence when the people had accepted the covenant terms which, when written down, were witness to what they had undertaken.

43. See C. E. Woods, "The Sun-God Tablet of Nabû-apla-iddina Revisited," *Journal of Cuneiform Studies* 56 (2004): 23–103; translation by V. Hurowitz, "Boundary Stones: The 'Sun Disk' Tablet of Nabû-apla-iddina (2. 135)," in Hallo and Younger, eds., *Context of Scripture*, 2:364–68.

44. E. B. Pusch and S. Jakob, "Der Zipfel des diplomatischen Archivs Ramses' II," *Ägypten und Levante* 13 (2003): 143–53.

45. On the meaning of atonement, see Wenham, *Leviticus*, 59–63.

The definitive copy of the terms was that on the two tablets provided by the suzerain, which had to be kept in the Ark where the suzerain could be present. God's benevolent presence at the commissioning of the completed Tabernacle, with the tablets in place inside the Ark and covered with the atonement lid, indicated his acceptance of Israel (Exod 40). In order to secure the continuation of his goodwill, the terms of the treaty had to be observed. Failure to do so would breach the oath that had been sworn, releasing the curse implicit in the blood rite of Exod 24:6–8.

There need be no doubt about the contents of the two tablets inside the Ark. The biblical texts affirm that they contained the written terms of the covenant and the widespread ancient Near Eastern texts supports them.

It is a pleasure to offer this essay to Gordon Wenham whose perceptive commentaries, other writings, teaching and willing service to the Church have won him many friends and put many more in his debt.

MEMORY, WITNESSES AND GENOCIDE IN THE BOOK OF JOSHUA*

Pekka Pitkänen

Israel served Yahweh during the time of Joshua and the time of the elders who lived after Joshua and who knew all the deeds that Yahweh had done for Israel. (Josh 24:31)

In this study, we will first look at some issues that relate to history writing and identity. These will show the importance of history as a factor that defines the identity of a people and some problems that relate to events that might define that identity negatively. We will pay special attention to genocides, a feature often associated with the book of Joshua. From there, we will show how the Israelite author(s) of Joshua used references to the events relating to the conquest as he saw it through memorials and other contemporary manifestations, with the aim of making his audience remember the great acts of Yahweh so that they would follow him. Finally, we will return to the problem of genocide in the context of remembering a genocide as portrayed in the book of Joshua in present-day settings that are far removed from the original milieu of the book, arguing that the book at most refers to a single set of events in the past and does not need to be taken literally today, even though the problems of its rhetoric and Yahweh's action in history, and thus theodicy, still remain.

* I am pleased to dedicate this essay to Gordon Wenham, my esteemed mentor, who was and is a specialist in Pentateuchal and Old Testament studies, with a particular interest in Old Testament law and ethics. I had the opportunity to study with him in Cheltenham in the late 1990s and then join him as a colleague at the University of Gloucestershire until his retirement in 2005. I hope this essay may stimulate others to have an interest in this area, and in particular to benefit from Gordon Wenham's contributions to Old Testament studies.

1. *The Nature of History Writing*

What is history and why does it matter? The theoretical aspects that relate to history writing are complex and the literature is immense. Also, a number of the historical questions that people deal with at the present are the subject of lively debate, even controversy, especially when they relate to gross acts of violence, clearly an issue pertaining to the book of Joshua. For example, students of the Holocaust find it historically compelling, even while they deplore the horrors and brutality associated with it. And yet, we can ask why Holocaust studies continue to exert a greater fascination than, for example, studies of Japanese atrocities in East Asia in the early part of the twentieth century, the Cambodian massacres of the 1980s, and the conquest of the Americas and the decimation of the native peoples from 1492 on,[1] just to name a few.[2] While not denying the scale and horror of any of these events, we may ask, why is one, or a few, of them elevated to a special status?[3] Is it because of the event itself, or because of the audience of the studies, or for some other reason? For example, does the political and economic strength of the Jewish community in the USA explain why there are so many more centres devoted to the Holocaust than to the extermination of the Native Americans?[4] Does the fact that the Americans were victors in the Second World War, and thus not implicated in the Holocaust in Europe, contribute to the popularity of the subject, in comparison with the American holocaust? Is there a lasting audience in the west for the Cambodian massacres or the Japanese atrocities in East Asia? Why is it mainly only in Korea and China that there is alarm about the silence of Japanese historiography about massacres before and during the Second World War, while denial of the Holocaust causes outrage in the West, and is even criminalized in parts of it? Had Hitler won the Second World War, how much would we know about what happened to the Jews in Germany at the time?

1. For this, see, for example, the lively work by David E. Stannard, *American Holocaust: The Conquest of the New World* (Oxford: Oxford University Press, 1992).

2. Mark Levene asks the same question in slightly different words in the introduction to his *Genocide in the Age of the Nation State*. Vol. 1, *The Meaning of Genocide* (London: I. B. Tauris, 2005), 1–2. Levene's book includes considerations of definition regarding genocide, and reference to many of the numerous genocides that are known to have taken place in world history.

3. Cf. ibid., 11–12.

4. For the rest of this paragraph, cf. Levene's comments in ibid., 23–26. Levine in essence, asks similar questions.

These preliminary observations intend to illustrate the nature of historiography. Historiography is always selective and subjective, and often controversial;[5] even to pose questions such as those above may be contentious. Certainly, any events used to form an account of the past must have some kind of relevance and purpose for their audience, regardless of whether the writers or the audience consciously recognize this. Moreover, the audience, while emphasizing or even stylizing matters of importance, may block some material, and even not tolerate certain honest and straightforward questions about the past if they are deemed to be offensive. In particular, historiography relating to contentious and potentially uncomfortable matters such as war and genocide may be significantly biased towards a specific interpretation.[6]

Against this background, ancient Israelite historiography, and the book of Joshua in particular, raise a number of questions. Why has this account of the past been written? To whom has it been addressed? What does the material want to say to its audience? How does the selection of the material serve the purposes of the writer? Is there any conscious or unconscious hiding or exaggeration of material, or even outright distortion of events or fictional creation of the past? Naturally, every reader of a text like Joshua will form their own understanding of it, reacting to it and consciously or subconsciously answering these kinds of questions in different ways. And, when we as contemporary readers are distant in time and culture from the original events and audiences, the task of interpretation becomes even more difficult. We do not know much if anything about the author and the original audience, and some of our informed guesses must proceed based on the text itself in a kind of hermeneutical spiral where the text, together with any possible extra-textual material, provides us with clues which we then take up and feed reflectively into the reading process in order to make sense of the material.

A further relevant factor is history's role in forming the identity of a people. As Hutchinson and Smith point out, "shared historical memories, or better, shared memories of a common past or pasts, including heroes,

---

5. There can, of course, be exaggeration and embellishment, even outright falsification of material.

6. Cf. Levene, *Genocide*, 31 (and passim), on how genocidal actions are "airbrushed" if they imply fault on "our own side." See also Stannard, *American Holocaust*, 256, for a specific example in the USA from the early 1990s where members of the US Senate "were threatening to cut off or drastically reduce financial support for the Smithsonian Institution because a film project with which it was marginally involved had dared to use the word 'genocide' to describe the destruction of America's native peoples."

events and their commemoration" are one aspect of ethnicity.[7] In other words, memory provides people with one aspect of their identity. And, whether conscious or subconscious, oral or written, we may say that this cultivation of corporate memory is likely to be as old as humanity. This aspect of identity formation also explains many of the features relating to history writing. For example, why is it that in the corporate record criticism is often directed at external targets, rather than individuals or groups within the community itself? Here it helps to bear in mind that ethnicity is an extension of family which itself is formed of individuals,[8] and there is a link between history writing in the context of ethnic groups and in the context of individuals and their characteristics and outlook on life. A nation may consist of one or more ethnic groups. In the case of more than one ethnic groups, such as in modern Britain, the overall identity is an amalgamation and combination of the constituent groups' views of their identity.[9] In this formation of an overall identity, there is constant renegotiation. All this said, it will be helpful to keep in mind the link between individual and group identities and behaviour when looking at features and characteristics of history writing.

2. *Memorials in Joshua*

As regards Old Testament studies, it first needs to be acknowledged that various modern reading communities have their own identities. Academic communities, for their part, have conducted a long debate about the historicity of the Old Testament narratives. Broadly speaking, in twentieth-century critical scholarship the Old Testament narratives were

---

7. John Hutchinson and Anthony D. Smith, eds., *Ethnicity* (Oxford Readers; Oxford: Oxford University Press, 1996), 6–7. The full list given by Hutchinson and Smith is: (1) a common proper name, to identify and express the "essence" of the community; (2) a myth of common ancestry, a myth rather than a fact, a myth that includes the idea of a common origin in time and place, and that gives an ethnie a sense of fictive kinship, what Horowitz terms a "super-family"; (3) shared historical memories, or better, shared memories of a common past or pasts, including heroes, events and their commemoration; (4) one or more elements of common culture, which need not be specified but normally include religion, customs, or language; (5) a link with a homeland, not necessarily its physical occupation by the ethnie, only its symbolic attachment to the ancestral land, as with diaspora peoples; (6) a sense of solidarity on the part of at least some sections of the ethnie's population.

8. Donald L. Horowitz, *Ethnic Groups in Conflict* (repr., Berkeley and Los Angeles: University of California Press, 2000 [1985]), 55–92.

9. As a simple example, compare the way Chinese and Indian food have become part of modern British culture and identity.

thought to provide some historical reminiscences from the time of Judges on, with the book of Joshua regarded as less reliable, especially since the collapse of the Albrightian conquest model in the latter part of the century. Recently, however, even this has been disputed, with the most sceptical scholars doubting that there are any reminiscences of real history of Israel from before the time of the Babylonian exile.[10] The challenge of the so-called "minimalists" to the rest of scholarship has also spawned a number of treatments on method.[11] In a related development, the conventional archaeological dating of early Iron Age II has been challenged, potentially resulting in a radical re-evaluation of the history of the early monarchy.[12] The issue and its implications have been the subject of lively scholarly debate over the past five to ten years.[13]

Under these circumstances, the discussion of the historiography of ancient Israel is currently in flux. While, as indicated above, there has been scepticism about the historical value of the book of Joshua, a few recent studies have suggested that the book may have something to say historically if read in an appropriate way.[14] In any case, even where the book is not regarded as possessing referential historical value, it remains possible to examine what kind of historical picture it provides. I propose chiefly to attempt the latter here, yet at the same time to be alert to any possible intended specific historical referents (as further specified below), since in some cases the historicality of a narrative may belong to its meaning. To return to the example of the Holocaust, everyone is likely to agree that it makes a difference that the narrative of it is based on real events. But, we can also go beyond such a question and ask: What kind

10. See, e.g., Niels Peter Lemche, *The Israelites in History and Tradition* (Library of Ancient Israel; Louisville, Ky.: Westminster John Knox, 1998).

11. See, e.g., V. Philips Long, David W. Baker and Gordon J. Wenham, eds., *Windows into Old Testament History* (Grand Rapids: Eerdmans, 2002), among many others.

12. See Israel Finkelstein and Neil Asher Silberman, *The Bible Unearthed: Archaeology's New Vision of Ancient Israel and the Origin of Its Sacred Texts* (New York: Simon & Schuster, 2001), for a semi-popular exposition and a bibliography.

13. One example of such a lively (even polemical!) debate is William G. Dever, *What Did the Biblical Writers Know and When Did They Know It? What Archaeology Can Tell Us About the Reality of Ancient Israel* (Grand Rapids: Eerdmans, 2001).

14. E.g. K. Lawson Younger, *Ancient Conquest Accounts: A Study in Ancient Near Eastern and Biblical History Writing* (JSOTSup 98; Sheffield: Sheffield Academic Press, 1990), and Pekka Pitkänen, *Central Sanctuary and Centralization of Worship in Ancient Israel: From the Settlement to the Building of Solomon's Temple* (2d ed.; Piscataway, N.J.: Gorgias, 2004); Pekka Pitkänen, "Ethnicity, Assimilation and the Israelite Settlement," *TynBul* 55 (2004): 161–82.

of picture are we and should we be presenting about the Holocaust? In one respect, the building of memorials to it helps to reinforce the message of the immense potential for human evil and that such events should never happen again. However, in another respect, it is perhaps difficult (in the West) to dissociate this universal implication from the memory that it was ended in a war by America and its allies. Thus, besides serving as a warning to future generations, the remembrance of the Holocaust can be seen to serve towards positive identity formation for America (and its allies). This is history written by the winners and history writing with a purpose in the context of a nation and of a culture, whether or not such a purpose is expressed explicitly or even recognized consciously.[15]

Various aspects of the book of Joshua have of course been studied extensively over the past 200 years.[16] However, it appears that the possible role of historical referents suggested by the author in the context of the book as a whole has not been brought forward in full.[17] In particular, let us consider the following. In Josh 3 and 4, the narrative describes how twelve stones are picked from the river and set up in Gilgal, with the intention that they are to remain there as a witness (memorial![18]) for the coming generations (4:20–24).[19] In fact, the narrative states that the stones remain there "until this day" (4:9). The rhetorical device of future childrens' questions also plays a part.[20] Next, we note that the Israelites are circumcised at Gibeath-haaraloth, translated as the "hill of foreskins" (5:2–3). This suggests that the place name reminds its later hearer about this event, even if the story was created, or at least embellished, for the

---

15. As the United States went on to win the Cold War and became the world's most powerful country at the beginning of the twenty-first century, its interpretation (or interpretations) of history features all the more prominently in the contemporary world.

16. For a summary, see, e.g., Ed Noort, *Das Buch Josua: Forschungsgeschichte und Problemfelder* (Darmstadt: Wissenschaftliche Buchgesellschaft, 1998).

17. However, Brevard Childs, "A Study of the Formula 'Until This Day,'" *JBL* 82 (1963): 279–92, and P. J. van Dyk, "The Function of So-Called Etiological Elements in Narratives," *ZAW* 102 (1990): 19–33, come close to a number of aspects of what we will indicate below in this respect.

18. Compare the use of memorials in the USA or Britain (and many other countries) today to commemorate past events (e.g. Trafalgar Square and statue of Nelson, the Lincoln memorial and many others).

19. This regardless of what one thinks about the somewhat confusing information in 4:9, which suggests that stones, or *the* stones, were set up in the river itself.

20. See especially J. Alberto Soggin, "Kultätiologische Sagen und Katechese im Hexateuch," *VT* 10 (1960): 341–47; Pitkänen, *Central Sanctuary*, 207–8.

place name, as Alt and Noth suggested,[21] or vice versa. Similarly, Gilgal's name is said to have been based on the event of the circumcision and the accompanying removal of the shame (חרפה) of Egypt from upon the Israelites.[22] Thus, the name is intended to create memories about the conquest in the minds of its later hearers according to the book of Joshua.

Another possible case is Joshua's curse on Jericho, recorded in Josh 6:26. Usually what is noted in this connection is that the curse is said to come true in 1 Kgs 16:34 in the context of the Deuteronomistic History.[23] However, one may also think here that the writer of Joshua may imagine that his readers, upon seeing or hearing about the state of Jericho,[24] will think about the events of the conquest.

In relation to Ai, the writer states that there is a heap of stones over the bodies of Achan and his family, and that it is there to this day (7:25). The heap of stones reminds those who see it about the story of Achan, which itself refers back to the conquest. The place name Valley of Achor (7:26) is a further reminder of the events. Anyone hearing the story needs to be aware that there is a valley somewhere in the area and a heap of stones which confirms the story. Also, when Ai itself is destroyed, it is made a heap of ruins, "until this day" from the perspective of the author (8:28). The smaller heap in front of the bigger one reminds of the fate of the king of Ai (8:29).

In 8:30–35 an altar is built on Mt Ebal. The author does not indicate whether the altar still exists, but if some remains were left intact, this would also serve as a reminder of the ceremony that took place there.[25]

In Josh 9, the Gibeonites are said to have been designated as water-drawers and woodcutters for the altar of Yahweh "until this day." Joshua 9 is often taken to be an etiological story explaining the existence of

21. See Childs, "Formula"; Noort, *Josua*, 94–95; Martin Noth, *Das Buch Josua* (2d ed.; Tübingen: J. C. B. Mohr, 1953), passim.

22. The word Gilgal is a Pilpel of גלל (thus *HALAT*, 186, noting the same [rare in the Old Testament] form of גלל in Jer 51:25).

23. See, e.g., Noth, *Josua*, 41.

24. Without going into details, Jericho has some poor remains from the Late Bronze Age, was then apparently abandoned, and rebuilt in Iron Age II. See Kathleen Kenyon, *Digging Up Jericho* (London: Ernest Benn, 1957), 262–64, for a summary, and Piotr Bienkowski, *Jericho in the Late Bronze Age* (Warminster: Aris & Phillips, 1986), for a detailed consideration of the Late Bronze evidence in particular.

25. For a summary of archaeological issues relating to Mt Ebal, see my *Central Sanctuary*, 167–85, among other works. The excavator's preliminary report can be accessed from Adam Zertal, "Mount Ebal: Excavation Seasons 1982–1987, Preliminary Report," *Tel Aviv* 13–14 (1985–86): 105–65.

Gibeonites, a different ethnic group, in the midst of the Israelites.[26] Whether or not this is correct, we note for our present purposes that the existence of the Gibeonites is clearly tied to the time of the conquest (cf. 2 Sam 21:2). From here, it is not difficult to think that the Gibeonites also serve as a reminder of the conquest, and, in fact, partially as a reminder that the Israelites failed to consult Yahweh at the time (Josh 9:14).

The "scholarly" reference to another source, the "Book of Yashar" (Josh 10:12–13), presumably seeks to lend credibility to the story of Joshua at Gibeon and the accompanying miracle (10:10–11). It is as if the writer is saying, "I did not make this up, read the poem in the Book of Yashar!" In the same narrative, the stones in front of the cave at Makkedah where the bodies of the kings lay are said to remain "until this day" (10:27).

The tribal allotments (chs. 13–19) do not at first seem relevant to our discussion. However, if they are in any way based on real borders of the tribes, which is possible at least to some extent,[27] it is unmistakable that the tribal borders are shown to have their basis on the conquest. In other words, any Israelite thinking about the tribal borders should, according to the book, realize that they were decreed by Yahweh through Joshua at the time of the conquest. The same goes for the cities of refuge (ch. 20) and the Levitical cities (ch. 21). We should also note a couple of smaller points here. The existence of Jebusites in Jerusalem (15:63), the Canaanites in Gezer (16:10) and the Geshurites and Maacathites in Transjordan (13:13) "until this day" is according to the author an unfortunate situation not originally intended, and thus these situations too are tied to the conquest. Even the story of the Danites and the existence of the city of Dan outside the intended area of the Danites serve as a reminder of the conquest (Josh 19:47; cf. Judg 18:1, 27–30). Caleb's ownership of Hebron is also linked to the same event (Josh 14:13–14).[28]

The case of the Transjordanians in ch. 22 follows the tribal allotments. The book of Joshua (cf. Num 32 and Deut 3:12–22) emphasizes the importance of the Transjordanians and stresses that they are part of Israel. They are said to have received their land east of Jordan on the basis of a command of Moses (Josh 13:8), are portrayed as having taken

26. See Noth, *Josua*, 53.

27. There has been extensive discussion and debate about these lists, including their origin and date. Work done respectively by Alt, Noth and Mowinckel can be seen as foundational for the inquiry, and there has of course been much further discussion since. However, no firm conclusions have been reached. For a summary, see Noort, *Josua*, 181–97. See also my *Central Sanctuary*, 228–40, for an attempt to date the material based on an analysis that is linked to rhetorical considerations.

28. Cf. Childs, "Until This Day," 287.

part in the conquest in Joshua (1:12–18; 4:12; 13:8–32) and are then allowed to go back by Joshua in 22:1–8. The altar incident, which starts with a possible conflict, ends with a twist confirming the unity of Cisjordan and Transjordan. The altar is to serve as a reminder throughout generations about this unity (22:21–29). Again, the unity here is tied to the events of the conquest, and in this case even to events before the conquest.

Finally, in ch. 24, the stone (and perhaps the accompanying book) in the sanctuary at Shechem (24:26–27) serves as a witness about the last words of Joshua to Israel where Joshua exhorts Israel to keep the covenant of Yahweh (24:2–24). Even if the formula "until this day" or the like is not used, the text may well imply that the sanctuary or holy place is still in existence (cf. Gen 35:4; Judg 9:6). The graves of Joshua (24:30), Eleazar (24:33) and Joseph (24:32) may also serve as reminders about the conquest.[29]

3. *The Memorials and the Interpretation of the* חרם

Thus, at least based on a text-centred reading, even if the book of Joshua were a collection of etiological stories, in their present arrangement in the book of Joshua they can be seen to serve as a powerful testimony about the Israelite conquest for its readers. It is tempting to suppose that the writer did this intentionally in a time when there were no footnotes and cross-references in the literature that was produced. The writer tied events to localities, not haphazardly, but as a powerful testimony about the saving acts of Yahweh for the Israelites. For the writer, reading and hearing about these events was to remind the Israelites about who Yahweh is and what he has done for them, so that the Israelites would keep his laws and statutes. This is history writing with a purpose. It is ancient Israelite history writing intended to convince its readers to follow the god Yahweh and to keep away from those who might compromise such loyalty. As Josh 24:31 states, "Israel served Yahweh during the time of Joshua and the time of the elders who lived after Joshua and who knew all the deeds that Yahweh had done for Israel." The book of Joshua refers to living memory and implies that it itself is a substitute for this living memory for the ancient Israelites of a later generation. The book also refers to such witnesses as the stones at Gilgal, the Hill of Foreskins and the Book of Yashar that remain after living memory has been extin-

29. Cf. the supposed tomb of Abraham in Hebron today, and other places attesting to biblical events, even though one inevitably encounters such issues as modern tourism when considering these.

guished. In fact, the author arguably states, or at least tries to create an impression, that there is evidence available at the time of writing to support his claims.[30] The later generation is to know the great and veritable deeds of Yahweh so that they can follow his laws and statutes. Of course, the laws proper are mainly promulgated in the last four books of the entity we call the Pentateuch, that is, in the books of Exodus, Leviticus, Numbers and Deuteronomy. But, they are alluded and referred to here with great rhetoric and persuasion. They are connected with the great injunction to Joshua at the beginning of the book, "Do not let this Book of the Law depart from your mouth: meditate on it day and night, so that you may be careful to do everything written in it. Then you will be prosperous and successful" (Josh 1:8). This means reading the law, meditating on it, and following it completely. Even negative lessons of failure by the Israelites serve to reinforce this message.[31]

Here it must be emphasized that the book of Joshua is history as written by a Yahwistic author (or authors), and it would seem logical that he did not act alone but was part of a group (or community) of Yahwists. The Yahwistic author of the book of Joshua strongly argues for an exclusive devotion to his god, including a threat and a mandate to kill anyone within Israelite society who does not subscribe to such devotion and way of life. Recent anthropological studies have pointed out that heightened rhetoric often occurs precisely when a segment of society wants to "internalize" their views throughout the whole of society.[32] This fits in perfectly when one keeps in mind that the Yahwists were by no means dominant in ancient Israelite society, rather the contrary, as many recent studies have demonstrated.[33] Thus, the Yahwists wanted to employ the strongest possible rhetoric, accompanied by a programme of very forceful measures in order to get others to follow their vision of a perfect society based on a Yahwistic theocracy.[34] And, whenever it might have

30. Similarly van Dyk, "Function," 22–23.

31. For "subversion" in the narrative of Joshua to show that things were not as ideal as first might appear, see Daniel L. Hawk, *Every Promise Fulfilled: Contesting Plots in Joshua* (Louisville, Ky.: Westminster John Knox, 1991).

32. This aspect is well dealt with in Glen Taylor, "Supernatural Power, Ritual and Divination in Ancient Israelite Society: An Examination of Deuteronomy 18" (Ph.D. diss., University of Gloucestershire, 2006).

33. See, e.g., William G. Dever, *Did God Have a Wife? Archaeology and Folk Religion in Ancient Israel* (Grand Rapids: Eerdmans, 2005), and the selection of works cited there. The Bible itself, of course, gives many hints about a number of people worshipping other gods than Yahweh.

34. It is best to keep in mind that the concept of a secular state would have been (at least practically) unthinkable in the ancient Near East at the time.

been that the Yahwists began their programme,[35] history has shown that their view eventually prevailed. In particular, their writings survived and took a pre-eminent position in Israelite society, going on to form a canonical collection that became a foundation for the identity of the Israelite community. From there, through Christianity and Islam and other offshoots of the Israelite communities, the ideology of the Yahwists has probably spread much farther than its original promulgators might have imagined.

Herein lies an important problem. The text has spread far and wide throughout the ages into many contexts that are quite different from the situation that ancient Israel found itself in. How does and should this testimony of the Yahwistic winners then matter to later readers who are (and have been) faced with the ancient text in new contexts? In particular, at the present time, there are those among such readers who may still in some way see themselves as belonging to the tradition in question, who see that tradition as contributing to their identity, and who may think that others, and even the world, should know and remember. In this context, while it is easy to appropriate the idea that Yahweh has power to help and save, a particularly difficult issue that modern readers face is the question of violence, and of genocide.[36] They naturally wonder why they should remember and pay attention to an account of a holocaust composed by its perpetrators as an object lesson of good practice.[37] Even allowing for a measure of understanding for the intended "internalization" of Yahwistic views and a desire to create a perfect Yahwistic society, the text employs the rhetoric of destroying the opposition regardless of whether and to what extent the genocidal events described in Joshua took place.[38] In fact, the more one speaks for the historicity of

35. There has been much debate, and many studies, about the emergence of Yahwism. See, e.g., Mark S. Smith, *The Early History of God: Yahweh and Other Deities in Ancient Israel* (2d ed.; Grand Rapids: Eerdmans, 2002), for the issues involved. See also Dever, *Did God Have a Wife?* I have personally argued for the possible early origin of this ideology through an examination of the central sanctuary in Israel, and related redating of Joshua and Deuteronomy, in my *Central Sanctuary*. See also my "Ethnicity, Assimilation and the Israelite Settlement."

36. Levene, *Genocide*, 157, notes how genocide seems not to have been perceived as so great a moral problem in premodern times, including in the ancient world.

37. Cf. the comments in ibid., 150–52 about genocide in the Old Testament. While no serious Christian theologian today thinks that Joshua may be taken to mandate genocide, history has demonstrated that the canonical texts have been read by Christians to support genocidal activities (for this, see, e.g., Stannard, *American Holocaust*, 149–246 and passim).

38. Appeal to the sinfulness of the Canaanites can be seen to be part of a standard strategy of demonization and dehumanization of the opposition in comparable

the events, the bigger the theological problem for those confessing Jews and Christians (and any others) who wish to retain a personal attachment to the narratives. And yet, it also has to be remembered that no real critical discussion about genocides, or their legitimacy from the perpetrator's perspective, is known to survive from contemporary documents of the ancient Near East. Any such discussions are a rather modern concept.[39] But, even if one were to plead the ignorance and lack of sophistication of the ancients, one may nevertheless ask: What does this tell about the ancient societies and how does this relate to any positive modern appropriation of the book, including by faith communities, especially if one wishes to have a high view of Scripture? How is it possible for such communities and their individual members to admit fully that "their own side" has engaged in gross violence and in genocidal activities (if only rhetorical)[40] when they would really like to see their faith and its heritage from a positive, even reverential perspective as a foundational part of their identity?[41] It is a difficult dilemma.

This dilemma has of course been pointed out by commentators in the past, most of them concentrating on the concept of חרם (*herem*),[42] which

situations in order to rationalize the acts of violence (for this, see, e.g., Stannard, *American Holocaust*; Levene, *Genocide*). Another point to mention here is that we do not seem to see this rhetoric against Canaanites in the prophetic or wisdom literature, not even in the book of Kings. Under the conventional method of arguing about the dating of the Old Testament documents, this would then speak of Joshua (and Deuteronomy) originating in a different milieu from this literature, and thus possibly even from a different time. I have argued for a possible earlier date for other reasons in my *Central Sanctuary*. See also below for further issues involved in the difference between the portrayal of the early and later time.

39. Cf. comments in Levene, *Genocide*, 157. But note how Levene comments about the drafting of the UN definition of genocide so that those who drafted it would not need to be called into account about their own wrongdoings (ibid., 36–42), and other comments about how modern nations try or have tried to hide their actions (ibid., 157 and passim).

40. It would be so much easier if they were victims rather than perpetrators!

41. It is good to remember here that the problem of "excessive" violence by one's "own side" is of course not confined to the book of Joshua and the conquest tradition. See, e.g., David's "two thirds" act in 2 Sam 8:2, etc.

42. There have been numerous studies about חרם. Two may be mentioned here, which include references to further literature: Norbert Lohfink, "*herem*," *TDOT* 5:180–99, and Richard D. Nelson, "*Herem* and the Deuteronomic Social Conscience," in *Deuteronomy and Deuteronomic Literature* (ed. M. Vervenne and J. Lust; Festschrift C. H. W. Brekelmans; Leuven: Leuven University Press, 1997), 39–54. In essence, I agree with Nelson's interpretation that חרם is a special social-anthropological category of belonging to Yahweh, necessitating either the destruction of its object or (permanent) transfer to nonsecular use.

is closely tied to the Israelite conquest ideology and the destructions of populations portrayed in the Old Testament. In search for a solution, three views are worth focusing on.[43] R. W. L. Moberly[44] has suggested that חרם should be read metaphorically, to indicate a heightened rhetoric expressing devotion to Yahweh, without however taking the actual killings literally. Moberly argues for this on the basis that, for example, the focus of Josiah's reform is on the destruction of non-Yahwistic religious objects and any killing is marginal.[45] According to N. Lohfink, the concept of חרם was created by the Deuteronomists around the time of Josiah to explain the distant past in terms that were affected by Assyrian brutality, in contrast to Israel's actual current practice which was far more civilized.[46] It also suited the exilic revisers of the Deuteronomistic History to create a distant past where the Israelites had failed to follow Yahweh's commandments to obliterate the original inhabitants, who then contributed to Israel's apostasy and sin which was the cause of the exile.[47] Nelson suggests that, "In Israelite culture, חרם was not really a matter for human ethical choice, but part of the natural order of things, part of Israel's culture map. As such it can hardly be compared to genocide, brutal tactics intended to terrorize the foe, or the prosecution of total war."[48] In other words, Moberly sees חרם as metaphorical, Lohfink as essentially theological-fictional, and Nelson as part of what was the natural order for the Israelites, which cannot be compared with genocide, terror or total war.

However, in response to Moberly, for example, 1 Kgs 9:20–21 interprets חרם as implying that the destruction of non-Israelites should have taken place during the time of the conquest, even though such an attitude did not prevail any more during the time of Solomon. In other words, while it may be correct to consider the Deuteronomic injunctions as invalid subsequent to the conquest, there is reason to believe that they were seen to apply to the period of the conquest itself. The problem of the חרם in the conquest remains therefore. In any case, even if the events were not historical, in the case of genocides generally, fully fledged violence is often preceded by hostility and conflict of lesser

---

43. I thank Gordon McConville for drawing my attention to these.

44. R. W. L. Moberly, "Toward an Interpretation of the Shema," in *Theological Exegesis: Essays in Honor of Brevard S. Childs* (ed. C. Seitz and K. Greene-McCreight; Grand Rapids: Eerdmans), 124–44.

45. Ibid., 137.

46. Lohfink, *"herem,"* 197.

47. Ibid., 198.

48. Nelson, *"Herem,"* 54.

intensity.[49] In other words, rhetoric that refers to violence can be dangerous even if not intended literally. Certainly, to return to American history, the biblical rhetoric was interpreted as giving a licence for genocide by the Puritans.[50]

The suggestion of Lohfink is in many ways ingenious. In this case too, if the conquest never took place, that part of the problem is solved, but we are still left with a rhetoric that can easily be misunderstood. And yet, such studies as Younger's[51] have pointed out that conquest accounts with accompanying claims of total destruction of enemies (at least in the context of a single battle if not more, and even if a total destruction was often not the case) are part of an ancient Near Eastern heritage that is very much older than the neo-Assyrian period. In this light, it would be quite natural to consider taking the Israelite rhetoric according to its meaning in its ancient Near Eastern context. Moreover, if the book of Joshua (and Deuteronomy) were to be dated earlier,[52] the setting of the rhetoric would have to be modified from what Lohfink suggests.

Finally, while Nelson's interpretation of חרם has much to commend it, that חרם is merely a part of Israel's culture map, based on assumptions about the natural order, does not mean that it could not be seen as a cause for violence. In fact, that non-Israelites and non-Yahwists were seen as falling under חרם precisely gives the grounds, in fact compulsive reasons, for their destruction and thus genocide according to the books of Deuteronomy and Joshua. Also, the rhetoric of Deuteronomy is not limited to חרם and its social construction as a concept. For example, the "demonization of the opponent" that Deuteronomy advocates is precisely something that accompanies genocides.[53] This then in fact speaks for the conceptual plausibility of the historical occurrence of the events portrayed in Joshua.[54] In addition, that genocides are often triggered by war

---

49. This is probably correct in regard to how Jews were treated from the time Hitler came into power from 1930s on.

50. Cf. Nelson, "*Herem*," 39, who refers to Cotton Mather, the Puritan leader.

51. Younger, *Ancient Conquest Accounts*.

52. I have argued that this is at least possible in my *Central Sanctuary*.

53. Cf. above, n. 38.

54. In this vein, Levene's comments about the psychology of the victims and perpetrators and the role of power are insightful (Levene, *Genocide*, 90–143). In particular, his analysis of how the perpetrators perceive the victims as a grave threat, even if they often have even well nigh absolute control over them (they can sometimes be practically powerless, as with disabled people), is captivating (see ibid., especially 135–43). It is also worth noting that the victims often have no particular agenda! As regards the portrayal of an incomplete conquest in Joshua, one may imagine a very plausible scenario. Even though the Canaanites were seen as a

or some other severe crisis[55] also speaks for the conceptual plausibility of the events portrayed in Joshua.[56]

We have seen some attempts, therefore, to mitigate the difficulty posed to modern readers by the account of the חרם in Joshua. It is certainly right, I believe, to try to show that the genocide of the Canaanites (whether real or imaginary) was a unique set of events and that the biblical material should not be read as giving licence for repeating it. However, I have argued too that the theological difficulty of the חרם is not mitigated by arguments against its historicity, since the text has in any case shown its capacity to mandate violence against peoples. The

great threat by the rhetoric of Deuteronomy and Joshua, they may not by any means have been as powerless as in many other cases of genocide around the world in differing circumstances and historical settings (cf. Levene's comments in ibid., 151– 52, about the biblical [Old Testament] material and situations). Therefore, the genocide did not happen, at least on a large scale, due to the Yahwistic party's lack of power (both within Israel society "proper" and without) to implement its programme, whether during the time of the events portrayed or the time when the book was written, and later. Instead, there was mutual coexistence as the book of Judges and later canonical books describe, and, apparently, as I have argued in my "Ethnicity, Assimilation and the Israelite Settlement," assimilation. Further on the role of power, according to the biblical tradition in the book of Exodus in particular, the Israelites sojourned in Egypt and were subsequently oppressed by Egyptians and suffered a genocidal campaign by them. If so, soon after liberation the oppressed Israel became in turn the oppressor in the transition from Egypt to Canaan. Here it may be of interest to consider possible parallels with American history where the oppressed European Puritans who emigrated to the "new" continent in search of (religious) freedom became (among others) perpetrators of violence against the native peoples. The New England Puritans wanted to found a kind of theocracy, and, while it is true that there were missionary efforts towards the Native Americans, ultimately hostility prevailed, including rhetoric by at least some about God's help in destroying the natives, by analogy with the Canaanites (see Stannard, *American Holocaust*, 237–38; Cecelia Tichi, "The Puritan Historians and Their New Jerusalem," *Early American Literature* 6 [1971]: 143–55; and Zubeda Jalaljai, "Race and the Puritan Body Politic," *The Society for the Study of Multi-Ethnic Literature of the United States [MELUS]* 29, nos. 3–4 [2004]: n.p. Online: http://www.findarticles. com/p/articles/mi_m2278/is_3–4_29/ai_n9507933, accessed June 5, 2006; Nelson, "*Herem*," 39. (I am grateful to Heath Thomas for bringing my attention to the articles by Tichi and Jalaljai and for reading through the first draft of the present article before its publication).

55. Levene, *Genocide*, 135–43.

56. One might of course ask why the later Israelite wars did not trigger genocides, but, as Levene points out and as is also known from elsewhere, wars or crises do not always trigger genocides. In fact, a full understanding of what catalyses a genocide still remains a mystery (and so one cannot predict the occurrences of genocides in order to try to prevent them; cf. ibid., passim).

theological issue, therefore, is essentially one of theodicy, and thus part of a problem that needs to be addressed more broadly across the Old Testament and indeed the New Testament.

But we also saw that the book of Joshua advocates a vision where an important part of achieving an ideal society was to destroy anyone or anything not compatible with its central tenet of Yahwism. When we keep in mind that many of the known genocides that have taken place across the globe have stemmed from the desire of one people group to take forceful measures against another group that may be different from it and may have different ideals, the book of Joshua reminds us of our common humanity and our propensity as humans to exclusivity and to pushing through our views and visions forcefully against those who may not be compatible with them.

TOWARDS A COMMUNICATIVE THEOLOGY
OF THE OLD TESTAMENT*

J. W. Rogerson

Old Testament theology is a German Lutheran invention that was made at the end of the eighteenth century. It came about when the emerging discipline of modern biblical criticism finally succeeded in snapping the link that had traditionally made the Old Testament theologically subservient to the New Testament. That link had been under pressure for some considerable time prior to the end of the eighteenth century, as thinking people found it increasingly difficult to accept the justification for the immoral behaviour of central Old Testament characters such as David, the massacres of whole populations of cities by Joshua, and claims such as that Solomon had seven hundred wives and three hundred concubines (1 Kgs 11:3). In Britain, indeed, there were those who asked at the beginning of the eighteenth century whether there was any use for the Old Testament at all. If God could be known from reason and nature, what was the point of seeking him "in the 'historical' annals of an illiterate Semitic tribe"?[1]

It is worth asking at this point why, if some thinkers in Britain had broken the link between the testaments a hundred years earlier than scholars in Germany, Old Testament theology did not become a British invention. The answer lies in the fact that the Old Testament was an important political document in eighteenth-century Britain and was used to justify the established Protestant religion and monarchy at a time when there was still a Stuart, Catholic claimant to the throne. The established church needed the link with the New Testament to show that the Old was divinely inspired because it contained prophecies that were fulfilled in

* A lecture delivered as the first of the Thomas Burns Memorial Lectures in the University of Otago, Dunedin, New Zealand in August 2006.
1. B. Willey, *The Eighteenth Century Background* (Harmondsworth: Penguin, 1962), 14.

the coming of Christ. This, indeed, was the political agenda of Handel's *Messiah*, and why *Messiah* begins with the prophecies of Isa 40, and not with the fall of mankind in Gen 3.[2] Further, the theological and philosophical culture of Britain made it resistant to the emerging discipline of biblical criticism in Germany, and to its questioning of traditional views of the authorship of books of the Old Testament. Jesus had accepted that Moses was the author of the Pentateuch (cf. Mark 10:5–6). If it was denied that Moses had written it, this was an attack upon the divinity of Jesus because it attributed an error to him. For much of the nineteenth century in Britain, in church circles the defence of the view that Moses wrote the Pentateuch became the defence of the first dyke that ultimately protected Christian belief in the divinity of Jesus.[3]

It would be wrong to assume that biblical criticism was accepted in Germany without a struggle.[4] A rearguard action was fought against it in the middle of the nineteenth century, and the most famous embodiment of this reaction was the commentary on the whole of the Old Testament by Keil and Delitzsch. This work is still highly regarded by American evangelicals and is still available in print and online. However, the distinctive philosophical and theological culture of Protestant parts of Germany ensured that biblical criticism made progress without this leading to the abandonment or downgrading of the Old Testament as part of the Christian Bible.

If we ask how German exponents of Old Testament theology understood their task, the answer is that they saw it as a value-free historical and descriptive enterprise. Baumgarten-Crusius, writing in 1828, explained it as the study of the Old Testament "without prior views to which it must conform, and without regarding it as a supernatural unity, or containing a double (spiritual) sense through divine inspiration."[5] Old Testament theology "needed to give an account of the historical development of the biblical ideas as opposed to how they were used in the church and in dogmatics."[6] A similar view was expressed by Steudel in 1840. Old Testament theology is "the systemic overview of the religious ideas which we find in the books of the Old Testament, including the

2. R. Smith, *Handel's Oratorios and Eighteenth-Century Thought* (Cambridge: Cambridge University Press, 1995), 148–52.

3. See H. P. Liddon, *Life of Edward Bouverie Pusey* (London: Longmans, Green & Co., 1897), 4:40–42.

4. See J. W. Rogerson, Old Testament Criticism in the Nineteenth Century: England and Germany (London: SPCK, 1984).

5. L. F. O. Baumgarten-Crusius, *Grundzüge der biblischen Theologie* (Jena: Friedrich Frommann, 1828), 7 (my translation).

6. Ibid., 9.

Apocrypha."[7] However, these writers who saw their task in historical, descriptive terms also sincerely believed that they were doing justice to the Old Testament as divine revelation. Thus Steudel could insist that what was discovered in this overview of religious ideas was not a self-revelation of the human spirit, but divine revelation. Christianity, he declared, was "the completed development of the Old Testament idea of God."[8]

It is necessary at this point to dwell on these beginnings and their implications because this will help to explain why Old Testament theology has been a German speciality and how a communicative theology is different.

The first point to consider is the importance of history in the task of Old Testament theology. In an intellectual climate shaped by philosophers such as Schelling and Hegel, it was natural to believe that history was an objective "thing" and that God was involved in influencing and directing it. This, indeed, appeared to be the view of the Bible itself, expressed classically in the words of Joseph to his brothers when he finally revealed to them his true identity:

> do not be distressed, or angry with yourselves, because you sold me here; for God sent me before you to preserve life…so it was not you who sent me here, but God. (Gen 45:5, 8)

But if this was apparently the view of the Bible, it was confirmed by the researches of secular historians such as B. G. Niebuhr who, in his *History of Rome* (1811–12), clearly saw the hand of God at work in particular times of crisis in that nation's history. Heinrich Ewald, whose *History of Israel*, begun in 1843, was the first great work of that genre, wrote at the beginning of his opening volume:

> The history of this ancient people is in reality the history of the growth of true religion, rising through all stages to perfection…finally revealing itself in full glory and power, in order to spread irresistibly from this centre, never again to be lost, but to become the eternal possession and blessing of all nations.[9]

We can summarize this view as follows: God's involvement in history was such that scholarly reconstruction of history, especially that in the

7. J. F. C. Steudel, *Vorlesungen über die Theologie des Alten Testaments* (Berlin: G. A. Reimer, 1840), 1 (my translation).
8. Ibid., 3 (my translation).
9. H. Ewald, *Geschichte des Volkes Israel* (Göttingen: Dieterichs Buchhandlung, 1843), 1:9. English translation, *History of Israel* (London: Longmans, Green & Co., 1876), 1:5.

Old Testament, could make visible both what God had done, and the goal to which he was directing history. This was tremendously appealing to practitioners of biblical criticism. They had begun to dismantle the view of Israel's history as it was presented in the Old Testament, in order to re-present it in the light of scholarly research and discovery. An extreme view at the time, represented by de Wette, was that very little of what the Bible attributed to Moses had actually been done by him. Israel's sacrificial and priestly institutions were late developments, not things instituted by Moses near the beginning of the nation's history.[10] Ewald was not so minimalist and allowed much more scope for the contribution of Moses. But even he could not accept Abraham, Isaac and Jacob as historical figures. The stories about them concerned dealings between various social groups, and in so far as they were presented as characters, they were ideal types rather than historical figures. It is easy to understand how attractive the view was in critical biblical circles, that what criticism was doing was not destroying the Bible but using it positively to discover God's self-revelation in history.

This view of the task of critically informed Old Testament theology lasted through the nineteenth century and well into the twentieth, and convinced some of the most acute and able scholars in the field. The Scot, William Robertson Smith who, after all, had obtained the most significant parts of his theological outlook from Germany and was the most original and outstanding British Old Testament scholar of the nineteenth century, was fully convinced that the history of ancient Israel as reconstructed by critical scholarship was a history of God's grace.[11] As late as 1961, a group of German scholars including Rendtorff and Pannenberg published a collection of essays entitled *Offenbarung als Geschichte*.[12]

The second point to make about the view that Old Testament theology was a value-free historical and descriptive enterprise was that it brought assumptions with it to the task. These included belief in God as supremely revealed in Jesus Christ, and belief in the Old Testament as a record of God's dealings with ancient Israel. What was regarded as objective and value-free was in fact to some extent circular. I say this not in order to

10. See J. W. Rogerson, *W. M. L. de Wette, Founder of Modern Biblical Criticism: An Intellectual Biography* (JSOTSup 126; Sheffield: Sheffield Academic Press 1992).

11. W. R. Smith, *The Old Testament in the Jewish Church* (Edinburgh: A. & C. Black, 1881), 15–16.

12. W. Pannenberg, (ed.), *Offenbarung als Geschichte* (Göttingen: Vandenhoeck & Ruprecht, 1961); English translation, *Revelation as History* (London: Sheed & Ward, 1969).

bring a charge of dishonesty or hypocrisy, but to point out how odd this claim to objectivity sounds today in a world where we are all very aware of our subjectivities and how our gender, ethnic and political orientations, to name only three, affect our perception of reality. This point will become important later on.

The third matter arising from the nineteenth-century critical understanding of Old Testament theology is that the Old Testament as text and narrative was downgraded. This point has already been partly made in the remarks about history, and how the picture of Israel's history was partly dismantled in order to make way for a critical scholarly reconstruction. But the preoccupation with history spread to the treatment of "non-historical" parts of the Old Testament. The prophetic books came under close scrutiny in order to recover the actual words of the prophets and to eliminate later and editorial glosses. There was little value in these *literary* processes (i.e. later inner-biblical editorial revision and expansion), whereas what prophets had said in concrete historical circumstances was part of the historical process through which God was at work. Not surprisingly, books such as Proverbs had little or nothing to contribute to a history-driven approach to the Old Testament, and even narratives such as the book of Ruth were of value only if they could be fitted into an historical scheme, in the case of Ruth as an alleged protest against the policies of Ezra and Nehemiah.

The fourth point about the nineteenth-century development of Old Testament theology is that it opened a gap between the Old Testament and its modern readers. The task of Old Testament theology was to describe the past: what people had once *believed*, how the faith of Israel had *developed*. How one got from the past to the present, assuming that this was possible, was not the concern of Old Testament scholarship. That was the province of systematic and practical theology, for which biblical scholarship provided the raw material according to what has been called the "pass the baton" model. To be fair to Old Testament scholarship, the problem of how the writings of the old covenant related to the people of the new covenant was a long-standing one, and not the fault of the eighteenth or nineteenth centuries. It was odd, however, to describe as theology something that was in reality a history of past religious beliefs or ideas, and this fact certainly influenced the development of Old Testament theology as a branch of study in Britain.

Before I proceed, however, I want to quote a passage from Bultmann's *New Testament Theology* because it throws down a challenge that the present essay will try to take up. Bultmann wrote in his *Epilegomena*:

> Because the New Testament is a document of history, and in particular, of the history of religion, its interpretation requires the work of historical investigation, whose methods were developed from the time of the Enlightenment, and which bore fruit in the investigation of early Christianity and the interpretation of the New Testament. Such work can only be carried out from two standpoints, either from that of reconstruction or that of interpretation. Reconstruction is concerned with past history, interpretation with the writings of the New Testament; and clearly, one cannot be done without the other. They always work mutually together. But the important question is which of the two is the servant of the other. Either the writings of the New Testament can be treated as "sources" which the historian uses in order to reconstruct early Christianity as a phenomenon of the historical past, or the reconstruction serves the needs of the interpretation of the New Testament writings, on the assumption that these writings have something to say to the present. The historical investigation involved in the picture that is presented here is put at the service of the latter view.[13]

Bultmann's observations apply just as much to Old Testament scholarship as to the study of the New, as does his identification of the two alternatives that such study is confronted with. Adapting his language, we can say:

> Either the writings of the Old Testament can be treated as "sources" which the historian can use in order to reconstruct the religion of ancient Israel as a phenomenon of the historical past, or the reconstruction serves the needs of the interpretation of the Old Testament writings, on the assumption that these writings have something to say to the present.

If my account of the origins of Old Testament theology in the eighteenth and nineteenth centuries is correct, then we can say that critical scholars opted for the first alternative, that of using the Old Testament as a source or sources for the reconstruction of the religion of ancient Israel as a phenomenon of the ancient past. To be fair to them, these scholars believed that their reconstructions of the past would uncover the workings of God in human history, and to that extent would be divine revelation. The price that was paid, as I have already said, was a downgrading of the actual text; and what they were doing was a long way from Bultmann's aim of interpreting the text on the assumption that it had something to say to the present.

Why did Old Testament theology become a German speciality and an enterprise hardly even undertaken in Britain? The answer lies, I think, first in the fact that Germany had and still has a tradition of systematic

---

13. R. Bultmann, *Theologie des Neuen Testaments* (9th ed.; Tübingen: J.C.B. Mohr [Paul Siebeck], 1984), 600 (my translation).

theology that has never been approached in British theology, and second that the Lutheran idea of the Bible as the Word through which God communicates has been so deeply rooted in German biblical scholarship that the Old Testament could never ultimately become merely a source or sources for reconstructing the past. In Britain, on the other hand, there was a long tradition going back to the Deists of the seventeenth century of subjecting the Old Testament to moral criticism that saw it at best as preparation for the New Testament, and in any case as falling far short of its teaching.[14] Whether or not this is correct, it remains a fact that no major Old Testament theology was produced by a British scholar in the twentieth century as opposed to the German and German-speaking efforts of König (1922), Sellin (1933), Procksch (1949–50), Eichrodt (1933–39), von Rad (1957–60), Zimmerli (1972), Preuss (1991–92), Rendtorff (1999–2001) and Kaiser (1993–2003), to name only those that come readily to mind. There were, of course, important contributions to the subject especially from British scholars from the Baptist tradition. One thinks here of H. H. Rowley's *The Unity of the Bible* (1953) and the *Faith of Israel* (1956), H. Wheeler Robinson's *Inspiration and Revelation in the Old Testament* (1946) and Ronald Clements's *Old Testament Theology: A Fresh Approach* (1978).

This essay will attempt to undertake Bultmann's second alternative, to interpret the Old Testament writings on the assumption that they have something to say to the present. Underlying this attempt will be three assumptions that I shall now discuss in turn: (1) the gap between past and present can be bridged; (2) history is essentially narrative; (3) we need to learn from theories of cultural memory.

1. *The Gap Between Past and Present Can Be Bridged*

The section in von Rad's 1957 *Old Testament Theology* entitled "The Subject-Matter of a Theology of the Old Testament" was critical of attempts to present the "theologically important views, thoughts and ideas of the Old Testament."[15] He did not dispute that their description belonged somehow to Old Testament theology, but he doubted whether they did justice to it since they were abstractions and systematizations and could not do justice to the complexity and many-sidedness of ancient Israelite experience. What von Rad was complaining about was the fact that Old Testament Theologies had been organized according to system-

14. See Rogerson, *Old Testament Criticism*.
15. G. von Rad, *Theologie des Alten Testaments* (Göttingen: Vandenhoeck & Ruprecht, 1957), 1:124.

atic categories, in spite of their commitment to historical investigation. Thus Steudel, whom I have already quoted, had three main sections covering "The Doctrine of Man," "The Doctrine of God," and "The Doctrine of Divine–Human Relationships." Eichrodt had attempted to find a scheme that arose from the Bible itself, and had chosen the notion of Covenant as the organizing principle of his theology. This left him open to the charge that Covenant was not necessarily the central idea of the Old Testament and that in any case there was much that could not be brought under its aegis.[16] For von Rad, the subject-matter of an Old Testament theology was the "*Zeugniswelt*" of ancient Israel, by which he meant the Old Testament's own witness to its belief in God, as expressed in its historical and prophetic traditions, and his theology was organized along these lines.[17] Von Rad believed that ancient Israel had confessed its faith by telling and re-telling its own history. The task of an Old Testament theology was to expound this telling and re-telling in the light of modern scholarship.

This may not seem to have much to do with bridging the gap between past and present, but I want to point out two things. First, von Rad's approach was an expression of the scholarship of his day, a scholarship which, in Germany in the work of Martin Noth and von Rad himself, was especially concerned with tradition history—the investigation of the process of the growth of the biblical traditions. Second, the ideas of witness and kerygma, terms that appeared frequently in von Rad's theology, had their setting in the Confessing Church with which von Rad had been involved from the beginning of its activities in 1934, even though he did not formally become a member until 1939.[18] It is, perhaps, an obvious and even trivial observation that the research of scholars cannot be separated from the times and burning questions in which they do their work, but it serves my purposes here; and in any case it was Wilhelm Vatke who pointed out as long ago as 1835 that there could be no such thing as objective study of the past entirely free from subjective considerations.[19]

---

16. G. von Rad, "Offene Fragen im Umkreis einer Theologie des Alten Testaments," in his *Gesammelte Studien zum Alten Testament II* (TBü 48; Munich: Chr. Kaiser, 1973), 291–92.

17. Von Rad, *Theologie*, 1:124.

18. R. Smend, *Deutsche Alttestamentler in drei Jahrhunderten* (Göttingen: Vandenhoeck & Ruprecht, 1989), 236.

19. W. Vatke, *Die biblische Theologie wissenschaftlich dargestellt*. Vol. 1, *Die Religion des Alten Testaments nach den kanonischen Büchern entwickelt* (Berlin: G. Bethge, 1835), 15.

I would not go so far as to say that history is actually the study of the present with the help of the symbols of the past, but I would want to say that *how* the past is studied and used is a function of the present; that however objective we may try to be we cannot escape from the fact that the agendas that we bring to the study of the past are part of the way we are situated in the present. This is also true for Old Testament theology. We may claim that we are studying ancient texts with a view to discovering, say, how they conceived of God, but *how* we do this is affected by who we are and where we are located. Our study is a dialogue between past and present, and to this extent a two-way communication is taking place. A Communicative Theology of the Old Testament begins by recognizing this process: that there is a dialogue between past and present, and that the outcome, the written theology, is a part of the present that will interact with those who read it in the present and future. But we must go further than this, which brings me to the next point.

2. *History is Essentially Narrative*

Our knowledge of the past is very incomplete and in some cases dependent upon chance discoveries. We have only to think how much light has been shed by the Dead Sea Scrolls upon the Judaism from which Christianity emerged to realize how fortunate it was that Cave 1 was quite accidentally discovered by a Bedouin Arab boy, apparently in 1947. At the time of writing this essay (February 2006), it has been announced that a completely intact burial has been found in the Valley of the Kings in Egypt, a burial of whose existence the experts had no prior inkling. This discovery will no doubt add to our knowledge of the history of ancient Egypt.

What we do know about the past comes by way of narrative. In the first instances there are documents such as treaties, wills, laws, chronicles and letters. There are also ancient narratives which incorporate and preserve some of these things. One thinks of the ecclesiastical history of Eusebius from the fourth century or of the Venerable Bede from the eighth. Even where history is based upon archaeological discoveries, the artefacts and objects discovered have to be brought to life and accessibility by being incorporated in a narrative. The narrative is necessarily an interpretation of what has been found, and an interpretation that is necessarily shaped and conditioned by the knowledge available to the interpreter. New discoveries and new knowledge can sometimes demand a completely different interpretation of archaeological remains. A fierce debate that is currently raging in Old Testament studies is whether

Jerusalem was in fact inhabited in the tenth century B.C.E. when, according to the Bible, it was captured and occupied by David.

My own view is that we must distinguish between history as the past,
and history as narrative about the past, and that our only, very incomplete, access to history as the past is via narrative or narratives.[20] These
will change in the light of new research and discoveries and in any case
will inevitably reflect the interests of those who construct them. Granted
that our access to the past is only via narrative, it will be clear that I
cannot agree with those nineteenth- and twentieth-century scholars who
believed that God acted in history and that the Old Testament was a
source for recovering God's self-disclosure in this history. They assumed
that history was an objective "thing" with which God was involved, and
that it was possible to speak of God revealing himself in history. I find
such language and ideas meaningless. However, because my position can
be easily misunderstood, I must try to make some things clear. I am not
denying that people have had, and indeed continue to have, encounters
and experiences in their own lives, or the lives of groups to which they
belong, in which they sincerely believe that God has been dealing with
them. I am not denying that Jerusalem was destroyed by the Babylonians
in around 587 B.C.E. and that groups in the land sensitive to the words of
the prophets saw in this event the judgment of God upon the nation. My
point is that it is only through the narratives that have been preserved that
we know *both* that Jerusalem was destroyed *and* that some groups saw in
the happening the judgment of God. If God is revealed, it is not in some
objective "thing" called the past, but in the narratives that both describe
and interpret the happenings in the past. To put it another way, the
definition of history as "fact plus interpretation" overlooks the point that
there is no such thing as an uninterpreted fact.[21]

All this, perhaps strangely, brings me very close to the position of von
Rad in his Old Testament theology, for all that von Rad did believe that
history was an objective "thing." For von Rad, the problem was how to
bridge the gulf between the actual history of Israel and that recorded in
the Bible or, as I would put it, between a scholarly reconstructed narrative about Israel's past and the Bible's narrative. Critical scholarship had
opened a gap between the two narratives, a gap which, incidentally, has

20. See J. W. Rogerson, "Can a Doctrine of Providence Be Based on the Old
Testament?," in *Ascribe to the Lord: Biblical and Other Studies in Memory of Peter
C. Craigie* (L. Eslinger and G. Taylor; JSOTSup 67; Sheffield: JSOT Press, 1988),
529–43.
21. J. Lauster, *Religion als Lebensdeutung: theologische Hermeneutik heute*
(Darmstadt: Wissenschaftliche Buchgesellschaft, 2005).

grown wider in the almost fifty years since von Rad's theology appeared. Von Rad's solution, for which he was severely criticized, for example, by Eichrodt, was to sever all connection between "actual" history and that narrated in the Bible, and to regard the latter as the locus of revelation. The datum of Old Testament theology was not God's revelation in history as the past, but Israel's witness to its faith as expressed in its own narratives about its past, whether or not these corresponded to the kind of narrative that would be produced by modern critical research. In my opinion, von Rad was right to take this line. What he was unable to do was to place it within a theory of cultural memory.

3. *Cultural Memory*

The idea of cultural memory was introduced into scholarly literature by Maurice Halbwachs in 1925 with the words "*mémoire collective.*"[22] He had been a student of Durkheim and his main contribution was to investigate the communal and social aspects of remembering. A work entitled *La mémoire collective* appeared posthumously in 1950, Halbwachs having been murdered in the concentration camp at Buchenwald in March 1945. His work was taken up and developed in the 1990s by the German Egyptologist Jan Assmann.[23]

It is necessary to distinguish between individual remembering and corporate remembering. Individuals who remember do so as part of their engagement with a past of which they were part and a present that has to some extent been formed by that past. There is a strong communicative element to their remembering. They engage with memories of the past and they interact with fellow human beings by recalling the past and by speaking about it. It is one of the ways in which individuals embed themselves in the social milieu in which they live. An important aspect of individual remembering is that it is unstructured. Unless a person writes an autobiography which attempts to present a life as a connected whole, individual memories are larger or smaller fragments or episodes unrelated to each other. Individual memory is limited in time. It stretches back over two or three generations, and exists after death only partially in the memories of those still alive.

22. For what follows I am indebted to the account in J. Assmann, *Das kulturelle Gedächtnis. Schrift, Erinnerung und politische Identität in frühen Hochkulturen* (Munich: C. H. Beck, 1997), 34–48.
23. See also J. Assmann, *Religion und kulturelles Gedächtnis* (2d ed.; Munich: C. H. Beck, 2004).

Corporate or cultural memory stretches back much further than individual memory. It can be located or perpetuated in ceremonies or customs or religious practices. While it depends on specialist individuals
such as priests or scribes or the tellers of epics it embodies the interests
of social groups, not individuals. Insofar as it is concerned with the past,
it deals not with what modern scholars would call factual history, but
with remembered history—a way of recalling the past which can change
with the changing needs and situations of a given social group. This
remembered history exists not because there is an interest in the past as
such, but because the remembering enables a group to understand itself
in the present and to generate hopes for the future. A point emphasized
by Halbwachs is that an important aspect of remembering is forgetting,
of discarding memories that do not contribute to self-understanding in
the present, and of selecting those memories that best achieve this aim.
Assmann argues that in the Old Testament the stories of the Patriarchs,
the Exodus from Egypt, the wilderness wanderings, the conquest of
Canaan and the Babylonian exile are what he calls *Erinnerungsfiguren*,
memories that in some cases were perpetuated through celebrations such
as the Passover, and which served to shed light on the present situation
of those who remembered and celebrated them. In later chapters Assmann investigates how such memories were united first, with what he
calls textual coherence (i.e. a meaningful and connected story) and later
with canonical form.[24]

The theory of cultural memory as developed by Assmann is not, at
first sight, dissimilar from von Rad's insistence that Old Testament
theology should deal with "Israel's" own account of its history, and not
its history as reconstructed by critical scholarship; but there are two
important differences. Von Rad, in accordance with the critical scholarship of his day, believed that there had been a "Solomonic Enlighten-
ment" in Israel in the tenth century B.C.E. and that "historians" such as
the Yahwist had set about producing Israel's histories.[25] It was not
uncommon at the time for books to be published with titles such as *The
Yahwist: The Bible's First Theologian*, an indication of the extent to
which biblical scholarship was still in thrall to positivistic ideas of history and history writing.[26] Second, for all his undoubted enormous
theological sensitivity, von Rad was not able convincingly to cross the

24. Assmann, *Das kulturelle Gedächtnis*, 200–2.
25. Von Rad, *Theologie*, 1:62–70.
26. See P. Ellis, *The Yahwist: The Bible's First Theologian* (London: Geoffrey
Chapman, 1969).

gap from his interpretation of the Old Testament traditions to the time and world in which he was writing.

Before I conclude by saying how I think that the theory of cultural memory helps us to do this, I need to mention the work of another Old Testament scholar whose work seems to come close to what Assmann is saying, and that is Brevard Childs, whose canonical approach has focussed upon the intentionality that according to him has driven the Old Testament to assume the canonical forms that the Hebrew text has taken.[27] I have never been convinced by Childs's argument that there was an intention to produce Scripture in the way that the Old Testament reached its final form and that this intentionality can guide us in producing a confessional interpretation of its texts. I find Assmann's theory more helpful, and free from the confessional constraints implicit in Childs's approach; which brings me to say what I think a Communicative Theology of the Old Testament is about.

It begins from the view that Old Testament texts are instances of cultural memories, probably from a number of different times and circumstances. These cultural memories utilized the past in order for the groups responsible to understand the present and articulate hopes for the future. To that extent they had a communicative purpose within their own milieu. An Old Testament theology can engage critically and constructively with these cultural memories. It will do so by bringing to the encounter an agenda necessarily shaped by the concerns and interests of the writer or writers involved. In my own case, this agenda will be drawn from a concern with modern social and political issues, and the result will look nothing like traditional Old Testament theologies with their sections on the doctrine of God or the nature of humanity.

I am well aware that I may be accused of confusing theology with anthropology; of putting humanity where God ought to be. I would reply as follows. In the first of Schiller's plays in the Wallenstein trilogy, *Wallensteins Lager* (Wallenstein's Camp), Wallenstein, the tragic general on the Catholic side in the Thirty Years War, never appears in the play at all. Yet he is the absent presence, whose personality affects and permeates every part of the play. If a Communicative Theology concentrates upon the Old Testament treatment of human dilemmas integral to modern existence, this will not exclude God any more than Wallenstein is excluded from *Wallensteins Lager*. When all has been said and done, the only test that remains is that of the challenge thrown

27. See, e.g., B.S. Childs, *Old Testament Theology in a Canonical Context* (London: SCM Press, 1985).

down by Bultmann. Either we use our scholarship to make the Bible tell us about the past, or we use it on the assumption that the Bible has something to say to the present. Whether or not our attempts to meet the second part of the challenge succeed, it is one that we cannot afford to ignore.

BIBLIOGRAPHY OF THE WRITINGS
OF GORDON J. WENHAM

1. *Dissertation*

Wenham, Gordon J. "The Structure and Date of Deuteronomy: A Consideration of Aspects of the History of Deuteronomy Criticism and a Re-Examination of the Question of Structure and Date in the Light of That History and of the Near Eastern Treaties." Ph.D. diss., King's College, University of London, 1970.

2. *Books: Authored and Co-authored*

Wenham, Gordon J. *Faith in the Old Testament*. Leicester: Theological Students' Fellowship, 1976.

——*The Book of Leviticus*. NICOT. Grand Rapids: Eerdmans; London: Hodder & Stoughton, 1979.

——*Numbers: An Introduction and Commentary*. TOTC. Leicester: Inter-Varsity; Downers Grove, Ill.: InterVarsity, 1981.

Wenham, Gordon J., and Richard Winter. *Abortion: The Biblical and Medical Challenges*. London: CARE Trust, 1983.

Heth, William A., and Gordon J. Wenham. *Jesus and Divorce: Towards an Evangelical Understanding of New Testament Teaching*. London: Hodder & Stoughton, 1984. American ed.: *Jesus and Divorce: The Problem with the Evangelical Consensus*. Nashville, Tenn.: Thomas Nelson, 1985. 2d ed.: Biblical and Theological Classics Library 9. Carlisle: Paternoster, 1997. 3d ed.: Carlisle/Waynesboro, Ga.: Paternoster, 2002.

Wenham, Gordon J. *Genesis 1–15*. WBC 1. Dallas, Tex.: Word, 1987. British ed.: Milton Keynes: Word (UK), 1991.

Poole, M. W., and Gordon J. Wenham. *Creation or Evolution: A False Antithesis?* Oxford: Latimer House, 1987.

Wenham, Gordon J. *Genesis 16–50*. WBC 2. Dallas, Tex.: Word, 1994.

——*Numbers*. OTG. Sheffield: Sheffield Academic Press, 1997.

——*Story as Torah: Reading the Old Testament Ethically*. OTS. Edinburgh: T. & T. Clark, 2000. American ed.: *Story as Torah: Reading Old Testament Narrative Ethically*. Grand Rapids: Baker Academic, 2004.

——*The Pentateuch*. Exploring the Old Testament 1. London: SPCK, 2003. American ed.: *A Guide to the Pentateuch*. Exploring the Old Testament 1. Downers Grove, Ill.: InterVarsity, 2003.

Wenham, Gordon J., William A. Heth and Craig S. Keener. *Remarriage After Divorce in Today's Church: 3 Views*. Edited by Mark L. Strauss. Grand Rapids: Zondervan, 2006.

298   *Reading the Law*

3. *Books: Edited and Translated*

Wenham, Gordon J., and Colin Brown, eds. *History, Criticism and Faith: Four Explora-tory Studies*. Leicester: Inter-Varsity, 1976.
Kaye, Bruce, and Gordon J. Wenham, eds. *Law, Morality and the Bible: A Symposium*. Leicester: Inter-Varsity; Downers Grove, Ill.: InterVarsity, 1978. Korean ed.: 1985.
Neuer, Werner. *Man and Woman in Christian Perspective*. Translated by Gordon J. Wenham. London: Hodder & Stoughton, 1990.
Hess, Richard S., Philip E. Satterthwaite and Gordon J. Wenham, eds. *He Swore an Oath: Biblical Themes from Genesis 12–50*. Cambridge: Tyndale House, 1993. 2d ed.: Carlisle: Paternoster; Grand Rapids: Baker, 1994.
Wenham, Gordon J., J. Alec Motyer, Donald A. Carson and R. T. France, eds. *New Bible Commentary: 21st Century Edition*. Leicester: Inter-Varsity; Downers Grove, Ill.: InterVarsity, 1994. Vietnamese ed.: 2004.
Satterthwaite, Philip E., Richard S. Hess and Gordon J. Wenham, eds. *The Lord's Anointed: Interpretation of Old Testament Messianic Texts*. Carlisle: Paternoster; Grand Rapids: Baker, 1995.
Hess, Richard S., and Gordon J. Wenham, eds. *Make the Old Testament Live: From Curriculum to Classroom*. Grand Rapids: Eerdmans, 1998.
—*Zion, City of Our God*. Grand Rapids: Eerdmans, 1999.
Long, V. Philips, David W. Baker and Gordon J. Wenham, eds. *Windows into Old Testament History: Evidence, Argument, and the Crisis of "Biblical Israel."* Grand Rapids: Eerdmans, 2002.

4. *Articles and Essays*

Wenham, Gordon J. "The Inspiration of Scripture—A Received Tradition?" *Churchman* 84 (1970): 286–88.
—"Trends in Pentateuchal Criticism Since 1950." *Churchman* 84 (1970): 210–20.
—"The Deuteronomic Theology of the Book of Joshua." *JBL* 90 (1971): 140–58.
—"Deuteronomy and the Central Sanctuary." *TynBul* 22 (1971): 103–18.
—"Legal Forms in the Book of the Covenant." *TynBul* 22 (1971): 95–102.
—"*Bᵉtûlāh*: 'A Girl of Marriageable Age.'" *VT* 22 (1972): 326–58.
—"Were David's Sons Priests." *ZAW* 87 (1975): 79–82.
—"History and the Old Testament." Pages 13–75 in *History, Criticism and Faith: Four Exploratory Studies*. Edited by Gordon J. Wenham and Colin Brown. Leicester: Inter-Varsity, 1976.
—"The Biblical View of Marriage and Divorce 1—The Cultural Background." *Third Way* 1, no. 20 (20 October 1977): 3–5.
—"The Biblical View of Marriage and Divorce 2—Old Testament Teaching." *Third Way* 1, no. 21 (3 November 1977): 7–9.
—"The Biblical View of Marriage and Divorce 3—New Testament Teaching." *Third Way* 1, no. 22 (17 November 1977): 7–9.
—"Clarifying Divorce." *Third Way* 1, no. 25 (29 December 1977): 17–18.
—"Daniel: The Basic Issues." *Themelios* 2, no. 2 (1977): 49–52.
—"The Coherence of the Flood Narrative." *VT* 28 (1978): 336–58. Reprinted in pages 436–57 of *"I Studied Inscriptions From Before the Flood": Ancient Near Eastern and Literary Approaches to Genesis 1–11*. Edited by R. S. Hess and D. T. Tsumura. SBTS 4. Winona Lake, Ind.: Eisenbrauns, 1994.

—"Grace and Law in the Old Testament." Pages 3–23 in *Law, Morality, and the Bible: A Symposium*. Edited by Bruce Norman Kaye and Gordon J. Wenham. Leicester: Inter-Varsity; Downers Grove, Ill.: InterVarsity, 1978.

—"Law and the Legal System in the Old Testament." Pages 24–52 in *Law, Morality, and the Bible: A Symposium*. Edited by Bruce Norman Kaye and Gordon J. Wenham. Downers Grove, Ill.: InterVarsity, 1978.

—"Leviticus 27:2–8 and the Price of Slaves." *ZAW* 90 (1978): 264–65.

—"The Marriage Bond and the Church: A Summary and Evaluation of the Recent Church of England Report on Divorce and Remarriage." *Third Way* 2, no. 11 (1 June 1978): 13–15.

—"The Ordination of Women: Why Is It So Divisive?" *Churchman* 92 (1978): 310–19.

—"The Restoration of Marriage Reconsidered." *JJS* 30 (1979): 36–50.

Wenham, Gordon J., and J. Gordon McConville. "Drafting Techniques in Some Deuteronomic Laws." *VT* 30 (1980): 248–52.

Wenham, Gordon J. "The Religion of the Patriarchs." Pages 157–88 in *Essays on the Patriarchal Narratives*. Edited by A. R. Millard and D. J. Wiseman. Leicester: Inter-Varsity, 1980.

—"Aaron's Rod (Numbers 17:16–28)." *ZAW* 93 (1981): 280–81.

—"May Divorced Christians Remarry?" *Churchman* 95 (1981): 150–61. Reprinted in *Evangelical Review of Theology* 6 (1982): 118–30.

—"The Theology of Unclean Food." *EvQ* 53 (1981): 6–15.

—"Christ's Healing Ministry and His Attitude to the Law." Pages 115–26 in *Christ the Lord: Studies in Christology Presented to Donald Guthrie*. Edited by Harold H. Rowdon. Leicester: Inter-Varsity, 1982.

—"The Symbolism of the Animal Rite in Genesis 15: A Response to G. F. Hasel." *JSOT* 22 (1982): 134–37.

—"A Biblical Theologian Looks at Abortion." Pages 3–8 in *Abortion: The Biblical and Medical Challenges* by Gordon Wenham and Richard Winter. London: CARE Trust, 1983.

—"Recent Old Testament Study: An Evangelical Assessment." *Themelios* 8 (1983): 25–26.

—"Why Does Sexual Intercourse Defile (Lev 15,18)?" *ZAW* 95 (1983): 432–34.

—"Matthew and Divorce: An Old Crux Revisited." *JSNT* 22 (1984): 95–107.

—"Gospel Definitions of Adultery and Women's Rights." *ET* 95 (1984): 330–32. Reprinted in *Evangelical Review of Theology* 9 (1985): 151–55.

—"The Date of Deuteronomy: Linch-Pin of Old Testament Criticism. Part One." *Themelios* 10, no. 3 (1985): 15–20.

—"The Date of Deuteronomy: Linch-Pin of Old Testament Criticism. Part Two." *Themelios* 11, no. 1 (1985): 15–18.

—"Sanctuary Symbolism in the Garden of Eden Story." *PWCJS* 9 (1986): 19–25. Reprinted in pages 399–504 of *"I Studied Inscriptions From Before the Flood": Ancient Near Eastern and Literary Approaches to Genesis 1–11*. Edited by R. S. Hess and D. T. Tsumura. SBTS 4. Winona Lake, Ind: Eisenbrauns, 1994.

—"The Syntax of Matthew 19.9." *JSNT* 28 (1986): 17–23.

—"Heterosexuality in the Bible." Pages 17–26 in *Sexuality and the Church: The Way Forward* by Tony Higton. Eastbourne: Kingsway, 1987.

—"Homosexuality in the Bible." Pages 27–38 in *Sexuality and the Church: The Way Forward* by Tony Higton. Eastbourne: Kingsway, 1987.

—"Interpreting Genesis 1–3." Pages 22–33 in *Creation or Evolution: A False Antithesis?* by M. W. Poole and G. J. Wenham. Oxford: Latimer House, 1987.

—"The Perplexing Pentateuch." *Vox Evangelica* 17 (1987): 7–21.

—"Genesis: An Authorship Study and Current Pentateuchal Criticism." *JSOT* 42 (1988): 3–18.

—"Marriage and Divorce in the Old Testament." *Didaskalia* 1 (1989): 6–17.

—"The Place of Biblical Criticism in Theological Study." *Themelios* 14, no. 3 (1989): 84–89. Reprinted in *The Best in Theology* 4 (1990): 11–22.

—"Contemporary Bible Commentary: The Primacy of Exegesis and the Religious Dimension." *PWCJS* 10 (1990): 1–12.

—"Original Sin in Genesis 1–11." *Churchman* 104 (1990): 309–28.

—"Method in Pentateuchal Source Criticism." *VT* 41 (1991): 84–109.

—"The Old Testament Attitude to Homosexuality." *ET* 102 (1991): 359–63.

—"Divorce." Pages 169–71 in *The Oxford Companion to the Bible*. Edited by Bruce M. Metzger and Michael D. Coogan. Oxford: Oxford University Press, 1993.

—"The Face at the Bottom of the Well: Hidden Agendas of the Pentateuchal Commentator." Pages 185–209 in *He Swore an Oath: Biblical Themes from Genesis 12–50*. Edited by Richard S. Hess, Philip E. Satterthwaite and Gordon J. Wenham. Cambridge: Tyndale House, 1993. 2d ed.: Carlisle: Paternoster; Grand Rapids: Baker, 1994.

—"Weddings." Pages 794–95 in *The Oxford Companion to the Bible*. Edited by Bruce M. Metzger and Michael D. Coogan. Oxford: Oxford University Press, 1993.

—"Genesis." Pages 54–91 in *New Bible Commentary: 21st Century Edition*. Edited by Gordon J. Wenham, J. Alec Motyer, Donald A. Carson and R. T. France. Leicester: Inter-Varsity; Downers Grove, Ill.: InterVarsity, 1994.

—"The Pentateuch." Pages 43–53 in *New Bible Commentary: 21st Century Edition*. Edited by Gordon J. Wenham, J. Alec Motyer, Donald A. Carson and R. T. France. Leicester: Inter-Varsity; Downers Grove, Ill.: InterVarsity, 1994.

—"Reading Genesis Today." *Word and World* 14 (1994): 125–35.

—"The Akedah: A Paradigm of Sacrifice." Pages 93–102 in *Pomegranates and Golden Bells: Studies in Biblical, Jewish, and Near Eastern Ritual, Law, and Literature in Honor of Jacob Milgrom*. Edited by David P. Wright, David Noel Freedman and Avi Hurvitz. Winona Lake, Ind.: Eisenbrauns, 1995.

—"Divorce." Pages 315–17 in *New Dictionary of Christian Ethics and Pastoral Theology*. Edited by David J. Atkinson and David H. Field. Leicester: Inter-Varsity; Downers Grove, Ill.: InterVarsity, 1995.

—"Holiness Code." Page 445 in *New Dictionary of Christian Ethics and Pastoral Theology*. Edited by David J. Atkinson and David H. Field. Leicester: Inter-Varsity; Downers Grove, Ill.: InterVarsity, 1995.

—"The Theology of Old Testament Sacrifice." Pages 75–87 in *Sacrifice in the Bible*. Edited by R. T. Beckwith and Martin J. Selman. Carlisle: Paternoster, 1995.

—"Biblical Criticism." Pages 138–50 in *New Bible Dictionary*. Edited by Derek R. W. Wood. 3d ed. Leicester: Inter-Varsity; Downers Grove, Ill.: InterVarsity, 1996.

—"Clean and Unclean." Pages 209–12 in *New Bible Dictionary*. Edited by Derek R. W. Wood. 3d ed. Leicester: Inter-Varsity; Downers Grove, Ill.: InterVarsity, 1996.

—"Creation." Pages 239–51 in *New Bible Dictionary*. Edited by Derek R. W. Wood. 3d ed. Leicester: Inter-Varsity; Downers Grove, Ill.: InterVarsity, 1996.

—"Law: In the Old Testament." Pages 672–75 in *New Bible Dictionary*. Edited by Derek R. W. Wood. 3d ed. Leicester: Inter-Varsity; Downers Grove, Ill.: InterVarsity, 1996.

—"Pentateuchal Studies Today." *Themelios* 22, no. 1 (1996): 3–13.

—"Aaron." Pages 346–58 in vol. 4 of *New International Dictionary of Old Testament Theology and Exegesis*. Edited by W. A. VanGemeren. 5 vols. Grand Rapids: Eerdmans, 1997.

—"Cain and Seth." Pages 454–56 in vol. 4 of *New International Dictionary of Old Testament Theology and Exegesis*. Edited by W. A. VanGemeren. 5 vols. Grand Rapids: Eerdmans, 1997.

—"Flood." Pages 640–52 in vol. 4 of *New International Dictionary of Old Testament Theology and Exegesis*. Edited by W. A. VanGemeren. 5 vols. Grand Rapids: Eerdmans, 1997.

—"The Gap Between Law and Ethics in the Bible." *JJS* 48 (1997): 17–29.

—"Teddy-Bear Sacrifices: Selling the Old Testament in a Religious Studies Department." Pages 101–10 in *Make the Old Testament Live: From Curriculum to Classroom*. Edited by Richard S. Hess and Gordon J. Wenham. Grand Rapids: Eerdmans, 1998.

—"Hope and the New Millennium." Pages 13–16 in *The Fifth Times Book of Best Sermons*. Edited by Ruth Gledhill. London: Cassell, 1999.

—"The Old Testament and the Environment: A Response to Chris Wright." *Transformation* 16, no. 3 (1999): 86–92.

—"Pondering the Pentateuch: The Search for a New Paradigm." Pages 116–54 in *The Face of Old Testament Studies: A Survey of Contemporary Approaches*. Edited by David W. Baker and Bill T. Arnold. Grand Rapids: Baker, 1999.

—"The Priority of P." *VT* 49 (1999): 240–58.

—"Relationships." Pages 41–57 in *The Fourth Times Book of Best Sermons*. Edited by Ruth Gledhill. London: Cassell, 1999.

—"Walter Brueggemann—An Old Testament Theology for the New Millennium?" *European Journal of Theology* 8 (1999): 169–76.

—"Life and Death and the Consumerist Ethic." Pages 118–34 in *Christ and Consumerism: Critical Reflections on the Spirit of Our Age*. Edited by Craig G. Bartholomew and Thorsten Moritz. Carlisle: Paternoster, 2000.

—"Rejoice the Lord is King: Psalms 90–106 (Book 4)." Pages 89–120 in *Praying by the Book: Reading the Psalms*. Edited by Craig Bartholomew and Andrew West. Carlisle: Paternoster, 2001.

—"Does the New Testament Approve Remarriage After Divorce?" *Southern Baptist Journal of Theology* 6 (2002): 30–55.

—"Purity." Pages 378–94 in vol. 2 of *The Biblical World*. Edited by in John Barton. London: Routledge, 2002.

—"Genesis." Pages 32–71 in *Eerdmans Commentary on the Bible*. Edited by James D. G. Dunn and John W. Rogerson. Grand Rapids: Eerdmans, 2003.

—"Biblical Ethics in a Multicultural Society." Pages 13–55 in *Tales of Two Cities: Christianity and Politics*. Edited by in Stephen Clark. Leicester: Inter-Varsity, 2005.

—"The Ethics of the Psalms." Pages 175–94 in *Interpreting the Psalms: Issues and Approaches*. Edited by Philip S. Johnston and David G. Firth. Leicester: Apollos, 2005.

—"Genesis, Book of." Pages 246–52 in *Dictionary for Theological Interpretation of the Bible*. Edited by Kevin J. Vanhoozer et al. Grand Rapids: Baker Academic, 2005.

—"Law." Pages 441–56 in *Dictionary for Theological Interpretation of the Bible*. Edited by Kevin J. Vanhoozer, et al. Grand Rapids: Baker Academic, 2005.

—"The Authorship of the Pentateuch." Pages 537–39 in *New Dictionary of Christian Apologetics*. Edited by Campbell Campbell-Jack and Gavin J. McGrath. Leicester: Inter-Varsity; Downers Grove, Ill.: InterVarsity, 2006.

—"No Remarriage After Divorce." Pages 19–52 in *Remarriage After Divorce in Today's Church: 3 Views* by Gordon J. Wenham, William A. Heth and Craig S. Keener. Edited by Mark L. Strauss. Grand Rapids: Zondervan, 2006. Also "A Response to W. A. Heth," pp. 85–89, and "A Response to C. S. Keener," pp. 121–25.

—"The Old Testament and Homosexuality." Pages 155–60 in *Guarding the Gospel: Bible, Cross and Mission*. Edited by Chris Green. Grand Rapids: Zondervan, 2006.

—"Towards a Canonical Reading of the Psalms." Pages 333–51 in *Canon and Biblical Interpretation*. Edited by Craig G. Bartholomew, Scott Hahn, Robin Parry, Christopher Seitz and Al Wolters. Scripture and Hermeneutics Series 7. Milton Keynes: Paternoster, 2006.

—"Prayer and Practice in the Psalms." Pages 279–95 in *Psalms and Prayers: Papers Read at the Joint Meeting of the Society of Old Testament Study and the Oud Testamentische Werkgezelschap in Nederland en België, Apeldoorn, August 2006*. Edited by Bob Becking and Eric Peels. OtSt 55. Leiden: Brill, 2007.

INDEXES

INDEX OF REFERENCES

INDEX OF AUTHORS

Reading the Law